WINCHESTER®
AN AMERICAN LEGEND

WINCHESTER®
AN AMERICAN LEGEND

R. L. WILSON

The Official History of
Winchester Firearms and Ammunition
from
1849 to the Present

Photography by

G. Allan Brown

CHARTWELL
BOOKS, INC.

OTHER BOOKS BY R. L. WILSON

Winchester Engraving
Winchester: The Golden Age of American Gunmaking and
   the Winchester 1 of 1000
The Book of Winchester Engraving
Samuel Colt Presents
The Arms Collection of Colonel Colt
L. D. Nimschke Firearms Engraver
The Rampant Colt
Colt Commemorative Firearms
Theodore Roosevelt Outdoorsman
Antique Arms Annual (editor)
The Book of Colt Firearms
The Book of Colt Engraving
Colt Pistols
Colt Engraving
Colt Handguns (Japanese)
Paterson Colt Pistol Variations (with P. R. Phillips)
The Colt Heritage
The Deringer in America (with L. D. Eberhart, two volumes)
Colt's Dates of Manufacture 1837–1978
Colt: An American Legend

Book design:
   Martin Moskof
Design Assistant:
   George Brady
Book Production:
   Linda Kaye

Printed in China
Reprinted in 2011, 2012

This book has been written with the cooperation of the
Winchester Division of Olin Corporation (owner of the trade-
mark WINCHESTER®) and the U.S. Repeating Arms
Company, Inc. (exclusive licensee and current producer of
WINCHESTER® firearms). Their participation is greatly
appreciated.

Library of Congress Cataloging-in-Publication Data

Wilson, R. L. (Robert Lawrence)
    Winchester: an American legend/by R. L. Wilson.
       p.   cm.
    Includes bibliographical references and index.
    ISBN-10: 0-7858-1893-6
    ISBN-13: 978-0-7858-1893-9
    1. Winchester rifle—History.   I. Title.
TS533.2.W57   1991
683.4′22—dc20   90-45257

This edition published in 2004 by
CHARTWELL BOOKS
A division of BOOK SALES, INC.
276 Fifth Avenue Suite 206,
New York, New York 10001

Published by arrangement with R. L. Wilson

Endpapers: Cross section of the Winchester legend. *Upper left*,
Volcanic lever-action pistol by Smith & Wesson, rights to which
were bought by O. F. Winchester. Lever-action musket with
bayonet, a Model 1873, an all-time classic. Rifle beneath, the
Model 1904 .22 rimfire bolt-action, representing one of dozens
of .22s of various types built by factory over the years. *Lower
left*, the Model 50 automatic shotgun, landmark sixteen-
millionth Winchester (gift to General LeMay, Outdoorsman of
the Year, 1957, by John M. Olin). *Center right*, Grand American
Model 21 side-by-side shotgun, top of the line, delivered to client
Gary Hansen, 1990. O. F. Winchester commemorative Model
94, among the most popular of factory issues for a whole new
breed of collector. Ammunition became a bread-and-butter
product over the years and continues to be produced today by
the Winchester Division of Olin Industries. Fly-fishing rod and
reel represent non-gun Winchester products, mainly in sporting
goods and hardware. The Winchester horse-and-rider logo was
originally painted by artist Philip Goodwin, c. 1935. Catalogue
at upper right from 1933.

Frontispiece: Evolutionary landmarks, and memorabilia, in the
Winchester legend. *Left to right*, iron-framed Volcanic pistol, by
Smith & Wesson, one of the earliest lever-actions. Model 1873, a
musket, with its angular steel bayonet. Model 1904, .22 rimfire
bolt-action rifle, evolved by Winchester from its first .22 bolt, the
1900 invented by John M. Browning. Sixteen-millionth Winchester is the Model 50 automatic, presented by John M. Olin to
General Curtis LeMay, 1957. The Grand American Model 21
side-by-side double-barrel shotgun was delivered to client in
1990. O. F. Winchester commemorative Model 94 was among
the most popular of factory issues for collectors. Ammunition
has been a staple Winchester product since the 1860s. Fishing
reel represents non-gun Winchester products, primarily in
sporting goods and hardware.

In memory of
O. F. Winchester,
T. G. Bennett,
and John M. Olin,
and in honor of
the tens of thousands
of Winchester employees
who built and sold
the Winchester
arms and ammunition
which made the legend

AND

With apologies
to Christopher and Stephen—
this is why Dad
couldn't take you fishing.

Theodore Roosevelt on safari in East Africa, with a mammoth bull black rhinoceros, taken with a Winchester Model 1895 in .405 caliber. Rhino a specimen for the Smithsonian Institution, long before the species was on the endangered list.

The Winchester . . . is by all odds the best weapon I ever had,
and I now use it almost exclusively. . . .
It is as handy to carry, whether on foot or on horseback,
and comes up to the shoulder as readily as a shotgun;
it is absolutely sure, and there is no recoil to jar
and disturb the aim, while it carries accurately
quite as far as a man can aim with any degree of certainty. . . .
The Winchester is the best gun for any game to be found
in the United States, for it is as deadly, accurate,
and handy as any, stands very rough usage, and
is unapproachable for the rapidity of its fire
and the facility with which it is loaded.

Theodore Roosevelt
Hunting Trips of a Ranchman, 1885

Contents

NEW HAVEN ARMS COMPANY,

NEW HAVEN, CONN.,

U. S. A.,

Manufacturers of

Henry's Repeating Rifles,

CARBINES, MUSKETS AND SHOT GUNS,

AND

FIXED AMMUNITION

FOR THE SAME.

HENRY A. CHAPIN, Sec'y.   O. F. WINCHESTER, Pres't.

Introduction

Firearms have been major instruments in the course of history since their first primitive appearance in the fourteenth century. In all that time no maker of longarms can equal the international image of adventure attached to the name *Winchester*. The historian, collector, or curator who pursues the Holy Grail of Winchester belongs to a select group of devotees of one of the most fascinating marques in Americana. Arguably it is the Winchester that won the West. And the two most glamorous and sought-after blue chips in gun collecting worldwide are Colt, primarily a handgun maker, and Winchester, primarily a maker of shoulder guns.

Designed with mechanical ingenuity and made with advanced manufacturing techniques—mass production decades before Henry Ford and the automobile—most Winchesters were graceful and handsome in line and form. And for the lover of

New Haven Arms Company trade card, c. 1863.

decorative arts, a prized portion of production has the extra merit of hand decoration: checkered or carved select-grain stocks, special finishes, engraving and precious-metal inlaying, and sometimes elegant casings. A few were presentations, even gifts of state.

Tracing its origins back to 1849, Winchester is the oldest maker of lever-action repeating firearms in the world, and at its peak in the twentieth century was the largest gunmaker in the world with over 18,000 employees. As an ammunition manufacturer, Winchester remains the world's largest. The marque is also possessor of one of history's most famous brand names. In many respects Winchester is to firearms and ammunition as Ferrari is to automobiles and Tiffany is to silver.

Winchester: An American Legend pays tribute to the romance and legacy of this remarkable heritage in a pictorial review of the deluxe and the standard, the historic and the everyday working tool. Herein is a collection which no museum or enthusiast

could ever hope to assemble in today's spellbinding market. Increasingly the most prized Winchesters are leaving private hands and becoming permanent exhibits in museums. *Winchester: An American Legend* exclusively brings together these dazzling arms and their history.

Period photographs and original art were chosen to complement the exquisite color photography of G. Allan Brown, specially commissioned for this book and shot to convey the mechanical and artistic merit of the firearms and the unique aura of Winchester and its galaxy of guns.

The author is indebted to the officials of the Winchester Division of the Olin Corporation and the U.S. Repeating Arms Company, and to the many collectors and museums who have shared their prized firearms with Allan Brown's 4×5 Schneider lens to make *Winchester: An American Legend* a reality.

—*R. L. Wilson*

WINCHESTER®
AN AMERICAN LEGEND

Chapter I
Genesis of the Winchester

New York City inventor Walter Hunt held a patent for a unique bullet he called the Rocket Ball, with the powder within the lead projectile, and the primer from a separate device actuated by the hammer. The gun he designed to fire his rockets was an ugly but intriguing lever-action breech-loader, which he named the Volitional Repeater. From this awkward arm evolved the Jennings, the Smith & Wesson, the Volcanic, the Henry, and the Winchester lever-action firearms. But only one Hunt rifle is presently known, and that has been part of the Winchester factory's museum collection since the days of O. F. Winchester himself. Al-

---

Pioneers preceding the Winchester. *From the top*, the only known Hunt Volitional Repeater, the first of millions of Winchester firearms to follow. *Second and third* rifles are the Jennings—the First Model (breech-loading and single-shot, with ring trigger and triggerguard) and the Second Model (a magazine repeater, with ring trigger and automatic pill primer). At *bottom*, a rare iron-frame promotional rifle by Smith & Wesson, an early Volcanic of exquisite quality exhibiting features prescient of the Henry rifle.

though the Hunt proved quite impractical, the seeds for an incredible enterprise had been sown.

The Hunt never entered into production, but the basic design was improved by a talented gunsmith named Lewis Jennings and patented on Christmas Day, 1849. Jennings worked in New York for businessman George Arrowsmith, who had taken an interest in the Hunt concept and later became an investor in its future. It was not Arrowsmith but another New Yorker, Courtland C. Palmer, who bought the rights to the Hunt and Jennings, and then contracted with the Robbins and Lawrence factory in Windsor, Vermont, to manufacture 5,000 guns in a historic building which now houses the American Precision Museum. (The foreman at the plant was one B. Tyler Henry, who was later to be a key player in the rapid growth of Winchester and its predecessor companies.)

The Jennings rifle, of .54 caliber, had a tubular magazine under the barrel, used an improved lead projectile, and had an ignition system dependent on an automatically-fed pill primer. Only three models of Jennings were made: the First type, a

breech-loading single-shot; the Second type, a repeater with improvements by Horace Smith; and the Third, a single-shot muzzle-loader. Two pioneer American gunmakers who also had prominent roles in the Jennings were Horace Smith and D. B. Wesson, who were later to become the renowned revolver manufacturers Smith & Wesson.

Jennings rifles were made from approximately 1850 to 1852, and only about 1,000 were completed. Too complex, ugly, and underpowered, these arms were a commercial failure. But as the first Winchester made in any quantity, they are of historical and technical importance.

The Smith & Wesson and Volcanic Repeaters

After the Hunt-Jennings-Arrowsmith effort, Horace Smith and D. B. Wesson carried on with investor Courtland C. Palmer and formed a new company, first named Smith & Wesson and later the Volcanic Repeating Arms Company. The basic patent for the so-called toggle-link action was awarded to inventors Smith and Wesson on February 14, 1854. Initial production of the S&W "Volcanic"

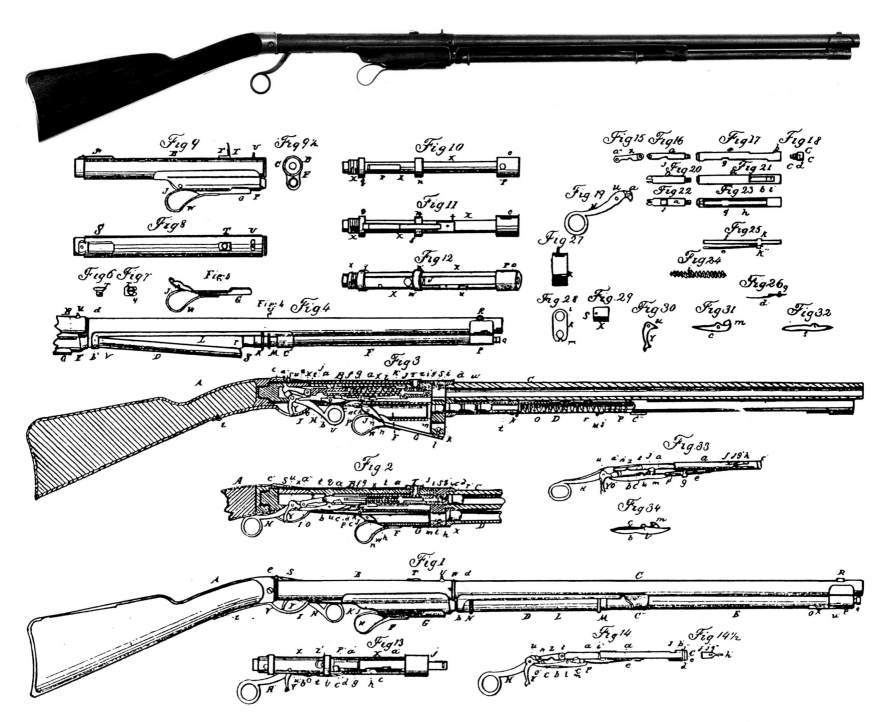

4

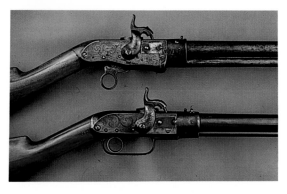

At *bottom*, the First Model Jennings, a single-shot breechloader, operated by pulling the hammer to half cock; loading-port cover is opened, and the cocking lever/trigger is slid forward to move the breech bolt rearward. The pill primer is automatic as the lever is moved. When rearward, the bolt is locked and priming has been achieved, and the hammer is then pulled to full cock. A final pull on the trigger fires the rifle. At *top*, operation of the Second Model Jennings, a pill-primed repeater, is basically the same as above, except that the forward and rearward movement of the cocking lever/trigger also feeds the cartridge from the magazine tube beneath the barrel. Primer on both guns is at the top of the frame, adjacent to the hammer, and covered by a disk. The Third Model, a muzzle-loader, is standard with hand-applied percussion-cap priming. Both the First and Third Models have ramrods beneath the barrel, in place of the magazine tube of the Second Model.

The complexities of Walter Hunt's patent of August 21, 1849, for his Volitional Repeater, are evident in this specification drawing. The lever near the trigger was for cocking, the forward lever for loading cartridges from the magazine. The one known example (*inset*) may have survived because it was likely seldom fired.

was in Norwich, Connecticut, and the guns were lever-action. These early, iron-framed arms were limited to handguns, in calibers .30 and .38, with hollow projectiles that contained both powder and primer. The Smith & Wesson period arms number only about 1,000 total and are marked with the patent date and SMITH & WESSON NORWICH, CT. Ironically, they are the first S&W firearms as well as being pioneer Winchesters.

In July of 1855 the business was restructured, and the company changed its name to the Volcanic Repeating Arms Company. But sales were slow, and the firm accumulated debt. One of the stockholders of the new firm was Oliver F. Winchester, then a shirtmaker living in New Haven. He had a fine hand at business, and by 1857 he had acquired the major share of Volcanic stock and had become president of the firm. In 1856, the factory and offices had moved to New Haven, and Horace Smith and D. B. Wesson dropped out of the business to concentrate on metallic-cartridge revolvers, an enterprise at which they would make their fortunes.

Volcanic arms, made from 1855 to 1857, had brass frames, are in .38 caliber, and fired self-contained and self-primed lead projectiles. Only about 3,000 guns were manufactured, and in only two models: a carbine and a lever-action Navy pistol (some with attachable shoulder stock). Their standard barrel marking is THE VOLCANIC REPEATING ARMS CO./PATENT NEW HAVEN CONN/FEB. 14, 1854.

The Third Model Jennings rifle was a muzzle-loading single-shot, using percussion caps. The magazine tube under the barrel was adapted to hold a ramrod. Note the distinctive trigger and triggerguard configuration.

In 1857 the firm adopted the name New Haven Arms Company, by which time O. F. Winchester had exclusive ownership of the patents, and 800 of the 1,900 shares issued were his. Not only was he president and chief stockholder, he also became treasurer. The new guns did not have the VOLCANIC markings in their barrel address, but Volcanic was the trade name applied to them, and that is how all these lever-action arms are generally termed by collectors. Total production was only about 3,200 handguns and longarms, and, despite an expanded line of rifles, sales were weak.

However, *Frank Leslie's Illustrated Weekly*, October 9, 1858, enthusiastically endorsed the Volcanic:

It combines every quality requisite in such a weapon, with many advantages which no similar invention has yet succeeded in attaining. It is placed beyond all competition by the rapidity of its execution. Thirty shots can be fired in less than one minute—a really marvellous rapidity, in which it far outdoes the best revolving firearms yet produced. Its ammunition has the advantage of compactness, lightness, and of being water-proof. . . . the entire charge consists in a bullet of the Minié pattern, in which both charge and priming

are contained, and of which sixty weigh only one pound. What an improvement upon the heavy cartridge of powder-flask that it has hither been necessary to carry! The balls may be soaked in water with perfect impunity, and can be kept any length of time in any climate, without losing their explosive force; nor can they be exploded by contact with flame. . . . The manufacture of these firearms—of which several sizes, as well pistols as rifles, are produced—was commenced in 1855, and is now carried on by the New Haven Arms Company, of New Haven, Conn., where a large factory is established, employing, on an average, some fifty hands. The depot of the company, a very handsome store, is at No. 267 Broadway, New York.

The iron frame, humped back-frame profile, and spurred cocking lever help to identify this .38-caliber pistol, known as No. 2, as made by Smith & Wesson, Norwich. A smaller pistol, known as No. 1, was .30-caliber and had a bag-shaped grip. Only about 1,000 total of both types were made.

Serial number 100 Volcanic carbine, with rare New Haven Arms Company brochure, with pistols and carbines listed. According to the list, the price of this plated and engraved gun was $33, $38, or $43, depending on barrel length.

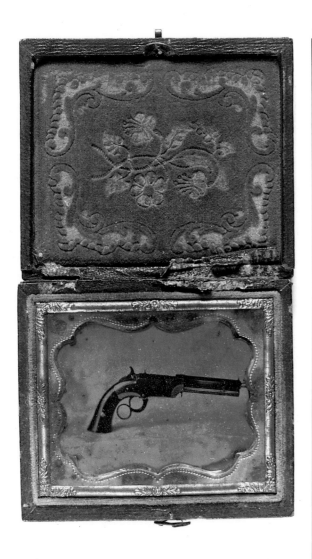

From the estate of Oliver F. Winchester, ambrotype of a .30-caliber Volcanic pistol, probably taken for advertising and promotional purposes. The only such period photograph known to the author.

New York dealer Joseph Merwin's broadsheet on the Volcanic provides full details of operation. The full array of pistols and longarms helps to date this rare document c. 1859. Calibers are .30 and .38.

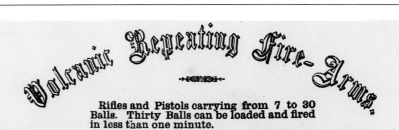

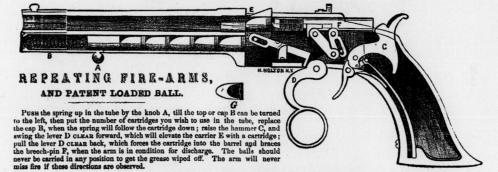

Volcanic Repeating Fire-Arms.

Rifles and Pistols carrying from 7 to 30 Balls. Thirty Balls can be loaded and fired in less than one minute.

REPEATING FIRE-ARMS,
AND PATENT LOADED BALL.

PUSH the spring up in the tube by the knob A, till the top or cap B can be turned to the left, then put the number of cartridges you wish to use in the tube, replace the cap B, when the spring will follow the cartridge down; raise the hammer C, and swing the lever D CLEAR forward, which will elevate the carrier E with a cartridge; pull the lever D CLEAR back, which forces the cartridge into the barrel and braces the breech-pin F, when the arm is in condition for discharge. The balls should never be carried in any position to get the grease wiped off. The arm will never miss fire if these directions are observed.

JOSEPH MERWIN,
267 BROADWAY, NEW YORK, Sole Agent.

The rapidity of execution of this Arm places it beyond all competition. The thirty-shooter can be loaded and fired in less than one minute—a quickness and force of execution which is as much superior to the best revolvers as they are to the old muzzle-loading single shooters.

The Ammunition is water-proof, hence it can be used in any weather, or loaded and hung up for months, or laid under water, and then fired with certainty.

Its safety from accidental discharge is a great consideration in its favor; for, while the magazine (a tube running the whole length of the barrel) may be filled with balls, and thus the gun, in fact, be loaded from breech to muzzle, it is yet impossible, from any carelessness in handling, to discharge it. *Its construction* is simple and its workmanship most perfect, hence it is not easily got out of repair.

Its proportions are light, elegant, and compact, and the barrels are all rifled with great exactness. It requires no cap nor priming, no bullet-mould nor powder-flask. The powder and cap is contained in a loaded "minnie" ball of the best form and proportions, and is as sure as the best percussion caps.

It shoots with accuracy and greater force than any other arm can with double the powder used in this. Directions for use accompany each arm. Balls are packed in tin cases, 200 each.

After this date, the price will be as follows, viz. :

No. 1,	4-inch Pocket Pistol,	$12 00,	Plated and Engraved,	$13 50,	Carrying 6 Balls.
No. 1,	6 " for Target Practice,	13 50,	" " "	15 00,	" 10 "
No. 2,	6 " Navy Pistol,	18 00,	" " "	20 00,	" 8 "
No. 2,	8 " "	18 00,	" " "	20 00,	" 10 "
No. 2,	16 " Carbine,	30 00,	" " "	33 00,	" 20 "
No. 2,	20 " "	35 00,	" " "	38 00,	" 25 "
No. 2,	24 " "	40 00,	" " "	43 00,	" 30 "

AMMUNITION.

No. 1 Balls, 130 to the Pound, $10 per Thousand.   No. 2 Balls, 66 to the Pound, $12 per Thousand.
No. 1 Arms require No. 1 Balls.   No. 2 Arms require No. 2 Balls.)

A liberal discount to the trade.   Your orders are respectfully solicited.   (TURN OVER.)

Volcanic pistols by the Volcanic Repeating Arms Company and the New Haven Arms Company are brass-framed, the engraved examples standard silver-plated and blued. Navy pistol, at *top*, with rosewood grips, pocket pistol with walnut. Compared with that on contemporary Colt firearms, the engraving was rather primitive.

Oliver F. Winchester's own deluxe pair of ivory-gripped Volcanic Navy pistols, serial numbers 1401 and 1506—the only firearms known to the author as having been owned by Winchester himself, who passed them down through the family. Gold Tiffany & Co. watch belonged to son-in-law T. G. Bennett, who joined Winchester in 1870. These artifacts are directly associated with the two driving forces in Winchester history, spanning the years from the 1850s to the 1920s. O. F. Winchester and T. G. Bennett *made* Winchester.

The attachable shoulder stock was appropriate for the 16-inch barrel of the .38-caliber Navy pistol, one of the most rare of Volcanics.

Volcanic rifle of .38 caliber, in original pasteboard packing box, with cartridges.

The Henry Rifle

But from the Hunt, Jennings, Smith & Wesson, and Volcanics would soon evolve one of the most note-worthy of all pioneers in the Winchester story: the Henry rifle. B. Tyler Henry, inventor-gunmaker-mechanic and plant superintendent, had an involvement with the lever gun from as early as 1857. In October of 1860, Henry was issued a patent covering his design of a new rifle employing a rimfire metallic-cased cartridge, to replace the impractical self-contained lead-powder-and-primer bullet of the Volcanics. The use of this new ammunition was the key to making the new gun practical—so important were these developments that the new arm came to be called the Henry, and its cartridge bore an H headstamp in honor of the inventor. The Henry was of .44 caliber, with a 216-grain conical bullet, backed by a 26-grain powder charge.

With continued financial backing from O. F. Winchester, tooling up proceeded at a relatively rapid pace, and, fueled by the Civil War market, the first Henrys were in the field by mid-1862. But the revolutionary new repeater had to prove itself. The Chief of Ordnance, Brigadier General James W. Ripley, was decidedly of a boldly looking backward mentality toward any newfangled repeaters (even though President Lincoln was so intrigued by them that he test-fired a Spencer repeater on the White House lawn). Ripley actually warned the Secretary of War, in December of 1861, of "a great evil . . . in regard to . . . the vast variety of new inventions. . . . the weights of the arms with the loaded magazines [is] objectionable, and also the requirement of special ammunition rendering it impossible to use the arms with the ordinary cartridges or with powder and ball." Single-shot guns could be loaded and fired quickly enough, he added.

The future of the Henry was likely boosted by special presentations to Secretary of War Edwin Stanton and Secretary of the Navy Gideon Welles, and even a gift to President Lincoln—all guns with single-digit serial numbers, richly engraved and inscribed, and fitted with rosewood stocks. The Henry was even tested at the Washington Navy Yard (conveniently, Secretary Welles was from Connecticut), reported in May of 1862: 187 shots were fired in three minutes and thirty-six seconds (not counting reloading time). and one full fifteen-shot magazine was fired in only 10.8 seconds. A total of 1,040 shots were fired, and hits were made from as far away as 348 feet, at an 18-inch-square target— quite impressive accuracy with open sights. The report noted, "It is manifest from the above experi-

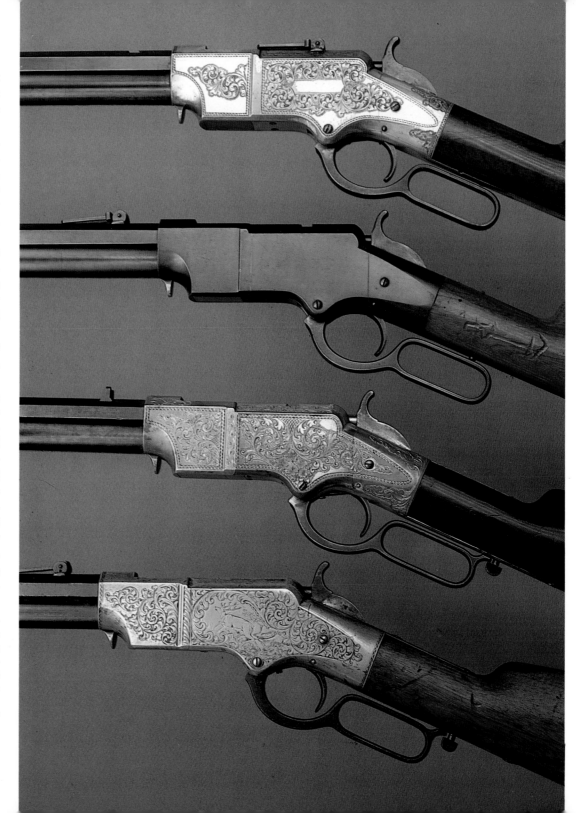

From the *top*, Henry rifle serial number 11, with variant factory scroll, border engraving, and rosewood stock. Note early-style lever, without locking latch, a feature also evident in the iron-frame Henry number 73 (*next*), one of the finest examples known to collectors. This factory-engraved Henry has the rare combination of gold-plated frame and rosewood stock. *Bottom*, an example of engraving by Louis D. Nimschke, who was active in New York in the second half of the nineteenth century.

ment that this gun may be fired with great rapidity, and is not liable to get out of order. The penetration, in proportion to the charge used, compares favorably with that of other arms."

By July of 1862 the Henry was on the market, and it quickly found popularity with both civilian and military purchasers—except for the federal government, sales to which totaled only 1,731, spread over the period July 1863 to November 1865.

A July 14th, 1862, newspaper report, in the *Louisville Journal*, written by its editor George D. Prentice, was highly laudatory:

> In these days, when rebel outlaws and raids are becoming common in Kentucky, when guerillas are scouring different counties nightly, and practising the most atrocious outrages, when even the central positions of our State are openly threatened, and when it is understood in high quarters that secret companies are on foot for a sudden and general insurrection at some favorable moment, it behooves every loyal citizen to prepare himself upon his own responsibility with the best weapon of defense that can be obtained. And certainly the simplest, surest, and most effective weapon that we know of, the weapon that could be used with the most tremendous results in case of an outbreak or invasion, is one that we have mentioned recently upon two or three occasions, the newly invented rifle of Henry, now on exhibition, and for sale at Messrs. Jas. Low and Co.'s, Sixth street.
>
> This rifle, as we have stated, can be loaded in eight or ten seconds with fifteen cartridges, and the whole number can be fired in fifteen seconds or less, so that one man, with the weapon, is equal to fifteen armed with ordinary guns. . . . It may lie loaded for a week at the bottom of a river, and, if taken out, will then fire with as much certainty as if it had been kept perfectly dry all the time. It is remarkably simple, not liable to get out of order, and is utterly free from the objection sometimes urged against other repeating rifles that two or more charges are liable to be fired at once.

Prentice believed so strongly in the Henry that he brought several hundred of them to resell to clients who were faithful to the Union cause.

Besides in Kentucky, early sales were especially brisk in the border states, Illinois, Missouri, and Indiana. Other sites and sellers included leading arms dealers J. C. Grubb of Philadelphia, Hartley & Graham of New York, William Read & Son of Boston, and R. Liddle of San Francisco.

An extraordinary encounter between seven Confederates and Captain James M. Wilson, commanding officer of Company M of the 12th Kentucky Cavalry, was widely publicized, appearing in various advertisements and journals. H.W.S. Cleveland's *Hints to Riflemen* gives an account:

> Capt. Wilson had fitted up a long crib across the road from his front door as a sort of arsenal, where he had his Henry Rifle, Colt's Revolver, etc. One day, while at home dining with his family seven mounted guerillas rode up, dismounted and burst into his dining room and commenced firing upon him with revolvers. The attack was so sudden that the first shot struck a glass of water his wife was raising to her lips, breaking the glass. Several other shots were fired without effect, when Capt. Wilson sprang to his feet, exclaiming, "For God's sake, gentlemen, if you wish to murder me, do not do it at my own table in the presence of my family."
>
> This caused a parley, resulting in their consent that he might go out doors to be shot. The moment he reached his front door he sprang for his cover, and his assailants commenced firing at him. Several shots passed through his hat, and more through his clothing, but none took effect upon his person. He thus reached his cover and seized his Henry Rifle, turned upon his foes, and in five shots killed five of them; the other two sprung for their horses. As the sixth man threw his hand over the pommel of his saddle, the sixth shot took off four of his fingers; notwithstanding this he got into his saddle, but the seventh shot killed him; then starting out, Capt. Wilson killed the seventh man with the eighth shot.
>
> In consequence of this feat the State of Kentucky armed his Company with the Henry Rifle.

Wilson's company was not the only one to be armed with the Henry, but the issuing of such arms was counter to War Department policy. Assistant Secretary of War Peter Watson wrote to O. F. Winchester (August 9, 1862) that "companies arming themselves with Henry's repeating rifle, will [not] be allowed to retain them in the field . . . as great inconvenience has resulted from promises heretofore given in other cases to furnish companies of troops with special arms. If you choose to arm and equip a whole regiment at your own expense, or the regiment chooses to arm itself, it will be accepted with the condition that it shall be at liberty to use its own arms and equipments exclusively."

Despite the War Department objections, 240 Henrys were purchased by the federal government for the 1st District of Columbia Cavalry. Inspired by that moral victory, O. F. Winchester gleefully wrote to Brigadier General Ripley stating, "If these arms were used as efficiently by the men who are to receive them as they have been by our Union friends in Kentucky, the country will have no cause to regret the expenditure."

Still another federal government purchase was 800 more Henrys, to equip the eight companies of Maine cavalry assigned to the 1st District of Columbia Cavalry. Armed also with Spencer rifles, the First Maine had ample opportunity to demonstrate the superiority of breech-loading, metallic-cartridge repeaters.

The regimental chaplain, Samuel H. Merrill, wrote in his memoir on the First Maine and the 1st District cavalry units:

> This regiment was distinguished by the superiority of the carbines with which it was armed. It was the only regiment in the Army of the Potomac armed with "Henry's Repeating Rifle." . . . After having witnessed the effectiveness of this weapon, one is not surprised at the remark, said to have been made by the guerilla chief. Mosby, after an encounter with some of our men, that "he did not care for the common gun, or for Spencer's seven shooter, but as for these guns that they could wind up on Sunday, and shoot all the week, it was useless to fight against them."

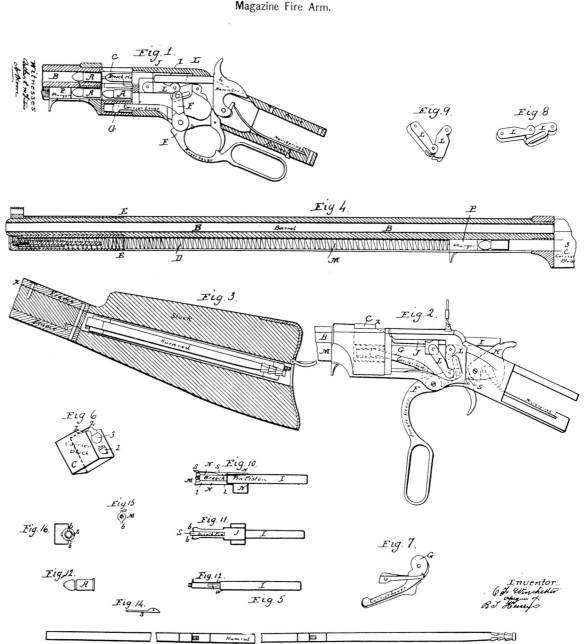

Oliver Fisher Winchester, November 30, 1810–December 10, 1880. From New England farm boy to world-renowned industrialist and entrepreneur. In addition to his role in building the Winchester Repeating Arms Company, he was a generous patron of Yale University and a founder of the Yale National Bank and the New Haven Water Company, and he was elected lieutenant governor of Connecticut in 1866. The New Haven *Palladium* eulogized him as "an eminent citizen, to whose public spirit and private enterprise [New Haven] is indebted for much of her present prosperity. . . . The great establishment which he organized, and to which he gave his name, stands to-day as a monument to the great ability and enterprise which marked his whole business career."

The master drawing from B. Tyler Henry's patent of October 16, 1860, showing the mechanism open and closed, the bolt, extractor, and carrier block, the cartridge and magazine, and even the sectional hickory-and-metal cleaning rod and its compartment in the buttstock. Note toggle-link connection to the bolt, and automatic cocking of the hammer as the lever is lowered. Not shown is the means by which the magazine plunger is slid manually to the muzzle, allowing the loading aperture to be twisted to the side to allow for front loading of cartridges.

Reports of the successful use of Henrys in the Civil War are numerous, both from the Union point of view and from the Confederates who forced the incessant fire. The incredible firepower, especially in comparison to the muzzle-loading single shots, is evident in Major William Ludlow's account of the Battle of Allatoona Pass:

What saved us that day . . . was the fact that we had a number of Henry rifles. . . . These were new guns in those days and [the commander] had held in reserve a company of an Illinois Regiment that was armed with them until a final assault should be made. When the artillery reopened . . . this company of 16-shooters sprang to the parapet and poured out such a multiplied, rapid, and deadly fire that no men could stay in front of it, and no serious effort was thereafter made to take the fort by assault.

Endorsed by the President of the United States, the Spencer repeating rifle had a better following than the Henry. The Spencer, loading through an aperture in the butt, was referred to by General Ripley's succeeding Chief of Ordnance (1864) as "the cheapest, most durable, and most efficient," in comparison to the Colt revolving rifle ("both expensive and a dangerous weapon to the user") and the Henry ("expensive and too delicate for service in its present form"). This preference is easily noted in the purchase totals: U.S. Ordnance acquired just over 94,000 Spencer carbines, but only about 4,600 Colt revolving rifles, and a total of only 1,731 Henrys. An interesting and revealing further statistic: from January 1, 1861, to June 30, 1866, the Ordnance Department acquired approximately 4,600,000 .44 Henry cartridges, as compared to over 58 million cartridges for the Spencer.

Finally, at the end of the war, in March of 1866, a major ordnance test was held for the Army's adoption of a breech-loading firearm system. Several single-shot firearms were tested, but only two magazine repeaters, the Henry and the Spencer. Tested for rapidity of fire, endurance, bullet penetration,

and other factors, the Henry experienced such problems as burst cartridge casings, a burst cartridge in the magazine, and a locked breech pin (only movable "by blows"). Other problems encountered were relatively weak penetration (seven 1-inch pine boards by the Henry, ten by the Spencer), failure to work practically as a single-shot rifle, weak mainspring, and "imperfect" connector "between the arm and the platform that raises the cartridge." Tests for dust were acceptable, but the results of the rust test were not favorable.

The final report favored the Spencer, stating it was "the best service gun of this kind yet offered."

O. F. Winchester's reaction to the report was to publish his own comments, making disparaging observations on the Spencer, and even stating that his reaction was addressed specifically to the Secretary of War. But Winchester probably did not stay mad for long: the glut of arms on the market following the end of the Civil War led to the demise of the Spencer, as prices for surplus arms plummeted. Despite the endorsement of the Ordnance Department, by 1868 the Spencer firm had gone under. Winchester acquired its assets, and buying out the competition became a preferred practice in the evolution of Winchester.

Despite the fact that only two basic types of Henry rifle were made, some details on these arms are still obscure. But first, what is generally known: the initial production was of iron-frame rifles, serialized in their own range, from 1 up through approximately 400.* The buttplates are also of iron, and the loading levers have no extension to engage a locking latch. The profiles of the stocks and frames are noticeably different from these on the standard Henrys, which were made with brass frames and buttplates and have the latch design for the levers, although some specimens below the serial range of approximately 2500 do not have the latch feature.

The brass Henrys are serialized from 1 up into

the 14000 range, and thus overlap with the next model, the 1866 Winchester. Blued barrels were standard on both the iron- and brass-framed Henrys, and the barrels were marked

HENRY'S PATENT. OCT. 16. 1860
MANUFACT'D BY THE NEW HAVEN ARMS CO.
NEW HAVEN. CT.

Henrys marked by the U.S. government ordnance inspector are much sought-after; the guns, from various serial-number ranges, all have brass frames and are marked C.G.C. on the breech of the barrel and on the stock. Also much sought are engraved rifles; none to date have been found in the iron-frame variation, but several hundred were made in the brass-frame Henrys. Some striking examples are featured in the accompanying photographs, including presentations made for high-ranking government officials and B. Tyler Henry's own rifle.

Since Henrys were sold with a sectional cleaning rod of brass, iron, and hickory, some specimens will be found with that feature still present, secured in a compartment in the buttstock and accessible through a trapdoor in the butt. Shaking the gun will reveal whether or not the cleaning rod is present.

The practical matter of manufacturing the Henry with its magazine integral with the octagonal barrel was addressed by gunmaker Aldo Uberti, with Val Forgett of Navy Arms Company, when tooling up for modern Henry production. Uberti surmised that the original manufacture was done by milling the barrel from a bar of steel, and then bending flat wings of metal on the sides around a mandrel to form the magazine (the technique he introduced for the .44-40-caliber rifles he and Navy Arms Co. have been producing since the 1970s). The ingenuity of nineteenth-century—and twentieth-century—gunmakers is one of the more appealing aspects of arms collecting.

*Unless stated otherwise, new models were standard commencing with serial number 1.

New Haven Arms Company factory, c. 1859.

President Lincoln's Henry rifle, serial number 6, is one of the Smithsonian Institution's great treasures. The frame and buttplate are plated in gold; the stock is of lustrous rosewood. The President was intrigued by firearms and was a competent marksman.

Presentation Henry rifles of signal importance. *Top*, serial number 9, inscribed for the Secretary of the Navy, and serial number 1, for the Secretary of War. The stocks are rosewood, the frames and buttplates silver-plated. The promotional use of such arms was relatively rare in O. F. Winchester's *modus operandi*; in this he differed from his contemporary Samuel Colt, for whom gift guns played a central role.

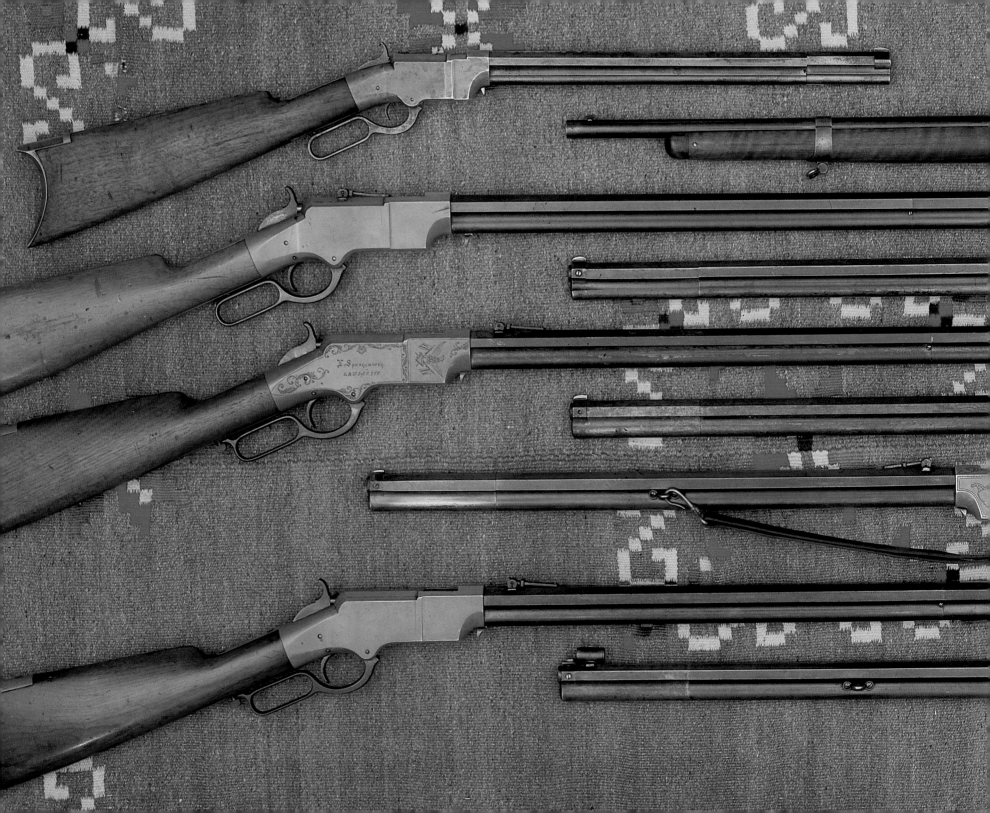

Tzi-kal-tzn, reputed to be the son of Captain William Clark of the Lewis and Clark Expedition, holds a Henry rifle (which apparently had a repair at the wrist) in this photograph by William H. Jackson (c. 1871).

An extraordinary panorama of Henry rifles. *From the top*, the serial number 1 Volcanic carbine. A rare French copy of the Henry, with iron frame. Serial number 21, with early lever and butt profile. Henry 1216 with factory engraving and silver plating. The Civil War Henry of J. Spangenberg, "Co. B. 3d Rgt. U.S.V." *Sixth*, the Civil War Henry of Louis Quinius, Co. B., Wisconsin Sixty-sixth Infantry. Number 8291, engraved and silver-plated, with rare sling, is credited with having been used by photographer Mathew Brady. Number 8816 is of the standard configuration of most of the second half of production. *Bottom* rifle bears presentation silver plaque, to J. E. Chapman, from employees of the Back Bay Gravel Works. High serial number 14262, from last of production.

SIXTY SHOTS PER MINUTE

HENRY'S PATENT

REPEATING

RIFLE

The Most Effective Weapon in the World.

This Rifle can be discharged 16 times without loading or taking down from the shoulder, or even loosing aim. It is also slung in such a manner, that either on horse or on foot, it can be **Instantly Used,** without taking the strap from the shoulder.

For a House or Sporting Arm, it has no Equal;

IT IS ALWAYS LOADED AND ALWAYS READY.

The size now made is 44-100 inch bore, 24 inch barrel, and carries a conical ball 32 to the pound. The penetration at 100 yards is 8 inches; at 400 yards 5 inches; and it carries with force sufficient to kill at 1,000 yards.

A resolute man, armed with one of these Rifles, particularly if on horseback, CANNOT BE CAPTURED.

"We particularly commend it for ARMY USES, as the most effective arm for picket and vidette duty, and to all our citizens in secluded places, as a protection against guerilla attacks and robberies. A man armed with one of these Rifles, can load and discharge one shot every second, so that he is equal to a company every minute, a regiment every ten minutes, a brigade every half hour, and a division every hour."—*Louisville Journal.*

Address   JNO. W. BROWN,

Gen'l Ag't., Columbus, Ohio,

At Rail Road Building, near the Depot.

R. NEVINS' Steam Printing Establishment, No.'s 36, 38 and 40 North High Street, Columbus, Ohio.

Advertising art promoting the Henry rifle, also featuring its .44 Henry rimfire cartridge, c. 1862.

Oglala Chief Sitting Bull (not *the* Sitting Bull of General Custer fame) was the recipient of this Henry from President U. S. Grant. The presentation was made in June of 1875, when the Henry was already relatively obsolete.

John W. Brown's flier helped in spreading the word on "The Most Effective Weapon in the World," and he accounted for over 500 rifles sold.

Extraordinary Mathew Brady photograph of the color bearers and color guard, 7th Illinois Volunteer Infantry, armed with Henry rifles (and proud of it).

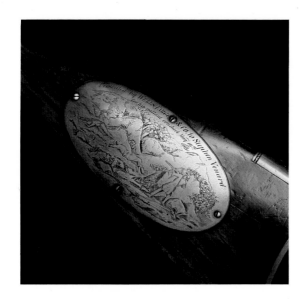

Wells Fargo & Company rewarded Stephen Venard with a presentation Henry and $3,000 for pursuing and killing three outlaws after they had stuck up a stagecoach near Nevada City, California. This Henry, now a featured exhibit at the Wells Fargo Bank History Room, San Francisco, has an engraved frame and buttplate and a richly decorated stock plaque of German silver. Venard, a former Nevada City town marshal, had used his own Henry in dispatching the outlaws.

Louis D. Nimschke's distinctive scroll and border engraving graces this silver-plated Henry, its stock of varnished walnut. Characteristic of Nimschke is the sculptural scrollwork and the neatly punched dot background. A scrapbook kept by Nimschke documents several Henrys embellished by him, some of which even bore his signature in stamped or engraved initials.

Accompanying a standard late-model Henry is a stagecoach-style carrying case, with pinstripes to match the coach's decor. This unique accessory was displayed at the Gene Autry Western Heritage Museum, Los Angeles, in a 1990 loan exhibition of coaches and memorabilia, "Stagecoach! The Romantic Western Vehicle."

The Model 1866 Winchester

Although only about 13,000 Henrys were made, the name became so popular that for a year the firm was called the Henry Repeating Rifle Company. However, in 1866–67, since O. F. Winchester had majority control, the name was changed to the Winchester Repeating Arms Company, and the company absorbed all the assets of previous firms in which Winchester had invested substantial sums. Making guns had become more important than making shirts. And with the Henry's successor, the Model 1866, his investments began to pay off handsomely. Known popularly as the "Yellow Boy" in reference to its bright brass frame, the 1866 was the first of hundreds of models to bear the name Winchester.

One of the most popular of all Winchester arms, the 1866 was widely used in opening the West and, in company with the Model 1873, is the most deserving of Winchesters to claim the legend "The Gun That Won the West." It was also with this model that the factory engravers first created elaborate and exquisite masterpieces, some for exhibitions and a few for special presentations. The engraving dynasty of the Ulrich family, active primarily at Winchester for over eighty years, was effectively launched with the Model 1866.

Model 1866 production would reach a total in excess of 170,000, with its serial numbering continuing that of the Henry rifle. The run continued until 1898, despite the appearance of several newer, more modern lever-actions within its production span. All 1866s were in .44 rimfire caliber, and all frames were brass. Most steel parts were blued, though some barrels were browned, and the levers and hammers were standard case-hardened.

Nelson King's celebrated 1866 patent covering improvements in loading, for which he was rewarded $5,000 by a vote of the board of directors ($4,000 of which he took in company stock). Note the lack of a forend and the Henry-style frame, to which a hinged loading port was attached.

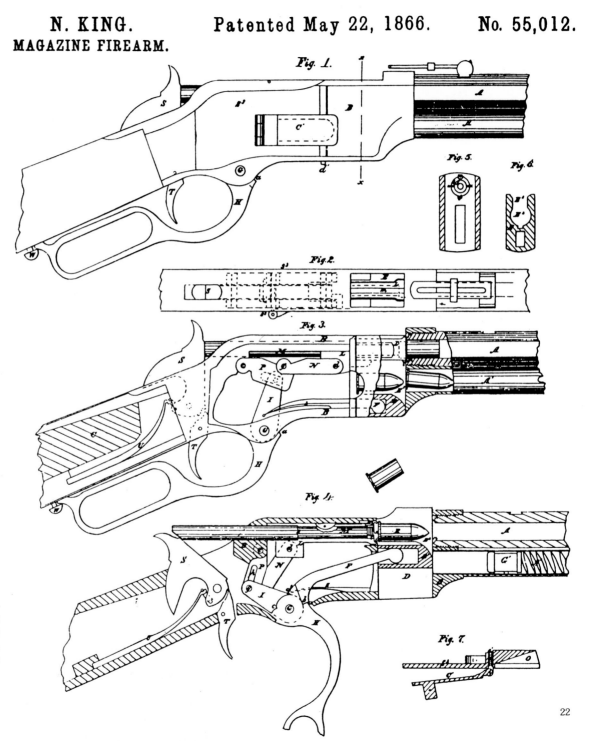

N. KING.   Patented May 22, 1866.   No. 55,012.

MAGAZINE FIREARM.

Fig. 1.

Fig. 5.   Fig. 6.

Fig. 2.

Fig. 3.

Fig. 4.

Fig. 7.

As on the Henry, the model designation does not appear on the gun. However, the barrel markings are distinctive. Through serial range 23000 the first roll stamping was simply

HENRY'S PATENT—OCT. 16. 1860.
KING'S PATENT—MARCH 29. 1866.

The remaining production carried the longer marking:

WINCHESTER'S—REPEATING ARMS. NEW HAVEN. CT.
KING'S—IMPROVEMENT
PATENTED—MARCH 29. 1866. OCTOBER 16. 1860.

Giving credit where credit was due appears to have been a hallmark of Oliver Winchester's attitude toward his leading employees. B. Tyler Henry's improvements which created the Henry rifle were acknowledged in the earlier roll marking, as well as by the H headstamp on the cartridges. The reference to King's improvement identifies a major contribution of Nelson King, who became superintendent of the Winchester factory late in 1866 (in Bridgeport) and remained so after the return to New Haven, 1871, not leaving the post until approximately 1875. King's prime improvement was designing a practical system for storing cartridges in a tube under the barrel, and for loading the tube through a gate on the right side of the frame. In the inventor's own words:

Beneath the barrel I place a thin metal tube extending along the barrel nearly its entire length, its rear and entering the frame. . . . Within the tube I place a follower and close the upper end of the tube by a plug or otherwise, and between the follower and the plug I place a helical spring, the tendency of which is to force

Comparison of three of the key stages in Winchester evolution. *From the top,* a Volcanic with standard engraving style and silver-plated frame. Standard engraving pattern on a silver-plated, brass-framed Henry rifle. The Model 1866 has its brass frame gold-plated and engraved by one of the Ulrich family. The loading port at frame center was the 1866's prime improvement over its predecessors.

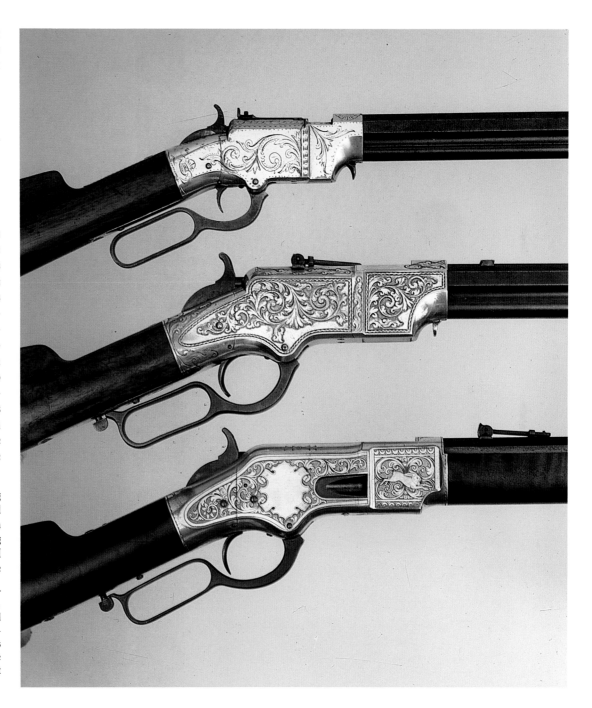

the follower toward the lower or rear end of the tube. Through one of the plates (preferring that one upon the right hand side) I form an opening . . . so as to communicate through the frame directly to the chamber in the carrier-block. Through this opening, and while its carrier-block is down . . . insert the cartridges, front first . . . the second cartridge pressing the first into the magazine, and so on. . . .

The patent drawing shows a hinged loading gate, but the production arms had a flat (later grooved) plate held firm by a spring.

So important were King's improvements that the firm's board of directors voted him a $5,000 bonus, most of which he took in company stock. King was second only to O. F. Winchester in company salary.

Despite the model designation of 1866, production quantities did not reach the market until 1867. The board had voted to authorize 5,000 rifles and carbines in a resolution of early March 1867, and another 10,000 were voted in mid-February 1868. The first Model 1866s were commonly known in the arms trade as "improved Henrys." References to the 1866 in newspapers and in journals were generous and not infrequent. The *Scientific American* of October 14, 1868, noted: "We have lately examined the Winchester repeating rifle . . . which was submitted to a series of trials by the Federal Military Commission of Switzerland. . . . The rifle is elegant in appearance, compact, strong, and of excellent workmanship. On examination we find its working parts very simple, and not apparently liable to derangement."

The 1866 was advertised in carbine, rifle, and musket (with bayonet lug) configurations, but they are divided by today's collectors into four basic technical variations:

First Model—Tang serial marking hidden by buttstock, Henry-style profile at hammer area of frame, flat cover to loading gate, barrel marking with Henry and King patent dates, flattish frame

These magnificent rifles help demonstrate the evolution of the lever-action and its decoration, from the Henry (at *top*, serial number 9) through the 1866. *Center* rifle, number 26283, is a masterpiece and likely was made as a factory show gun by Gustave Young, America's foremost arms engraver of the nineteenth century. The Goddess of Liberty was inspired by banknote engraving. *Bottom* rifle, 1866 number 79944, is a showpiece by a Young protégé, C. F. Ulrich (and so signed). Inspiration for the female nude was sculptor Hiram Powers's *The Greek Slave*, or a similar sculpture of the period.

Earliest-pattern cartridge board (21" × 23") by Winchester, c. 1874. All are rimfire cartridges except for the .44-40 centerfire at bottom. The cartridges were mounted on the lithographed background and then framed for exhibit by dealers and distributors. Thus began the tradition of cartridge boards, continued to this day by the Winchester Division of Olin Corporation.

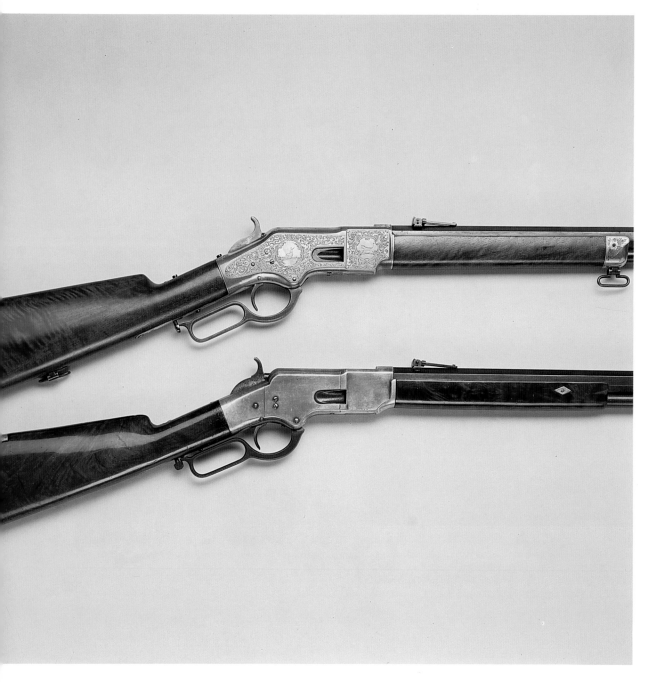

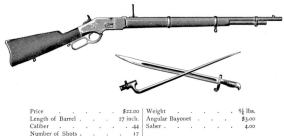

Price	.	.	.	.	$22.00	Weight	.	.	.	.	8¼ lbs.
Length of Barrel	.	.	.	27 inch.	Angular Bayonet	.	.	.	$3.00
Caliber	.	.	.	.	.44	Saber	.	.	.	.	4.00
Number of Shots	.	.	.	17					

does not flare to meet forend, two screws on upper tang, serial number range from 12476 (first 1866) to approximately 15500, made only in carbine and rifle configurations.

Second Model—Tang serial marking hidden by buttstock (through c. 19000 serial range), frame flares upon meeting forend, more graceful curve to frame at hammer area, most specimens with Henry and King patent barrel marking, approximate serial range 15500–25000, only in rifle and carbine style.

Third Model—Serial marking on lower tang behind trigger, less pronounced frame profile at hammer area, King's Patent and New Haven barrel marking, frame flares to meet forend, approximate serial range 25000–149000.

Fourth Model—Script serial number on lower

The 1866 musket, as pictured in the factory's September 1st, 1882, catalogue. The bayonet styles were termed saber and angular.

Bottom, rare First Model or "Flatside" 1866 rifle, number 15109, with such early features as diamond-escutcheoned forend lacking forend cap, Henry styling to areas of the frame, and serial numbering on side of tang (covered by buttstock). Even earlier rifles had flat loading-port covers. The *top* rifle, number 36259, is one of the earliest examples of signed engravings by C. F. Ulrich; the initials C.F.U. are minutely inscribed on frame bottom behind the trigger.

tang at area of lever latch, frame flares to meet forend, frame profile less pronounced than predecessor, Third Model barrel marking, approximate serial range 149000–170101.

By 1868 the Yellow Boy already had a wide reputation. In his book *Buffalo Land*, William E. Webb wrote of his 1866 carbine, which he carried across the plains:

> I became very fond of a carbine combining the Henry and King patents. It weighed but seven and one-half

Chief Poundmaker of the Crees and his Model 1866 rifle, with sling attached.

Model 1866 advertisement shows the rifle and carbine versions, and the rimfire cartridge with H headstamp. Note the artist's desire to show the loading port and saddle ring on the carbine; only the latter belongs on the left side.

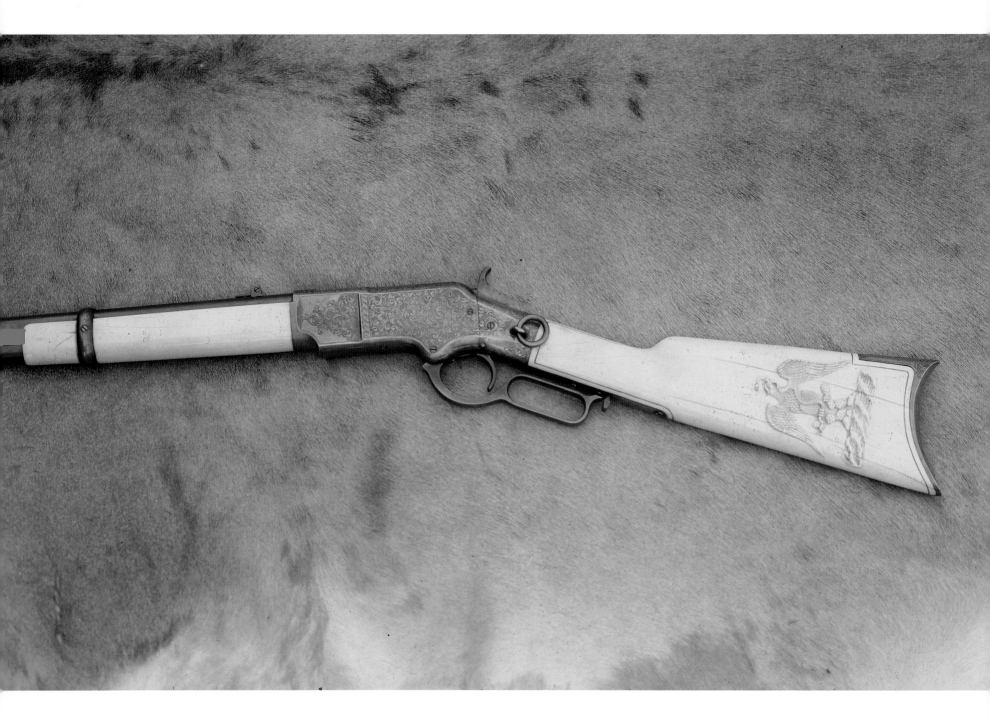

The butt of this trapper's 1866 carbine has Indian-style tack decorations. Contemporary photograph by J. F. Rowe of Portage la Prairie, Manitoba, Canada.

From the private arms collection of Mexican President Porfirio Díaz, Model 1866 number 21921 boasts a Mexican eagle carved in relief on the ivory stock. Ivory-stocked longarms rank high in American firearms rarities. So rare is the Díaz carbine that it is known to collectors as *the* ivory-stocked Winchester.

Unusual Victorian decorative motifs with running deer and a female nude grace this C. F. Ulrich–engraved show gun. Barrels were seldom decorated on the Model 1866, and the scrollwork and silver band inlays on this specimen are added indications of exclusivity.

Serial number 79863 is an Ulrich masterpiece, and has been attributed to John. A near twin to this cased rifle, number 84015, bears the signature of John's brother Conrad F. Since both John and Conrad studied under Gustave Young, it is not surprising to find such closeness of style, quality, and execution. The casing is of bird's-eye maple, with special hardwood edging, and the interior is lined with green velvet. Such period cases are much sought-after.

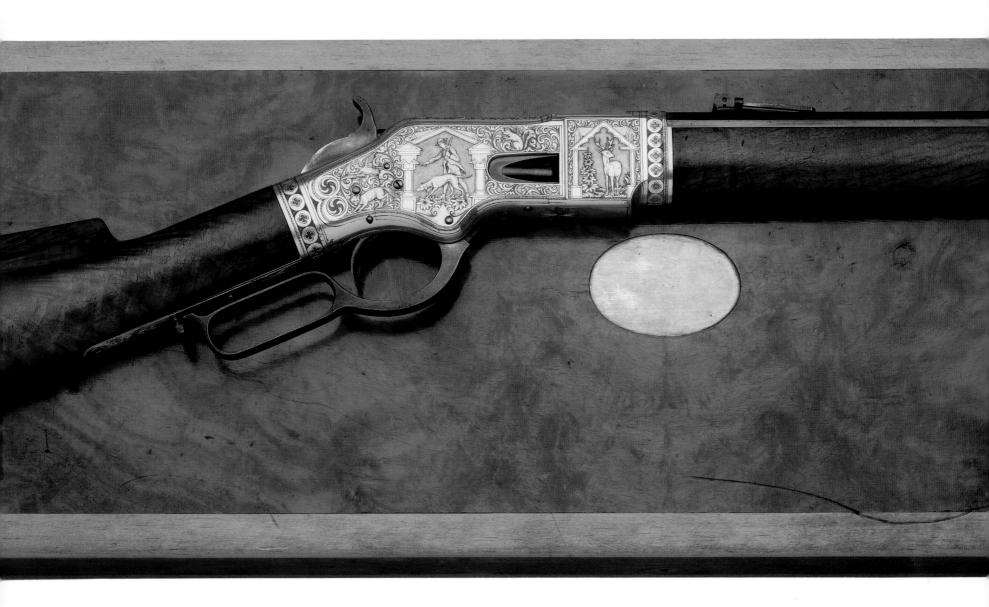

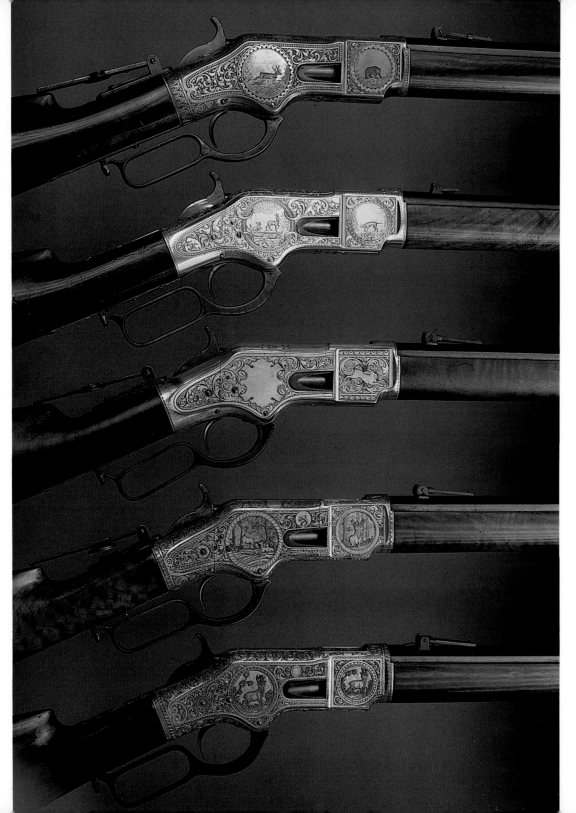

pounds, and could be fired rapidly twelve times without replenishing the magazine. Hung by a strap to the shoulder, this weapon can be dropped across the saddle in front, and held there very firmly by a slight pressure of the body . . . with a little practice, the magazine of the gun may be refilled without checking the horse. So light is this Henry and King weapon that I have often held it out with one hand like a pistol, and fired.

In response to the rapid-fire capability of the 1866, and indeed to the Henry, the Indians labeled these guns the "many shots" or "heap-firing." Model 1866 and Henry rifles were used against General George Armstrong Custer at the famous Last Stand; besides being outnumbered, Custer's men were generally outgunned—a Henry or an 1866 having far more firepower than the single-shot Springfield trapdoor carbines which were the issue longarm for the cavalrymen.

Some comments in a Winchester broadside of the late 1860s noted certain of the advantages of the 1866:

The advantage that this Gun possesses over all others for *single individuals* traveling through a wild country, where there is reason to expect a sudden attack either from *robbers* or *Indians*, cannot be *over-estimated*, as it is well known to all who have used a gun to any extent . . . that there is a *little* uncertainty of its going off; but with this Gun there can be no such feeling, because even though a Cartridge should miss fire, it is drawn from the barrel with *unfailing certainty*, and another placed in its stead, and fired in just *half a second*, thereby giving two chances, even though the enemy should be within twenty feet at the firing of the

A distinguished lineup of deluxe Model 1866 rifles, each of show-gun quality, and each with a gold-plated frame. Attributed to John and Conrad F. Ulrich, with the possibility of at least one by brother Herman. No signed rifles by Herman have been located by collectors.

Titans of the overland rails. A. J. Russell's c. 1868–69 photograph shows a Union Pacific directors' meeting in a private railroad car. Seated staring imperiously at the camera is Thomas C. Durant, with John Duff on his left and Sidney Dillon on his right. Both Duff and Dillon later became UP presidents. Consulting Engineer Silas Seymour is at *far left*. Above the central mirror are crossed pairs of Model 1866 rifles and 1851 Navy Colts. At the directors' feet, spittoons at the ready.

L. D. Nimschke's engraving masterpiece the "Solid Silver" Winchester, made for presentation from the President of Peru, José Balta, to the President of Bolivia, Mariano Melgarejo. Frame, forend, buttplate, and carrier block are all of silver, which is believed to have been supplied to Winchester from the rich mines of Peru. Signed by the engraver seven times, including on frame bottom: L. D. NIMSCHKE ENG. N.Y. Photographed on a page documenting the rifle, from the author's book *L. D. Nimschke Firearms Engraver*, a reprint edition of Nimschke's own engraving scrapbook.

22. PERU. *Engraved on solid Silver frame of Henry's Patent Rifle.
Impressions of Barrel see page Nº 20.*

1868.
L. D. Nimschke

first shot, which is something that no other Rifle yet built is capable of doing. . . . this Gun is what has long been wanted; it is so simple in its construction, that a child ten years old can with half an hours instruction, load and fire it with perfect safety, it being impossible to get a cartridge into it otherwise than right.

A quite pointed recommendation of the Model 1866 was made by Vice Admiral Jasper H. Selwyn, Royal Navy, who stated (1882, London):

I have been for a long time a consistent advocate of the magazine gun known as the Winchester, or the Winchester-Henry as it is also called. . . . I saw personally in Turkey during the [Russo-Turkish War of 1877] the Circassian cavalry all armed with the Winchester-Henry [1866] carbine. My friend Reouf Pasha . . . told me he was reconnoitering at Yeni Zahrah with only his personal bodyguard of some thirty Circassians. A Cossack regiment, some 600 strong, came down and surrounded him. It was toward nightfall; he got his Circassian guard off their horses and made them all lie down, they and their horses. He said to them: "Now, my children, we are in a mess, and must sell ourselves dearly to the Ruski." The Cossacks formed around them, thinking they had only to prevent their escape, but in five minutes so many of the Cossacks were killed, not one of the Circassians being touched, that the Cossacks decided to leave them alone and to go away. That shows the value of magazine weapons.

Henry M. Stanley, in *How I Found Livingstone in Central Africa*, alluded to his leaving Zanzibar with a Winchester and a Henry "sixteen shooter." The

Winchester appears to have been a Model 1866 rifle, with which he shot at hippopotamus: "The Winchester rifle (calibre 44), a present from the Hon. Edward Joy Morris—our Minister in Constantinople—did no more than slightly tap them." When leaving Livingstone, Stanley left the Henry, a revolver, two rifles, and 1,500 cartridges. The grateful recipient later acknowledged his appreciation by letter. He thought the Henry's cartridges were "not satisfactory, but everything else gives so much satisfaction that I could not grumble though I were bilious."

Although the international sales for the 1866 were substantial, the major market for the guns was North America, and the prime sales were in the West. Among the agents were such renowned frontier emporiums as Freund & Brother, with stores in Salt Lake City, Cheyenne, and Laramie; Liddle and Kaeding of San Francisco; John P. Lower of Denver; and C. S. Kingsley of Idaho City. Not a few sales came from the powerful jobbers and dealers of the major Eastern and Midwestern cities, among them Cooper & Pond, John P. Moore & Sons, and Schuyler, Hartley & Graham of New York, William Read & Sons of Boston, J. C. Grubb & Company of Philadelphia, Charles Folsom of Chicago, and William Golcher of St. Paul. In St. Louis (with an office in New York as well), Henry Folsom & Company was still another Winchester outlet.

A statistical analysis of factory shipping ledgers undertaken by the late author John E. Parsons revealed some interesting facts about the Model 1866s of serial range 125000 and above. Of the 44,739 guns shipped, 35,402 were carbines, 3,914 were muskets, and 5,423 were rifles. Nickel-finished carbines numbered only 420, rifles only twenty-three, and muskets eighty-six; for half-nickel finishes the totals were thirteen carbines and thirteen rifles. Silver-plated guns totaled 245 rifles and two carbines; sixteen carbines were gold-plated, as were seven muskets and two rifles; nine

Stagecoach king Ben Holladay was the proud owner of 1866 number 38586, and of the accompanying gold-inscribed canes and elegant silver-and-gilt punch bowl. The bowl was a gift from Lewis Leland, proprietor of the Occidental Hotel, San Francisco. The side shown is engraved with a stagecoach scene; the other side of the bowl is engraved with a steamship motif. These items were later prized by pioneer Western gun and memorabilia collector Parker Lyon, whose Pony Express Museum, Pasadena, exhibited over one million objects of the Old West.

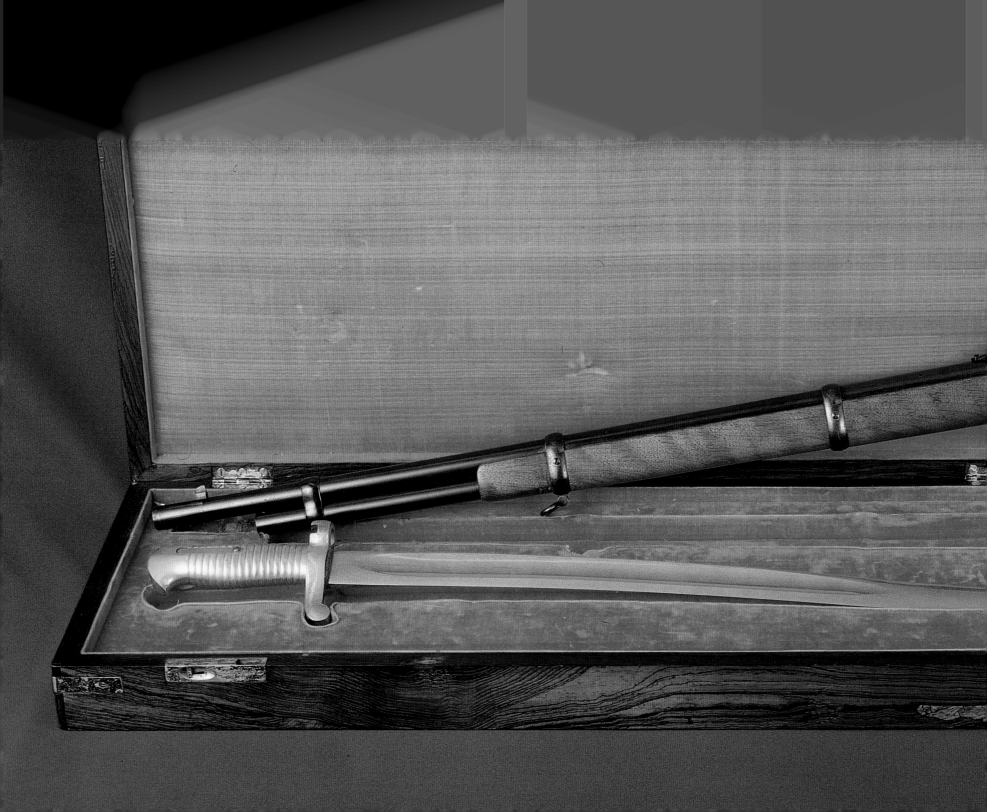

Cased, engraved, and gold-plated Model 1866 musket number 78143 features the Three Graces (after sculpture by Canova), elephant, dog, and fox panel scenes, and attribution of presentation to Thomas Witherell Palmer, businessman, philanthropist, U.S. Senator, U.S. Minister to Spain, and president of the Chicago World's Fair Commission. Signed C. F. ULRICH twice, on the lower tang. This musket is also pictured on the dust jacket of this book.

rifles had half-plating in gold. A total of eighty-one carbines, ninety-one rifles, and fifty-three muskets were plated and factory-engraved. Only five guns were factory-inscribed, each with initials. Research suggests that more than half of the engraved 1866s have yet to be discovered and entered into the collector market.

Discoveries of surviving guns by collectors and dealers, and the Model 1866s in museums around the world, testify to this model's being the first Winchester to spread the name internationally. The Army Museum in Constantinople displays some of the most exquisite of engraved Model 1866s, and Turkey was also a major client. The deluxe arms likely served as presentations to whet the appetite of Turkish generals and colonels. If so, the results were well worth the expense on Winchester's part: 5,000 carbines and 45,000 muskets were ordered by the Turks in 1870 and 1871.

Oliver F. Winchester (*inset*) and two views of his palatial mansion on Prospect Street, New Haven. The mansion was demolished in the early twentieth century; the site is now occupied by the Yale Divinity School. Still standing—and the next estate south—is the mansion of Winchester's shirt-making partner John M. Davies. The two houses were quite similar, and may have been designed to reflect their long-standing partnership and association, first in the shirt business and later in firearms.

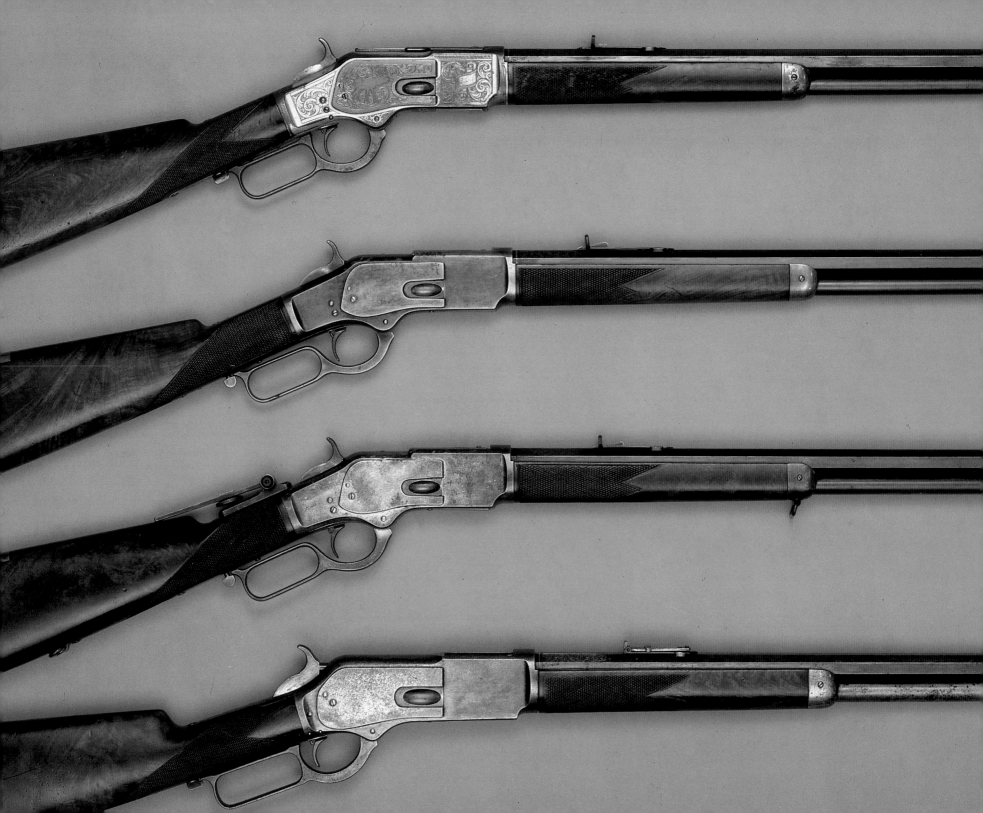

Chapter II
Frontier Rifles:
The 1873 and 1876

The fortunes of Oliver Winchester and his rapidly growing firearms company surged during the banner years of 1873 and 1876. Joining the already highly popular Model 1866, the new rifles caught the public's fancy immediately upon reaching the market. The Model 1873 looks like a smaller brother to the 76; both have iron frames and raised sideplates, and overall graceful lines. The 73 offered the newly developed (by the W.R.A. Co.) .44-40 centerfire cartridges, and the 76 was Winchester's first big-game rifle, taking the mighty .45-75. These new models, in carbine, rifle, and musket versions, were part of the evolution of the firm as the dominant American maker of lever-action repeating firearms.

Three deluxe Model 1873 rifles, and, at *bottom*, a deluxe 1876. The *top* two and the 1876 are One of One Thousands; *second from bottom* is a One of One Hundred. The mammoth frame size of the 1876 is immediately evident.

The Model 1873
While the factory was still hoping to land military contracts for lever-action repeaters, the production for foreign military markets and for national and international civilian sales was burgeoning. The company's 1875 catalogue noted that the Model 1873 was built for "the use of a longer [than its Model 1866 predecessor] and a centerfire cartridge, holding a charge of 40 grains of powder [and there was a sliding breech cover at top] to keep dirt and snow out of the lock." For a while the Model 1866 was discontinued, only to return again in 1875 (first serial number of 124995); its revitalized sales were likely influenced by a reduction in price.

A most practical accessory which greatly boosted the 1873's usefulness was the William Wirt Winchester (Oliver's son) invention of a reloading tool (patented October 18, 1874). The 1875 catalogue stated, "The Reloading Tool, as constructed, removes the exploded primer, inserts the new primer, and fastens the ball in the shell, at the same time swaging the entire cartridge to the exact form, and with absolute safety."*

Winchester Model Room mechanic and designer Luke Wheelock had invented a safety sear (patent issued December 1, 1868), which was actuated by contact between the cocking lever and a release mounted near the trigger. Model 1873s with that feature postdate 1880, and similarly equipped 1876s postdate 1878.

Quite a few variations were made in the long production run of the 1873, which was the first Winchester offering a wide variety of options and custom or special-order features. The 1878 catalogue offered the following array of options, which were also available for the 1866 and 1876 but, as a practical matter, were most often to be found on the 1873:

*Illustrated at right center of page 173

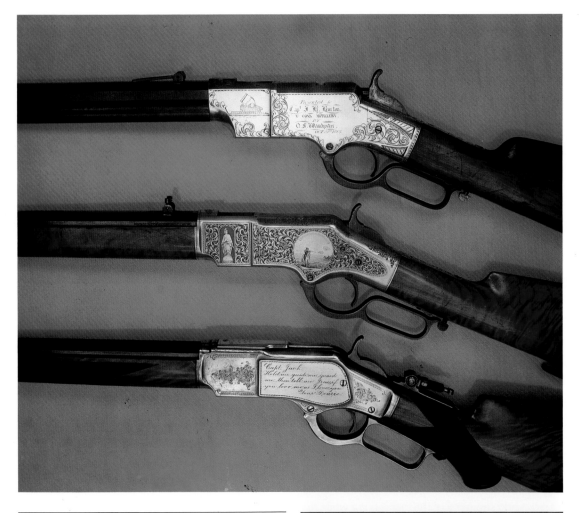

PRICE LIST

	Model '66.	Model '73.	Model '76.
Sporting Rifle, Octagon Barrel,	23.00	27.00	35.00
" " ½ " "	23.00	27.00	35.00
" " Round "	22.00	25.00	32.00
Musket,	22.00	26.00	30.00
Carbine	20.00	24.00	27.00

EXTRAS

All deviations from standard styles and sizes involve a large proportional outlay for hand labor, and when ordered will be subject to the following charges:

For additional length of barrel and magazine, add to price $1.00 per inch over the regular lengths, as quoted in preceding pages.

Extra heavy barrels, round or octagon, increasing the weight of the gun from one to two pounds, can be furnished at an additional cost of $5.00.

Engraving, from $5 to $100 additional, according to style and quality.

Full Nickel Plating,	$ 5.00
Nickel Plating Trimmings,	3.00
Silver " "	5.00
Gold " "	10.00
Set Triggers,	4.00
Mortise Cover Slide, Model 1876,	1.00
Fancy Walnut Stock,	5.00
Checking Butt Stock and Forearm,	5.00
Pistol Grip Stock, Model 1876 only, Fancy Walnut, Checked,	15.00
Case Hardening,	1.00
Swivels and Sling Strap,	1.50

Fancy Wood, Leather and Canvas Cases, Cartridge Boxes and Belts; furnished to order at moderate prices.

Comparison of the Henry, the 1866, and the 1873, in three exceptional rifles. *From the top,* the Henry, serial number 1978, was presented to Captain J. R. Burton, 1st Connecticut Artillery, by O. F. Winchester, and is so inscribed. The 1866, number 26283, was an exhibition piece engraved for Winchester by Gustave Young. The 1873, number 99609, was given by the Winchester factory to Captain Jack Crawford, the "Poet Scout of the Black Hills." Known as the author of "sincere but banal verse," Captain Jack was a Buffalo Bill look-alike, with a distinguished Civil War record, and the successor to Cody as chief of scouts in the Sioux campaign of 1876. The "Captain Jack" rifle is the .22-caliber variation of the 1873.

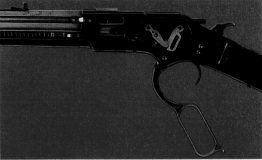

Factory cutaway showing the Model 1873 with its lever lowered. Examples of factory cutaways are supremely rare. Besides demonstrating how a firearm functioned, they reveal the extraordinary ability of gunmaking machinists.

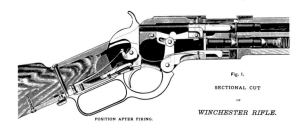

Fig. 1.

SECTIONAL CUT

OF

WINCHESTER RIFLE.

POSITION AFTER FIRING.

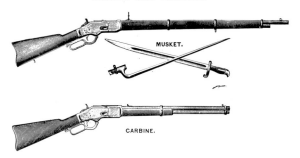

MUSKET AND CARBINE.

MUSKET.

CARBINE.

MODEL 1873.

SPORTING RIFLE, OCTAGON BARREL, PLAIN TRIGGER.

SPORTING RIFLE, SHORT MAGAZINE, HALF OCTAGON BARREL, PLAIN TRIGGER.

A "sectional cut" of the Model 1873, from the company's September 1882 catalogue. The basic toggle-link mechanism that began in the Volcanics continues.

Carbine, rifle, and musket, as pictured in the September 1882 catalogue.

Six Winchester Model 1873s are in the gun room at Sandringham, England, remnants of royal presentations (apparently a total of fifteen rifles and fifteen carbines) given by Edward, Prince of Wales, while traveling through India in 1875. The guns had come to His Royal Highness through the London Armoury Company, agents for Winchester. Serial numbers of these Sandringham pieces are 3972, 4161, 6597, 6604, 6618, and 31244; all but one are rifles. All have select walnut stocks and fine quality finishes, and three have brass plaque inlays engraved with the monogram and crest illustrated. Prince Edward, later King Edward VII, was a keen sportsman, especially fond of shooting. These and other royal firearms are the subject of David J. Baker's *The Royal Gunroom at Sandringham*, with a foreword by H.R.H. the Duke of Edinburgh.

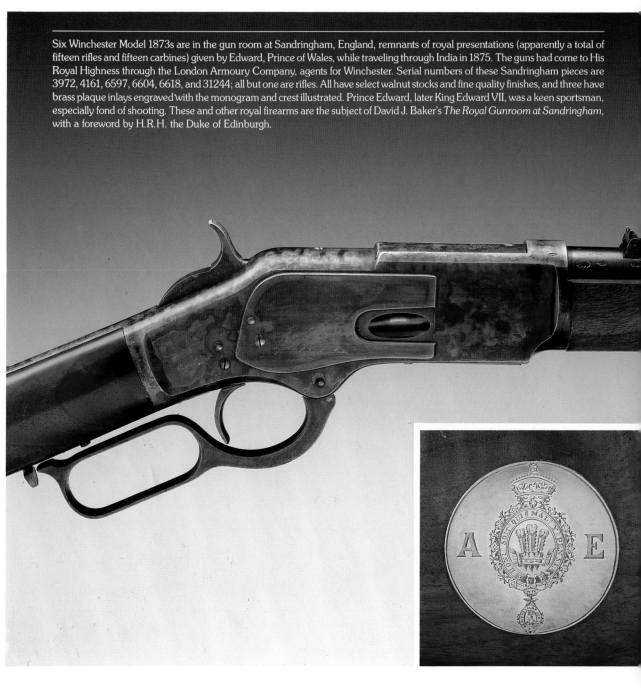

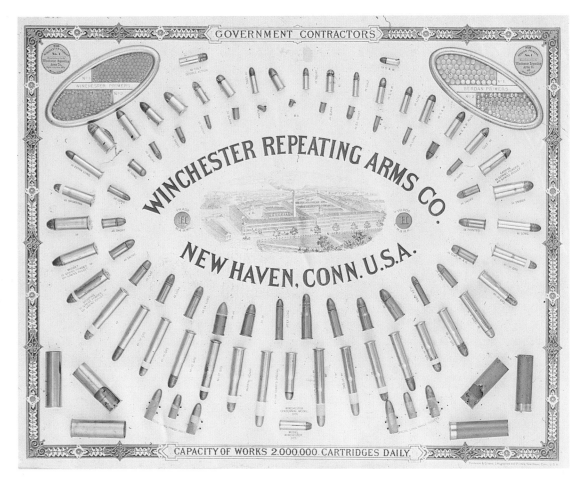

An 1879 cartridge board, 25″ × 31″, with thirty-one rimfires forming the inner circle and forty-six centerfires forming the outer circle and corners. Primers, shotshell cases, and bullets are also included. Note the legend: "Capacity of Works 2,000,000 Cartridges Daily." Collectors term this the "Double Oval" board. Interestingly, at the time, the factory produced a total of ninety-nine cartridge variations.

(The number of options later increased, but began decreasing in the twentieth century, as was true with most models.)

Standard on the upper tang was the roll marking MODEL 1873, the first Winchester to be marked with its model and introductory-year designation. Serial numbering continued sequentially to 720610. These arms were made over a forty-seven-year period, and the model was not formally discontinued until 1924—one of the longest production runs of any gun in the firm's history. Soon to join the .44-40 caliber were the .38-40 and .32-20, and for a twenty-year period beginning in 1884, a total of nearly 20,000 Model 1873s were made for .22 Short and Long rimfire cartridges. The Model 73 was the first American-made repeating rifle chambered for the .22 rimfire, the most popular and widely used rifle or handgun cartridge in history.

The barrel inscription continued with the later marking standard on the Model 1866, although variations occur in time. Calibers were standard marked on the carrier block and/or on the breech of the barrel. Sights were standard in rifle, carbine, and musket configurations, setting a pattern which continued into the twentieth century on various Winchester lever-action models. Most guns were made with a blued finish and with case-hardened hammers, levers, and buttplates. Case-hardened frames are found and, in an original state, are of exquisite quality and color. The high quality of manufacture was a hallmark of these arms and remained so throughout production. The fit of metal to wood, the finesse in machining, finishing, and final assembling, and the overall beauty of design are all factors which explain the particular attraction the 1873 had for the original owners and users, as well as for the present-day collector.

The technical breakdown which identifies the major variations are as follows:

Early First Model—Serial range 1 to approximately 28000; note dust cover having guide

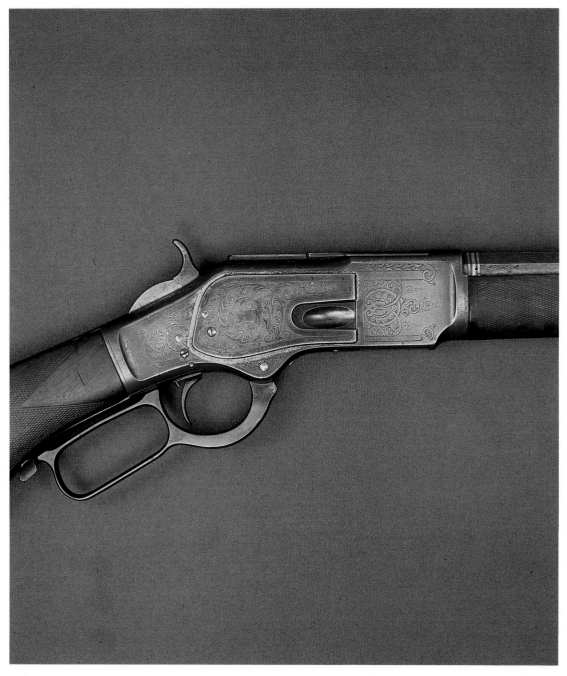

One of the most fascinating of historic Winchesters, number 33669 was given to Kansas cowtown marshal Henry Brown, a member of Billy the Kid's outlaw gang who had turned straight, but not for long, as Brown later used this rifle in an attempted bank robbery in Medicine Lodge, Kansas. He and his sidekicks were captured, and that night a lynch mob attacked the jail; three of the outlaws were lynched, and Brown was shot while trying to escape. In his jail cell, hours before his death, Brown wrote a haunting letter to his wife, in which he urged her to sell his property, but "keep the Winchester." The rifle now belongs to the Kansas State Historical Society, Topeka, and is considered among the museum's prized exhibits.

Members of the posse which captured Henry Brown and his gang of Medicine Lodge bank robbers, 1884. Most of the group are holding Model 1873 Winchesters.

Armed with a Model 1873 carbine and a single-action Colt, Billy the Kid posed for this historic tintype picture at Fort Sumner, New Mexico, c. 1879–80. The loading port visible on the left side of the carbine proves the image to be reversed; thus, the Kid carried his revolver on his right hip, which would suggest that he was right-handed. His killer, Sheriff Pat Garrett, also owned a Model 1873 carbine, and shot the Kid with a Colt single-action revolver, 1881.

grooves at front of frame, separately attached oval thumbrest on dust cover, two screws above trigger on frame.

Late First Model—Approximate serial range 28000–31000; note similar-style dust cover with oval thumbrest checkered on cover; trigger pin now under two frame screws, over trigger.

Second Model—Approximate serial range of 31000–90000; note center rail mount for dust cover at frame rear, checkered oval thumbrest panel later replaced by serrated edges.

Third Model—Serial range approximately 90000 to end of production; note dust-cover rail mount integral with frame, two frame screws and pin near trigger absent.

.22 Rimfire Caliber—.22-caliber markings, no loading gate on frame (load through front of magazine).

The most glamorous and appealing of all the Model 1873 variations are the One of One Hundred and One of One Thousand series. The factory catalogue of 1875 was the firm's initial public announcement of the type:

> The barrel of every sporting rifle we make will be proved and shot at a target, and the target will be numbered to correspond with the barrel and be attached to it.

> All of those barrels that are found to make targets of extra merit will be made up into guns with set-triggers and extra finish, and marked as a designating name "one of a thousand," and sold at $100. The next grade of barrels, not quite so fine, will be marked "one of a hundred," and set up in order in any style at $20

The R. S.-monogrammed, checkered stock, set trigger, Beach and peep sights, case hardening, and half-octagonal barrel are detailed in factory records for rifle 67517, shipped in May, 1881. Monograms are of even greater rarity than scroll engraving, judging from factory records and from surviving nineteenth- and early twentieth-century arms.

advance over the list price of the corresponding style of gun as shown in price-list.

So venerated are these rifles by today's collectors that a book was written to tell their fascinating story, the author's *Winchester: The Golden Age of American Gunmaking and the Winchester 1 of 1000*.

These special rifles helped capture for Winchester an image of prestige, quality, and performance, an image the brand name has kept into modern times. However, only 133 Model 1873 One of One Thousands were made, and only eight One of One Hundreds. Of the Model 1876, only fifty-one One of One Thousands were built, and seven One of One Hundreds.

The Winchester factory ledger records the entire original production, giving variations in barrel types and lengths, calibers, finishes, stocks, triggers, sights, slings and/or swivels, engraving, and special magazines.

Among the distinguished owners of One of One Thousands in the Model 1873 were Montana pioneers Granville and Thomas Stuart, Wild West show marksman Doc Carver, the outlaw Teton Jackson, and various stagecoach drivers, lawmen, and sportsmen.

Cowboys from Buffalo Bill's Wild West, photographed on Staten Island, New York, 1886. *Lower left*, Johnny Baker, the "Cowboy Kid," with 1873 rifle.

At *top*, dated 1876 beneath a low-relief E.R.G. monogram, rifle 23385, a One of One Thousand, also features CENTENNIAL inscribed on top of frame; likely a factory display piece at the Philadelphia Centennial Exposition. Signed J. ULRICH on the lower tang. At *center*, Montana pioneer Thomas Stuart's One of One Thousand, serial number 5611, has rare inscribed sideplate and early scroll embellishments. Stuart's brother Granville also had a deluxe One of One Thousand 1873. *Bottom* rifle, number 127938, has the so-called half-nickel finish (frame, buttplate, and forend), with the balance of steel parts blued or case-hardened. The small screw behind each trigger is to set the trigger pull.

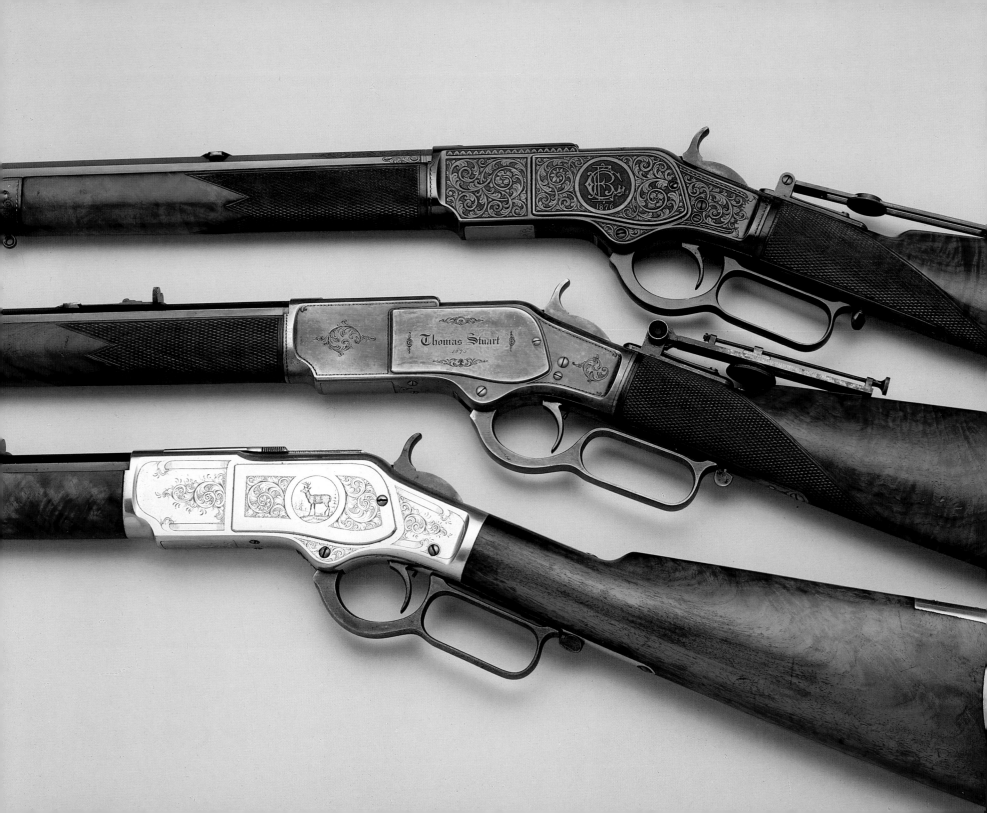

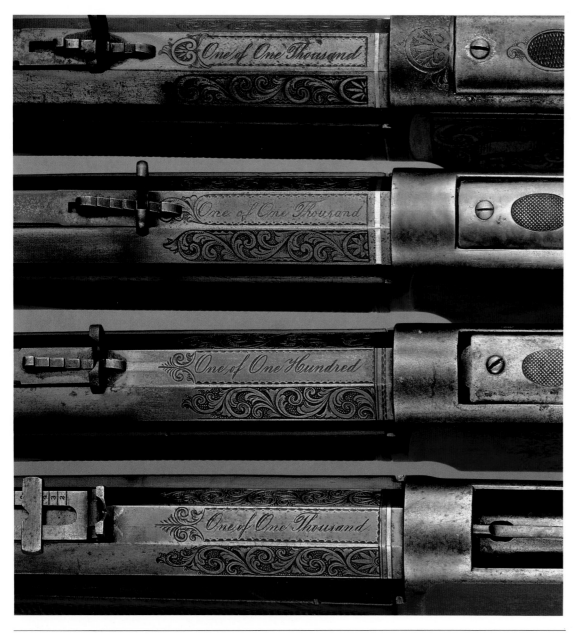

Standard script markings on the barrel breeches of One of One Hundred and One of One Thousand rifles. *Top three* are the Model 1873; at *bottom*, the Model 1876 (see also page 40, showing side views of all four rifles). Mortise covers on the 1873s show two types of thumbgrip stylings.

Model 1873 rifles. *From the top*, numbers 18070 (One of One Thousand), 27179 (One of One Hundred), and 435498 (One of One Thousand, with rare cheekpiece). Among special features are the half-round, half-octagonal barrels on the One of One Thousands and the heavy barrel on the One of One Hundred.

It was the One of One Thousand which inspired the only Hollywood Western movie ever named for a specific model of Winchester: *Winchester '73*, starring James Stewart. As part of the nationwide promotion of the film (which was released in 1950 and is still shown on television), Universal Pictures and Winchester launched a nationwide search for One of One Thousand rifles. Owners of the first twenty guns discovered were given a Model 94 carbine. To locate the rifles, 150,000 "Wanted" posters were printed and sent to Winchester dealers (there were then some 50,000 of them) and to "20,000 chiefs of police, daily and weekly newspapers, radio stations . . . rifle club[s] . . . and . . . approximately 7,000 motion picture theaters." The campaign was instrumental in adding to the ranks of firearms collectors, as well as locating over two dozen One of One Thousand 1873s.

Following the Custer massacre of June 25, 1876, complaints over the single-shot Springfield trapdoor carbine, combined with 4th Cavalry Colonel Ranald S. Mackenzie's request for ordnance issue of Winchesters, led to a Springfield Armory test. The findings showed the .44-40 Winchester 1873 had insufficient power in comparison to the .45-70 trapdoors, and the Model 1866 carbine also generally did not fare well. Both the 1866 and the 1873 performed their best at a range of 100 yards.

Despite the continued diffidence of the military brass, sales of the 1873 were faring admirably. Comments from the field, and especially the West, were encouraging. Frontiersman John Cook had a .44-40 in New Mexico in 1874, and said it was "the first magazine gun I had owned. I had practiced with it until it had gained my confidence completely as *the* gun." Texas Ranger James B. Gillett bought an 1873 carbine after a battle with Apaches who were armed with repeaters. In his memoirs Gillett noted his purchase of December 1875:

The new center-fire 1873-Model Winchester had just appeared on the market and sold at $50 for the rifle

This young marksman is believed to be a son of Adam Bogardus, the showman and champion shooter who pioneered trapshooting in America.

Best-armed of what appear to be Army scouts is the center figure, with his 1873 rifle. All guns appear to be cocked in this photo of c. 1880.

Gentleman marksman and his 1873 rifle with half-round, half-octagonal barrel, Lyman tang peep sight, and custom front sight.

John Y. Nelson, driver of the Deadwood stagecoach in Buffalo Bill's Wild West; photo believed taken during the Chicago World's Fair, c. 1892–93.

Very rare Trapper's Model 1873 carbine, the barrel about 14 inches. The holstered revolver is likely a Colt six-shooter in matching caliber.

Well-armed Wells Fargo & Company expressmen at the Reno, Nevada, office, c. 1890.

Eagle Eye and his wife, Neola, likely a trick-shooting team, not only well-armed but nattily attired.

Lady bandit Pearl Heart, in photo believed taken after release from the Yuma Territorial Prison, Arizona, where she served time for stage robbery.

These men are possibly members of a city militia. One has his carbine attached to his shoulder sling.

and $40 for the carbine. A ranger who wanted a Winchester had to pay for it out of his own pocket and supply his own ammunition as well, for the State furnished cartridges only for the Sharps [single-shot] gun. However, ten men in Company D, myself included, were willing to pay the price to have a superior arm. I got carbine number 13401, and for the next six years of my ranger career I never used any other weapon. I have killed almost every kind of game that is found in Texas from the biggest old bull buffalo to a fox squirrel with this little .44 Winchester.

Easily one of the most treasured endorsements of the 1873 was from Colonel William F. "Buffalo Bill" Cody, whose letter from Fort McPherson, Nebraska, was published in Winchester's 1875 catalogue:

I have been using and have thoroughly tested your latest improved rifle. Allow me to say that I have tried and used nearly every kind of a gun made in the United States, and for general hunting, or Indian fighting, I pronounce your improved Winchester *the boss*.

An Indian will give more for one of your guns than any other gun he can get.

While in the Black Hills this last summer I crippled a bear, and Mr. Bear made for me, and I am certain had I not been armed with one of your repeating rifles I would now be in the happy hunting grounds. The bear was not thirty feet from me when he charged, but before he could reach me I [put] more lead [in him] than he could comfortably digest.

Believe me, that you have the *most complete* rifle now made.

However, the lack of power in the .44-40 cartridge was a disadvantage to Winchester sales. Experienced hunter J. Mortimer Murphy's comments reflected a generally held opinion of big-game hunters:

I have found the Winchester magazine or repeating rifle very convenient for general shooting; but that also had its faults, not the least of which was that the bullet would sometimes tilt as soon as it reached the breech from the magazine, at seemingly the most critical mo-

The always photogenic William F. "Buffalo Bill" Cody, taken by Eugene Pirou. Paris, 1889.

Signed J. ULRICH, Model 1873 number 148025 was inscribed on the left sideplate: "Presented to George P. Bissell. Colonel 25th Regt. C. V. by members of the Regiment at the Regimental reunion, April 14, 1884 as a slight testimonial of affection for their old commander."

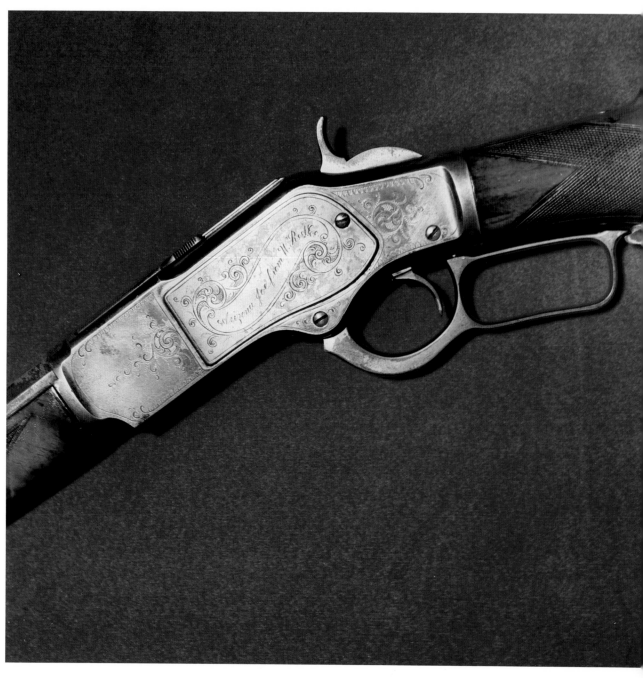

Showman Arizona Joe Bruce was presented deluxe 1873 rifle number 510607 by Winchester in 1897. Joe was the subject of a dime novel by Colonel Prentiss Ingraham, entitled *Arizona Joe, the Boy Pard of Texas Jack . . . [the] History of the Strange Life of Captain Joe Bruce, a Young Scout, Indian Fighter, Miner, and Ranger, and the Protégé of J. B. Omohundro, the Famous Texas Jack*. The rifle in the Zimmerman & Company photograph is undoubtedly the factory presentation.

ment; and ere it could be extricated and placed in its proper position, the game would probably be out of sight. I was compelled to leave a buffalo hunt on two occasions on account of this. . . . Another fault that it possessed for shooting heavy game was that the charge of powder it carried was too small . . . but it atoned in some respect for this by the rapidity with which it could be fired. . . .

The Centennial Rifle: The Model 1876

Winchester addressed objections to the 1873's lack of power by devising the 1876, a nearly identical-looking model but larger overall, the frame alone measuring an extra 1½ inches in length. The new cartridge, the .45-75, had substantially more punch, firing a 350-grain bullet. The cartridge measured 2¼ inches, as opposed to the 1⁹⁄₁₆ inches of the .44-40.

Winchester first displayed the new rifle at the Philadelphia Centennial Exhibition of 1876, where it drew rave notices. The exhibit itself was described in the book *Souvenir of the Centennial Exhibition* (1877):

> The Winchester Repeating Arms Company of New Haven had a rich and extensive display of weapons, consisting of magazine rifles, field, sporting, and target models. . . . The cases containing them were upright, forming three sides of a square, with projecting counter cases, and in the center an upright, octagonal case. . . . Another case contained a rifle exquisitely inlaid in gold tracery on blued steel, the floor of the case being a mirror, reflecting the reverse side, and thus exhibiting the whole piece. The exhibit included a total of nearly 200 guns, representing about 50 different styles. The cost of the cases alone was $3000, and this represents but a fraction of the value of the exhibit.

Unfortunately, no photograph showing the display has survived, as have photographs of the dramatic Colt showcase, which was back-to-back with Winchester's, in the Main Building off the center aisle.

Judges of the Centennial Exhibition awarded Winchester a citation for "the best magazine rifle for

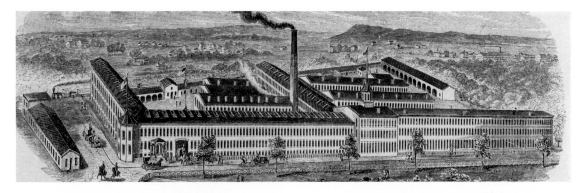

The Winchester Repeating Arms Company, c. 1876. Note the railroad immediately behind the factory. At this time the company did approximately $1,812,500 in net sales, made a profit of approximately $444,500, and paid dividends to stockholders of $50,000. The company then had about 690 workmen.

Rare photograph shows firearms displays at the Philadelphia Centennial Exhibition, 1876. *Upper center*, Winchester Repeating Arms Company, back-to-back with Colt's.

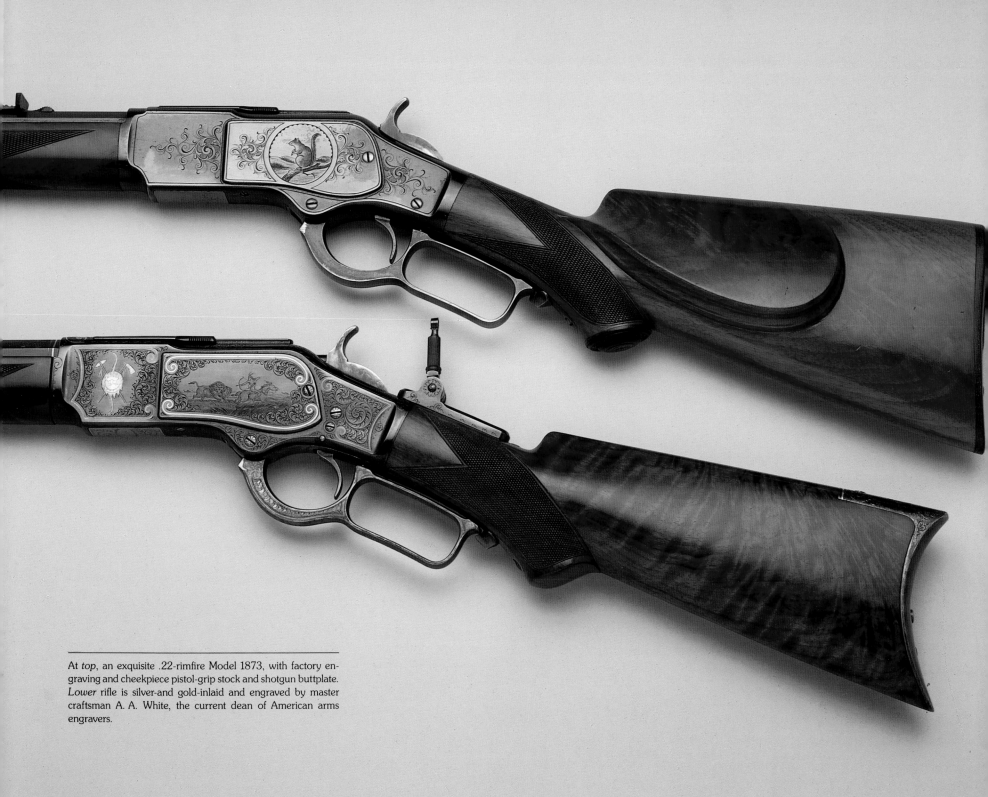

At *top*, an exquisite .22-rimfire Model 1873, with factory engraving and cheekpiece pistol-grip stock and shotgun buttplate. *Lower* rifle is silver-and gold-inlaid and engraved by master craftsman A. A. White, the current dean of American arms engravers.

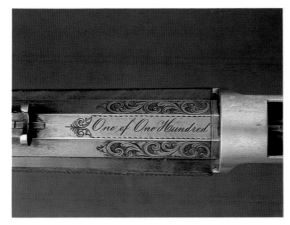

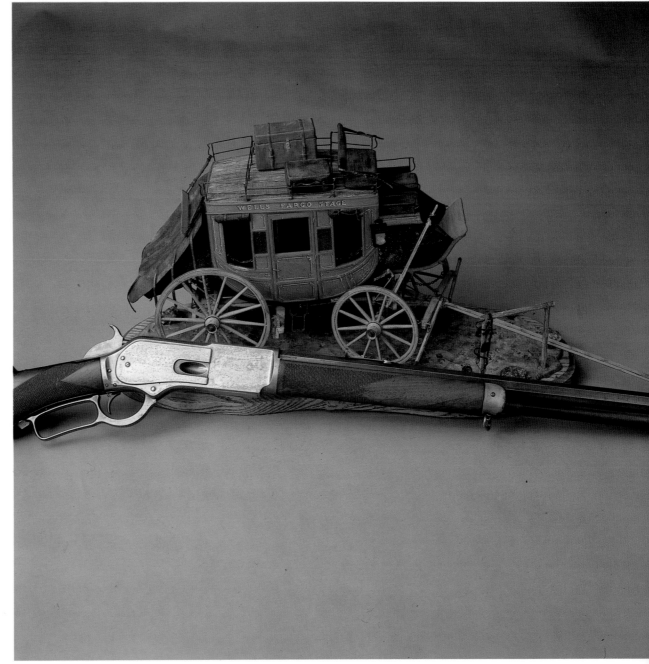

Property of stagecoach driver and operator John Kelsey, serial number 713 Model 1876 One of One Hundred left the factory in November of 1877. Kelsey was also a lookout at a Montana gambling house, bailiff in federal court, and guard for the U.S. Marshal's office, Montana. Of the seven One of One Hundred 1876 rifles made, all but one had three-digit serial numbers. All One of One Hundreds were .45-75 caliber, with 28-inch barrels; six had set triggers, one a plain trigger. Model 1876 Ones of One Thousands totaled fifty-one, in 24-, 26-, 28-, and 30-inch barrels, the majority of .45-75 caliber and most with octagonal barrels, set triggers, and case-hardened frames.

Some variations of the Model 1876; from the *top*, the .50-95 rifle; a .40-60 rifle; and a .45-75 musket. *Next*, a North West Mounted Police .45-75 carbine, and a .45-60 carbine. Serial numbers range from 11542 at bottom to the highest, the North West Mounted Police carbine, number 44172.

Carbine Rear Sight.

For Models 1866 and 1873.

Price, $1.50.

Musket Rear Sight.

Graduated 100 to 900 yds.

Price, $1.50.

Sporting Leaf Sight.

Graduated 100 to 800 yds. for Model 1873.
Graduated 100 to 1,000 yds. for Model 1876.
Graduated 100 to 1,000 yds. for Hotchkiss.

Price, $1.75.

Military Wind Gauge Sight.

Price, $2.50.

Sporting Rear Sight.

Graduated from 50 to 300 yds.

Price, $1.00.

AS OPEN.   AS GLOBE.

Winchester Reversible Sight.

Price, $1.50.

Lyman's Patent Combination Sight.

Complete with base . . . $5.00
Without base 3.00

Any of the above rear sights will be furnished with
Clover Leaf, Buckhorn, or any desired shape.

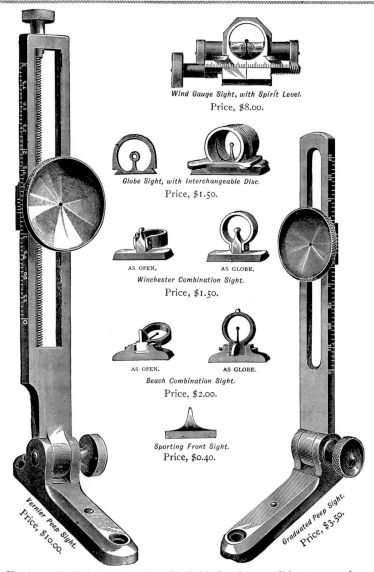

Wind Gauge Sight, with Spirit Level.

Price, $8.00.

Globe Sight, with Interchangeable Disc.

Price, $1.50.

AS OPEN.   AS GLOBE.

Winchester Combination Sight.

Price, $1.50.

AS OPEN.   AS GLOBE.

Beach Combination Sight.

Price, $2.00.

Sporting Front Sight.

Price, $0.40.

Vernier Peep Sight.

Price, $10.00.

Graduated Peep Sight.

Price, $3.50.

Vernier and Wind Gauge Sights, with Spirit Level, extra disk, etc., complete
in morocco case, $18.00.

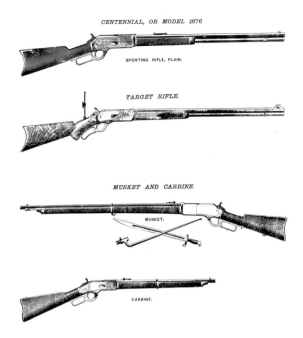

CENTENNIAL, OR MODEL 1876

SPORTING RIFLE, PLAIN.

TARGET RIFLE.

MUSKET AND CARBINE.

MUSKET.

CARBINE.

Four variations of the 1876, as pictured in the September 1882 catalogue.

Selections of sights, primarily for the Models 1873 and 1876, from the September 1882 catalogue.

Brilliant case hardening was a hallmark of Winchester. The effect was achieved by quenching polished parts, which had been heated to a very high temperature, in an oil bath. At *top*, Model 1886 serial number 66675, a .40-82; with number 106102, in .40-65. Both are Fancy Grade rifles, surviving over a century in exquisite condition.

Captain Jack Crawford with a Model 1876 rifle, the stocks checkered and deluxe. Like many of his celebrated contemporaries, Crawford was a devotee of firearms and assembled quite a private collection. He sought out examples from such sidekicks as Wild Bill Hickok and George Armstrong Custer, and an inventory exists which lists several of the guns in the Crawford collection.

Superbly case-hardened Model 1876 short rifle, against an antique Western saddle.

Theodore Roosevelt's stalwart Model 1876 half-magazine .45-70 rifle, number 38647. Cover illustration on author's book depicts TR in his Dakota rancher buckskins, photographed in a New York studio. He is holding this 1876 rifle, and has a sterling silver Bowie knife (made for him by Tiffany & Co.) in his belt. Roosevelt wrote his sister Anna in 1884 that he looked "like a regular cowboy dandy, with all my equipments finished in the most expensive style. . . ."

Roosevelt's best Western revolver, the single-action .44-40 number 92248, with its hand-tooled holster, and .40-60 Model 1876 carbine, number 45704. Both guns were embellished by L. D. Nimschke on custom order, likely through New York dealers Schuyler, Hartley & Graham. The .40-60 was used by Roosevelt as a "saddle gun for deer and antelope" and was carried by him in the pursuit and capture of boat thieves, Dakota Territory, 1886. Accompanied by scarce first edition of TR's second book on his adventures in the West. From the Gene Autry Western Heritage Museum.

Indisputably one of the most spectacular and historic of all Winchesters, number 14327 is a John Ulrich masterpiece, signed by him in each panel. It is a half magazine .50-95 Express rifle, with special sights, set trigger, and select French walnut pistol grip and checkered stocks. General Phil Sheridan distinguished himself in the Civil war and in Indian fighting, and his friend W. E. Strong was president of the Peshtigo Lumber Company, Chicago.

" 'Hands Up'— The Capture of Finnigan," a drawing by Frederic Remington for Roosevelt's *Ranch Life and the Hunting Trail.* "When [the boat thieves] were within twenty yards or so we straightened up from behind the bank, covering them with our cocked rifles, while I shouted to them to hold up their hands. . . ." The Winchester that Roosevelt used is believed to have been the .40-60 Model 1876 carbine.

A Roosevelt neighbor and fellow rancher in the Dakota Territory, the Marquis de Mores was every bit as arrogant as he looks. Like Roosevelt he favored the 1876 Winchester, and had an ivory- or pearl-handled Colt six-shooter. The two men came close to having a duel, which would have been fought with Winchester rifles at a distance of twelve paces! Instead the two met for dinner at the Marquis's thirty-room mansion in Medora, and the threatened duel never took place.

Rare, beautiful, and in new, unfired condition, Model 1876 number 53072 was a gift to Colonel Gzowski, an aide-de-camp to Queen Victoria, in Canada. The velvet-lined casing of bird's-eye maple is equipped with a full complement of accessories. Rifle bears signature stamping J. ULRICH.

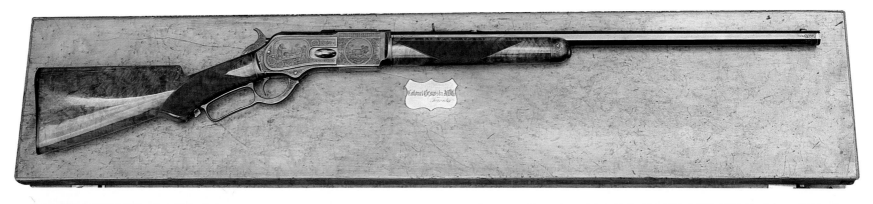

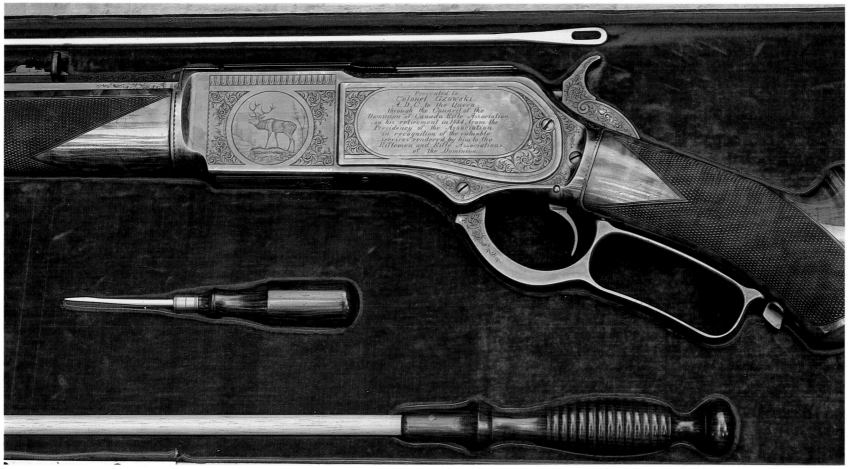

sporting purposes yet produced." In an August 1877 factory price list, the "Centennial" rifle was described as "finished same as Model 1873 with wrought iron mountings, uses a cartridge 45 calibre, with 75 grains of powder, and 350 grains of lead, nearly corresponding with the charge used in United States Government rifles."

Although cartridges added to the line were the .45-60 and .50-95 Express (1879) and the .40-60 (1884), the reference to "Government rifles" was important, since the firm was still hopeful of garnering lucrative government contracts. Even military endorsement of the product would have given impetus to sales.

But the best that Winchester could do for contract sales was with the Canadian government, for issue to the North West Mounted Police. An initial order of fifty had been supplied to the force in 1878, when the entire command was only 300-strong. In that year the commissioner noted that the "Winchester rifles . . . supplied are admirable weapons for our service. . . . I am in hopes that we may be supplied with fifty more rifles this year . . . as all ranks are very desirous of practicing with the new and popular arm." A further fifty 1876 carbines had been issued for the NWMP by 1880, and by then the commissioner had some observations based on field experience:

The Winchester rifle, which is a repeating one, and capable of receiving eight cartridges in the magazine, has many good points, and is a favorite arm with the western prairie men. I do not, however, consider it a good military weapon. The system of rifling is good, but the rifle is altogether too weak in construction to meet the rough handling that at times it is impossible to prevent its receiving. As an example of its weakness: some time ago a man on sentry at night slipped and fell; in doing so the barrel of his rifle was broken at the joint where it is secured into the breech apparatus. Other similar instances have occurred. The back sight on the Winchester rifle is *badly* attached to the barrel.

The sight slides readily from one side the other, which, of course, interferes with accurate shooting.

In May 1882, 300 of the specially marked (NWMP with an arc cartouche on stock) carbines were acquired, followed by 446 in April 1885. And, despite the shortcomings, the carbine remained in service as late as 1914.

The sportsman most often associated with the 1876 Winchester is Theodore Roosevelt. In *Hunting Trips of a Ranchman*, Roosevelt, a keen enthusiast of firearms and ballistics as well as an experienced and dedicated hunter, wrote of his favorite 1876 rifle that it was

stocked and sighted to suit myself. [It] is by all odds the best weapon I ever had, and I now use it almost exclusively, having killed every kind of game with it, from a grizzly bear to a big-horn. . . . the Winchester is the best gun for any game to be found in the United States, for it is deadly, accurate, and handy as any, stands very rough usage, and is unapproachable for the rapidity of its fire and the facility with which it is loaded.

Because of the heavy calibers, export sales—primarily to Africa, India, and Canada for big-game use—were notable. The large cartridges were needed for such heavy game as the brown and grizzly bears, Cape buffalo, rhinoceros, and elephant. In Canada the big bears were best confronted with an 1876—to do so with an 1873 or an 1866 was tantamount to suicide.

Mechanically the 1876 was the last of the toggle-link-style lever-actions, a system dating back to the Volcanics and the Henry. But the 76 also launched the new era of lever-action repeaters firing heavy-caliber cartridges. In the line through 1897, the total production of the Model 1876 was just under 64,000. Standard features were the MODEL 1876 upper-tang roll marking, Winchester barrel marking of name and address and King's improvement patent dates, and caliber markings on the barrel

breech and the bottom of the carrier block.

The major variations are as follows:

First Model—Lacks dust cover to top of frame; serial range to approximately 3000.
Early Second Model—Frame top with dust cover, its oval thumbpiece diestruck, guide rail of cover attached to frame top with screws, approximate serial range 3000–7000.
Late Second Model—Knurled finger grip at rear of dust cover, oval discontinued, approximate serial range 7000-30000.
Third Model—Dust-cover guide rail now integrally machined on frame, serial range approximately 30000 to end of manufacture.
North West Mounted Police guns—Carbine configuration, .45-75 caliber, 22-inch barrel, in serial ranges beginning approximately 8000, but most are in range 23801–24100 and 43900–44400.

Theodore Roosevelt: Conservationist and Hunter

One of the most vital lives in American history was led by Theodore Roosevelt—twenty-sixth President of the United States, soldier, statesman, conservationist, hunter, rancher, explorer, and recipient of the Nobel Peace Prize. An accomplished sportsman and naturalist, he was as serious about his guns and his hunting as he was about conservation of the world's natural endowment. No one did more for conservation in America than Roosevelt, and his status in the hunting world is legendary.

As each new lever-action was announced by Winchester. Roosevelt would add one (or more) to his growing collection. No amateur of arms, he was as expert on shooting and ballistics as most of his contemporaries, and often more experienced in the field. Most of Roosevelt's game shooting was in the West, but several Winchesters accompanied him and his son Kermit on their great African safari of 1909–10. TR's correspondence with the Winchester factory in outfitting that trip reveals how dedicated, knowledgeable, exacting, and experienced he was.

His love for the hunt was movingly expressed:

No one but he who has partaken thereof, can understand the keen delight of hunting in lonely lands. For him is the joy of the horse well ridden and the rifle well held; for him the long days of toil and hardship, resolutely endured, and crowned at the end with triumph. In after-years there shall come forever to his mind the memory of endless prairies shimmering in the bright sun; of vast snow-clad wastes lying desolate under gray skies; of the melancholy marshes; of the rush to mighty rivers; of the breath of the evergreen forest in summer; of the crooning of ice-armored pines at the touch of the winds of winter; of cataracts roaring between hoary mountain masses; of all the innumerable sights and sounds of the wilderness; of its immensity and mystery; and of the silences that brood in its still depths.

Roosevelt owned at least three Model 1876s: a carbine and rifle in .40-60 caliber, and his favorite, a rifle in .45-75. Each of these was specially engraved and built at his request, and he wrote of his .40-60 carbine in the March 1886 issue of *Outing* magazine:

A ranchman . . . with whom hunting is of secondary importance, and who cannot be bothered by carrying a long rifle always round with him on horseback, but who, nevertheless, wishes to have some weapon with which he can kill what game he runs across, usually adopts a short, light saddle-gun, a carbine, weighing but five or six pounds, and of such convenient shape that it can be kept under his thigh alongside the saddle. A 40-60 Winchester is perhaps the best for such a purpose, as it carries far and straight, and hits hard, and is a first-rate weapon for deer and antelope, and can also be used with effect against sheep, elk, and even bear, although for these last a heavier weapon is of course preferable.

Few sportsmen in the Eastern or Western United States could rival Roosevelt's collection of fine guns

A scout with Model 1876 across lap, single-action Colt on his left hip. The back of photograph is marked for "Rev. Mr. Kirby," presumably the recipient.

Carte de visite of frontier character, leaning on his Fancy Grade Model 1876 rifle. Note ax, Bowie knife, and Colt single-action.

Plains Indian braves with a superb beaded pipe/tomahawk and brand-new Model 1876 rifle.

Company D, Texas Rangers, most armed with 1873 carbines and Colt six-shooters, c. 1887. Standing, second from left, is Bass Outlaw, later killed in a gunfight.

Nearly dwarfed by the giant 1876 rifle, the sportsman in this picture by Payne of Santa Fe appears to be wearing a Winchester cartridge belt.

Studio shot of a burly huntsman with elk trophy, 1876 rifle, and skinning knife. Photograph by Davidson, Portland, Oregon.

The Sportsmen's Depot of John P. Lower, Denver, an emporium for a variety of firearms, ammunition, and equipment.

In this 1885 photograph the Dennis Scouts of the North West Field Force are well armed with Model 1876 NWMP issue carbines.

Not only a leading source for arms and ammunition, the Freund Armory, Cheyenne, also customized guns and made special sights for sportsmen like Theodore Roosevelt.

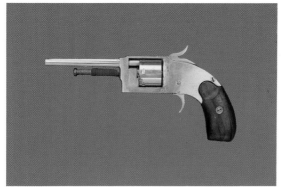

William Mason's single-action revolver (1883) built at Winchester and potentially a direct competitor to the Colt Army single-action. Mason had ample experience at Colt and had been intimately involved in designing its single-action.

Double-action Winchester prototype revolver, chambered for heavy-caliber cartridges and attributed to former Smith & Wesson inventor William Wetmore. The factory design drawing reveals much of the action's mechanism.

Patent model of the Winchester swingout-cylinder revolver, the patent issued to Stephen W. Wood, January 1877. The gun was built without a triggerguard, since the model was intended to demonstrate the practicality of the swingout design. Pulling forward and to the side on the knurled pin beneath the barrel released the cylinder, allowing for extraction or loading.

and accouterments. The highlights of these masterfully built objects were his Winchesters, a couple of deluxe Colt six-shooters, and a silver-mounted Bowie knife custom-made by Tiffany & Co., New York. The 1873 and 1876 Winchesters had captured Roosevelt's dedication to the marque. But developments at the Winchester factory and at a little-known gunshop in Ogden, Utah would give big-game sportsmen the ultimate repeating lever-action rifle up to that time: the Model 1886. Roosevelt's first rifle of this model came from winning a tennis match, and he "turned my share of the cup to a new Winchester rifle that I have been longing for."

Theodore Roosevelt's new Winchester was a Model 1886 .45-90 deluxe rifle, which he wrote about in *Ranch Life and the Hunting Trail*:

> Now that the buffalo have gone, and the Sharps rifle by which they were destroyed is also gone, almost all ranchmen use some form of repeater. Personally I prefer the Winchester, using the new Model [1886], with a 45-caliber bullet of 300 grains, backed by 90 grains of powder, or else falling back on my faithful old standby, the 45-75 [Model 1876]. . . .

The new rifle did yeoman service as Roosevelt's big-game gun from 1887 through 1894. He took over one hundred head of North America game with it and initially relied on factory loads for ammunition. But he soon switched to doing his own handloading, using a hybrid 300-grain hollow-point bullet with 85 grains of Orange Lightning smokeless powder. The same year that he purchased his new .45-90 rifle, TR organized the Boone and Crockett Club, an organization still actively engaged in wildlife conservation today. Among the eminent charter members were the artist Albert Bierstadt and the naturalist George Bird Grinnell. As the club's first president, Roosevelt was a driving force for its activities.

WINCHESTER REVOLVERS

One of the most intriguing episodes in the annals of Winchester is the company's brief foray into the specialized world of its own-design revolvers. The first such attempt was in 1876, and credit for the developmental efforts go to William Wetmore and Stephen W. Wood. A bit more than a dozen specimens have been studied in museum and private collections, most operating on the single-action system, with swingout cylinders and .44-caliber chamberings. These were the earliest American-made revolvers with swingout cylinders and cylinder-pin ejection, coming about thirteen years before Colt's first model of the same basic system, the 1889 Navy. The early Wetmore and Wood guns also were chambered for the .44-40-, .44-, and .38-caliber centerfire cartridges. Inspiration for the designs was Winchester's desire to garner lucrative U.S. and foreign—including Russian—government contracts. At least one sample went to the U.S. Navy for trials, and another to Colonel Ordinetz of the Czar's ordnance department.

A long-standing tradition suggests that Winchester used prototype revolvers, including a rather practical one designed in 1883 by William Mason, to persuade Colt to discontinue manufacture of its Burgess lever-action rifle of 1883. Edwin Pugsley's own narrative, based on information told to him in his forty-one years at Winchester, stated:

> Mr. [T. G.] Bennett . . . went to [William] Mason and asked him to make a couple of .44 revolvers. Mason went to work and made up some revolvers . . . and Mr. Bennett went up to Colt with these . . . guns in his satchel. He was cordially received by the President of Colt and they talked about a little of everything and finally Mr. Bennett said, "We would like it very much if you could help us out; we're in a dilemma and I know that if you would, you could help us greatly. We are thinking about going into the pistol business and I've got a couple of models here and if you'll just criticize them and tell us where they are wrong from the trade standpoint, you'll save us an awful lot of money and time." Mr. Bennett got the pistols out and they discussed the various merits and demerits . . . and then they got to talking about rifles in general. The President of Colt sent for whatever cost figures they had and the two men worked over them all afternoon, and when they got through, Colt was surprised to find that they had never made any money in rifles—there just was no money in rifles and he had been able to prove to Mr. Bennett that he'd lose his shirt if he went into the pistol business. There was absolutely no money in the pistol business and so as a result, Winchester never went into the pistol business and Colt dropped the lever action rifles.

It must have been the lever-action Colt Burgess rifle which annoyed Winchester, since Colt entered vigorously into the pump-action rifle business (beginning production in 1884, and remaining active in the market through 1904).

There are those who debunk the Winchester-Colt trade-off story, but Edwin Pugsley—married to a granddaughter of O. F. Winchester, and a Winchester employee since 1911—was certainly in a position to have heard the story from T. G. Bennett himself. In any event, it is ironic that revolvers are among the rarest of all Winchesters.*

---

*The author met Mr. Pugsley in 1964, one Saturday afternoon at an antique arms show. But it never occurred to him at the time to ask this most learned and experienced gentleman about the Winchester revolvers. His self-introduction was very much in the nineteenth-century tradition: "Pugsley's the name."

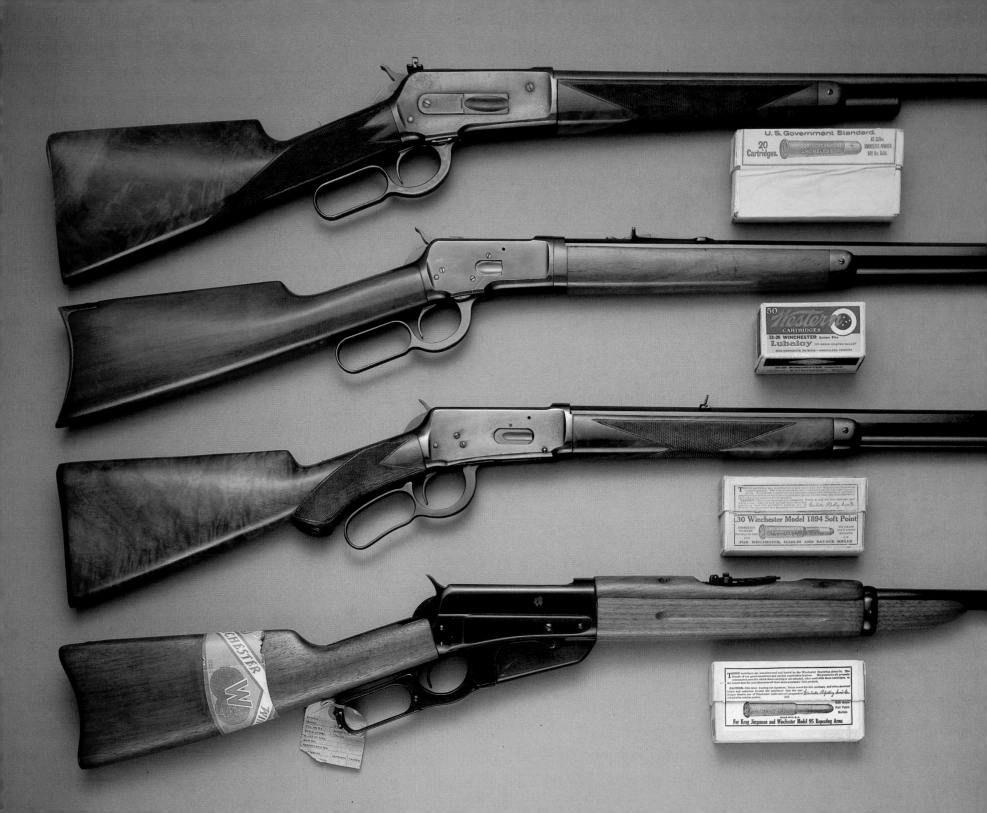

Chapter III
Perfecting the Lever-Action: The Browning Connection

Another vital life of the times was the inventor of the new rifle which Theodore Roosevelt held in such high esteem. John Moses Browning was one of twenty-two children of Mormon gunmaker Jonathan Browning. Five sons carried on the gunmaking traditions of their father, opening their own firm—the Browning Gun Factory—in Ogden, Utah Territory, in 1879. They set out to manufacture an innovative single-shot rifle invented by John, which was patented by him in late 1879. It was this new rifle which led to the nineteen-year Winchester/Browning association and launched John's meteoric career as arguably the most extraordinary and influential inventor in the history of firearms.

The four key models of the "Browning connection" lever-action Winchester rifles. *From the top*, Model 1886, a half-magazine deluxe rifle with shotgun butt. A Model 1892 rifle with takedown feature (note two-piece construction where frame meets barrel mounting). The Model 1894 has a Fancy Grade pistol grip and shotgun butt. The Model 1895 carbine has rare factory tag and stock wrapper. All ammunition by W.R.A. Co., except the Western .32-20s with the Model 1892. Note comparative frame sizes, the larger accommodating more potent cartridges.

No other gun inventor or designer can rival John Browning's string of achievements. He owned 128 gun patents covering eighty different firearms; he sold approximately forty gun designs to Winchester, and guns of his design were produced not only by Winchester but by Remington, Colt, Savage, and Fabrique Nationale de Guerre, of Liège, Belgium. He invented the automatic pistol, rifle, and shotgun, and was also a pioneer in the development of machine guns and automatic cannon. Often termed the Thomas Edison of firearms, this inventive genius created a record which remains unmatched—and unmatchable. His legacy continues through the Browning Arms Company, and through the many models and types of arms of his invention still in production, by various manufacturers, to this day.

Browning's association with Winchester began with the single-shot falling-breech rifle of 1879, followed by designs which became the lever-action rifles Models 1886, 1892, 1894, and 1895, as well as pump-action rifles and shotguns, a bolt-action rifle, and even a lever-action shotgun.

It was Thomas Gray Bennett, Winchester vice

president and a son-in-law of O. F. Winchester, who first bought patent rights for the factory from Browning. So vital was a single-shot rifle for Winchester's product line that Bennett, on hearing in 1883 of Browning's invention, made the nearly week-long trip from Connecticut to Utah to meet the twenty-eight-year-old inventor. Bennett perceived that the Browning shop was potential competition, and so laid the groundwork for an association which would last until the early twentieth century.

In a deal made on the spot in Browning's shop, and for the reasonable sum of $8,000, Winchester acquired exclusive rights to the single-shot, and the first refusal on a remarkable new lever-action rifle for big-game cartridges. Fortunately for Winchester, there was no royalty agreement with Browning: flat (and often fat) fees were conventionally paid for patent and production rights, and Browning was to give Winchester the privilege of first refusal on all future designs of rifles and shotguns. The shooting public would remain largely unaware of Browning's important role in Winchester's development, as the Browning name was not marked on guns based on

his design. And for Winchester, to prevent other firms from invading its turf, its practice was to acquire the rights to every design submitted to it by Browning—at an estimated average price of $15,000. Winchester would see to obtaining the patents, in Browning's name but assigned to the W.R.A. Co. More than three fourths of the inventor's designs were never put into production, but those that were served as the foundation of Winchester's product line from the mid-1880s until well into the twentieth century. One model continues to this day, and is the most widely known and used of all Winchesters: the Model 94 lever-action.

When Bennett traveled to Ogden in 1883, he knew the Winchester line needed a single-shot rifle—one capable of the big-caliber cartridges used in guns made by the rival Remington Arms Company—that would take up the slack left by the failure of the Sharps Rifle Company, which went

Theodore Roosevelt's fifth Winchester of record was Model 1886 number 9205, a .45-90. The richly case-hardened rifle had a half-round, half-octagonal barrel, half magazine, deluxe pistol-grip stock, shotgun buttplate, and crescent cheekpiece—all features favored by this experienced, no-nonsense rifleman.

From this seemingly cluttered workbench came the creations of the genius John Browning. Photographed c. 1900; note prototype semiautomatic shotgun near vise. From this simple Ogden setting came concepts and mechanisms which forever changed the world of firearms.

This photograph from about 1882 captures the unprepossessing beginnings of the Browning firearms dynasty. *From left to right,* Sam, George, John, Matt, and Ed Browning and gunsmith Frank Rushton, all with Browning single-shot rifles.

Three generations of Winchester heirs: Thomas Gray Bennett with son Winchester Bennett and grandson T. G. Bennett II. Photograph taken in 1909, a year in which the firm sold over 262,000 firearms. A tribute to T. G. Bennett published on the occasion of his forty-eighth anniversary with W. R. A. Co. (April 10, 1919) recognized him for being "a leading figure in the community and closely associated with the development of Yale University. In his service with the Company Mr. Bennett has been particularly interested in the manufacturing part of the organization and he is to-day known as a man possessing the fullest practical knowledge of small arms and ammunition in this country or in the world."

Total of 119 cartridges, both rimfire and centerfire, for rifles and pistols, form a decorative pattern on this 1886 factory cartridge board (35″ × 46″), known to collectors as the "Inverted V Board." The back was marked "Compliments of Winchester Repeating Arms Company, New Haven, Conn. USA." Paper and brass shotshells are also shown, with a cutaway of each. Similar board made in 1888 has two additional cartridges, a .38-56 W.C.F. and a .40-65 W.C.F., one above each of the primer tins at *far left* and *far right*.

Some basic variations of the Model 1886. *From the top*, first-model carbine with long forend; number 22713, .40-82 caliber. Later-model carbine has standard forend; serial number 81734, .45-90 caliber. The rare musket, number 82373, is in .45-70 caliber, with angular bayonet. Octagonal-barreled rifle is in .38-70 caliber, number 123616. At *bottom*, special-order Fancy Grade rifle, number 136937, a .45-70, with shotgun butt, lightweight rapid-taper barrel, half magazine, and a Lyman sidesight mounted on frame near hammer.

under in 1881. The fact that John Browning was then creating a lever-action rifle for the larger calibers (which the Models 1866 and 1873 could not accommodate, and for which the 1876 was found inadequate) made Bennett's trip doubly productive. It was this new invention which became the rifle Theodore Roosevelt was so fond of—the Model 1886.

The $8,000 single-shot rifle deal was a godsend for the Brownings, not only in beginning the lucrative Winchester association, but in allowing John the financial freedom to concentrate on his firearms inventions. The extent of his productivity thereafter is nothing less than mind-boggling. He never stopped until 1926, dying at the Fabrique Nationale factory in Liège while working on still another gun

design. Fast, productive, intense, lost in his world of invention, John sometimes created a number of new gun designs in the course of a single year.

The basic simplicity and directness of the man is reflected in the unadulterated functionalism of his designs. There were no frills; everything was reduced to the basics. Browning used to say that "anything that can happen with a gun probably *will* happen, sooner or later." His guns were sturdy, supremely practical, and functional. And, in accordance with the adage of form following function, they were generally supremely handsome, even graceful.

He had no formal education as a mechanic or engineer, but he had a fundamental knowledge of firearms and machinery. He could fix, and improve upon, virtually anything. He did not draw blueprints, and his sketches were crude; it was a mental image which was his chief guide. Whistling and singing were part of his working routine; when he was stymied for a while, there would be silence.

Amazingly, the precision design tools the Browning brothers used were quite basic: a compass, a foot rule (in 64ths of an inch), a caliper for inside and outside measurements, and a small spirit level. The finished model guns would be tested in the countryside near Ogden. The Brownings were hunters, so sometimes the models were field-tested. John was an excellent shot, and he and his brother Matt, with G. L. Becker and A. P. Bigelow of Ogden (the "Four B's"), were the leading trap and live-bird shooting team of Utah in the 1890s.

The Model 1886 Lever-Action
Traditionally the sum of $50,000 is accepted as the price Winchester paid John Browning for the patent and production rights to what became the Model 1886. Browning had applied for a patent on this new repeater in May of 1884; it was granted the following October. Soon thereafter he and brother Matt took the train to New Haven, presenting the model to Bennett and his team at Winchester. The

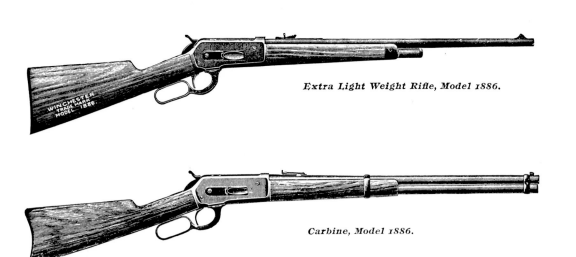

Extra Light Weight Rifle, Model 1886.

Carbine, Model 1886.

Sporting Rifle, Model 1886.

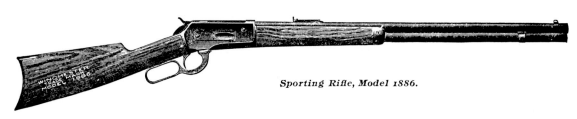

Fancy Sporting Rifle, Model 1886.

RIFLE TAKEN APART.

Action Closed.

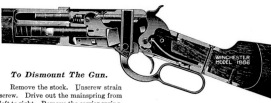

To Dismount The Gun.

Remove the stock. Unscrew strain screw. Drive out the mainspring from left to right. Remove the carrier spring. Take out the hammer screw and tang with sear attached. Draw out the hammer. Remove the spring cover. Drive out the finger lever pin and bushing. Draw the locking-bolts out from below. Pull back the breech-bolt until the lever connecting pin shows at the rear of the receiver. Drive out the pin. Draw out finger lever and carrier attached by the carrier hook. Remove the cartridge guide and magazine stop.

Action Open.

To Assemble The Gun.

Put in the magazine stop finger lever with the carrier below. Enter the breech-bolt finger lever into its place in the pin. To do this it will be necessary in the ejector corresponds with Push up the locking-bolts from below. See that the cartridge guide enters its notch in the spring cover. Lay the hammer in place, and push in the tang, drawing back the trigger, so that its point may not catch on the hammer. Push in the hammer screw. Replace the carrier spring. Replace the mainspring and stock.

and cartridge guide. Connect carrier and hook, and put them into the receiver from at the rear, and press the upper end of the breech-bolt. Push in the lever connecting the pin. Push the bolt forward into the gun. Replace finger lever pin and bushing. Replace the

---

Still in the line and selling well after thirty years, the Model 1886 was pictured prominently in these cuts from the factory's fiftieth anniversary catalogue, 1916. The solid mechanism is revealed in schematics of the action open and closed, and the takedown version is shown taken down.

The factory c. 1889, a year in which Winchester sold about 72,000 firearms and had over 1,200 employees.

Brownings had stopped briefly in New York City and had informally shown the 1886 prototype to an expert from Schoverling, Daly & Gales, then one of the country's leading sporting goods and gun jobbers and dealers. The brothers were then told quite frankly that the gun "was the best rifle in the world" and that they were "holding the future of the Winchester Company" in their hands!

Bennett and the Brownings agreed on the sale of the rights to the new lever-action rifle, and immediately Bennett asked for a design of a lever-action shotgun. To his surprise the new design would be completed in a matter of months. In quick succession, from 1883 to 1885, Winchester acquired what became the Model 1885 single-shot rifle (covered further in Chapter V), the Model 1886 lever-action rifle, and the Model 1887 shotgun, and from October 1884 to September 1886, W.R.A. Co. acquired eleven new firearms designs from Browning. As a devout Mormon, he did take off two years for missionary work—in March of 1887, with an assignment in Georgia. His return to his Ogden workbench marked a renewal of his creative brilliance, which was basically uninterrupted until his death in 1926.

Model 1886s are standard with the model designation roll-marked on the upper tang, with variations in the Winchester name and patent dates on the barrel. Serial numbering reached nearly 160000 during the impressive manufacturing run,

The 1886 rifle at *left* would prove more than helpful to these two claimants to a townsite staked between the Santa Fe Depot and the Land Office, soon after the Town Lots Run of April 22, 1889. Photo taken in Guthrie, Oklahoma Territory.

Exhibiting the ultimate in published engraving, inlaying, and stocking, number 111070 Model 1886, a .45-70 takedown, bears the signature of engraver John Ulrich and was made and shipped in 1897. In the same year the factory published "Highly Finished Arms," a catalogue devoted to various grades of custom embellishments.

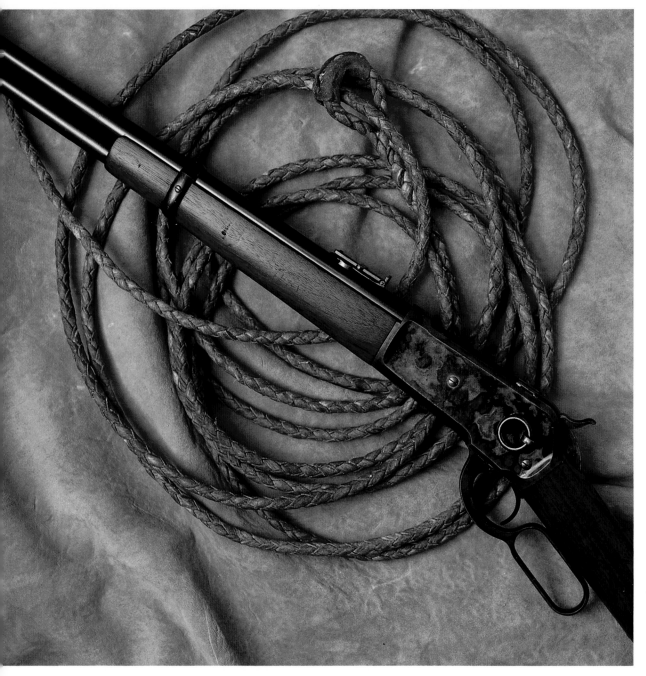

Brilliant case colors are evident on the Winchester Model 1886 in this charming portrait of a young man with his dog. One shot with the powerful rifle would likely jolt the little fellow rearward a step or two. Photographed by Burns of Eau Claire, Wisconsin, c. 1890.

Shipped in 1899, Model 1886 serial number 115315 is of .45-70 caliber and has striking case-hardened colors.

Identified in an old factory photograph as by engraver Angelo J. Stokes, Model 1886 number 145592 was embellished c. 1908, and is a takedown, in .33 W.C.F. caliber. Carved stock in factory Style D. English proofmarks reveal sale or possibly display there. Some Winchesters were sold through such prime London gunmakers as Holland & Holland, Ltd., and Boss & Co., and were at times engraved with their names, having been tested for sale to their clientele.

Model 1886 rifle serial number 120528 is one of perhaps three turn-of-the-century Winchesters with Tiffany-designed embellishments. The sterling silver buttplate mount bears Tiffany & Co. markings, and the firm's archives include a drawing for a similarly embellished 1886. Tiffany's traditions in firearms and edged weapons date back to the Civil War era, at which time the company even served as agents for Colts and the genuine Henry Deringer pistols. From 1890 to 1909, Tiffany, New York, advertised in its Blue Book catalogue "Revolvers of the most improved types, mounted in silver, carved ivory, gold, etc. with rich and elaborate decorations . . . . Cases, boxes, belts and holsters made in appropriate styles for presentations." The arms of Tiffany rank among the most striking, beautiful, and fascinating objects in the history of firearms.

which finally ended in 1935. Calibers varied from the smallest, .33 W.C.F., to the largest, .50-110 Express; of the ten choices, the .45-70 proved most popular. Intriguing design features were the vertical locking bolts to the breech and the relatively short frame (especially in comparison with the long and bulky Model 1876). Rifles were standard with 26-inch round or octagonal barrels, the carbines with 22-inch round barrels, and the musket with 30-inch round barrels. Of all models of lever-actions made in musket styling, the 1886 is the rarest, as only about 350 were made.

A variation which captured the imagination is the "Take Down" rifle, a type also adapted to subse-

quent Browning-designed lever-actions. Still another desirable variant is the "Extra Light Weight" rifle, with a 22-inch round and tapered barrel, a half magazine, and a buttplate of hard rubber, and available only in .45-70 and .33 calibers.

A successor to the 1886 was the Model 71, which evolved from the 1886 in order to take the .348 Winchester cartridge. These arms were made from 1935 to 1957, in a total of slightly more than 47,000, but were serialized in their own range. Despite its relatively modern manufacture, the 71 has a strong following with collectors. (Note that though many model designations employed the year of introduction, often—as with the Model 71—an arbitrary number was assigned.)

The Model 1892 Lever-Action
Browning so dominated Winchester's production capacity that for much of the nearly two-decade association, the firm's own engineers were mainly occupied with improving and adapting his designs for manufacture and in developing cartridges. John Browning was a satellite model shop, and on each trip he and Matt made to New Haven, Bennett and his staff would enjoy the surprises of the bundle of model guns brought from their Ogden associates. John enjoyed the ritual of cutting the cord which secured each wrapped package before showing off each new creation. On average, the

Likely a factory sample piece, Model 92 carbine number 60909, a .44-40, exhibits $25 worth of engraving, and went in and out of the factory several times. Rare factory casing of wood and fabric, lined in green felt, with seldom observed combination of gold- and nickel-plated finishes.

Annie Oakley, "Little Sure Shot," with a deluxe and engraved Model 1892 rifle, the barrel half-round, half-octagonal. Miss Oakley's extraordinary marksmanship and showmanship made her one of the world's most famous women, and she was the darling of Buffalo Bill's Wild West Show. Her career began as a market hunter, in Ohio. She joined the Cody troupe in 1885, with Frank Butler, her husband, manager, and fellow exhibition shooter. Winchesters were a favorite of Miss Oakley's, but she did not use them exclusively.

Posted at the Shafter mines, Big Bend district, these Texas Rangers were in pursuit of outlaws, c. 1890. Center foreground, Model 1892 short rifle; at *right*, carbine with Captain John R. Hughes.

Now on display at the Gene Autry Western Heritage Museum, Model 1892 number 278806 was presented by Pawnee Bill Lilly to pioneer country singer Jimmie Rogers. The barrel is a smoothbore, and the hammer spur was cut down so as to facilitate shooting aerial breakable targets. The upside-down mounting of the plaque on the stock is likely so the inscription could be read when the gun was in a saddle scabbard. The heavy casing was necessary for extensive traveling to show sites. Pawnee Bill was partner for many years with Buffalo Bill Cody and was himself one of the more renowned personalities of the Old West.

brothers made a trip or two each year, despite warnings from their Aunt America, who was fearful John would be poisoned by East Coast business-men. Among the brothers these trips came to be known, jokingly, as "raids" on New Haven. But John observed:

> Bennett knows what he's doing. I sell him a gun—the 86, for instance. He pays a lot of money for it, and has a big investment in plant and materials. It would be a serious blow to him if somebody should come out with a pretty good gun of the same general type as the 86. I'm just building some protective fences for Bennett. That's what these guns are that he buys and never expects to make—fences . . . And he pays me pretty well for the fences too.*

Winchester was securing its position as the dominant manufacturer of repeating firearms in the world. And John Browning was the creator of the prototypes which made that possible.

While in New Haven (c. 1890), Bennett requested that John design a successor rifle to the Model 1873, basically a scaled-down version of the Model 1886, chambered for .44-40 and similar cartridges. To urge John along, he offered $10,000 for the design if completed within a three-month period, or $15,000 if it could be in New Haven within two months.

John's reaction was that he would "have the rifle in . . . thirty days for twenty thousand or [I'll] give it

*John Browning and Curt Gentry, *John M. Browning: American Gunmaker.*

Model 1892s sequentially by serial numbers. *From the top*, a standard rifle in .44-40, number 16652. Number 438479, with its distinctive .25-20 cartridge, is a round-barreled rifle. The saddle-ring carbine, 952211, is in .44-40, and similar to that held by thespian Ronald Reagan in studio shot at *lower left*. The fancy saddle-ring, a *t*25-20, serial 982130, is inscribed *Bernardine Clark* on the frame. Takedown rifle, *bottom*, reveals the simplicity of that system, and also has a silencer attached to the muzzle; serial 984182. The Roosevelts at Sagamore Hill used a Model 1894 with silencer for dispatching rodents and similar pests without disturbing neighbors.

to you." The deal was made, and the Model 1892 prototype was being tested in Ogden in two weeks' time, and was delivered complete to New Haven a few days later, comfortably before the thirty-day deadline. The $20,000 stipend reached Ogden in a matter of days. Considering that just over one million Model 92s were made over a fifty-year period, Bennett's $20,000 was well spent.

Model 1892 calibers were primarily .44-40. .38-40. and .32-20. but a .25-20 was also available, as was the relatively scarce .218 Bee. Serial numbering will be found on the bottom of the frame toward the front. The upper tang bears the MODEL 1892 marking, with Winchester and other markings. There were barrel markings as well, and calibers are standard at the breech.

These arms found a substantial export market, and many remain in shooters' hands to this day. The smoothness of the action is familiar to any who have seen John Wayne swing his large-loop Model 1892 carbine in movies from *Stagecoach* (1939) to *True Grit* (1969). The dramatic prop was also adopted by Chuck Connors in the television program *The Rifleman*. The author tried the maneuver with Chuck's show gun and—lacking the long arms of the former baseball star and all-round athlete—managed to tear his Brooks Brothers shirt with the front sight.

Rifles were standard with 24-inch round or octagonal barrels, the carbines with 20-inch round barrels, and the muskets with 30-inch round barrels. A rare and sought-after variant is the Trapper's Model carbine, with barrels as short as 14 and 15 inches. Takedown models are one of the more intriguing variations.

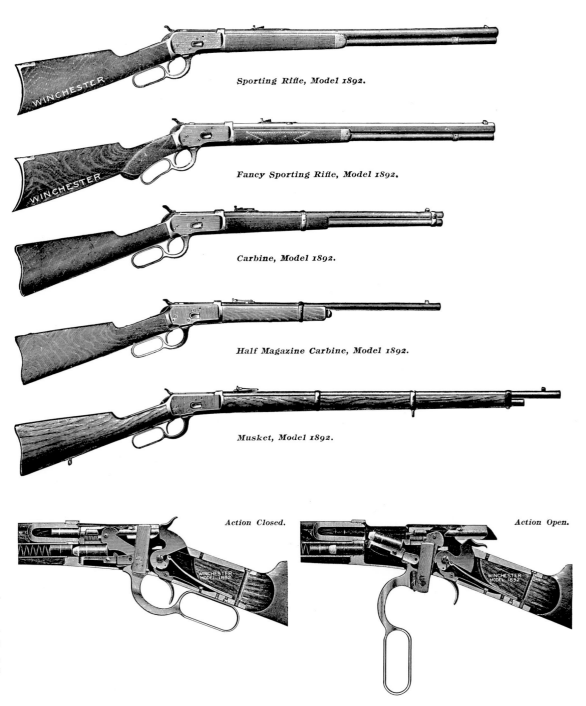

Sporting Rifle, Model 1892.

Fancy Sporting Rifle, Model 1892.

Carbine, Model 1892.

Half Magazine Carbine, Model 1892.

Musket, Model 1892.

Action Closed.

Action Open.

Five variations of the 1892, from the 1916 catalogue.

The 1892 mechanism, revealed with certain similarities to the Model 1886. The action is shorter and more compact on the 92, accommodating shorter and less potent cartridges. From the factory's 1916 catalogue.

David Henry Haight, of Goshen and of New York City, New York, with snowshoes and his trusty Model 92 carbine. Unusual turn-of-the-century photo showing outdoor regalia.

Of 1927-period manufacture, Trapper's Model carbine, serial number 978409, is one of an estimated 325 Model 1892 carbines with barrels factory-built at lengths of 18 inches or shorter; this .44-40 has a 14-inch barrel. Trapper's models in any lever-action are keenly sought by collectors.

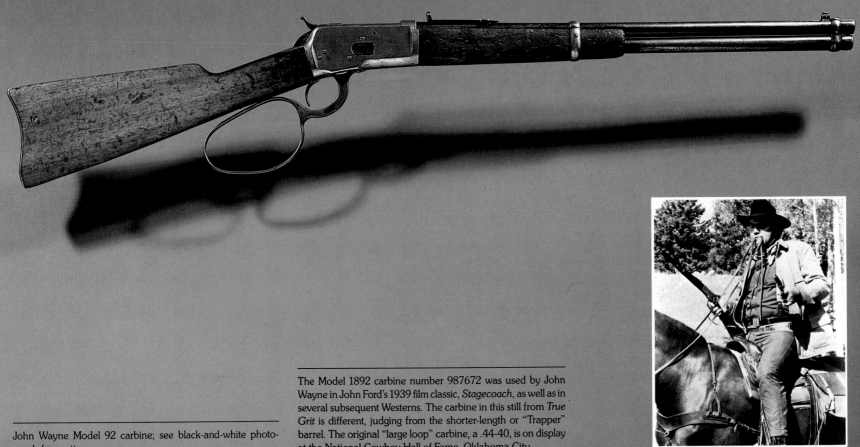

John Wayne Model 92 carbine; see black-and-white photograph for caption.

The Model 1892 carbine number 987672 was used by John Wayne in John Ford's 1939 film classic, *Stagecoach*, as well as in several subsequent Westerns. The carbine in this still from *True Grit* is different, judging from the shorter-length or "Trapper" barrel. The original "large loop" carbine, a .44-40, is on display at the National Cowboy Hall of Fame, Oklahoma City.

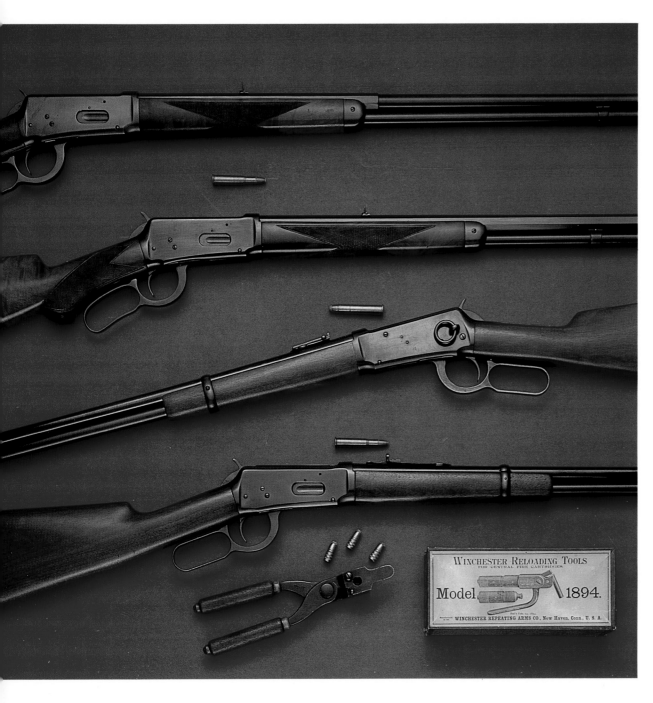

Related to the 1892 is the Model 53, which was in the line for eight years, from 1924, and made in a total of nearly 25,000. The 53 utilized the 92's frame and was within the 92's serial range. The MODEL 53 designation appears on the left side of the barrel, with the Winchester name and address on the right side. And still another version of the Model 92, the Model 65, appeared in 1933, and continued through 1947. Its production was limited to just under 6,000 rifles, and it too was serial-numbered within the Model 92 range. The left side of its barrel includes the marking MODEL 65.

The Model 1894 Lever-Action

Smokeless powder, a vast improvement over the gray-cloud-producing black powder which had propelled bullets for centuries, was a significant element in the formula for the next John Browning design for Winchester: the Model 1894. Visually the new gun differed from the Model 1892 in having the straightish profile to the frame bottom, since it did not utilize the vertical locking system. Serial numbering has continued sequentially since 1894, except for special-issue guns such as the commemoratives. On the upper tang are model designation marks, as well as the Winchester name and trademark stampings. The tang and barrel markings vary; caliber stampings are standard on the barrel breech. No major design changes have been made in the long production run of this most venerable of Winchesters, except for the rimfire Model 9422 and

Model 1894 variants in styles and grades. *From the top*, number 152281, a Fancy Sporting Rifle, .30-30 caliber, with half-octagonal barrel and special-order sights. Note pistol-grip stock, and checkering. Serial number 46516, same caliber, is a factory show gun short rifle, also Fancy Grade. Serial 660750, a standard carbine, is in .38-55 caliber. *Bottom*, carbine number 1457155, also standard and of post–World War II production. Bullet mold of early date; a valued accessory for the legions of shooters who loaded their own ammunition (among them Theodore Roosevelt).

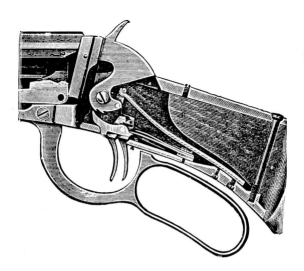

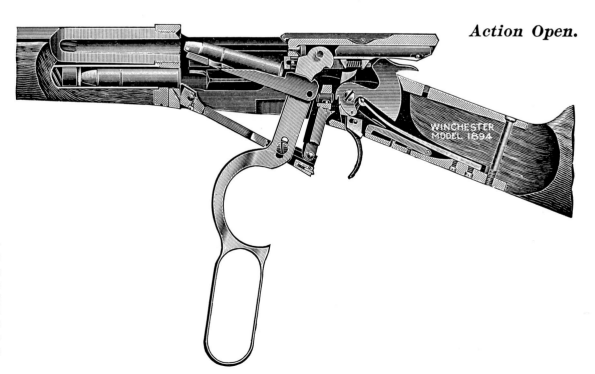

The flat plate pivoting at the bottom of the breech immediately distinguishes the Model 94 from preceding and succeeding lever-actions. Schematic picture is from the 1916 catalogue, as is the set trigger detail. The double trigger functions by pulling rearward on the second trigger until a click is heard. The forward trigger is then set, and ready to fire with a light touch. Single-set triggers were also used; they were set by pushing forward to click in place. A tiny screw behind the trigger served to adjust the pull.

Sporting Rifle, Model 1894 "Take Down," .32-40 And .38-55.

Carbine, Model 1894, .32-40 And .38-55.

Sporting Rifle, Model 1894, .32-40 And .38-55.

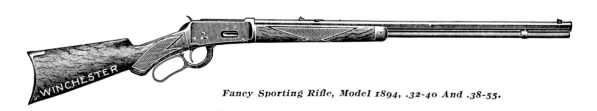

Fancy Sporting Rifle, Model 1894, .32-40 And .38-55.

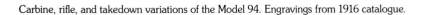

Carbine, rifle, and takedown variations of the Model 94. Engravings from 1916 catalogue.

Photographed by the Gem Studio, Tacoma, Washington, this hardy soul may have been headed to Alaska seeking his fortune in gold, armed with a Model 1894 and a Model 1878 Colt Frontier double-action, the types sharing common chamberings of .32-30, .38-40, and .44-40.

the .375 Winchester Big Bore Model 94 (which have their own serial number ranges) and the introduction of side ejection. Rifles were standard with 26-inch octagonal or round barrels, carbines (often found with saddle rings on the left side of the frame) with 20-inch round barrels, and the Trapper's Model with such barrel lengths as 14, 16, and 18 inches. The musket was not a standard variation in the 1894, but takedown rifles were built, as were extra-light-weight rifles, with 22-to-26-inch round and rapidly tapering barrels and a shotgun-style buttplate.

This new rifle came out first in .32-40 and .38-55 black-powder loads, but by August of 1895 it was marketed in the .25-35 Winchester and .30-30 Winchester smokeless-powder cartridges—the first lever-action repeater made and marketed specifically for smokeless-powder ammunition. The .30-30 has become the classic deer-hunting cartridge of all time, and the Model 94—the classic deer rifle—has continued without interruption with that chambering.

From 1924 through 1932, over 20,500 of a late variation of the 1894 were made, designated the Model 55. These are so marked on the barrel, and were basically a continuation of the Model 94 rifle, while the 94 was thereafter advertised only in the carbine version. Still another 94 offspring, the Model 64, was in the line from 1933 to 1957, with over 66,700 made. The rifle bore MODEL 64 and other markings, and was the successor to the Model 55. But the Model 94 outlived its offspring, and it continues to do so.

Winchester's announcement of the Model 1894 in the November 1894 catalogue certainly proved prophetic:

> We believe that no repeating rifle system ever made will appeal to the eye and understanding of the rifleman as this will and that use will continue to warrant first impressions.

As of 1991, total production is in excess of

Deluxe carved stocks (a variation of the factory-advertised Style A, $60 in 1897) and gold and platinum inlays (Style No. 2, then $175) grace this Model 94, a rifle that probably served as a factory sample and display piece.

These Texas Rangers, including the Paul Newman look-alike at *left* (Herb Carnes), favor the 94 Winchester and Colt single-action. Seated at *right* is the "Border Boss," Captain John R. Hughes, one of the best-known of all Rangers.

5,500,000 Model 94s, the vast majority in .30-30 caliber. In 1994 this legendary gun will join those limited ranks of arms which have continued in uninterrupted production for a century. The 94 is the best-selling Winchester centerfire rifle ever made.

Texas Rangers nattily posed with their Model 1895 carbines.

Made in 1901, Model 1895 number 30512 was a factory display rifle, with the seldom-seen bird's-eye-maple stock, nickel-plated frame, barrel, and sights, and gold-plated buttplate, bolt, lever, trigger, and hammer. From 1901 through 1911, this striking piece was sent out at least a dozen times for exhibits in various parts of the country. In 1912 it was placed in the factory's exhibition showcase. It resurfaced at an antique arms show in the 1980s and is now prized by a private collector.

These Wells Fargo expressmen bristle with Model 94 rifles, sawed-off double-barrel shotguns, and Colt single-actions. Note that one of them holds two shotgun shells, no doubt charged with buckshot.

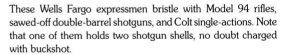

Nat Love, also known as "Deadwood Dick," was one of thousands of black cowboys from the late nineteenth century. The saddle, chaps, neckerchief, hat, cartridge belt, and Model 94 are incongruous with the "Saturday-night special" at his hip— surely a prop supplied by the photographer.

Texas Rangers Frank Hamer (left) and Duke Hudson (c. 1918), complete with Model 1894 carbines and single-action Colts. The near-legendary Hamer tracked down and killed the notorious Clyde Barrow and Bonnie Parker.

So esteemed is the 94 that milestone guns have been specifically engraved over the years: serial number 100000 went to President Harry S. Truman, number 200000 to President Eisenhower; and number 350000 was gold-inlaid and engraved by A. A. White for the factory, and in turn was sold at a gala auction. It is the only gun to be featured on the cover of both this book and the author's *Winchester Engraving*. It ranks among the finest and most noteworthy of arms in the company's long history. One of the most lavishly embellished Winchesters was the Model 1894 done in silver with rosewood stocks by Tiffany & Co. for display at the Paris Exposition, 1900.

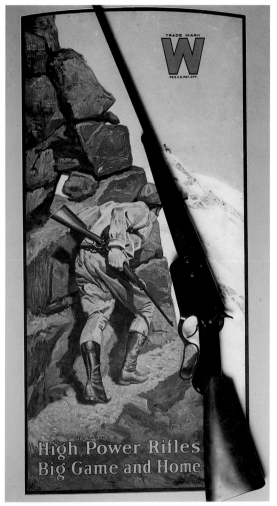

Early Model 1895 rifle, the so-called Flatside, serial number 3841, posed on scarce contemporary poster of hunter nearing the moment of truth, a bighorn sheep in the distance.

Theodore Roosevelt on a bear hunt with his Model 1894 rifle with two-third magazine, deluxe cheekpiece stock, and shotgun buttplate.

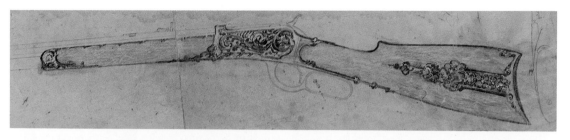

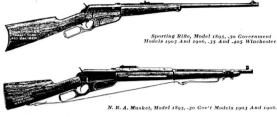

Winchester Repeating Rifle, Model 1895.

Sporting Rifle, Model 1895, .30 Government Models 1903 And 1906, .35 And .405 Winchester.

N. R. A. Musket, Model 1895, .30 Gov't Models 1903 And 1906.

Carbine, Model 1895, .30 Army, .30 Gov't Models 1903 And 1906, Or .303 British.

The Model 1895 Lever-Action

Last of the Winchester lever-action rifles to be created by John Browning is the Model 1895, featuring the new box magazine, chambering for high-powered smokeless cartridges, and a distinctively handsome profile. The first lever-action repeater with a box magazine to meet commercial success,

Sporting rifle, National Rifle Association musket, and carbine versions of the Model 1895; engravings from the 1916 catalogue.

Original Tiffany & Co. design drawings for the Paris Exposition "Hunting Set" Model 94 Winchester. Mountings on side of buttstock inspired by patch boxes found on Kentucky rifles.

Proudly displayed by Tiffany & Co. at the Paris Exposition (1900), this elaborate Model 1894 takedown rifle bears the renowned jeweler's markings and is documented by the factory's design drawing, identifying the project as number 11589. Exotic hardwood stocks, with the ultimate in Art Nouveau embellishments for an American longarm of the period.

Tiffany's own photograph documented the Paris Exposition Art Nouveau Model 94 rifle and its accompanying accessories, the "Hunting Set."

TIFFANY & CO. EXHIBIT
PARIS EXPOSITION 1900
HUNTING SET

NEG. NO. 1949

½ FULL SIZE

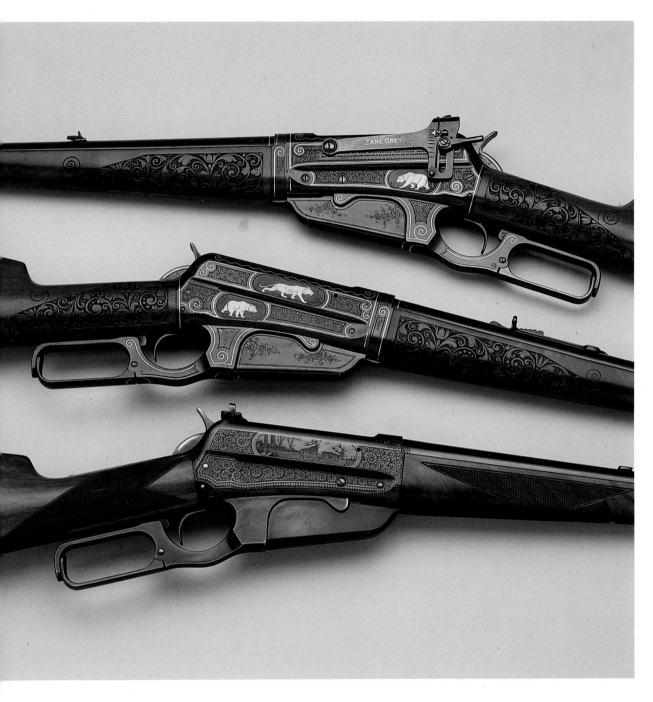

Posse, seated in a railroad car, in pursuit of the Wild Bunch (Butch Cassidy, the Sundance Kid, and henchmen). Three of the rifles can be identified as the Model 1895.

Author Zane Grey's Model 1895 deluxe, chambered for the .30-06 cartridge, bears the J.U. signature of John Ulrich on the lower tang; serial number 88044. At *center*, a similarly decorated takedown rifle, number 78191, in .405 caliber, bears the J. ULRICH signature on its lower tang (usually so small that magnification is needed to detect the stamp, and it can only be observed by looking carefully behind the trigger area, with the gun held upside down). The *bottom* rifle, number 87943, also in .405, is likely by Angelo Stokes, a member of the W.R.A. Co. engraving staff from approximately 1905 to 1917.

the 1895 was a big-game gun, relatively heavy, and was more costly than the 94 and 92 predecessors. Its biggest single purchaser was, however, the czarist government of Russia: over 293,000 muskets in 7.62 Russian caliber were built on contract in 1915–16, and these guns saw service in World War I.

The 1895 in .405 caliber also proved a powerful rifle for Africa and India. Teddy Roosevelt and son Kermit had three .405s and one .30-40 along on

Showing the ravages of nine months on safari in the East African bush (1909–10), this Model 1895 rifle was part of the Theodore and Kermit Roosevelt arsenal for the expedition. Winchester played a key role in equipping the adventure, an elaborate correspondence taking place with the President, mainly writing from the White House. O. F. Winchester's grandson Winchester Bennett was directly involved in accommodating the wishes of the Roosevelts. A detailed analysis of Winchester's role in the expedition's preparations occupies over thirty pages in the author's *Theodore Roosevelt Outdoorsman* (Winchester Press, 1970), listing in detail firearms, ammunition, and sundry equipment. Three .405s (what TR termed his "medicine gun" for lion) and one .30-40 Krag accompanied the expedition. When the rifles reached the President prior to departure for the Dark Continent, he wrote to Winchester: "The rifles have come. They are beautiful weapons and I am confident will do well."

Crates of ammunition and firearms packaged for the Roosevelts by Winchester. On each crate was a number and, stenciled in red, THEODORE ROOSEVELT. Delivery was made to the S.S. Hamburg, New York, on March 22, 1909.

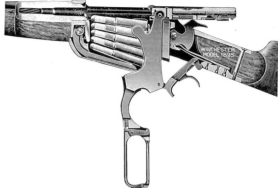

their African safari; they practiced for the great adventure on the White House lawn and relied on Winchester to handle many of the firearms-related details of the trip. In *African Game Trails*, Roosevelt clearly stated his esteem for these Winchesters, with such affectionate allusions as "my medicine gun for lion," "the beloved Winchester," and "the faithful Winchester." The Winchester public relations and advertising staff couldn't have been happier: endorsements from not only the former President of the United States, but a recognized authority on guns and shooting and the world's leading conservationist.

The practice of launching a new model with its own serial range, commencing with 1, was continued with the 1895. From 1896 through 1931, nearly 426,000 95s were made, in nine different calibers ranging from the .30-03 up to the .405. The upper-tang marking varies, but always in-

Factory schematic from the 1916 catalogue shows open action of the Model 1895, one of the most distinctive mechanisms in the Winchester series of lever systems.

Rare cutaway Model 95 rifle, set on calendar art by N. C. Wyeth for Winchester. The hunters are armed with the Model 95 rifle (at *left*) and a self-loading rifle of the type introduced by the company in 1905.

Model 1895s in four distinct variations. *From the top*, .30 U.S.–caliber Flatside rifle, number 3792. Standard-frame rifle, number 59351, is in .303 British and has side-mounted receiver peep sight. The saddle-ring carbine, number 400369, is in .30 Government caliber and exhibits particular forend and butt styling. The *bottom* Model 1895 is a National Rifle Association musket, in .30-06 caliber (serial 95397) and with saber-style bayonet.

"Our three bulls were fine trophies," Roosevelt wrote in his chronicle of the safari, *African Game Trails. Left to right*, with Cape buffalo from a hunt at Hugh H. Heatley's Kenya farm: R. J. Cunninghame, Kermit, TR, Edmund Heller, and Heatley. Kermit holds a Model 1895, and his father the celebrated Holland & Holland .500/.450 double rifle. Note American flag, which accompanied the expedition and was carried at the head of the 200-man force when camp was moved.

cludes the Winchester name and the model designation. Except on the early models, the Winchester address and patent, dates appear on the left side of the frame.

Most desired of all variations is the Flatside Model—the frames lack flutes or scallops, the cocking lever is one-piece, the magazine is two-piece, and the serial numbers range to approximately 5000. The standard production 95s had scalloped frame sides, the levers were two-piece and the magazines one-piece, and the serial numbers ran from about 5000 on up. Rifles were of varying barrel lengths (even up to 36 inches), the carbines in 22-inch round and the muskets in round lengths usually from 28 to 30 inches. Several musket variations were made. The first was a Flatside, and, as mentioned, is the rarest and most desirable. Others were the standard musket, the U.S. government (.30-40 only, and US marked on the frame), the U.S. Army National Rifle Association (in three models), and the Russian Model, the latter with special imperial ordnance stamps.

The long and historic Winchester-Browning connection did not come to an end until 1902, over a disagreement concerning Browning's innovative design for a semiautomatic shotgun. In a departure from the many previous transactions, Browning asked for a royalty on production. The conservative Bennett refused to acquire the rights under that arrangement, concerned that it would establish an unacceptable precedent, and Browning took his design to Fabrique Nationale of Belgium and the Remington Arms Company. The agreements that were made proved highly profitable for both firms, and for John Browning, his family, and the Browning heirs. Both Browning and Remington still manufacture semiautomatic shotguns based on Browning's designs, but Winchester has yet to capture that lucrative market, and failing to deal with the Brownings on this gun was a prophetic and costly mistake—for Bennett, and especially for Winchester.

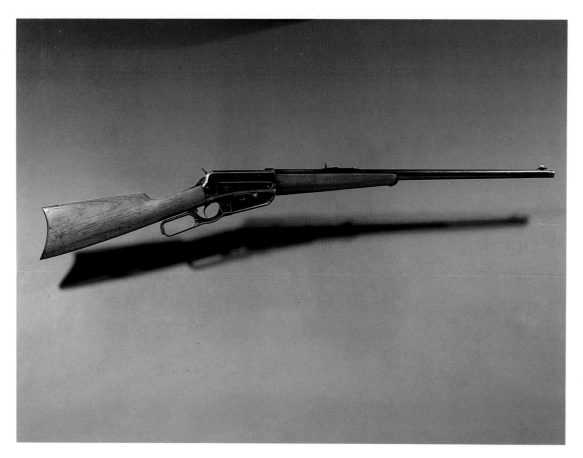

Cowboy artist Charles M. Russell tried his hand at engraving Model 1895 number 65903 for his friend Frank Linderman. The story of its engraving is told in Linderman's *Recollections of Charley Russell*: "Charley . . . reached for my rifle, which had caught his eye. He fondled it, turning it slowly in the firelight. 'You're a dead-center gun an' a meat getter . . . You roar like a cannon an' I bet ya kick like an army mule. Lemme cut some fresh meat on the old gal?' . . . I nodded and he opened the small blade of his jackknife . . . . I [watched] the point of the blade bite into the steel of the rifle's frame without hesitation, without a slip, and make the 'fresh meat'—a buffalo skull, a buffalo cow and calf, a bull elk, a mountain sheep, and a grizzly bear. They seemed to walk out of the metal as though pricked into life by the blade. 'C.M.R.–1913,' the knife recorded, and then his mark, a buffalo skull . . . . 'There she is,' he chuckled and handed me the rifle. 'Now the old gal will always have fresh meat in sight.' "

With engraving styles variations of No. 1, and stocks carved in Style B, these deluxe Winchesters, a Model 1895 takedown rifle (*top*), and Model 1910 self-loading rifle (*bottom*), represent the rich embellishments for which the firm became internationally renowned. To quote from the introduction to "Highly Finished Arms": "The ornamenting of Winchester Rifles affords excellent opportunities for displaying both fine engraving and artistic carving. . . . We have no arbitrary styles of ornamentation for our guns, those shown being only suggestive."

Chapter IV
"Highly Finished Arms"

In promotion and advertising, Winchester has traditionally been as good as—and often better than—any other firm in the firearms field. In the promotion of engraving, the firm has outdone all other American gunmakers, with its sole rival being the venerable firm of Colt.

The first Winchester engraving catalogue was that of 1897; it presented a collection of designs for engraving, inlaying, and stockmaking which had been collected by the Ulrichs and other craftsmen over a period of several years. This booklet is now one of the most rare and sought-after pieces of all Winchester literature.

Judging from early Winchester catalogues and price listings, the company did not find the marketing of engraved arms to be a matter of any difficulty. The demand was substantial, partly because of the tradition in the arms field that decorated sporting firearms, of quality manufacturing, were an expected part of the line.

In a late-1890s catalogue, Winchester stated its pride in making beautiful guns:

> The Winchester Repeating Arms Co. have unsurpassed facilities for producing fancy finished guns of all prices and descriptions. Inlaying in gold, silver, or

Conrad F.'s business card made no bones about his versatile talents. No doubt he himself engraved the copper plate from which the card was printed (c. 1870–80).

platinum, gold or silverplating, engraving, carving or fancy checking, is done in the most artistic manner by the company's own employees. Stocks of fancy woods can be supplied, if desired, at special prices.

Clients and engravers today still call upon the "Highly Finished Arms" catalogue as inspiration for the creation of beautifully embellished modern Winchesters. Since the catalogue appeared in 1897, it has never been reprinted with accompanying color photographs of arms decorated with its designs. Some of the Winchesters on the pages that follow were used for the catalogue pictures, but most were done based on the inspiration of the original catalogue. This gallery of arms presents an array no collector or museum could assemble in today's highly competitive world of the connoisseurs of rare and exotic Winchesters.

An original well-worn handle from an engraving hammer of John Ulrich. Silver plaque gives background of relic. Ulrich reputedly had a sliding-panel-covered peephole in his shop door, which was usually kept locked. If someone knocked, he would open the panel and peer through the peephole. If the visitor was not welcome, Ulrich would close the panel and continue working, ignoring the visitor—no matter who he was.

Front cover for the 1897 "Highly Finished Arms" catalogue, annotated with the name of the factory employee who used it for promotion and sales of deluxe Winchesters.

PRESS OF SPRINGFIELD PRINTING AND BINDING COMPANY, SPRINGFIELD, MASS.

Back cover of "Highly Finished Arms."

The ultimate in factory-decorated Winchesters, Model 1892 number 11009 is so richly engraved and inlaid with gold and platinum that it exceeds all published grades of factory embellishments. Signed J. ULRICH on the lower tang, this .44-40 rifle may have been built for the Emperor of Japan. Note the Grecian-key motif inlaid in gold at breech and muzzle of frame, intricacy of stock carving, and inlays on the hammer and lever.

② HIGHLY FINISHED WINCHESTER RIFLES.

THE ornamenting of Winchester Rifles affords excellent opportunities for displaying both fine engraving and artistic carving. The ornamental work shown here was done at our armory by our own employees, under our own immediate supervision.

We have no arbitrary styles of ornamentation for our guns, those shown being only suggestive. We can reproduce any of these styles of engraving, inlaying, carving, or checking which may be desired on any of our rifles, excepting on the model 1890 and on the Single Shot, or we can substitute, without extra charge, other animal scenes where the style of ornamentation permits it, provided such substitution does not involve a greater amount of work. Monograms, coats of arms, or special designs, either original or copied, can be reproduced upon any of our rifles, the price depending upon the amount of skill and work required.

The butt stocks and forearms of the guns shown in the illustrations are made of the choicest figured American walnut. We make our fancy stocks of this wood as it has a more beautiful curly grain than either the English or Circassian walnuts, and as it also takes a much higher finish. If they are desired, we can, however, supply stocks of bird's-eye maple or other fancy woods at special prices. In addition to the styles of fancy rifles shown, we can furnish them plated with gold, silver, or nickel. The system we employ in ornamenting our rifles in no way weakens them or decreases their efficiency.

The prices named cover only the engraving of the metal parts of the gun, and the carving or checking of the wood; *such prices are to be added to the list of the rifle* to ascertain the

③ HIGHLY FINISHED WINCHESTER RIFLES.

AN ELABORATELY ORNAMENTED MODEL 1886 WINCHESTER RIFLE.

Style of Engraving
No. 1, $250.00. *286.50*

This ornamentation embraces inlaying, engraving, damaskeening, and hand carving. The receiver is richly engraved on both sides with arabesque scrolls set off by artistic border work. The light unbroken lines show the inlaying in gold and platinum. The animal scenes, and the vignette on the underside of the receiver, are damaskeened in solid gold and silver.

The barrel is engraved at the breech and muzzle with scrolls and inlaid with bands of gold and platinum. The finger lever, hammer, breech bolt, and butt plate are engraved and inlaid with gold and platinum lines. The rear and front sight bases and all the screw heads are suitably engraved.

④

price of the completed arm. For instance : The standard Model 1886 Octagon barrel rifle with plain stock is listed at $21.00; to this add for pistol grip stock and forearm of fancy walnut, $10.00; for hand carving stock and forearm, $60.00; for engraving and inlaying, $250.00, making total price of the gun, as shown on page 4, $341.00.

Special finishes are subject to the same trade discounts as the arm to which they are added.

The price of engraving, and of carving and checking are given separately to enable the purchaser to combine any style of engraving with any style of carving or checking which may be preferred. Our 136 page illustrated catalogue, which describes all the rifles, shotguns, and different kinds of ammunition that we manufacture, will be sent to any address upon request.

WINCHESTER REPEATING ARMS CO. *[?] 1st [?]*
Engraving & Inlaying plain letters 70% list NEW HAVEN, CONN., U.S.A.
Ulrich Charges Company 5°° for inlaying monogram in Gold

PRICES OF SPECIAL FINISHES BESIDES THOSE SHOWN IN THE ILLUSTRATIONS.

Full Nickel-Plating,	$4.00
Nickel-Plating Trimmings,	2.50
Silver-Plating Trimmings,	4.00
Gold-Plating Trimmings, *Gold + Silver Trimmings $14°° Nov 28/11*	10.00
Engraving Scrolls on Barrel at Breech and Tip,	2.50
Engraving Scrolls on Barrel and inlaying Gold or Platinum Bands at Breech and Tip,	5.00
Fancy Walnut Stock and Forearm,	5.00
Matted Barrels,	5.00
Fancy Wood Cases Furnished to Order. *4.00 list*	

⑤ HIGHLY FINISHED WINCHESTER RIFLES.

AN ELABORATELY ORNAMENTED MODEL 1886 WINCHESTER RIFLE.
REVERSE SIDE.

Style of Carving
A, $60.00. *68/6*

A selection for the sides of the receiver may be made from any of the styles or scenes shown on page 25, or a monogram will be inlaid without extra charge if preferred. A monogram or initials may be substituted for the vignette on the underside.

Price of this style of Inlaying and Engraving, $250.00.

The butt stock and forearm of this rifle are beautifully carved with scroll work in relief especially designed to harmonize with the ornamentation of the other parts.

Price of this style of Carving, $60.00.

Any of the styles of carving or checking shown on page 24 may be substituted if preferred, the price being as stated on that page.

Model 1886 number 131188 is nearly identical to the rifle used to illustrate Style No. 1 engraving and Style A carving in the catalogue. Signed J. ULRICH on the bottom of the frame (in front of trigger). The inlays are gold and platinum. Both rifles are takedowns, but minor differences in decoration are evident on close comparison.

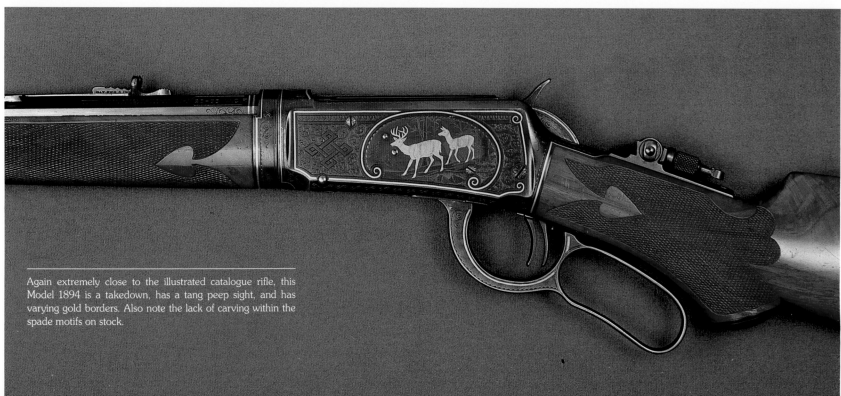

Again extremely close to the illustrated catalogue rifle, this Model 1894 is a takedown, has a tang peep sight, and has varying gold borders. Also note the lack of carving within the spade motifs on stock.

Question there price on guns with Nickel Steel receivers —

HIGHLY FINISHED WINCHESTER RIFLES.

A FANCY FINISHED MODEL 1894 WINCHESTER RIFLE.

220.50 July 1919 adv 26%
200.55

Style of Engraving
No. 2, $175.00.

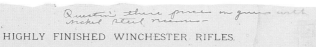

The ornamentation shown here is of the same general style as that of the Model 1886 previously described, but not quite so elaborate. It includes engraving, inlaying, and damaskeening, checking, and scroll carving. The inlaying is in gold and platinum, and the animals are damaskeened in gold. The receiver of the Model 1894 does not permit a vignette on the under side, but the link which forms that part of the arm is inlaid with platinum.

Scroll and border engraving are prominent in the ornamentation of the receiver, it being set off by inlaid borders of gold and platinum. The barrel is engraved at the breech and muzzle, also inlaid with lines of platinum and gold. The hammer and rear sight base are engraved and inlaid with platinum.

HIGHLY FINISHED WINCHESTER RIFLES.

A FANCY FINISHED MODEL 1894 WINCHESTER RIFLE.
REVERSE SIDE.

Style of Carving
F, $7.50.

The finger lever, butt plate, and fore-arm tip are engraved and inlaid with gold. The front sight and all screw heads are engraved.

If desired, a monogram or vignette can be substituted in place of one of the scenes on the receiver.
Price of this style of Engraving, $175.00.

The butt stock and forearm of this rifle are handsomely checked, the outlining of the checking with carved line work making a very effective finish. Either of the more costly styles of carving or checking shown on page 24 will harmonize with the ornamentation on this rifle.
Price of this style of Checking and Carving, $7.50.

Quoted for this style engraving on 1912 Shot Gun with water fowl scene substituted for animal (similar to that on 1912 Argan)
W. Bingham Co. Quote 175.00
July 20/15
Labor 65.00 (3 hrs)
Material 5.00
70.00 cost of gun 2

Question on gun with Nickel steel receiver

HIGHLY FINISHED WINCHESTER RIFLES.

AN ARTISTICALLY ORNAMENTED MODEL 1892 WINCHESTER RIFLE.

Style of Engraving
No. 3, $125.00.

8
175.00 cost
157.50 July 1919 adv 26%
142.50

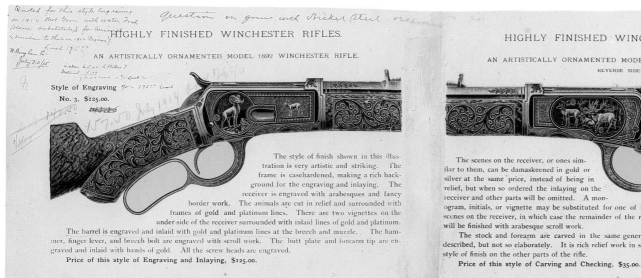

The style of finish shown in this illustration is very artistic and striking. The frame is casehardened, making a rich background for the engraving and inlaying. The receiver is engraved with arabesques and fancy border work. The animals are cut in relief and surrounded with frames of gold and platinum lines. There are two vignettes on the under side of the receiver surrounded with inlaid lines of gold and platinum.

The barrel is engraved and inlaid with gold and platinum lines at the breech and muzzle. The hammer, finger lever, and breech bolt are engraved with scroll work. The butt plate and forearm tip are engraved and inlaid with bands of gold. All the screw heads are engraved.
Price of this style of Engraving and Inlaying, $125.00.

HIGHLY FINISHED WINCHESTER RIFLES.

AN ARTISTICALLY ORNAMENTED MODEL 1892 WINCHESTER RIFLE.
REVERSE SIDE.

Style of Carving
B, $35.00.

40.11

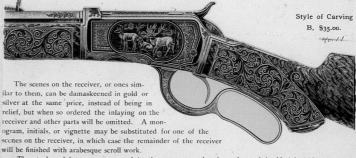

The scenes on the receiver, or ones similar to them, can be damaskeened in gold or silver at the same price, instead of being in relief, but when so ordered the inlaying on the receiver and other parts will be omitted. A monogram, initials, or vignette may be substituted for one of the scenes on the receiver, in which case the remainder of the receiver will be finished with arabesque scroll work.

The stock and forearm are carved in the same general style as those of the Model 1886, previously described, but not so elaborately. It is rich relief work in scroll and vine design, and is in accord with the style of finish on the other parts of the rifle.
Price of this style of Carving and Checking, $35.00.

[handwritten annotations at top of page]

HIGHLY FINISHED WINCHESTER RIFLES.

AN ENGRAVED MODEL 1894 WINCHESTER RIFLE.

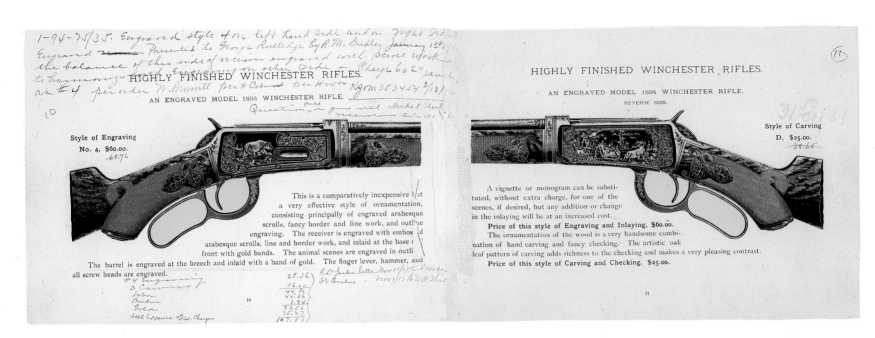

**Style of Engraving
No. 4, $60.00.**

This is a comparatively inexpensive but a very effective style of ornamentation, consisting principally of engraved arabesque scrolls, fancy border and line work, and outline engraving. The receiver is engraved with embossed arabesque scrolls, line and border work, and inlaid at the base in front with gold bands. The animal scenes are engraved in outline.

The barrel is engraved at the breech and inlaid with a band of gold. The finger lever, hammer, and all screw heads are engraved.

HIGHLY FINISHED WINCHESTER RIFLES.

AN ENGRAVED MODEL 1894 WINCHESTER RIFLE.
REVERSE SIDE.

**Style of Carving
D, $25.00.**

A vignette or monogram can be substituted, without extra charge, for one of the scenes, if desired, but any addition or change in the inlaying will be at an increased cost.

Price of this style of Engraving and Inlaying, $60.00.

The ornamentation of the wood is a very handsome combination of hand carving and fancy checking. The artistic oak leaf pattern of carving adds richness to the checking and makes a very pleasing contrast.

Price of this style of Carving and Checking, $25.00.

11

HIGHLY FINISHED WINCHESTER RIFLES.

A HANDSOMELY ENGRAVED MODEL 1895 WINCHESTER RIFLE.

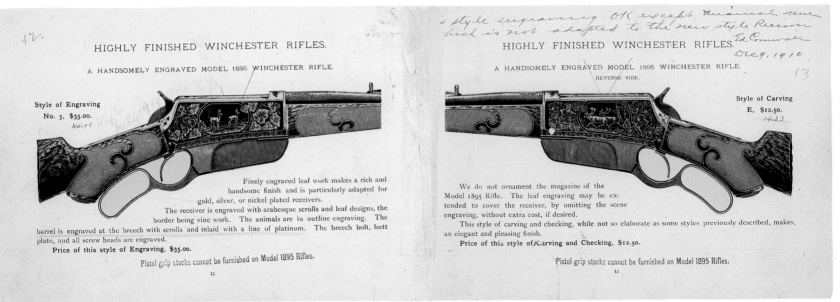

**Style of Engraving
No. 5, $35.00.**

Finely engraved leaf work makes a rich and handsome finish and is particularly adapted for gold, silver, or nickel plated receivers.

The receiver is engraved with arabesque scrolls and leaf designs, the border being vine work. The animals are in outline engraving. The barrel is engraved at the breech with scrolls and inlaid with a line of platinum. The breech bolt, butt plate, and all screw heads are engraved.

Price of this style of Engraving, $35.00.

Pistol grip stocks cannot be furnished on Model 1895 Rifles.

12

HIGHLY FINISHED WINCHESTER RIFLES.

A HANDSOMELY ENGRAVED MODEL 1895 WINCHESTER RIFLE.
REVERSE SIDE.

**Style of Carving
E, $12.50.**

We do not ornament the magazine of the Model 1895 Rifle. The leaf engraving may be extended to cover the receiver, by omitting the scene engraving, without extra cost, if desired.

This style of carving and checking, while not so elaborate as some styles previously described, makes an elegant and pleasing finish.

Price of this style of Carving and Checking, $12.50.

Pistol grip stocks cannot be furnished on Model 1895 Rifles.

13

Variations from "Highly Finished Arms" on number 161786 Model 1894 rifle. The client was given maple leaves instead of fine scrolls on the frame, and matching leaf coverage instead of scrolls on the carved stocks. The mountain sheep and elk game scenes remain as catalogued. The rifle is of .30 W.C.F. caliber, with a half-round, half-octagonal tapered barrel. On the lower tang is the signature J. ULRICH.

HIGHLY FINISHED WINCHESTER RIFLES.

Engraving Scrolls on S.S. Hammer (like Style #6) 1 Wrist & Comb — 11/27/15 (Chas. H. Wilson Md Pittsburg Pa) Can substitute #9 Vignette 250 2 Inflates

AN INEXPENSIVELY ENGRAVED MODEL 1892 WINCHESTER RIFLE.

Case Hardening S.S. Hammer 35¢ nt

Style of Engraving
No. 6, $25.00.
28.65

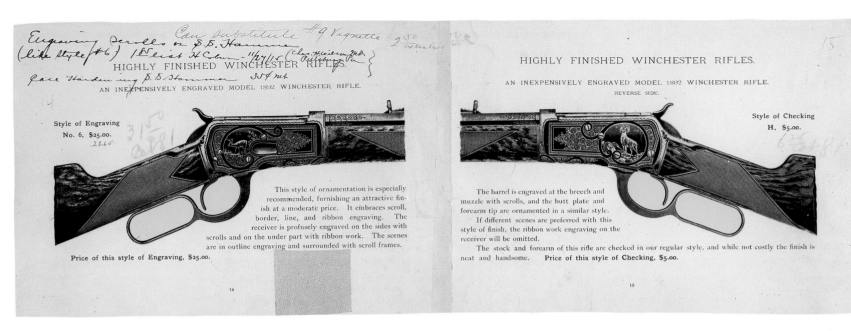

This style of ornamentation is especially recommended, furnishing an attractive finish at a moderate price. It embraces scroll, border, line, and ribbon engraving. The receiver is profusely engraved on the sides with scrolls and on the under part with ribbon work. The scenes are in outline engraving and surrounded with scroll frames.

Price of this style of Engraving, $25.00.

14

HIGHLY FINISHED WINCHESTER RIFLES.

AN INEXPENSIVELY ENGRAVED MODEL 1892 WINCHESTER RIFLE.
REVERSE SIDE.

Style of Checking
H, $5.00.

The barrel is engraved at the breech and muzzle with scrolls, and the butt plate and forearm tip are ornamented in a similar style.

If different scenes are preferred with this style of finish, the ribbon work engraving on the receiver will be omitted.

The stock and forearm of this rifle are checked in our regular style, and while not costly the finish is neat and handsome.   **Price of this style of Checking, $5.00.**

15

HIGHLY FINISHED WINCHESTER RIFLES.

A MODEL 1892 WINCHESTER RIFLE SHOWING STYLE OF FINISH PRICED AT $20.00.

Style of Engraving
No. 7, $15.00.

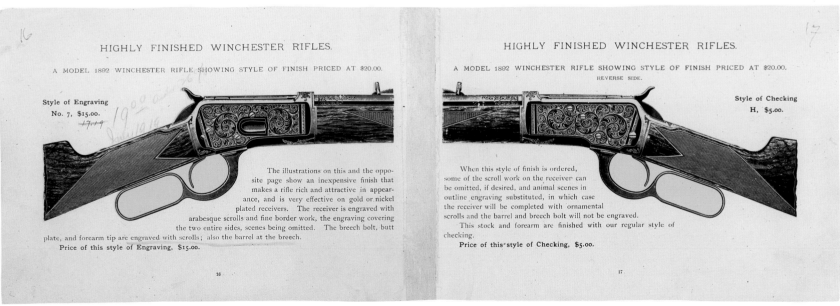

The illustrations on this and the opposite page show an inexpensive finish that makes a rifle rich and attractive in appearance, and is very effective on gold or nickel plated receivers. The receiver is engraved with arabesque scrolls and fine border work, the engraving covering the two entire sides, scenes being omitted. The breech bolt, butt plate, and forearm tip are engraved with scrolls; also the barrel at the breech.

Price of this style of Engraving, $15.00.

16

HIGHLY FINISHED WINCHESTER RIFLES.

A MODEL 1892 WINCHESTER RIFLE SHOWING STYLE OF FINISH PRICED AT $20.00.
REVERSE SIDE.

Style of Checking
H, $5.00.

When this style of finish is ordered, some of the scroll work on the receiver can be omitted, if desired, and animal scenes in outline engraving substituted, in which case the receiver will be completed with ornamental scrolls and the barrel and breech bolt will not be engraved.

This stock and forearm are finished with our regular style of checking.

Price of this style of Checking, $5.00.

17

124

HIGHLY FINISHED WINCHESTER RIFLES.

A STYLE OF ENGRAVING SUITABLE FOR THE MODEL 1890 WINCHESTER RIFLE.

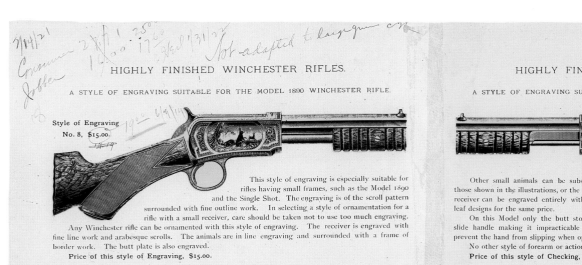

**Style of Engraving
No. 8, $15.00.**

This style of engraving is especially suitable for rifles having small frames, such as the Model 1890 and the Single Shot. The engraving is of the scroll pattern surrounded with fine outline work. In selecting a style of ornamentation for a rifle with a small receiver, care should be taken not to use too much engraving. Any Winchester rifle can be ornamented with this style of engraving. The receiver is engraved with fine line work and arabesque scrolls. The animals are in line engraving and surrounded with a frame of border work. The butt plate is also engraved.

Price of this style of Engraving, $15.00.

18

HIGHLY FINISHED WINCHESTER RIFLES.

A STYLE OF ENGRAVING SUITABLE FOR THE MODEL 1890 WINCHESTER RIFLE.
REVERSE SIDE.

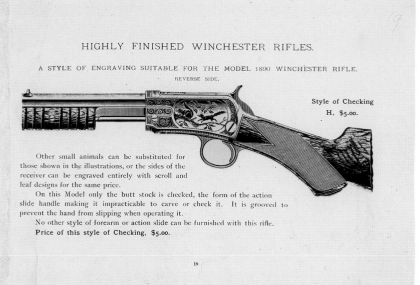

**Style of Checking
H, $5.00.**

Other small animals can be substituted for those shown in the illustrations, or the sides of the receiver can be engraved entirely with scroll and leaf designs for the same price.

On this Model only the butt stock is checked, the form of the action slide handle making it impracticable to carve or check it. It is grooved to prevent the hand from slipping when operating it.

No other style of forearm or action slide can be furnished with this rifle.

Price of this style of Checking, $5.00.

19

HIGHLY FINISHED WINCHESTER RIFLES.

A MODEL 1892 RIFLE ENGRAVED IN A STYLE PRICED AT $10.00.

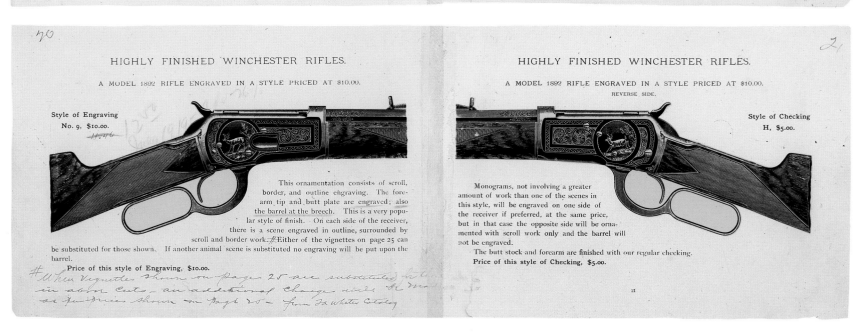

**Style of Engraving
No. 9, $10.00.**

This ornamentation consists of scroll, border, and outline engraving. The forearm tip and butt plate are engraved; also the barrel at the breech. This is a very popular style of finish. On each side of the receiver, there is a scene engraved in outline, surrounded by scroll and border work. Either of the vignettes on page 25 can be substituted for those shown. If another animal scene is substituted no engraving will be put upon the barrel.

Price of this style of Engraving, $10.00.

HIGHLY FINISHED WINCHESTER RIFLES.

A MODEL 1892 RIFLE ENGRAVED IN A STYLE PRICED AT $10.00.
REVERSE SIDE.

**Style of Checking
H, $5.00.**

Monograms, not involving a greater amount of work than one of the scenes in this style, will be engraved on one side of the receiver if preferred, at the same price, but in that case the opposite side will be ornamented with scroll work only and the barrel will not be engraved.

The butt stock and forearm are finished with our regular checking.

Price of this style of Checking, $5.00.

21

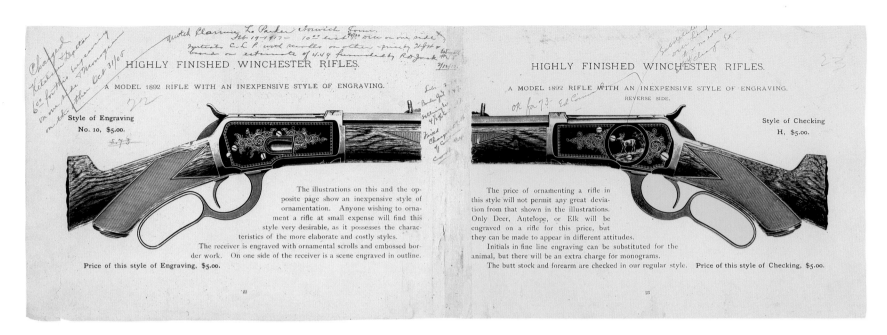

HIGHLY FINISHED WINCHESTER RIFLES.

A MODEL 1892 RIFLE WITH AN INEXPENSIVE STYLE OF ENGRAVING.

Style of Engraving
No. 10, $5.00.

The illustrations on this and the opposite page show an inexpensive style of
ornamentation. Anyone wishing to ornament a rifle at small expense will find this
style very desirable, as it possesses the characteristics of the more elaborate and costly styles.

The receiver is engraved with ornamental scrolls and embossed border work. On one side of the receiver is a scene engraved in outline.

Price of this style of Engraving, $5.00.

22

HIGHLY FINISHED WINCHESTER RIFLES.

A MODEL 1892 RIFLE WITH AN INEXPENSIVE STYLE OF ENGRAVING.
REVERSE SIDE.

Style of Checking
H, $5.00.

The price of ornamenting a rifle in
this style will not permit any great devia-
tion from that shown in the illustrations.
Only Deer, Antelope, or Elk will be
engraved on a rifle for this price, but
they can be made to appear in different attitudes.

Initials in fine line engraving can be substituted for the
animal, but there will be an extra charge for monograms.

The butt stock and forearm are checked in our regular style. Price of this style of Checking, $5.00.

23

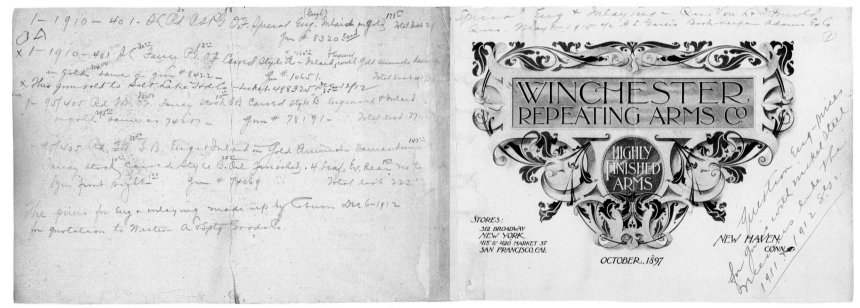

WINCHESTER
REPEATING ARMS CO.

HIGHLY
FINISHED
ARMS

STORES:
312 BROADWAY
NEW YORK
418 & 420 MARKET ST
SAN FRANCISCO, CAL.

OCTOBER, 1897

NEW HAVEN,
CONN.

WINCHESTER RIFLES.

NO effort is spared to produce the best, the most improved, and the most serviceable goods manufactured in our line.

The materials used are the best that can be obtained, and constant supervision and inspection insure the highest quality of mechanical work. No second quality goods are produced at the Winchester Armory. There is no difference in the material used in the manufacture of our highest priced and that used in our lowest priced arms. The difference in price is from exterior finish, ornamentation, and special features. The plain guns will do just as good work as the more elaborately finished.

All parts of our rifles and shotguns are strictly interchangeable, are carefully tested in process of manufacture, and when assembled in the completed arm are thoroughly inspected. Every arm is tried by being fired on our own ranges. No rifle or shotgun that does not pass all the required tests, and which does not make a target fully up to the standard, is allowed to leave the Armory.

In the manufacture of ammunition, these same principles are adhered to; we use our own guns to test our ammunition, or the proper arm for its ammunition, and our ammunition to test our guns, so by constant effort and experimenting we produce what we believe to be the best cartridges, primers, percussion caps, shot shells, wads, and loaded shells made. That Winchester goods are so well and favorably known throughout the world is a proof of the success of our efforts.

The first successful rifle on a repeating system was produced at the Winchester Armory, and as new ideas have been suggested, and the style of ammunition has changed, perfected models have been successively brought out.

GUNS MADE BY THE WINCHESTER REPEATING ARMS CO.

THE Model 1866 rifle was brought out before center fire ammunition was perfected. It uses the .44 caliber rim fire cartridge and is still in demand.

The Model 1873 rifle was the first to use center fire ammunition and is adapted to the .44, .38, and .32 Winchester Center Fire Cartridges. This is the gun which has made the "WINCHESTER" famous and more game has been killed with it in America than with any other rifle.

The Hotchkiss, Model 1883, rifle was brought out principally as a military repeating arm and uses the .45-70 ammunition. There has been an extensive demand for it, in Musket form, by foreign governments.

The Model 1886 rifle is adapted to heavy and powerful cartridges for large game and we believe it to be unexcelled, where a strong shooting arm is needed. It is the most popular large bore rifle on the market and more are used than of all other makes combined.

The Model 1890 rifle, adapted to the small .22 caliber cartridges, is novel and easy of manipulation; it is intended for target-shooting indoors and out, and for small game. It is safe in anybody's hands.

The Model 1892 rifle answers the same purpose as the model 1873. This arm was put upon the market to meet the growing demand for a rifle embodying the features of lightness combined with strength, and has met with unqualified success.

The Model 1894 rifle was brought out to use popular target cartridges, viz.: the .38-55 and the .32-40, for which, up to that time, no successful repeating rifle had been made. Subsequently, this model was adapted to the new smokeless powder cartridges .25-35 and .30 Winchester, now so extensively used for large game hunting.

The Model 1895 rifle is the only lever action, box magazine, rifle made. It is a powerful weapon, easy to handle and a strong, accurate shooter. The "Wimbledon Cup" was won with it in 1896. It is designed particularly for the new .30 caliber Government cartridge, but is also made for the .38-72 and the .40-72 Winchester cartridges, for large game and long range work generally. The demand for this arm is far exceeding our expectations.

The Lee Straight Pull Rifle 6 m/m (.236 caliber) is the arm of the United States Navy, manufactured by us, and for rapidity of action is unequaled by any military arm in the world. It is also made in the form of a sporting rifle.

Our single shot rifles are made in but one system. They are adapted to a very large variety of cartridges ranging from .22 to .50 caliber, enabling a selection for any kind of shooting that may be desired. For target use this rifle cannot be surpassed, and it is in the hands of the most popular shooters and prize winners in this country.

The Winchester Repeating Shotguns have steadily gained in popularity, and although low in price have proved their equality with the highest priced double barrel guns in the field and at the trap; as is evidenced by the steadily increasing demand for them by the leading marksmen and sportsmen generally.

The Lever action was the first brought out. It is made in both ten and twelve gauges and many shooters still prefer this style of weapon. The Winchester Repeating Shotgun has a marked advantage over the double barrel shotgun as the shooter has six cartridges at his command.

The Model 1897, the latest Sliding Fore Arm Action Shotgun, twelve gauge, is used by very many of the finest shots, and, as a trap gun, is unequaled.

WINCHESTER REPEATING ARMS CO.,
NEW HAVEN, CONN., U.S.A.

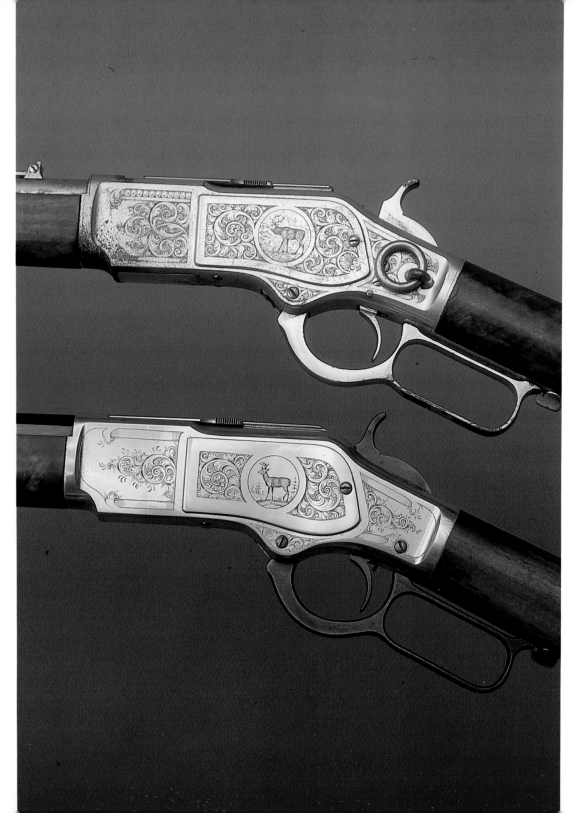

Gold plaque inlaid on Theodore Roosevelt's Model 1876 rifle number 38647 features a robust grizzly, believed based on Samson, a bear pictured in the book. Engraver Ulrich was paid the grand sum of 50¢ for doing the grizzly bear, item 3 on the page of vignettes. The factory's pricing to the trade was based on its cost from Ulrich at two fifths of list. Thus, the cost from Winchester was $1.25 for the grizzly, and $2.50 for such scenes as items 6 and 8 through 12. No doubt the original collection of such vignettes was put together by the Ulrichs and their associates by collecting prints directly from guns as they were engraved over the years.

Bugling elk on the Model 1873 carbine at *top* is either the source of or is based on the vignette at upper left of page 25. The whitetail deer motif on the rifle *below* is also a repeated motif, but is specifically represented in the "Highly Finished Arms" catalogue.

128

HIGHLY FINISHED WINCHESTER RIFLES.

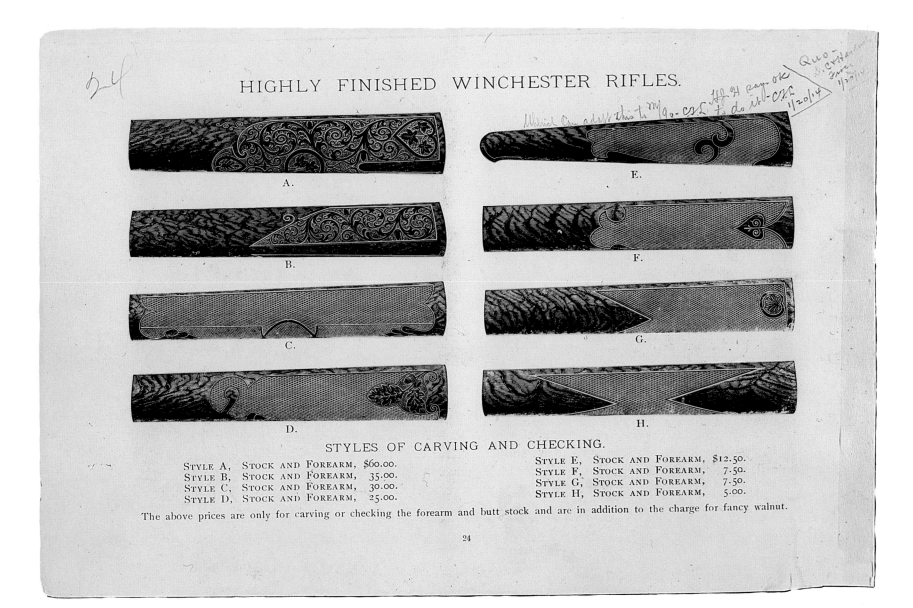

STYLES OF CARVING AND CHECKING.

STYLE A, STOCK AND FOREARM, $60.00.	STYLE E, STOCK AND FOREARM, $12.50.
STYLE B, STOCK AND FOREARM, 35.00.	STYLE F, STOCK AND FOREARM, 7.50.
STYLE C, STOCK AND FOREARM, 30.00.	STYLE G, STOCK AND FOREARM, 7.50.
STYLE D, STOCK AND FOREARM, 25.00.	STYLE H, STOCK AND FOREARM, 5.00.

The above prices are only for carving or checking the forearm and butt stock and are in addition to the charge for fancy walnut.

24

HIGHLY FINISHED WINCHESTER RIFLES.

APPROPRIATE SCENES AND VIGNETTES FOR REPRODUCTION ON ORNAMENTED RIFLES.

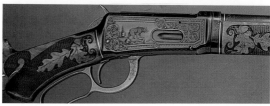

Believed to have once been owned by Theodore Roosevelt, this gold-plated Model 1892 saddle-ring carbine exhibits Style H checkering and Style No. 9 engraving, the whitetail deer at full tilt within a circular panel. Again, careful examination of the detail shows judicious use of hand-cut stamps to execute some of the repetitive border and scroll detailing.

This Model 1894 takedown rifle is close to the factory pattern No. 4 engraving, but shows variations in the carved oak-leaf motif on the stocks. Careful examination of the border at the top, bottom, and right of the frame sides show these to have been meticulously applied with hand-cut stamps. Scrollwork on lever likewise shows finely executed stampings for most of the design.

Deluxe 1894s with factory embellishments. Takedown rifle *second from top* is the subject of notations on page 10 of "Highly Finished Arms." *Bottom* 94's gold inlay of a running whitetail deer mirrors the frame oval from page 21 of the catalogue.

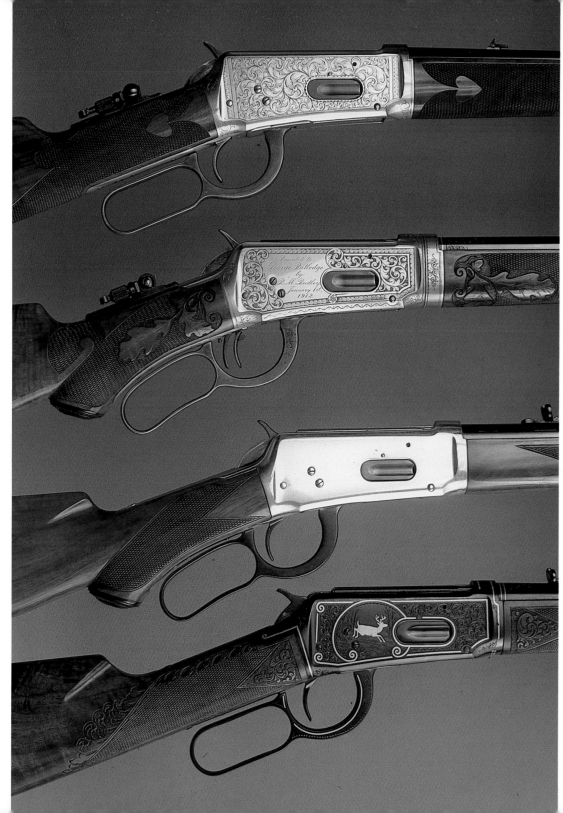

Chapter V
Into the New Century

Although already a thriving business—having sold over 100,000 lever-action repeaters by the early 1880s—Winchester was ready to expand its market with different-actioned firearms. The Hotchkiss, a bolt-action designed by American inventor Benjamin B. Hotchkiss and produced in hopes of military sales, appeared in 1883. In the same year, Winchester bought the rights to the falling block single-shot rifle invented and patented by John M. Browning.

Spawned by the Browning connection with Winchester, the single-shots appeared in the Winchester catalogue for 1885, and the announcement noted:

> This gun has the old Sharp's breech-block and lever and is as safe and solid as that arm. The firing pin is automatically withdrawn at the first opening movement of the gun and held back until the gun is closed. The hammer is centrally hung, but drops down with the breech-block when the gun is opened and is cocked by the closing movement. It can also be cocked by hand. This arrangement allows the barrel to be wiped and examined from the breech.
>
> In outline everything has been done to make the gun pleasing to the eye. It can be furnished either with or without set triggers, with barrels of all ordinary lengths and weights and for all standard cartridges, also with rifle and shotgun butt, plain or fancy wood, or with pistol grip.

The single-shot would not reach the market until 1885 and remained in the product line until approximately 1920. There are so many variations in calibers, barrels, overall configurations, finishes, triggers, sights, and other features that sportsmen, the military, and target shooters were all offered every variety of possible use for a single-shot rifle.

The number of cartridge chamberings for this model exceeds that of any other firearm made by Winchester: approximately sixty-five.

The single-shot was made at a time when target shooting was as popular as golf is today and a major match like the Creedmoor (on New York's Long Island) was very much the Masters of its day. Not only were the single-shots beautifully constructed and of a solid, virtually unbreakable design, but they were phenomenally accurate, used in international matches which were shot at distances up to 1,000 yards, with exquisitely constructed open sights and finely built tubular scope sights. The champion target shooters were international celebrities, and elaborate trophies were designed and built by such silversmiths as Gorham and Tiffany.

The Browning-Winchester single-shot rifles were also a favorite of sportsmen-hunters as the wide selection of chamberings meant that cartridges were available for every type of North American game animal. Then, as now, some hunters preferred the simplicity and reliability of a single-shot mechanism, as well as the challenge of having only one shot available, without the rapid-repeating ca-

New mechanical marvels in the Winchester line. *From the top,* the Model 1885 single-shot, a Deluxe Grade high-wall, with pistol-grip stock and folding Express-style sights. The slide-action, or pump, is a Model 1906, also Deluxe Grade, its .22 W.R.F. cartridges by Western. Both models were John Browning designs. *Next,* the T. C. Johnson–designed Model 1903 semiautomatic, in .22 Winchester Automatic Rimfire caliber, its cartridges designed specifically for the new gun. An extra-capacity ten-shot box magazine is on the Model 1907 .351-caliber self-loading rifle. *Bottom two* guns are cocked by pushing rearward on the device extending from the forend.

pability of magazine arms. Taking a grizzly bear with a nonrepeating rifle required cool nerves and a steady hand.

Variations in barrel types and weights were important aspects of Winchester's catering to single-shot clients. The barrel weights were Nos. 1, 2, 3, 3½, 4, and 5, ranging from 7 to 8 pounds (total for rifle) in the No. 1 up to approximately 12 pounds for the No. 5. The 3½ barrel, designed with a breech of the No. 4 size and a muzzle of the No. 3, was not brought out until 1910. There were extra charges for the special barrels, with the No. 5 barrel costing $10 in 1886.

Cutaway of a takedown single-shot high-wall rifle, revealing such features as the takedown system, floating firing pin, falling-block action, sundry springs and screws, and trigger mechanism.

Advertising the single-shot and the Model 1886, both new on the market, c. 1886. Winchester's New York and San Francisco stores received prominence.

Top, a Browning Brothers single-shot, serial number 509, in .40-70 caliber. *Bottom*, serial number 87 of the Winchester high-wall single-shot, with No. 3 barrel, in .45-70 caliber. Accompaniments, for the Browning, of mold, ladle, strips of lead, powder-measuring device, primers, shell casing, cast bullets, primer punch, and combination screwdriver.

"Take-Down" Single Shot Rifle

Made In Same Calibers As Solid Frame Rifle.

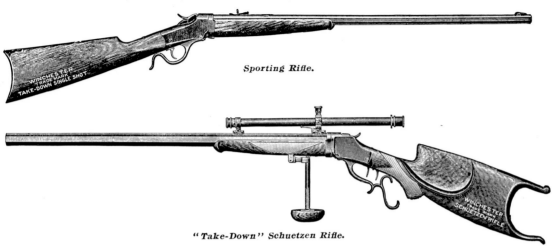

Sporting Rifle.

"Take-Down" Schuetzen Rifle.

Winchester Single Shot Rifle.

Made In All Desirable Calibers From .22 To .50.

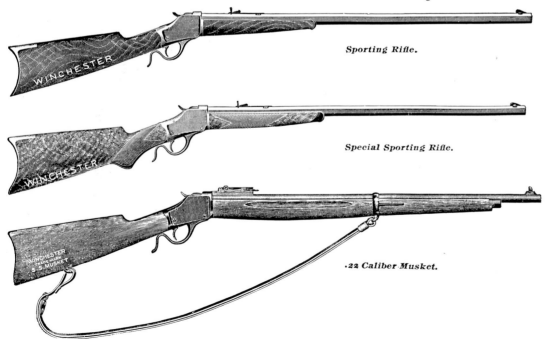

Sporting Rifle.

Special Sporting Rifle.

.22 Caliber Musket.

Pawnee Bill at *right*, Winchester low-wall (or possibly a Ballard single-shot) at the ready. At *left*, Buckskin Jim, armed with a Smith & Wesson Schofield. Note the substantial Indian influence in their attire.

Five of the several variants of the single-shot. Note all are high-walls, except the Takedown sporting rifle. From the 1916 catalogue.

136

The greatest variation of all was in the selection of cartridges: every standard cartridge then in production between .22 rimfire and .50 caliber was available, in both rimfire and centerfire (except rimless types, although a few rifles were built chambered for the rimless 6mm Lee and .30-06).

Two different frames were employed, and the frame profile is differentiated by being either of the high-wall or low-wall type. A datable variant is the change from a flat mainspring (attached to the barrel) to a coil type (attached to the breechblock and hammer). At the same time, the hammer was made to remain at half cock instead of at full cock after the action was closed, as a safety measure. The serial range for these changes was at about 100000 to 110000. The four stock types were the Plain Sporting, with rifle butt and straight grip; the Special Sporting, with rifle butt and pistol grip; the Schuetzen, with exaggerated profile and cheekpiece and elaborate buttplate and triggerguard/ lever; and the Musket, with military-style butt and forend. Rare were the carbine and the 20-gauge shotgun, each with variant stock styles.

Serial numbering attained a range of just under 140000. Calibers were marked on barrel breeches, and the numbers of the barrels appeared on the underside immediately in front of the forend.

When Winchester brought out a John Browning design, the company certainly got its money's worth. The $8,000 went a long way with the single-shot.

Single-shots and a sampling of barrels. *From the top*, a No. 3 octagonal with Beach combination front sight. A .50-110 high-wall with half-round, half-octagonal barrel and sporting rear sight. *Center*, the Beach front sight with its globe upright; *top* made with special matting to reduce glare when sighting. *Lower* rifle a high-wall, in .45-90 caliber, with No. 3 octagonal barrel, and Express-style rear sights; Fancy Grade stocks. Both rifles with rich case-hardened frame colors. *Bottom*, barrel from rifle with some customizing by gunsmith O. A. Bremer, San Francisco; heavily matted top and side angle flats, with adjustable wind-gauge front sight.

Interior view of firearms and ammunition emporium, likely in New York City, in the 1890s. Cartridge boards on view at *upper right*. The notched edging of showcases allowed longarms to stand without falling over.

Termed the "Single W," "Big W," or ".70-Caliber Board," this 142-cartridge classic, 38″ × 50″, dates from 1890. Note reference to New York and San Francisco sales offices, the first time these were marked on Winchester's cartridge boards. Circular arrangements *left* and *right* are rimfires; large W is composed of centerfires. Panel art is attributed to Frederic Remington. Large .70-150 cartridge at *top center* is found only on the Single W Board.

Three low-walls, and a high-wall takedown 20-gauge shotgun. *From the top*, a .25-20 with No. 2 barrel and single-set trigger; dual sighting of either tang peep or scope. The .22 Short rifle has a No. 3 barrel and identical set trigger. *Next*, a .22 Long takedown rifle. The shotgun reveals the simplicity of the takedown system. Black-powder shotshells have handsome period label.

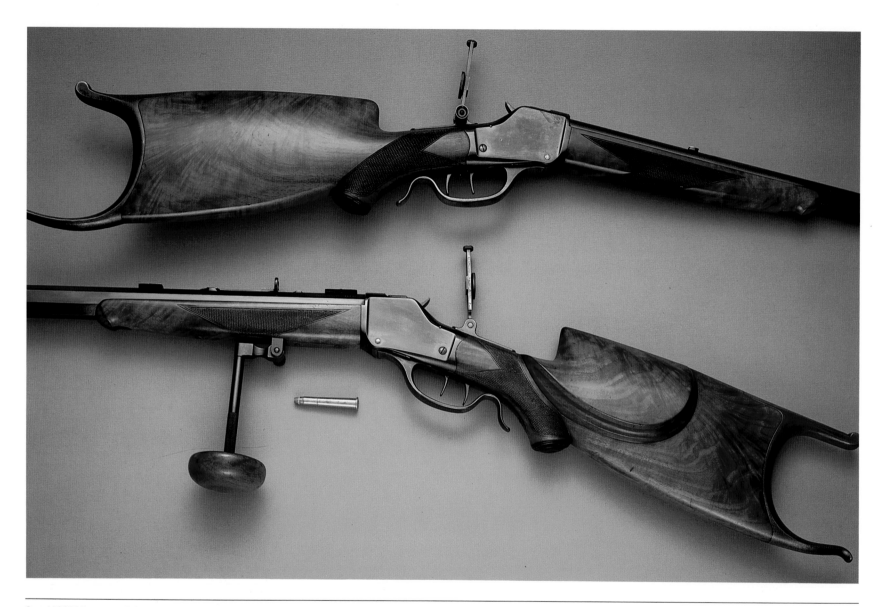

Serial 103300 at *top*, a Schuetzen single-shot with double-set triggers and No. 3 barrel, is chambered for .22 Hornet and has graduated rear peep sight. Number 110798, at *bottom*, a Schuetzen with palm rest, was built with scope mounts on the barrel, sporting rear *and* graduated tang peep sights; .32-40 caliber. Cheekpiece of typical substantial proportions, with massive iron buttplate.

Two of the most spectacular single-shot Winchesters ever made. At *top*, number 96428 bears two signatures by engraver John Ulrich (J. U. and J. ULRICH). The carved Style A stocks have the added richness of fine panels of checkering with a particularly fancy forend. *Lower* rifle, number 110806, is also signed by John Ulrich (J. U.), has two No. 3 barrels, is a takedown, and has a palm rest. Note the elegant and multicurved finger lever, engraved and gold-inlaid. Both the bear and moose panel scenes are based on the "Highly Finished Arms" catalogue.

Sights Adapted To Winchester Rifles.

FRONT.   SIDE.

Rocky Mountain Front Sight.
Price, $0.50.
Not adapted to M. '94, .30 Cal. Rifles.

AS OPEN.   AS GLOBE.

Beach Combination Sight.
Price, $1.00.

**Globe Sight,
With Interchangeable Disc.**
Price, $1.25.

**Wind Gauge Sight,
With Spirit Level And
3 Discs.**

Price,	$4.00
Without Spirit Level,	3.00
Spirit Level,	1.00
Spirit Level Bulb,	.15
Extra Discs, each,	.35
Traverse Screw,	.25
Base,	.75
Screw Caps to Level, each,	.15

Knife Blade Front Sight.
Steel or Ivory.
Price, $0.50.

Graduated Peep Sight.

Price,	$3.00
Extra Disc,	.75
Extra Disc Nut,	.25
Base only,	1.50
Thumb Screw,	.25
Leaf,	.75
Leaf with Disc and Nut,	2.00
Base Screws, each,	.05
Leaf Spring,	.30

**Winchester Four Leaf Express
Rear Sight Without Tangent.**
Price, $1.50 when sent out fitted to a new
rifle; $4.00 when furnished
separately.

Winchester Express.
Front Sight, Price, $0.50.

Winchester Express.
Rear Sight, ...Price, $1.50

Winchester Four Leaf Express.
Rear Sight, ...Price $4.00
When ordering sights always specify model and caliber of rifle, and for sights seated on
tang state whether stock is straight or pistol grip.

Sights Adapted To Winchester Rifles.

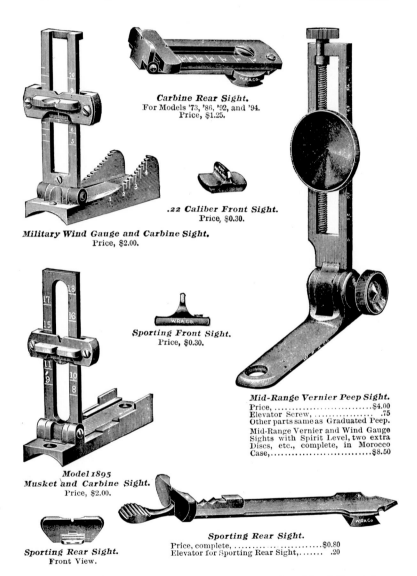

Carbine Rear Sight.
For Models '73, '86, '92, and '94.
Price, $1.25.

.22 Caliber Front Sight.
Price, $0.30.

Military Wind Gauge and Carbine Sight.
Price, $2.00.

Sporting Front Sight.
Price, $0.30.

Mid-Range Vernier Peep Sight.

Price,	$4.00
Elevator Screw,	.75

Other parts same as Graduated Peep.
Mid-Range Vernier and Wind Gauge
Sights with Spirit Level, two extra
Discs, etc., complete, in Morocco
Case, ...$8.50

**Model 1895
Musket and Carbine Sight.**
Price, $2.00.

Sporting Rear Sight.
Front View.

Sporting Rear Sight.

Price, complete,	$0.80
Elevator for Sporting Rear Sight,	.20

When ordering sights always specify model and caliber of rifle, and for sights seated on
tang state whether stock is straight or pistol grip.

104

Sights Adapted To Winchester Rifles.

Winchester Model 1890.
Rear Sight, Price, $0.60.

Winchester .22 Caliber.
Sporting Rear Sight, Price, $0.60.
Adapted to M. '90, '02, '04, '06 and Thumb Trigger.
Always specify Model when ordering.

LYMAN IVORY BEAD
FRONT SIGHT FOR MODEL
1895, .30 CALIBER.

Winchester Model 1890. Front Sight, Price, $0.30.

LYMAN HUNTING FRONT.

LYMAN IVORY BEAD FRONT.

LYMAN COMBINATION REAR SIGHT.

LYMAN RECEIVER SIGHT.

The Lyman Receiver Sight is intended for rifles having a long firing bolt, like the Model 1895 Winchester, which prevents the use of the Combination Rear Sight. It can be furnished for Models 1886, 1892, 1894, and 1895 rifles.

Price List of Lyman Sights.

Combination Rear Sight, ...$3.00	Wind Gauge Receiver Sight.............$5.00
Combination Rear Sight with Cup Disc, 3.50	Leaf Sight,.................... 1.00
Combination Front Sight,............. 1.00	Receiver Sight for Model 1895,........ 3.50
Ivory Bead Front Sight,........ .... 1.00	Ivory Bead Front Sight for .30 Caliber
Ivory Hunting Front Sight,........... .50	Model 1895,..................... .50
Wind Gauge Target Sight, ... 3.50	Receiver Sight for Models '05,'07,and '10, 4.50
Wind Gauge Sporting Sight,........... 3.00	Fitting Receiver Sights, net,........... .25

Marble Sights Adapted To Winchester Rifles.

Any of the Marble Sights given below can be attached to Winchester rifles when so ordered.

MARBLE'S REVERSIBLE FRONT SIGHT.

MARBLE'S IMPROVED FRONT SIGHT.

Reversible Front Sight, Ivory and Gold Bead,.............$1.50	Improved Front Sight,.............$1.00
Front Sight for Model 1894 Carbines using Black Powder,............. .50	Front Sight for Model 1895 Rifle, .30 Army and .303 British.... .50
Front Sight for Model 1894 Carbines using Smokeless Powder,........ .75	Stationary Front Sight,............. 1.00
	Adjustable Leaf Sight,............. 1.00
	Flexible Rear Sight,............... 3.00

A broad array of sights for a wide variety of Winchester rifles. Most were available only on special order. From the 1916 catalogue.

Three musket variations of the single-shot. *From the top,* military styling, .32-40 caliber. *Center,* .22 Short, civilian version of the so-called Winder, after marksman Colonel C. B. Winder, a champion shot who helped in the rifle's design. *Bottom,* .22 Long Rifle Winder, with military-style sights at barrel breech, in contrast to the adjustable peep sight of the *center* musket, and the sporting-style rear sight of the musket at *top.*

The Slide-Action .22 Rifle

Since the .22-rimfire version of the Model 1873 rifle had not proved as popular as hoped, the factory looked to John Browning for creating a repeater in that caliber. Among the disadvantages of the .22 Model 1873 was its substantial weight and cost. In June of 1888, John and Matt Browning were issued a patent for a slide-action magazine rifle, which—as the Model 1890—became Winchester's first rifle of that type. The slide, pump, or trombone action was already in production (since 1884) by the Colt company, used in its Lightning rifle series. It was up to Winchester to do some rapid catch-up.

The November 1890 catalogue announced the new rifle as the "Repeating Rifle Model 1890." Chambering was initially for the. 22 Short, the .22 Long, and the .22 W.R.F. (Winchester Rim Fire, a special cartridge created by Winchester for the 1890). These cartridges were not intermixable with the 1890, so that chambering was for each type cartridge only. As of 1919 the .22 Long Rifle was added, and, again, chambering was exclusively for that cartridge, and was not interchangeable. Despite this feature, the Model 1890, in two basic

The proud owner of a handsome trophy, with his prize-winning high-wall Schuetzen-style Winchester. Early telescopic sight had admirable magnification, and shootists of the day, despite using black-powder loads, were often amazingly accurate.

Pump- or slide-action .22s, in the Models 1890 (*top three*) and 1906 (*bottom two*). *From the top*, serial number 145, a .22 Long Rifle, is a Standard Grade rifle with plain walnut stocks. Serial number 134885, in .22 W.R.F., is Deluxe Grade, with checkered pistol-grip buttstock and takedown screw on frame near juncture with stock. Promotional envelope was a part of Winchester's comprehensive approach to advertising. The half-nickel rifle, serial number 378508A, is chambered for .22 Short. The flier advertises the Topperweins, who made trick-shooting history and were on Winchester's payroll for years. *Second from bottom*, Model 1906 number 256022B, was chambered for .22 Smoothbore. Model 1906 number 668869B has its action open. Note composition buttplates.

WINCHESTER
IMPORTANT INSTRUCTIONS
FOR
MODEL 61
SLIDE ACTION HAMMERLESS
REPEATING RIFLE

Olin
WINCHESTER-WESTERN DIVISION
NEW HAVEN 4, CONNECTICUT

MODEL
61
WINCHESTER
SLIDE ACTION HAMMERLESS
.22 REPEATING RIFLE

WINCHESTER
SUPER SPEED
.22 Long Rifle
50 Long Range Rim Fire Cartridges
STAINLESS   KOPPERKLAD

SIGHTER TARGET

FOR ALL SHOOTERS
25, 50, or 75 Feet
All Calibers   Any Sights

FOR ALL SHOOTERS
25, 50, or 75 Feet
All Calibers   Any Sights

DISTANCE
NO. OF SHOTS
TOTAL PLUS
TOTAL MINUS
SCORE
NAME
THIS TARGET COURTESY
WINCHESTER

WINCHESTER
IMPORTANT INSTRUCTIONS
FOR
MODEL 62
SLIDE ACTION REPEATING RIFLE

WINCHESTER
REPEATING ARMS COMPANY
Division of Olin Industries, Inc.
NEW HAVEN, CONN., U.S.A.

grades only (Sporting Rifle and Fancy Sporting Rifle, all having 24-inch octagonal barrels and rifle-style steel buttplates), remained in production through 1932, with a total production of nearly 850,000. The 1890 was Winchester's all-time sales leader in .22 rimfire, and many 1890s are still in use around the world.

As an economical version of the Model 1890, the factory brought out the 1906 pump-action. This new rifle differed mainly in having a 20-inch round barrel and a shotgun-style butt with composition buttplate. Initially, chambering was in .22 Short only, but as of 1908, alterations were made which permitted interchangeable use of .22 Short, Long, and Long Rifle cartridges—a move which accelerated sales considerably. And the 1906 thereby also became the factory's first rifle advertised and sold which accommodated the three cartridges interchangeably. A further sales factor was that all Model 1906s featured takedown capability. Basic grades were the Standard Sporting Rifle and the Expert Rifle, the latter sold in blue finish; in blue with nickel-plated fame, triggerguard, and bolt; and in full-nickel finish. All Expert Rifles had the additional features of a varying slide handle (no finger grooves) and pistol-grip stock.

Serial numbering on the 1906 was in its own range, and, like the 1890, the 1906 achieved an extraordinary sales total—nearly 850,000 made—before being discontinued in 1932.

In 1931, when Winchester was sold to Western Cartridge Company (and the Olin family interests), some models of guns were revamped and contin-

The lineage from the Models 1890 and 1906 is evident in these Model 61 (*top three*) and 62 pump .22s. *From the top,* number 18838, with octagonal barrel. A .22 smoothbore, serial number 161944, lacks rear sight. Number 345697 has its colorful model tag still attached. Serial number 98087A has a shorter forend than the *bottom* rifle, Model 62A number 264714 (with action open); note barrel marking denoting chambering for Short, Long, or Long Rifle.

Ernest Hemingway and his Model 61 .22 rifle, serial number 203648. Following his death in 1961, the writer's widow eventually commissioned Abercrombie & Fitch, New York, to sell this and other guns. Documents accompanying the rifle prove his ownership, and in 1964 Mary Hemingway wrote: "We had 18 to 20 guns with us on [our] 1953–54 Safari, including shotguns and various rifles from little .22s to big .375 elephant guns. . . . Our favorite .22 was a light pump-action gun which held, if I recall, 15 short-nosed shells in the tube which lived under the barrel. Ernest would have used this or any other .22 on small beasts such as bush-babies, rodents, or snakes, and also, on guinea fowl, which are such clever birds, they know shotgun ranges and keep outside of them. . . ." Their favorite .22 is shown in this photo of the Nobel Prize–winning author acquiring native arrows on safari in Uganda, 1954.

ued in production under their new styling and model designation. In 1932 the Models 1890 and 1906 were given new life as the Models 61 and 62.

The Model 62, which continued the visible-hammer design, featured interchangeable chamberings accommodating the .22 Short, .22 Long, and .22 Long Rifle, a shotgun butt (originally with a steel buttplate, but then changed to composition), a larger magazine capacity, and a 23-inch round tapered barrel, and it had mechanical improvements in the chambering and feeding as well as in the rifling. The entire production run from 1932—nearly 410,000 rifles—was of takedown type. Standard styles were the Sporting Rifle and the Gallery Rifle (which had a special loading port to allow for speedy loading with special tubes and was chambered for .22 Short only). The model remained in the line through 1958.

Introduced simultaneously with the 62, the Model 61 proved to be another highly popular .22-rimfire slide-action. It was a hammerless, with a choice of round or octagonal barrels; there was a .22 Long Rifle version (no rear sight, shotgun front sight), and additional chamberings in .22 W.R.F. only, and, from 1960, .22 Winchester Magnum rimfire. Throughout production the steel buttplate and the stock pistol grip were checkered. Even

Self-loading .22s, the Models 1903 (*top two*) and 63 (*bottom two*). *From the top*, serial number 14598, a Fancy Grade, with factory accessory loading tube. A few serial numbers away, *second* rifle is of Standard Grade. Model 63 with magazine tube drawn out of butt is serial number 2, in rare .22 Short (only a handful made); in-the-white barrel for testing. Serial number 169285, accompanied by model tag and factory instruction brochure. Knurled knob at back of frame for takedown.

though hampered because certain competitors had previously introduced a hammerless .22 pump, the Model 61 also had a remarkable sales total: over 342,000, through 1963.

The Models 1890, 1906, 62, and 61 proved again the wisdom of T. G. Bennett in aligning Winchester with John Browning and his brothers.

The Semiautomatic .22 Rifle

Thomas Crossley Johnson, a Winchester employee since 1885, developed the first blowback semiautomatic rifle to achieve commercial success in the United States, the Model 1903. Chambered for the new .22 Winchester Automatic Rimfire Smokeless cartridge (designed especially for the new gun), the 1903 also featured takedown capability. The 1903 was Winchester's first semiautomatic firearm of any type, as well as its first hammerless repeater. Loading was through a aperture on the right side of the buttstock, and the gun was cocked by pushing back a tubular extension at the front of the forend. A similar cocking mechanism would be used in the new larger-caliber semiautomatic rifles soon to appear in the Winchester line.

The blowback system operates by the force of the cartridge as it fires, pushing the carefully weighted breech bolt backward to eject the empty cartridge casing and automatically load the new round. Thus it is a recoil-operated mechanism, but since the bullet leaves the muzzle before the bolt is forced rearward there is no loss of energy or bullet velocity. It was necessary for Winchester to design the new .22 W.A.R., (Winchester Automatic Rimfire) cartridge as part of making the Model 1903 practical.

Styling of the 1903 was of two variants, known as the Plain and the Fancy, the latter featuring finer overall quality and a pistol-grip stock of select walnut. Barrels were 20-inches long and round, and serial numbers began with 1. Approximately 126,000 1903s were made in the model's twenty-

nine years of manufacture.

When the Olin family acquired Winchester, part of the general revamping of the line was an improved Model 1903, issued as the Model 63 automatic rifle. The new model chambered only the .22 Long Rifle cartridge, and this new chambering was instrumental in the increased sales over the Model 1903—nearly 175,000 during its production of 1933 to 1958. The Model 63 also simplified the takedown system: turning the takedown screw allowed pulling the rifle in half, whereas the Model 1903 (and the first few thousand of the Model 63) required pressing a takedown locking screw downward through the tang, which in turn released a lock on the takedown screw's collar.

Akin to the Model 1903 .22 W.A.R. rifle were the T. C. Johnson–designed centerfire blowback semiautomatic rifles—the Models 1905, 1907, and 1910. These new repeaters had box magazines fitted forward of the triggerguard and were otherwise mechanically quite similar to the Model 1903 .22.

The first of the series, the Model 1905, was also the first Winchester semiautomatic rifle built for centerfire cartridges and was the first made with a detachable box magazine. Chambering for the Model 1905 was .32 W.S.L. and .35 W.S.L. (Winchester Self-Loading); both of these new cartridges were created for the new rifle.

Weighing 7½ pounds in the Sporting Rifle configuration and eight pounds in the Fancy Sporting Rifle, the Model 1905 was noticeably heavy, as was its successor. Unfortunately the new cartridge lacked sufficient velocity, and, with the added factor of a relatively high price, sales of the 1905 were slow. It was made through 1920; only just over 29,000 were sold. Serial numbering began with 1.

Coinciding with the introduction of the 1905 was a new marking stamp, helpful in dating all models of Winchesters: beginning July 17, 1905, the proofmark WP within an oval was marked on the barrels of all guns in assembly (.22 calibers excepted).

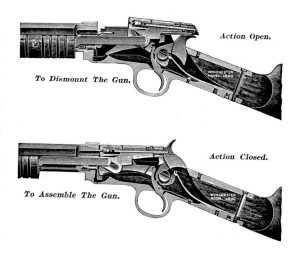

Open and closed action of the Model 1890 pump, with standard and Fancy Grade takedown types. Note relative size of .22 W.R.F. cartridge, as well as continued use of H (for Henry) on butt of shell casing. From 1916 catalogue.

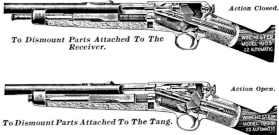

Action Closed.

To Dismount Parts Attached To The Receiver.

WINCHESTER MODEL 1903 22 AUTOMATIC

Action Open.

To Dismount Parts Attached To The Tang.

WINCHESTER MODEL 1903 22 AUTOMATIC

From July of 1908, the marking was also stamped on the frames, and starting in October, also on .22-caliber Winchesters. In order to differentiate mail-order guns from standard shipments, a special mail-order proof—P within an oval—was instituted in May 1913 and marked on barrels and frames of assembled guns shipped through the mail-order department.

Factory schematics from the 1916 catalogue show the mechanics and functioning of the Model 1903 self-loading rifle.

Used by Winchester promotional shooter Ad Topperwein, Model 1903 number 26292 lies across an "Uncle Sam" target, "sketched" by the remarkable shot in a matter of seconds. The Topperweins, Adolph and wife Elizabeth or "Plinky," natives of San Antonio, Texas, toured America for nearly forty years as featured exhibition shooters for the Winchester factory. In 1907 Topperwein set a world record which remained unbroken for over sixty years by shooting 72,491 2½-inch-square wooden blocks thrown as aerial targets. He did it over a ten-day period, shooting eight hours each day, using Winchester .22 rifles.

The Models 1905 (top), 1907 (center two), and 1910 self-loading centerfire rifles. From the top, .35 S.L.R. number 15751, a Deluxe Grade with checkered walnut stocks, with a box of .32 S.L. cartridges; .351 S.L.R. serial number 47686, an early model with flat cocking knob (cap to tube at front of forend); number 55697, also in .351 S.L.R., with later curved cocking aperture and ten-shot box magazine; and at bottom, serial number 18578, in .401 S.L. caliber, with scarce stainless-steel barrel.

Action Closed.

To Dismount Parts Attached To
The Receiver.

Action Open.

To Dismount Parts Attached To
The Guard.

The Self-Loading Centerfire Rifles

The Model 1907 self-loading rifle was built to fire the new .351 Winchester S.L. (Self-Loading) cartridge, which was of higher velocity than its .32 and .35 predecessors. The new rifle was somewhat heavier, and the 1907 became the best-selling of the 1905–1907–1910 series. A new variation added in the 1907 was the Police Rifle, its special features including an optional bayonet, special stocks, a checkered buttplate of steel, and a leather sling. It was the heaviest version, weighing nearly 11 pounds.

The 1907 was given its own serial number range, beginning with 1. Total production reached over 58,000 and continued through 1957. An intriguing market for the 1907 was created by Allied aviators in World War I, who used the rifles in cockpit-to-cockpit gun battles! Texas Rangers and other law enforcement forces found the semiautomatic rifle a useful tool against the evolving organized criminal element, and mavericks the likes of John Dillinger,

Closed and open action of the Model 1905 self-loading rifle, as pictured in the factory's 1916 catalogue. The bolt at rear of action allows for takedown.

Artist Philip R. Goodwin captured a surprised but ready hunter with an aggressive grizzly, the rifle a Model 1910 self-loading, as is serial number 2820, pictured in foreground.

Bonnie and Clyde, and Machinegun Kelly.

Last of the self-loading semiautomatic centerfire rifle trilogy was the Model 1910, even heavier than its predecessors, and firing its own newly developed cartridge: the .401 Winchester S.L., with an impressive 200- or 250-grain bullet. Like its predecessors, the 1910 included takedown capability, and was unduly heavy. The grades offered were Sporting Rifle, weighing 8¼ pounds, and Fancy Sporting Rifle, weighing 8½ pounds. Serial numbering began with 1 (thus all three models had their own range), and production ended in 1936, with nearly 21,000 made.

Business Changes in the New Century

Lever-action, pump-action, and self-loading repeating rifles, along with the single-shot and the ever-expanding line of ammunition, positioned Winchester into the new century as uniquely dominant in the American firearms industry. The company was seemingly impregnable, with a string of triumphs in a variety of models, ammunition sales at consistently high levels, and no significant business or production problems. However, in a surprising way, the company's course of history would be inexorably altered, because of a combination of factors brought on by an overwhelming demand for military arms during the First World War— many years after the disappointments in that market (at least from the standpoint of U.S. government orders) experienced by Oliver Winchester and by his successors as president, W. W. Converse and T. G. Bennett.

The back of this unusual photograph, c. 1910–15, bears the inscription "Compliments of the Biggest Crank in Montana, C. G. Williams." Several Winchesters are in his arsenal, among them the lever-action Models 1886 and 1895, a self-loading centerfire (the 1905, 1907, or 1910), the Model 1890 pump .22, and the 1903 self-loading .22. An itinerant dealer in firearms?

Chapter VI
Defending the Nation

Military sales could make an arms manufacturer quickly and wildly successful, as it did Samuel Colt with the Walker revolver in 1847. But with Winchester and its predecessor firms, there was no overnight order or single large contract which launched the company into immediate profits. U.S. Ordnance resistance to the "newfangled" repeaters was hard to overcome. The Jennings, Volcanic, and Henry all had problems, but the Civil War put to the test a myriad of metallic-cartridge breechloaders. From that crucible emerged the basis for volume sales of lever-action repeaters by Winchester.

First the Henry met with moderate success, largely through quantity purchases by the Union militia. Then the Model 1866 lever-action proved itself in the hands of both frontiersmen and Indians. But its first triumphs were in foreign military sales—most voluminously to the governments of Turkey (45,000 muskets and 5,000 carbines) and France (3,000 muskets and 3,000 carbines). France's purchases were made, strangely enough, through the Remington Arms Company.

Winchester's hopes for military sales are evident in the musket configurations (suitable for bayonet attachment) of the lever-action models of 1866, 1873, 1876, 1886, 1892, 1894, and 1895. Of these, by far the most impressive of lever-action military sales was the total of 293,816 of the 7.62mm Russian Model 1895 musket, sold to the Imperial Russian government in 1915–16. Military orders were also the impetus for the factory's experiments with revolvers. Smith & Wesson sold over 130,000 guns by contract to the Czar's ordnance in the 1870s, and no little effort was devoted by Winchester toward capturing a share of the potential military handgun market.

Oliver Winchester had an impassioned dedication to garnering military acceptance of his repeating firearms, and, as president of the firm, he lent much of his prestige and energy toward equipping U.S. forces with modern firearms. Winchester's championing of small-arms modernization was eloquently expressed in an appeal for the adoption of a breech-loading repeater for U.S. troops:

> What would be the value of an army of one hundred thousand infantry and cavalry, thus mounted and armed with a due proportion of artillery, each artilleryman with a repeating carbine slung to his back? Certainly the introduction of repeating guns into the army will involve a change in the Manual of Arms. Probably it will modify the art of war; possibly it may revolutionize the whole science of war. Where is the military genius that is to grasp this whole subject, and so modify the science of war as to best develop the capacities of this terrible engine—the exclusive control of which would enable any government (with resources sufficient to keep half a million of men in the field) to rule the world?

Other than lever-action sales to the Turkish and French governments and some undetermined

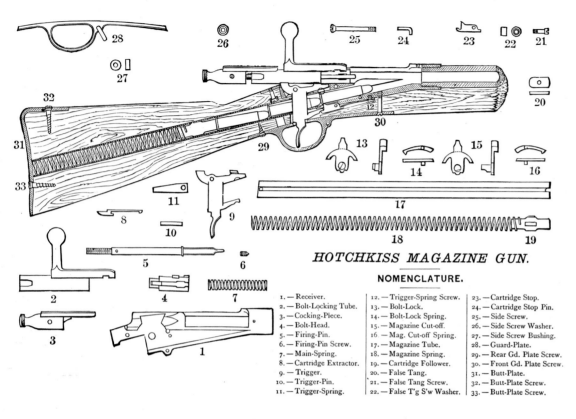

HOTCHKISS MAGAZINE GUN.

NOMENCLATURE.

1. — Receiver.	12. — Trigger-Spring Screw.	23. — Cartridge Stop.
2. — Bolt-Locking Tube.	13. — Bolt-Lock.	24. — Cartridge Stop Pin.
3. — Cocking-Piece.	14. — Bolt-Lock Spring.	25. — Side Screw.
4. — Bolt-Head.	15. — Magazine Cut-off.	26. — Side Screw Washer.
5. — Firing-Pin.	16. — Mag. Cut-off Spring.	27. — Side Screw Bushing.
6. — Firing-Pin Screw.	17. — Magazine Tube.	28. — Guard-Plate.
7. — Main-Spring.	18. — Magazine Spring.	29. — Rear Gd. Plate Screw.
8. — Cartridge Extractor.	19. — Cartridge Follower.	30. — Front Gd. Plate Screw.
9. — Trigger.	20. — False Tang.	31. — Butt-Plate.
10. — Trigger-Pin.	21. — False Tang Screw.	32. — Butt-Plate Screw.
11. — Trigger-Spring.	22. — False T'g S'w Washer.	33. — Butt-Plate Screw.

CARBINE AND MUSKET.

MUSKET.

CARBINE.

U.S. GOVT.45

quantities to the Chinese, Oliver Winchester never realized his ambitions to "modify the art of war" through Winchester repeaters. However, the Turkish, French, and Chinese sales also included millions of rounds of ammunition, and among other high-volume clients for cartridges was the government of Argentina.

A business coup was Winchester's signing a contract with the Turks for 200,000 Martini-Henry rifles. O. F. Winchester himself had been in Constantinople in 1872 and brought back the agreement, which he in turn sold to the Providence Tool Company of Rhode Island. One can assume that Winchester tried to sell the Turks on his lever-action repeaters and took the order for the Martini-Henry single-shot rifle somewhat disappointedly. However, he also garnered large contracts for ammunition: one in May 1874 for 87,500,000 primed Martini cartridge casings and bullets, and another in 1875 for 112,500,000; and in 1876–77, Winchester sold 80,100,000 Snider cartridges to the Turkish government.

The Martini rifle contract and the huge ammunition sales were instrumental in allowing Winchester to expand and grow as a world leader in arms and ammunition. However, from the late 1870s until World War I, military sales were relatively unimportant in the business of Winchester. Commercial

Intricacies of the Model 1883 Hotchkiss. The magazine is butt-loaded through the breech, with the bolt drawn rearward. From the September 1882 catalogue.

Carbine and musket variations of the Hotchkiss, accompanied by bayonets, the .45-70 cartridge, and data, from the September 1882 catalogue.

The Lee straight-pull Navy rifle, sporter at *top*, and two USN military muskets. A jerk on the bolt brought it back at a slight angle, for ejection and loading. The handsome bayonet, finished in bright steel, bears Winchester Repeating Arms Company markings on the crossguard, not visible in this view.

sales of firearms and ammunition proved the backbone of the firm's operations in those years.

The Hotchkiss Bolt-Action Repeater

A gun which had the potential to succeed commercially as well as militarily was the firm's first bolt-action firearm: the Hotchkiss repeating rifle, a specimen of which was on display at the Philadelphia Centennial Exhibition of 1876. The magazine was in the butt, and the bolt system was of greater strength than the toggle-link mechanism of the lever-actions. Drawing a favorable response from the military at the exhibition, Winchester made arrangements to buy Hotchkiss manufacturing rights in 1877.

In that same year, Congress voted funding for a military test of new firearms. For these trials, which commenced in April 1878, Winchester entered several Hotchkiss rifles to compete against twenty-eight repeating breech-loading firearms. To the delight of Winchester, the Hotchkiss emerged victorious. The trial board recommended that one hundred guns be built for testing. These rifles, made jointly by the Springfield Armory and Winchester, were, unfortunately, disappointing in the field. To quote Brigadier General S. V. Benét, 1880:

> The Hotchkiss has met with reverses, due to hasty manufacture and imperfect design in some of its minor parts, which can hardly be charged to the invention. It is believed that these defects, in which the mechanical principles of the invention were not involved, have been corrected in the new model, and more favorable results may not be anticipated. The manufacturer's experience with this gun proves that difficulties are ever to be met and overcome in perfecting a new invention that has to stand the severe test of field service. As a rule, a firstrate military arm must be of gradual growth; and be finally made up of successive improvements rendered necessary to correct defects developed in the hands of the soldier. The principle of

the Hotchkiss is a good one, but there seems to be some prejudice existing in our service against the bolt system and its awkward handle that time and custom may overcome.

Despite the failure of the Hotchkiss in the field test, the gun was released on the market in 1883, intended for both military and sporting sales. The bulk of sales were commercial, and the military Hotchkiss is identified by an eagle-head motif and markings of VP and U.S., all at the barrel breech. The guns were made in Army and Navy orders—carbines, rifles, and muskets for the Army, and rifles for the Navy.

Oliver Winchester died in 1880 without realizing his goal of successful U.S. military sales. And, in retrospect, it can be said that the commercial success of Winchester could have been even greater than it was, had not the president of the firm devoted so much time and energy to going after government contract sales. It is likely that Winchester himself recognized that chasing the rainbow of military sales had been largely wasted effort. The hint of that reality appears in the company's 1875 catalogue:

> One hundred and fifty thousand [Winchesters] have been sold without advertising or puffing, and they have everywhere given unqualified satisfaction, having earned their position solely by their merits.
>
> It has become a household word, and a household necessity on our western plains and mountains.
>
> The pioneer, the hunter and trapper, believe in the Winchester, and its possession is a passion with every Indian.
>
> They have found their way to every country in the world. In the armament of the explorer in the wilds of Africa, and other countries, they are sure to have a place.

The catalogue also concentrated more on the commercial factors in Winchester sales than on the military, by publishing a number of testimonial

letters on the Model 1866 and 1873 arms, written by satisfied shooters, many of them frontiersmen.

This increased concentration on commercial sales saw an increase in the number of Winchester dealers and jobbers. By the year of O. F. Winchester's death, the firm had over 150 Canadian and U.S. jobbers. These professionals in the field played an important role in building and maintaining the factory's leadership position. This management and manufacturing dominance was evolving at a time (c. 1873–79) when the United States was experiencing one of the worst business depressions of the nineteenth century.

Cartridge Sales and Acquisitions of Remington Arms Co.

Solidifying Winchester's business stature was an arrangement which by modern standards would be illegal, but in those days was quite acceptable: by 1870 the Union Metallic Cartridge Company was the largest cartridge maker in the world, and by 1873 Winchester had become much more active and competitive in the ammunition business. The two firms found areas of difference with patent rights on cartridge design and manufacture, and in 1873 they entered into an agreement in which claims "for the use of patents in manufacture of metallic cartridges . . . against each other up to this date are hereby cancelled, and set off one against the other." Further, "in the future [each party shall be] entitled to use the patents of the other so far as they may elect to do so. The royalty or compensation to be paid by each party to the other shall be fixed and determined by a Board of Arbitration." Agreement was also reached in payment of legal fees should there be suits brought against the firms on patents. The final significant point of this joint arrangement was limiting the deal "only to patent rights now in general use in the manufacture of cartridges, and . . . not . . . to any radically new mode of depositing metal by galvanic process."

The Winchester complex, c. 1915, a veritable city. Compare with the 1916 fiftieth-anniversary picture, on page 163. The growth during World War I was phenomenal in both extent and rate.

The agreement would remain in force for ten years, during which time both companies developed even closer ties.

One of the most remarkable developments in the history of gunmaking took place in 1888. The Remington Arms Company had suffered severe financial setbacks, mainly as a result of overexpansion, and by 1886 the firm was in receivership. Marcellus Hartley, who had built the Union Metallic Cartridge Company and shared with Winchester the bulk of the U.S. ammunition market, made a proposal.

Quoting from the minutes of the January 24th 1888, Winchester Board of Directors' meeting:

Messrs. Hartley and Graham [major gun dealers as well as owners of U.M.C.] . . . asked if our Company would consider entering a syndicate . . . for the purchase of a ⅗ or controlling interest in the Remington business and property which would probably require as our share $75,000. . . . On motion it was voted that the executive officers of the Company be authorized to go into the Remington transaction to the extent of $75,000 if it was thought advisable.

On March 7, Hartley and Graham purchased Remington, and Winchester assumed half of the $200,000 cost. Remington was jointly run by U.M.C. and Winchester until 1896, at which time Winchester sold its share to Marcelus Hartley. The deal gave Winchester a significant share in a key competitor, and also prevented Remington from ever becoming a manufacturer of lever-action firearms.

In an attempt to develop world markets—both commercial and military—Winchester relied heavily on Thomas Emmet Addis, who was appointed international salesman. Addis had considerable authority, and ranged so far and wide that he referred to himself as "World Traveller." Some fascinating comments based on his letters to New Haven were collected in a book of foreign contracts. Excerpts from 1887 and 1888 follow:

Japan: There is very little demand for sporting arms of any sort in Japan.

Bangkok, Siam: Siam would be a grand market for our goods were free importation permitted but the regulations are practically prohibitive as a permit must be obtained from the King himself who will only grant a permit where he is satisfied the arms will not be used against him. . . . A good many of our guns were imported before these regulations went into effect, and they are much liked. The King's Body Guard were at one time armed with them, but now use Martini-Henrys of Belgian make. . . . there is very little prospect of the Government purchasing our single shot muskets with bayonets and scabbards. . . .

Western Australia: T.E.A. does not think it advisable to visit there—no town of 5,000 inhabitants, and would require months time to make the trip.

Addis went on to note, "Sent an order for very finely finished carbines and shot guns intended for the King and Princess occupying high places. . . ."

At this time the major U.S. competitors to Winchester were the rifles by Colt and Marlin. And it appears that export sales in the 1880s and 1890s represented about 10 to 15 percent of total Winchester sales.

While the government sales of firearms were not what O. F. Winchester and other management would have hoped, ammunition proved to be increasingly profitable. A decisive factor in the profitability of ammunition sales was a little-known organization put together in 1883: the Ammunition Manufacturers' Association (AMA). The origin of the group was candidly explained by onetime Winchester executive Arthur Earle: "There had been very serious competition among the larger ammunition manufacturers. . . . they thought it would be much better for all hands to get together and make some money rather than spend their time and money and energy cutting each other's throats."

Not at all illegal at the time it was formed, the association included Winchester, the Union Metallic Cartridge Company, the Phoenix Metallic Cartridge Company, and the U.S. Cartridge Company. Winchester and U.M.C. held equal shares and owned nearly 75 percent of the stock. The main goals of the AMA were stated in incorporation documents:

. . . to buy and sell ammunition of all kinds and act as agent for others in the purchase and sale thereof; to make contracts with Manufacturers and Dealers in Ammunition for the purpose of producing and securing uniformity and certainty in their customs and usages and preventing serious competition between them; to settle differences between those engaged in the manufacture of or in dealing in ammunition, and to devise and take measurements to foster and protect their trade and business.

The members no longer were competing in terms of price, but continued to compete in quality, brand names, the preferences of dealers and jobbers, and related matters.

It has been estimated that the association had control of as much as 50 percent of the total sales of the ammunition industry. An idea of the importance of ammunition is evident by sales figures showing that Winchester's net sales from January 1, 1884, to December 31, 1888, were $9,500,000. The firm's net profit from this total was $2,200,000. Approximately half of these sales and half of the profit was from ammunition. What percent of the ammunition was intended for military use is unknown, but the variety of cartridges in the firm's line as of 1884 totaled approximately one hundred, plus primers, paper and brass empty shotshells, and felt gun wads.

Based largely on its substantial commercial sales of firearms and the large market for ammunition, Winchester's share of the arms and ammunition industry as a U.S. manufacturer went from 12 percent of the market (c. 1889) to 27 percent (c. 1899). In the same period the number of company employees more than doubled, from over 1,200 to nearly 2,800. Clearly W.R.A. Co. was an industry leader, not only domestically, but also as an international force.

T. G. Bennett Assumes Presidency

As of February 1890, Thomas Gray Bennett, son-in-law of Oliver Winchester and an experienced and educated gun man, became president of the firm. For the ten previous years, control had been under the able guidance of William W. Converse, a brother-in-law of William W. Winchester.* As O. F. Winchester had groomed his successors, so had Converse. The most qualified successor (who might even have taken over on O. F. Winchester's death in 1880, except for his youthful thirty-seven years) was T. G. Bennett.

T. G. Bennett would remain president for the next twenty-one years. He assumed control at a time of great company prosperity, with the firm in solid financial condition, well prepared to enter a new era characterized by the change from black powder to smokeless—a change that affected the design of both ammunition and the firearms themselves.

Under Bennett's presidency, W.R.A. Co. grew from approximately 1,430 employees to twice that by 1900, and twice again by 1914 (somewhat more than half of these workmen made firearms; the

---

*Though groomed to succeed his father, W. W. died of tuberculosis in March 1881.

From the *Winchester Record*, the company's in-house journal, an extraordinary photograph of Winchester employees heralding victory for the Allies in World War I.

The Winchester Repeating Arms Co. was awarded the Grand Prize - The Highest Possible Award - For All Kinds of Rifles, Shotguns, Metallic Cartridges and Loaded Shotgun Shells at the Panama Pacific International Exposition.

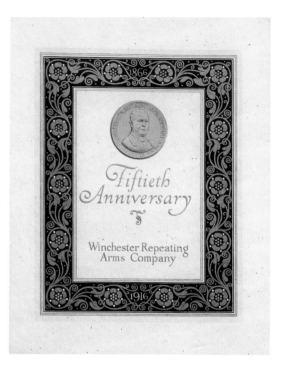

A superb tribute to the Winchester giant, from the firm's fiftieth-anniversary celebratory brochure. The Panama-Pacific Exposition award graced the back of this rare publication, embossed in gold.

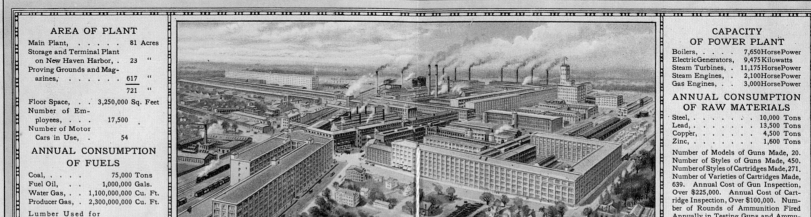

AREA OF PLANT	
Main Plant,	81 Acres
Storage and Terminal Plant on New Haven Harbor,	23 "
Proving Grounds and Magazines,	617 "
	721 "
Floor Space,	3,250,000 Sq. Feet
Number of Employees,	17,500
Number of Motor Cars in Use,	54

ANNUAL CONSUMPTION OF FUELS

Coal,	75,000 Tons
Fuel Oil,	1,000,000 Gals.
Water Gas,	1,100,000,000 Cu. Ft.
Producer Gas,	2,300,000,000 Cu. Ft.
Lumber Used for Cases,	6,000,000 Feet

CAPACITY OF POWER PLANT

Boilers,	7,650 Horse Power
Electric Generators,	9,475 Kilowatts
Steam Turbines,	11,175 Horse Power
Steam Engines,	2,100 Horse Power
Gas Engines,	3,000 Horse Power

ANNUAL CONSUMPTION OF RAW MATERIALS

Steel,	10,000 Tons
Lead,	13,500 Tons
Copper,	4,500 Tons
Zinc,	1,600 Tons

Number of Models of Guns Made, 20. Number of Styles of Guns Made, 450. Number of Styles of Cartridges Made, 271. Number of Varieties of Cartridges Made, 639. Annual Cost of Gun Inspection, Over $225,000. Annual Cost of Cartridge Inspection, Over $100,000. Number of Rounds of Ammunition Fired Annually in Testing Guns and Ammunition, Over 25,000,000.

THE Winchester Repeating Arms Co. was founded in May, 1866, by Oliver F. Winchester; therefore, this year it rounds out a half century of existence. From its organization down to the present time, the company has been owned and controlled by the same interests, and its management has been governed by one policy, namely, that of turning out a high-class product representing in every way all that is new, desirable and practical in the art of gun and ammunition making.

These fifty years have wrought many changes in guns and ammunition, and in all important developments the Winchester company has been a prominent factor. By intelligent and progressive management, the Winchester company early established itself as the leader in its line of manufacture, and throughout all the years of wonderful development since its organization, it has maintained this enviable position. From a very modest beginning the company has grown steadily and healthfully until to-day it is the largest manufacturer of sporting guns and ammunition in the world. Some idea of the growth and size of the plant, and the magnitude of its production, can be gained from the illustrations and statistics given above.

Honors upon honors have been bestowed upon Winchester—the W brand—guns and ammunition since they were introduced upon the market, the latest being the award of The Grand Prize—the highest possible honor—for all kinds of rifles, shotguns, metallic cartridges, loaded shotgun shells, etc., by the Panama-Pacific International Exposition. Appreciated as these honors are, they pale in comparison with the high esteem in which Winchester guns and ammunition are universally regarded by sellers and users of them the wide world over. At this time it is fitting, as well as a pleasure, to express thanks to our friends and customers for the many evidences of good will, and for the loyal support which has enabled our business to grow to its present proportions, and to further express the hope that these pleasant relations will continue in the years to come.

WINCHESTER REPEATING ARMS CO., - - - NEW HAVEN, CONN., U.S.A.

BY INVITATION MEMBER OF

Winchester's chief engineer's office, 1918, a Browning Automatic Rifle on the conference table. John Browning, seated at *center*, is accompanied by (*left to right*) Kenneth Browning, Edwin Pugsley, Fred Werme, Frank Burton, and W. C. Roemer. Pugsley's career at Winchester began soon after his graduation from Yale University in 1911, and he remained with the firm through 1952. A collector of firearms, he was instrumental in developing the Winchester factory collection and later sold his own collection to the firm.

balance produced ammunition). At the time of Bennett's beginnings, with Winchester (1870), sales totaled about 25,000 guns. When he retired as president in 1910, the annual production was about 300,000 guns.

His successor was George E. Hodson, with Bennett remaining as consulting director and his son Winchester Bennett appointed first vice president. Control of the firm remained in the Bennett family hands.* The most accelerated and substantial expansion of the company was about to begin.

World War I Changes Winchester Forever

With World War I impending, Winchester's business remained steady, showing very little change in the years preceding the outbreak of hostilities in 1914. Since the U.S. government's position was one of neutrality, the firm could do business with either side. Winchester Bennett made clear the company's sentiment in September 1914, when he wrote that it was "difficult to maintain in person the neutrality which our national position demands and one is inclined to feel from all one sees and hears, that the neutrality is of the nation and of the federal government only, for certainly much sym-

---

*At his death in 1880, O. F. Winchester had left 4,000 shares of company stock in trust to his widow (who already owned 475 shares). Their daughter, Mrs. T. G. Bennett, then owned 406 shares, and Mrs. William Wirt Winchester had 777 shares. When Mrs. O. F. Winchester died in 1897, the trust was evenly divided between Mrs. W. W. Winchester and Mrs. T. G. Bennett. Thus, as of 1904, the family held the following stock:

Mrs. T. G. Bennett—2,875 shares
Mrs. W. W. Winchester—2,777 shares
T. G. Bennett—32 shares
Winchester Bennett—6 shares
Total: 5,690

The two Winchester/Bennett women had the vast majority of stock, and since shares in the company totaled 10,000 common stock, the family retained control. In order to prevent a "hostile takeover" (it had been rumored that some New York investors were interested in doing so), in May 1905, the family formed the Winchester Purchasing Company, which was a holding company designed to prevent the family from losing controlling interest. They would retain control until the 1920s.

Honoring Winchester's contributions to World Wars I and II. The Browning Automatic Rifle, caliber .30-06 Springfield, was quickly put into production in New Haven in 1918. The color brochure recognized the factory workers' role as "soldiers of production" in World War II.

MR VAL BROWNING

1921

pathy [for Britain] is evident." All of Winchester's output was for the Allied cause.

Winchester offered a "Mauser type rifle, bolt action, which will be chambered for the .303 cartridge. This new military arm will be without question far superior to any other military arm now on the market or furnished by government arsenals to the troops." Along with this confidential information the British were told, "If any sort of rearmament idea were in view or a sufficiently large contract could be given, we would erect a new factory and install machinery to take care of a contract of any size. . . . [But] it will be several months before our preliminary work on this arm will be completed." The firm also noted that "in the course of a few months, we could deliver . . . up to two or perhaps over three million [cartridges] per week."

In November of 1914, two officials of the British government visited New Haven, and shortly thereafter an order was received for 50 million .22 Long Rifle cartridges (for training); negotiations had also begun for a rifle-making contract. Ammunition orders for the Belgian and British governments were also written with Winchester, on a subcontract basis from Remington-U.M.C. Further, the Baldwin Locomotive Works placed an order on behalf of the Russian government for 100,000 Model 1895 muskets, and the British government placed an order for 200,000 British Enfield bolt-action rifles. Amazingly, by the end of November, the total value of military orders was in excess of $16,700,000 and

Closely similar, the Enfield Pattern 14 bolt-action .303 British at *top* preceded the Model 1917 U.S. caliber-.30 rifle at *bottom*, which is turned somewhat to reveal the top of the breech. Close similarities are evident, including the front halves and bayonets, which are nearly identical in most respects.

John Browning's son Val posed for this BAR promotional picture in 1921; he was then serving in the U.S. Army Ordnance Corps.

the sum reached $47,500,000 by the end of 1915. The additional contracts had been negotiated by J. P. Morgan & Company, and these orders included another 200,000 Model 1895 muskets and 300 million 7.62mm cartridges for the Russian Imperial government, 44 million British .303 Mark VI cartridges, 9 million .44-40 cartridges, 1,500,000 French 7mm cartridges, and various orders for such matériel as 18-pound cannon cases and primers.

These contracts added the equivalent of five years of orders on the capacity of the existing factory. Night shifts and an expected decline in commercial sales would take care of the Russian Model 1895 order and the ammunition contracts, but in order to handle the British Enfield production, the company decided it would need to expand existing facilities. Records show that some $13,300,000 would be spent for the new plant expansion, a figure which wiped out much of the profits anticipated from the wartime orders.

It appears that management had in mind an extensive restructuring of the plant facility, paid for by the profits from World War I. Thus, older buildings were likely to be scrapped following the war, and were to be replaced by new structures. As matters developed, however, by November of 1915 Winchester was in need of financing in order to keep the production going and to pay for salaries and other costs. A company which had not yet had to rely on banks for anything but short-term loans was now faced with substantial cash shortages and the onerous necessity of having to reveal business information which had always been kept close to the vest.

Winchester turned to J. P. Morgan & Company, New York, from which $200,000 had been borrowed in 1907 during a Wall Street panic. In November 1915, the directors voted to permit a loan of not more than $1,500,000 from Morgan, a limit which was increased to $3 million by the end of the month. Early the following month, the loan authori-

zation was again increased, this time to $8,250,000. Winchester had spent $5,238,000 in the previous thirteen months on property, building construction, and building equipment, and $3,676,000 was spent on machinery, gauges, tools, and sundry equipment. Further, the inventory had increased in value to a total of $6,617,000.

Matters got even worse, partly because of delays in production. To borrow even more working capital, Winchester approached Kidder, Peabody & Company, of Boston, as it appears that Morgan was committed to the extent that it preferred to refer Winchester elsewhere.

The amount borrowed there was a staggering $16 million. Just over half of the sum was used to pay back Morgan; the balance was put to work immediately. The loan permitted Winchester to operate through completion of the wartime contracts, with the firm agreeing to limit plant expansion to what had already been planned and committed to.

Besides the rapid expansion of the plant and equipment (one of the buildings for the Enfield rifle contract was completed—from the foundation to the finished five stories—in just five weeks), the number of Winchester employees mushroomed dramatically. By the fall of 1914, the estimate of total workers was just over 5,600. In a year's time that had grown to in excess of 12,700, and by the winter of 1916 the labor force was over 17,000! With this rapid increase came a new element, for which traditional management had utter disdain: unions.

The delivery of the first Russian contract (via Baldwin Locomotive Works) of 100,000 Model 1895 muskets was two weeks late. The second order, for 200,000 Model 1895s, was completed by the end of 1916. However, problems occurred with the Russian government inspectors and the 7.62mm cartridges, and out of the 300 million cartridges ordered, the total delivered would be about 174 million. The balance of the contract was canceled.

The contracts (November 1914 and March 1915) through J. P. Morgan & Company for British Enfield rifles totaled 400,000 and represented $12,500,000 in orders. But delays had occurred for various reasons, and when Winchester was ready to begin assembly, the date was just four months prior to the agreed-upon cancellation date of May 31, 1916, when the British could cancel all orders for rifles which had not been delivered.

The British inspectors were very demanding; Winchester wrote to J. P. Morgan complaining that they were "not inclined to grant us any concession. . . . [Their attitude] is likely to be a serious handicap to our production."

Finally, in September 1916, the British authorities advised they were canceling all Enfield contracts. After considerable consternation, legal wrangling, and even a discussion by the British War Council in the Prime Minister's private office, an agreement was reached which brought no profit to Winchester, but did prevent the company from enduring a substantial loss. The total number of Enfield rifles delivered to the British by Winchester was nearly 246,000.

The pressure cooker of the World War I contracts and the increased costs of expansion left Winchester in a vulnerable position. Aggravating the situation was the ill health of Winchester Bennett and the aging and weakening of T. G. Bennett. By February 1916, T. G. Bennett was considering allowing the firm's control to pass into other hands. The terms of the $16 million loan gave Kidder, Peabody & Company the option of purchasing

Riot and trench guns, with military and police applications. *From the top*, Model 1893 riot gun, with 12-gauge brass shells. Model 1897 riot gun, issued to the Illinois State Police. *Bottom*, Model 1897 trench gun, fitted with carrying sling and bayonet, with packet of twenty-five military-issue shotshells. Ventilated hand guard over barrel helped in cooling when barrels heated up after repeated firing.

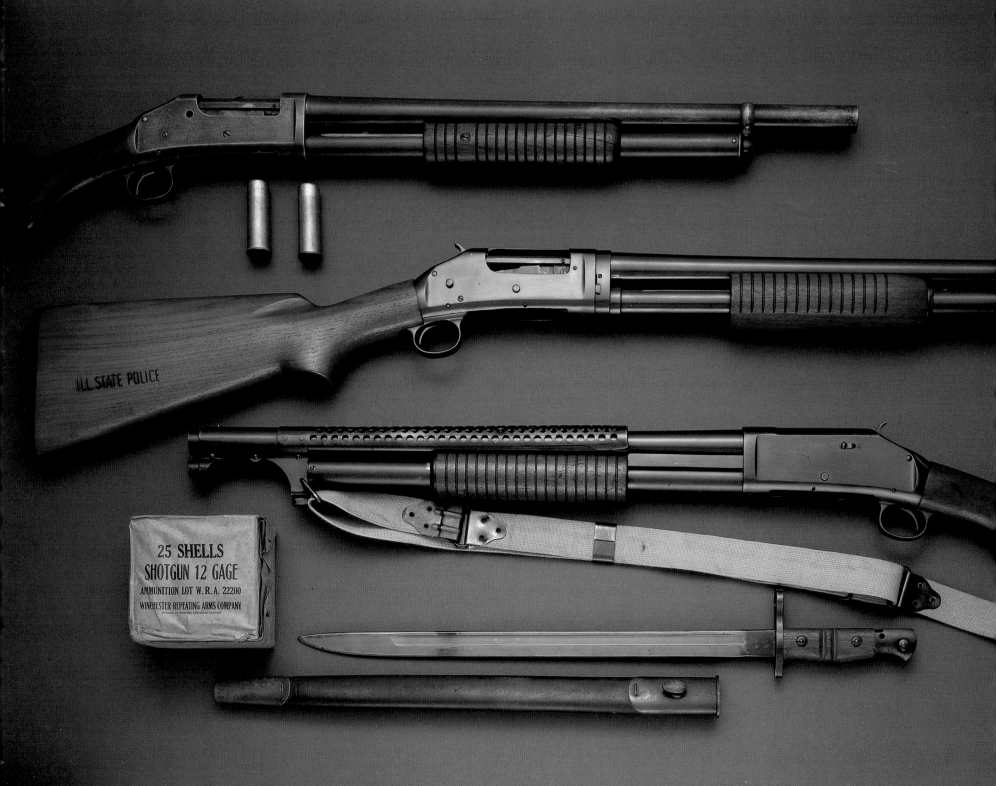

controlling interest in Winchester. Kidder, Peabody discussed this option with E. I. du Pont de Nemours & Company, but the deal fell through, since du Pont was interested only if contracts were extended and new orders taken.

At the same time, because of Bennett's ill health it was decided that a new chief executive would need to be selected. John E. Otterson, who had joined Winchester in 1915, was technically elected as "first vice president" in January 1917 but was, in fact, the chief executive.

When the United States entered the war, Winchester appeared to be in dire straits. To quote executive Edwin Pugsley, who had joined Winchester in 1911 and was married to a granddaughter of O. F. Winchester:

> At the end of 1916 and the early months of 1917 we had either completed or had cancelled practically all the work we had for foreign governments . . . so that the first part of 1917 found us with a plant entirely equipped for making small arms and ammunition and an organization completely trained and nothing to do. Great portions [of the factory complex] were idle.

Winchester had anticipated the U.S. entrance into the conflict, and, some two months before the U.S. declaration of war on April 6, 1917, had offered the company's plant and capabilities to the government. Winchester and Remington Arms recommended the British Enfield rifle be slightly modified to fire the .30-06 rimless cartridge. The equipment for making the Enfield had been sold back to the British government, but it was still in

place in New Haven and ready to go. Some few other alterations were also recommended for the gun, and in early May the Ordnance Department agreed to the suggested rifle and termed it the U.S. Rifle, Caliber .30, Model of 1917.

Winchester boldly went ahead with production even before receiving the formal contract. The company also rushed through production of the .30-06 ammunition, taking a chance by proceeding with some production even before getting precise specifications from the government. However, since the firm had manufactured the gauges used by government inspectors for testing the ammunition, W.R.A. Co. was on solid grounds.

Production for both rifles and ammunition was done on a cost-plus-10-percent basis. Winchester's efficiency in production was considered supreme, and the company's priming mixture for cartridges was of such quality that it became the norm for the government-ordered cartridges. The firm was also asked to help in cartridge development for use in machine guns mounted on U.S. aircraft. Machinery for testing these cartridges, synchronized to fire through the revolving propeller blades, was set up at Winchester with the cooperation of the U.S. Ordnance Department.

Winchester's wartime record was admirable: over 545,000 Model 1917 U.S. Rifles were built, and by July 1918, the company had 19,806 employees. Over $50 million worth of U.S. government contracts were completed in 1918 alone.

In September 1917, Winchester was instructed to commence tooling up for manufacture of the Browning Automatic Rifle (BAR). Edwin Pugsley, then manufacturing engineer, went to the Colt factory to see the only existing model. Since the BAR was needed at Colt's during the work week, it was borrowed for a weekend, and in that time drawings were made and the project begun. By the end of December the first Winchester BAR had been completed. Production was well along by March, and

by Armistice Day, November 11, 1918, Winchester had made approximately 47,000. Winchester also had begun construction of the Browning .50-caliber machine gun and had a working model completed within about two months. That gun, however, never entered into production, because of the end of hostilities.

Under pressure from the U.S. government to expand its production facilities to make, among other items, the Colt Model 1911 .45 ACP automatic pistol, the firm decided to attempt subcontracting. Arrangements were being made for five factories in the New Haven area, but the war ended and the plans were abandoned.

The total U.S. wartime contract business of Winchester was approximately $76 million. Nearly all of W.R.A. Co.'s business from mid-1917 through the fall of 1918 was military manufacturing.

Winchester management had hopes of financing the substantial plant expansion by profits from the wartime production. But, emerging from the war, the company was able to pay off one half of the $16 million owed Kidder, Peabody & Company, refinancing the $8 million balance for another year.

Control Passes from the Winchester-Bennett Family

In preparing for the future, a committee headed by T. G. Bennett made recommendations to the stockholders. The committee asked for a new infusion of capital ($3,500,000) in order to diversify Winchester by means of a broader product base, and not one limited to firearms and ammunition. From a committee letter dated October 26, 1918:

> We believe that if the plan is adopted the outstanding indebtedness will be taken care of and better provision made for future prospects, and that the stockholders will begin at once to receive regular dividends from the payment of the contemplated dividends on the new first preferred stock; whereas, in the absence of some such plan the financial situation of the Company will

Top and center, Model 1912 riot and trench guns, the former marked on the stock with an I monogram and ILLINOIS TOLLWAY. Accompanied by issue bayonet and military and civilian buckshot shell packages, and a Model 25 12-gauge riot gun at *bottom*. Model 12 types span c. 1912–63, the Model 25 c. 1949–54.

Meet the growing demand for packaged holiday goods with this fine assortment of Winchester products

From the in-house *Winchester Record*, an idea of the broad mix of products available from W.R.A. Co. in the 1920s.

Profusion of products which fit the category of Winchester memorabilia, most of them dating from the 1920s, when Winchester tried to switch from World War I military production to a broad-based gun, hardware, and sporting goods operation. Gray steel device at *right center*, is a reloading tool invented and patented by William Wirt Winchester, 1874.

be exceedingly unsatisfactory, and for a long time to come it is doubtful if the stockholders would receive any dividends as the earnings of the Company should be used in the business.

Financial control would no longer be in the Winchester-Bennett family, but in the hands of Kidder, Peabody & Company. Further, among the most influential of the new regime would be Otterson, as president (then only thirty-seven years old), and Louis K. Liggett, a renowned merchandiser who had made his fortune in the drug business and had organized a chain of drugstores (Rexall Stores, the United Drug Company).

Some shareholders resisted the deal, but the members of the Winchester-Bennett family and most others agreed. T. G. Bennett summed up the quandary in May 1919: "Without [the restructuring] we should today be in bankruptcy or so near it as to be helpless—drifting into bankruptcy because we had no working capital to go ahead. Now all our debts are paid and we have plenty of money to take care of current expenses and go ahead."

The new Winchester was headed by Otterson as president, T. G. Bennett as chairman of the board of the Winchester Company, and Liggett as a director of the Winchester Repeating Arms Company. Legally there were two Winchester firms, but both were operated as one.

Technically, Kidder, Peabody & Company owned the majority of the stock of the Winchester Company, which in turn owned 97.5 percent of the Winchester Repeating Arms Company's common stock. Beginning in 1919, there was what amounted to a five-year plan, headed by Otterson, with Kidder, Peabody & Company in *de facto* control.

Besides arms and ammunition, the new firm's production would include products requiring similar equipment to manufacture, items which could capitalize on the renowned Winchester name. The factory's experience in metallurgy and precision manufacturing with metals was called to the fore.

Further, quality was to be an important part of whatever was made, and the merchandising setup would need to be along the same lines as that used to sell firearms and ammunition.

Among the products selected were hardware tools, sporting goods, pocket and hunting knives, kitchen knives and related cutlery, fishing gear, flashlights, batteries, ice skates, and shears—all with the aim of top quality, but at a reasonable price.

Liggett's successes with the Rexall Stores chain served as the model for the merchandising and distribution scheme. The new Winchester organization was twofold: company-owned retail stores, and a dealer-agency scheme, allowing for direct sales and bypassing jobbers. Winchester would operate its own stores in cities larger than 50,000; in smaller cities the company would work directly with home-owned hardwares. Distribution of firearms and ammunition, however, would be through the traditional jobber arrangements.

The goal, simply put by Otterson himself, was to make "Winchester the largest single manufacturing institution in the world manufacturing sporting goods, cutlery, tools, and hardware specialities."

Winchester developed the product lines, set up the manufacturing, devised the merchandising, and launched into the new program with energy and dedication. Part of this evolution included purchasing existing companies, already experienced and many of them well known. In 1919, Eagle Pocket Knife, Napanoch Knife Company, Andrew B. Hendrix Company (fishing reels and lines), E. W. Edwards (fishing rods), Morrill Target Company (clay pigeons), Barney and Berry (skates), Lebanon Machine Company (auger bits), and Page-Storm Drop Forge Company (flat wrenches) were acquired. In 1920, the Mack Axe Company was added to the acquisitions list. A licensing and royalty arrangement was also set up which put Winchester into the battery business. By the end of

1920 Winchester had approximately 750 products either in production or in development stages.

The network of hardware and sporting goods outlets was developing at a rapid pace, but not without determined opposition from competitors. One of the most powerful of these was the well-known Simmons Hardware, perhaps the biggest of the wholesale hardware jobbers in the United States. The firm launched a counterattack against the Winchester program, and part of its strategy was accusing Winchester of being under the "centralized control [of] financial interests in Wall Street" and claiming that Winchester's success in its new program would lead to Wall Street's control of "the retail hardware businesses throughout the country."

Despite the attack by Simmons and others, Winchester had set up a system of 6,300 privately owned hardware stores by 1926. Winchester's own stores totaled only eleven, and were established by 1922, in New York, Providence, Boston, New Haven, and other cities.

For a variety of reasons—among them poor retail locations of many stores, lack of product expertise from management all the way down to store clerks, high cost of several Winchester products, and the depression—the ambitious dealer-agency plan was discontinued in 1929.

Still another major banking concern which had an involvement in Winchester's destiny in the 1920s was the Guaranty Trust Company of New York. A report done at Guaranty's request by a consulting engineer was critical of Winchester and its management, and although Otterson responded vigorously in defense, the report sowed seeds which were ominous for his administration.

The Merger with Simmons Hardware
As a means of reviving Winchester, a merger was arranged with an organization which not only was a competitor, but had voiced harsh criticism of Win-

chester's direct-to-dealers distribution program. The firm was the Associated Simmons Hardware Companies, St. Louis. Founded in 1864, Simmons was run by three sons of the founder at the time negotiations with Winchester began in approximately 1922. In June of that year a letter was sent to the stockholders announcing the merger:

The Winchester Company will operate as the manufacturing organization and the Associated Simmons Hardware Companies will operate as the distributing organization. . . . The combined interests will be operated through a holding company to be known as THE WINCHESTER-SIMMONS COMPANY. . . .

However, control of the new firm remained in the hands of Kidder, Peabody & Company. The Simmons brothers had been criticized by company insiders as know-it-all country-club college kids, and the deal would eventually neutralize their influence within the firm. On the occasion of the merger, George Simmons, who had previously been highly critical of Winchester's dealer-agency plan, explained away those objections, closing with the remarks:

I have discussed with several big manufacturers in the last five years just such an affiliation of producing and distributing organizations, and every one of them has been keen for it, but we have not found any other manufacturing concern big enough for us to tie up with because no other has the capacity for a broad variety of production that the Winchester Company has.

Among the new products Winchester was called on to produce with Simmons were Walden knives and Louisville Slugger–style baseball bats.

As of January 1924, Winchester-Simmons retail outlets totaled 5,600, representing approximately one fourth of all retail hardware stores in the United States. The same month, Otterson stated that approximately 1,000 new additions had been made to the Winchester product line over the previous

From the old to the new. Sergeant at *right* wears the World War I–era, doughboy-style helmet and is armed with the bolt-action U.S. Model 1903 service rifle. His counterpart at *left* is armed with the M1 Garand, with the style of helmet prevalent for U.S. troops in World War II.

year. He claimed for the firm "the most complete line of sporting goods placed on the market by any single manufacturer; also the most complete line of tools and hardware specialties."

However, 1923 had been a poor business year for Winchester, and an analytical team sent in by Liggett came to the shocking conclusion that the company should immediately go into receivership.

Instead, Otterson and Vice President R. E. Anderson resigned (June 1924), leaving the presidency to Frank Drew. But rather than turn to a top gun-and-hardware executive, Kidder, Peabody appointed Liggett president of Simmons Hardware Company and chairman of the board of Winchester Repeating Arms Company—succeeding T. G. Bennett, and thus ending his fifty-four years of association with the firm.

Among other appointments, Edwin Pugsley was made general superintendent of the Winchester factory. At least in him there was a key figure who, by marriage to a granddaughter of Oliver Winchester, was part of the Winchester-Bennett family. Pugsley was also a dedicated arms collector, a true expert, and a "gun man."

A rather impressive statistic is that the July 1924 Winchester catalogue offered 7,584 products, with virtually all but athletic goods made by Winchester. Still trying to build the dealer base, Winchester had approximately 6,300 stores by June—although Otterson's original goal had been 8,000.

Increasing Pressure from Debts and Poor Investments

In 1926, a partial purchase was made of the U.S. Cartridge Company. The agreement called for its product to be made by Winchester, but the distribution to continue through U.S. Cartridge's own outlets. It took eighty-three freight cars to ship the machinery to New Haven from the U.S.C. Co. plant in Lowell, Massachusetts. Radiator manufacture was part of U.S.C.'s operation, and this too was assumed by Winchester. As a result, in 1929 Winchester would make automobile radiators for Rolls-Royce.

Winchester also was briefly in the refrigerator business, but that proved a dismal and expensive failure, losing over $1,200,000 (1925–28). Still another project, washing machines, proved an even greater fiasco. In 1927 the promotional slogan "As Good as the Gun" was introduced, hoping to capitalize on the strength of the Winchester name.

In an atmosphere of ever-increasing pressure, Winchester abandoned the dealer-agency scheme early in 1929, and, to change to open-market sales and to refinance its debt of approximately $5,600,000, the firm was reorganized. The new organization was named Winchester Manufacturing Company, a Delaware corporation. The arrangements with the Simmons Hardware Company were also terminated.

These maneuverings effectively returned Winchester to where it had been in 1919. Poorly selling products were dropped, and distribution returned to an open-market arrangement, via jobbers. Kidder, Peabody & Company still retained financial control. But net worth of the firm had deteriorated from $22,500,000 in 1924 to about $8 million in 1931. Losses on new ventures alone accounted for over $3,300,000 of the difference. Finally, Kidder, Peabody would put no more money into Winchester, and on January 22, 1931, the firm went into receivership.

Sale to Western Cartridge Company—the Olins
Rumors of buyers included the Remington Arms Company, but it was the Western Cartridge Company that stepped in and absorbed the faltering giant. For $3 million cash and $4,800,000 of Western Cartridge Company stock (and for an assumption of Winchester's liabilities and costs of the receivership), the deal was closed in December 1931.

The new owners were in marked contrast to the controlling management of the humbled giant. The Western Cartridge Company had been founded by Franklin W. Olin in 1898, and had been preceded by the Equitable Powder Manufacturing Company, which Olin established in 1892. Olin, joined over the years by his sons Spencer T. and John M., expanded his companies into a powerful force in the ammunition business. And to think, some forty years previous to acquiring Winchester, Western had had the audacity to compete with the giant as a cartridge manufacturer.

For years the Olins—all of them keen gun enthusiasts—had considered acquiring a gunmaking firm and had also given thought to opening their own gun-manufacturing operation. The availability of Winchester proved irresistible to these entrepreneurial gun and cartridge experts, and despite the depression at its worst, they courageously took the biggest gamble of their business careers. To quote Edwin Pugsley: "Only those who passed through the financial depression can realize the courage of these three men in staking practically their entire fortune upon their judgment."

The Olins quickly assessed the status of their new acquisition and recognized among the strong points the creative design staff headed by T. C. Johnson, the patents for arms and ammunition, and developmental models and ideas awaiting production.

Of further value was the solid reputation of the Western Cartridge Company and that of the Olins, both as businessmen and for their proven expertise in the arms field. In the latter areas, those who had a record of success were invariably knowledgeable of the product—they were "gun men."

Several new models of firearms were introduced, as well as new cartridges. Among them was John Olin's favorite gun, the Model 21 side-by-side shotgun, and the Silvertip ammunition line was brought out. Also, manufacturing was streamlined throughout the factory—lines like radiator tubes,

radiators, cutlery, and tools were dropped. But flashlights, batteries, roller skates, and extruded tubes and heat exchangers were continued. A line of brass products, a development of Western Cartridge, was even added. Unlike its competitors, Western had its own brass mills and was in a unique position to control the quality of its cartridge brass.

Drawing near to the beginnings of World War II, Winchester's availability to the U.S. Ordnance Department would lead to a repeat of its patriotic role in World War I, but with a successful business emergence after the war's end.

Winchester and World War II
Winchester was a key factor in the development of the .30-caliber M1 carbine and in the production of the M1 rifle, the .30-caliber Garand (designed at the Springfield Armory). The Garand had been adopted in January 1936 as the new U.S. service rifle, succeeding the Model 1903 Springfield bolt-action.

Under a program known as an Educational Order, Winchester was awarded, in 1937, the contract to build 500 Garands. Even before the rifles had been completed, the Ordnance Department called for bids on quantity manufacture of the Garand. Winchester again was selected, and was awarded a contract for 65,000 rifles.

Throughout the war, Winchester was the only maker of Garands outside of the Springfield Armory. The first deliveries from New Haven were in 1940, and the total of Garands made by Winchester was over 513,500.

The .30-caliber M1 carbine was a major wartime

M1 Garand rifles. At *top*, gauge gun used by Winchester for setting up manufacture; no serial number, and possibly the first Winchester Garand ever made. *Bottom*, a sniper variation of the Garand, with scope and other amenities. *Center*, detail reveals muzzle configuration, bayonet, and forend.

achievement by Winchester. At the request of the Ordnance Department, Winchester officials were involved in the development of a 5-pound semi-automatic weapon. The cartridge requirement was between a .276 and a 7.65 Mauser. Prototype cartridges were developed, and the .30 caliber accepted by the Ordnance Department was a Winchester design. Gun designers were simultaneously invited to come up with designs for a weapon to fire the new cartridge. Preoccupied with the Garand, Winchester made no submission to the competition, but an initial Ordnance Department trial, in May–June 1941, failed to find a satisfactory rifle.

Winchester designer David Marshall Williams had been working on a gun which had a system known as the "short-stroke piston." A 7½-pound rifle of his creation worked well in Marine Corps tests, and Winchester advised the Ordnance Department that it was confident of creating a 5-pound .30-caliber gun.

Just thirteen days after Winchester received the order, the new carbine was ready for testing at Aberdeen Proving Ground, Maryland, where it performed admirably, and Winchester was asked to submit the gun for the formal trials to be held September 15, 1941.

To quote Edwin Pugsley:

Marksmanship training with the M1 Garand: explaining the sight picture for use with peep sights. In order to encourage marksmanship, special competitions have been organized for military rifles, under the aegis of the Director of Civilian Marksmanship. In the summer of 1916 the National Defense Act was passed, providing for government funding for civilian marksmanship training. The War Department was authorized to provide firearms and ammunition to civilian rifle shooting clubs, supervised by the National Board for the Promotion of Rifle Practice. Military personnel were made available for assisting these clubs, and government rifle ranges were opened to the civilian shooters. Funding was also provided for transporting civilian teams to the National Matches (held at Camp Perry, Ohio, since 1907).

By working around the clock, including Sundays, the parts of the new gun were assembled on the afternoon of Friday the 13th of September. On Saturday morning a call from the Ordnance Department informed Winchester that the gun must be in Aberdeen by the noon of the following day in order to undergo a firing test of 1,000 rounds before being submitted to the Test Board on Monday. It was not until early midnight on Saturday that the gun was operating satisfactorily. Six hours later it was on its way to Aberdeen.

On arrival at Aberdeen about 1:30 P.M. Sunday the gun was rushed through the preliminary trials required of all guns to be entered in the test. . . . As the test progressed, the Winchester gun pulled away from the field and at the end of the test, by unanimous choice, became the now worldwide known U.S. Carbine, Caliber .30, M1 of the U.S. forces and, under Lend-Lease, that of our many allies.

A total of 350,000 carbines were ordered from Winchester in November 1941, and by August 1942, the first ten production-model carbines had been made. To meet production goals, innovative manufacturing practices were instituted, such as using women in factory and workshop capacities for which they were not previously considered suitable. Pugsley stated that "the carbine was developed with a speed heretofore unknown in the arms industry," and the total produced under various contracts to Winchester was over 818,000.

Not long after the start of the war, Winchester voluntarily ceased production of all commercial products and concentrated entirely on contracts for government requirements. The company was the first in the U.S. gun industry to do so, but its major competitors soon followed suit.

Winchester also excelled in wartime ammunition production. The Finnish government placed the first orders, but the main production was for the U.S. government, and such allies as the British.* The combined labor force of Winchester and the Western Cartridge Company during World War II exceeded 61,000 at peak production, with over 13,600 at the New Haven facility alone.

The contributions of Olin companies in World War II included 15 billion rifle and machine gun cartridges, 1.5 billion pounds of cartridge metals, and 100 million pounds of aluminum, in addition to hundreds of thousands of M1 Garand rifles and M1 carbines. An extraordinary process for making smokeless ball powder underwater was developed by Olin's Dr. Fred Olsen, instrumental in making the cartridges for the M1 carbine and the post–World War II short-case NATO 7.62mm rifle cartridge.

Other than hundreds of millions of rounds of ammunition made on government order since the end of World War II, the main production by Winchester for the U.S. forces was the M-14 service rifle, 7.62mm caliber. The new gas-operated rifle, an improvement over the M1 Garand, was introduced in August 1960. This twenty-shot box-magazine arm fired the .308 NATO round and weighed 8.6 pounds. Winchester was awarded contracts, and when New Haven production of the M-14 ceased, over 350,500 had been built by the firm.

As a gunmaker, Winchester's involvement with the U.S. government also included subcontracted barrels for the AR-15 .223-caliber rifle. A total of 18,000 of these were built (c. 1961).

Present-day federal government business for the Winchester Division of the Olin Corporation is of such magnitude that Winchester is part of the larger corporate segment known as Defense and Ammunition. It is Winchester personnel who operate the government's Lake City Arsenal, Independence, Missouri (since winning the contract from the Remington Arms Company in 1985), and defense business changes brought about by the Cold War thaw (beginning 1989) were referenced in the 1990 Olin Corporation Annual Report. The solid position of

---

*See Appendix, page 390, for World War II production figures.

Proof firing an M14 rifle at the New Haven indoor test range.

U.S. Army combat photograph, southwest Pacific, Fall 1943. The infantrymen are armed with the M1 Garand rifle, and await word to advance.

Comparison of the .30-caliber M1 carbine (*top*, U.S. issue number 1032386), the M1 Garand (*center*, used at W.R.A. Co. ammo plant for testing, .30-06 caliber, number 2487840), and the M14 (.308 NATO caliber, serial number 3934, selector switch for full and semiautomatic).

Marshall "Carbine" Williams, inventor of the M1 carbine, pointing out the simplicity of his invention, the "short-stroke piston," an inspiration he had while serving time on a prison chain gang. The James Stewart film *Carbine Williams* paid tribute to this remarkable firearm's innovator and inventor.

Sniper (*top*) and paratrooper variations of the M1 carbine, the latter with collapsible skeleton buttstock which folds along the left side of gun.

General Mark W. Clark, commanding Fifth Army, congratulating Lieutenant Roland Gagnon and two men of the 34th Division, on taking of Leghorn, Italy, July 1944. The men are Japanese-Americans of the 442nd Regiment, of the 34th. At *left*, M1 Garand rifle; the lieutenant carries an M1 carbine.

XM21 adjustable ranging telescope on an M14 sniper rifle, aimed by a U.S. infantry marksman, at Fort Benning, Georgia, 1970.

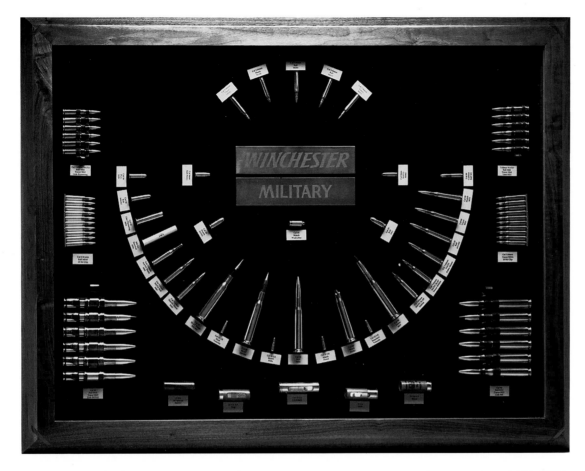

Rarely encountered by collectors are cartridge boards devoted exclusively to the military. Eighty-two cartridges demonstrate Winchester-Olin's comprehensive array, including various .22 Long Rifle and 5.56mm, 7.62mm, .30, and .50 longarm ammunition, 9mm, .38, and .45 pistol ammunition, .410-bore and 12-gauge shotshells, and a variety of tracer, match, wadcutter, blank, survival, line throwing, slap, ball, trap, and skeet shells. Only two of these boards were made, c. 1989.

Rear view of a "Parker" automatic loader at Winchester's center-fire facility, East Alton, c. 1990.

High-speed photograph capturing two .308 cartridges in flight, fired from the M14 rifle. Taken at Winchester's research laboratory, New Haven.

Array of military heavy machine gun cartridges, by the Defense and Ammunition Division (including Winchester) of the Olin Corporation. Sizes range from the .50 caliber on up to 30mm, color-coded to indicate various types of ammunition, *viz.*, blue (training), black (armor-penetrating), pink or red (incendiary), orange or yellow (high explosive), purple (dumbbell or proof load), and combined colors (*e.g.*, pink and black indicates incendiary and armor-penetrating).

Olin was neatly summed up by Donald W. Griffin, executive vice president, Defense and Ammunition: "Our leadership position in small and medium caliber ammunition that is supplied to the U.S. Government and its allies has been achieved through our superior technology, favorable cost position, and proven quality." Chapter IX presents a more detailed picture of Olin's extensive present business in defense-oriented ammunition and in related products and services.

Chapter VII
Bolt-Actions
for Sport and Target

The bolt-action breech-loading system originated with such European inventors as Von Dreyse and Mauser, but the system which became Winchester's first bolt-action, that of Benjamin B. Hotchkiss, was among the first made in America. Hotchkiss was an American living in France, with a factory near Paris. His invention was displayed at the Philadelphia Centennial Exhibition of 1876, and it so impressed Winchester executives that the rights to make and market the gun were bought by the New Haven gunmaker. So anxious was Winchester to promote the Hotchkiss that the May 1878 catalogue officially announced the new "Hotchkiss Re-

peater," noting, "These arms will not be in the market for some months, but models may be seen at our depot, 245 Broadway, New York."

The August 1880 catalogue referred to the rifle as the "Hotchkiss Magazine Gun." and finally, after improvements stretching over nearly eight years, the Hotchkiss was in the January 1884 catalogue as the "Winchester Model 1883," Winchester's first bolt-action, this gun is the ancestor of countless bolt-actions that have come from the New Haven factory since. It was the first and only centerfire bolt-action Winchester with a magazine in the butt. Sporting rifle, carbine, and musket configurations were standard. The caliber was .45-70 U.S. Government, and the production was in three models—the First and Second Models had a one-piece stock, the Third Model a two-piece. Production lasted through 1899.

Winchester had had little success with its lever-action repeaters in attracting U.S. Military orders, but the relatively simpler bolt-action seemed to have considerable military potential. The system

had caught on with certain European governments, with the Mauser on the way to becoming the standard of European-made bolt-actions. The .45-70 chambering for the Hotchkiss was a logical choice by Winchester, and government sales were relatively good. The Hotchkiss First and Second Models with U.S. military markings are believed to have been manufactured at the Springfield Armory. However, civilian sales were insignificant, with shooters preferring the lever-action models. Thus, from the total production in excess of 84,000, the vast majority were military carbines and muskets.

The Lee straight-pull rifle was also primarily a military firearm and was made by Winchester for the U.S. Navy. It was claimed to be the first clip-loaded rifle made in the United States. Only about 1,700 of the Lees were made as sporters, largely because of the relatively small 6mm caliber, with its light bullet weight. Further details on the Hotchkiss and Lee appear in the preceding chapter, "Defending the Nation."

Major steps in the evolution of bolt-action Winchesters. *Top to bottom*, Hotchkiss Model 1883 sporter, with .45-70 cartridge, and Model 1900 .22 rimfire single-shot, both rifles with cocking knobs at rear of bolts. Model 52 rifle, serial number 17, has military styling, with scope bases on the barrel and folding rear sight on frame. Fitted with an elaborate scope is a Model 54 target rifle. An early production Model 70 bears serial number 78328 and is c. 1948.

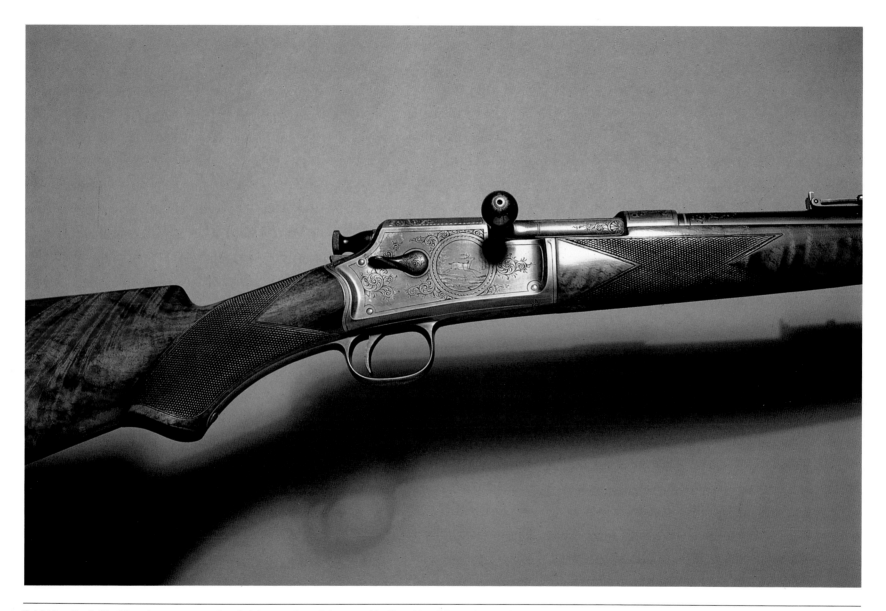

Exhibition Grade Hotchkiss, factory-engraved, with deluxe stocks and platinum-inlaid barrel band. It was displayed at various expositions and fairs, and at the Winchester San Francisco and New York offices. Very few Hotchkiss arms were engraved.

From the top, the Hotchkiss carbine, sporting rifle, and musket. Switch mounted on side was for the magazine cutoff, allowing for firing as either a single-shot or magazine repeater. Opposite side of gun has a bolt lock, a safety device which also locked the trigger. Musket muzzle with angular bayonet borders picture at *bottom*.

SPORTING RIFLES.

SPORTING RIFLE, PLAIN.

ROUND BARREL.		OCTAGON OR HALF OCTAGON BARREL.	
Price	$25.00	Price	$27.00
Length of Barrel	26 inch.	Length of Barrel	26 inch.
Caliber	.45	Caliber	.45
Number of Shots	6	Number of Shots	6
Weight	8¼ lbs.	Weight	8½ lbs.

SPORTING RIFLE, FANCY WALNUT CHECKED.

PISTOL GRIP STOCK.

26 inch Round Barrel . . . $40.00 | Octagon or Half Octagon Barrel . . $42.00

Two grades of Hotchkiss sporting rifles, from the September 1882 catalogue.

Variants of the pioneer Winchester small-caliber bolt-actions. *From the top*, the first Model 1900, .22 Short and Long. The butt of specimen at *right* is embossed WINCHESTER. The pistol was made by factory employees from the Model 1902 single-shot rifle, a specimen of which is *next* in sequence. At *center* a Model 36 with special 9mm shotshell; note bolt pulled back and firing pin cocked. The thumb-trigger Model 99 was a patented invention of T. G. Bennett. *Bottom*, the Model 1904 single-shot, with a colorful box of Winchester .22 Long Rifle cartridges. All the bolts have a knurled knob, which is pulled back to cock before firing.

The New Bolt-Action .22 Rifles

With the Model 1900 bolt-action .22-rimfire rifle, Winchester opened the floodgates of single-shot and repeating bolt-actions, some models of which were made in totals well into the hundreds of thousands. Appropriately, the Model 1900 was a John M. Browning design, bought by Winchester, but built on his patent of August 1899. Quoting from the first announcement, in a flier included with the August 1899 catalogue:

The Winchester Model 1900 single shot rifle is a serviceable low-priced gun designed to handle .22 Short or .22 Long Rim-Fire cartridges. Bullet breech caps [BB-caps] may also be used in it if desired.

It is "Takedown" and can be taken apart easily and quickly; the operation consisting simply of unscrewing the thumb screw located underneath the forearm which releases the barrel and action from the stock.

The action used on this gun is of the bolt type and is exceedingly simple, consisting of very few parts. When the gun is cocked, the action is locked against opening until the firing pin falls. This permits carrying the gun cocked without liability of the action jarring open. The gun is cocked by pulling rearward on the firing pin which is made with a knurled head to afford a good grip.

The barrel of this rifle is round, 18 inches long, bored, and rifled with the same care and exactness that have made Winchester rifles famous the world over for their accurate shooting. . . . Model 1900 rifles are fitted with open front and rear sights. . . . The length of the Model 1900 from muzzle to butt is 33¼ inches.

The Model 1900 can be furnished only as described above. We cannot fill orders for this gun calling for any variation whatsoever from the standard.

Interestingly, and like most of the .22 rifles to follow, these guns were made without serial numbers. Although approximately 105,000 Model 1900s were made, the production run was for only two years. Too light in weight and considered too much of an economy model, the 1900 was succeeded by the higher-grade Model 1902 single-shot rifle.

Best-known of all Winchester cartridge boards, the "Double W" dates from 1897 and exhibits 182 metallic cartridges. These boards, 40″×58″, have markings on the back showing a production number, the highest of which is about 1000.

The 1902 was quite similar to its predecessor, but featured a scroll-type triggerguard which simulated a pistol grip. In addition to being heavier, the gun had an improved trigger pull, a rear peep sight (back to an open rear in 1904), and a buttplate of blued steel (which was changed to composition in 1907). Chambering was increased in 1914 to accommodate interchangeably not only the .22 Short and Long, but the .22 Extra Long; the factory called the new variation the 1902-A.

Made from 1902 through 1931, the 1902 reached a rather astounding production total of over 640,000—with not a single one bearing a serial number. Expert sales were a significant segment of the rifle's success story, and, beginning in 1920, the Winchester Junior Rifle Corps Range Kit No. 1 included a Model 1902 rifle.

One of the most bizarre of all Winchesters was the next .22-rimfire to join the expanding line: the Thumb Trigger Model 99. A design of none other than President T. G. Bennett, the patent called for a system wherein the bolt was cocked by pulling back on the cocking knob; the gun was fired by simply pushing down on the knurled top trigger with the thumb. There was no conventional trigger or triggerguard. The Model 99 was otherwise basically a Model 1902, including its .22-caliber chamberings. Production continued into the early 1920s, with over 75,000 produced from 1904 through 1923. Export sales were substantial, and T. G. Bennett's creation had a ready market in Australia. Not surprising, the Model 99 was the only thumb-trigger firearm ever made by Winchester.

Next in Winchester's evolving and ever-growing line of .22-rimfire bolt-actions was the Model 1904, basically an upgraded Model 1902, with a 21-inch barrel of greater weight, a stock of larger proportions, and a knob forend. Its total weight was 4 pounds, a pound heavier than the Model 1902. It was in the line for twenty-seven years, and its production exceeded 302,000. Popular domestically and for export, both the Model 1902 and 1904 were widely copied by other manufacturers. The 1904 was part of the Winchester Junior Rifle Corps Range Kit No. 2, first marketed in 1920. The ever-rampant Australian rabbit population was kept in partial check by many thousands of Model 1902 and 1904 Winchesters, not a few of which are still in service there.

Winchester's next .22-rimfire rifle ranks among the most sophisticated of .22s made: the Model 52. Primarily a target-shooting rifle, the 52 was first shot competitively at the National Rifle Matches of 1919, at Camp Caldwell, New Jersey. As a consequence of America's involvement in World War I, many returning veterans had developed a keen interest in bolt-action target shooting. The 52's military styling was a natural carryover from wartime experience. The small caliber was ideal, since even then ranges for the larger calibers were not readily available.

Winchester's Model 52 responded to the demand, and it is considered the first of its type in America. Designed by T. C. Johnson, the 52 held its cartridges in a removable box magazine, which had a curved contour to accommodate the rimmed cartridges. Over the years the 52 was made in such configurations as standard Target, heavyweight-barrel Target, Sporting, Bull Gun (extra-heavy barrel), International Match Rifle, and International Prone Target Rifle. All rifles were chambered for .22 Long Rifle.

Model 52 barrels were made standard to accommodate telescopic sights; this was accomplished by drilling and tapping the barrels for Winchester scope bases. So many variations in features are known that the Model 52 demands a book of its own, but a recognized mechanical differentiation is the slow lock and the speed lock. The former was standard from the beginning of production through 1929; the speed lock was standard thereafter. The slow lock was cocked by pulling the knob at the rear of the bolt (as on the preceding .22 bolt-action Winchesters); the speed lock was automatically cocked when the bolt handle was worked.

Recognized as the leading factor in the evolution of competitive small-bore target shooting in America, the Model 52 had a long and successful reign. Total production was over 125,000, and the model was not discontinued until 1980, and some standard and heavyweight-barrel Model 52s remained available for a limited period thereafter.

A flurry of activity in the bolt-action .22 market saw a number of new models brought out by Winchester in the late 1920s and early 1930s. The Models 56, 57, 58, 59, 60, 60A, 67, 68, 69, 677, 72, and 75 all preceded World War II. Some were made before the purchase of Winchester by Western Cartridge Company, and others (60A and beyond) were brought out by the new Olin-owned Winchester. These rifles intended to claim their fair share of the increasingly competitive .22-rimfire bolt-action market. Of these, the Model 60 (over 165,000 sold), the Model 67 (over 383,000), the Model 68 (over 100,000), the Model 69 (over 355,000), and the Model 75 (over 88,000) reached respectable sales totals. General identifying information is provided in the picture captions and the tables in the appendix.

Subsequent models which Olin introduced in the World War II and postwar era are presented in Chapter IX. These include the Models 47, 121, 131, 141, 310, and 320 .22-rimfire bolt-actions.

Centerfire Bolt-Action Rifles

Despite the problems confronting Winchester in its post-World War I business, the design staff continued to create new models. One of the most desirable of these was the Model 54, a big-bore bolt-action at first chambered for .30-06 Springfield and the .270 Winchester. The styling was military-influenced, but the market would be primarily sporting. The newly designed bolt system used a box magazine, with a steel sheet (the "floorplate") set on the bottom of the stock, forward of the

triggerguard. As on previous bolt-actions, the frame was solid, with the barrel screwed into place.

An idea of the variants of the Model 54 is evident from the rapid introduction of types: in 1925, the Standard Rifle; in 1927, the Carbine; in 1929, the Sniper's Rifle; in 1931, the NRA Rifle; in 1934, the Super Grade, and in 1935, the Heavy Barrel Target Rifle and the National Match Rifle. Added to the original calibers were .30-30. 7mm, 7.65mm, 9mm, 250-3000 Savage, .22 Hornet. .220 Swift, and .257 Roberts. On the standard rifles and carbines, the frames were drilled and tapped for the fitting of telescopic sight bases. Match, Target, and Sniper types had sight bases mounted.

There was a fair degree of variation in stocks, barrels, sights, slings, and weights. The model had serial numbers from 1 on up; production continued through 1936, and over 50,000 were built. The Model 54 is a key bolt-action, since it was the firm's first big-bore, firing high-velocity cartridges capable of taking big game, and for use in so-called big-bore target matches. It was also the predecessor to one of the classics of all Winchesters: the Model 70.

Several models of .22 rimfire rifles, sequentially from the mid-1920s to the late 1930s; all are bolt-actions with manual cocking device at bolt rear. *From the top*, the Model 56, a removable-box-magazine repeater. The Model 57 has a similar magazine; both rifles with target scopes. The Model 58 was an economy continuation of the Model 1902 and 1904 single-shots. Rifle with light-colored stock is a Model 59 single-shot made only in 1930. *Second from bottom*, a Model 60A variant with grooved forend, *above* a Model 60A target rifle with barrel band, target sights, and apertures for shoulder sling. Cartridges, grease, and knives by Winchester.

Further evolution of the bolt-action .22 single-shot Winchester. *At left*, Model 67, a variant chambered for .22 Smoothbore. *Next*, Model 67A, a Junior Boys rifle with short barrel. *Center* rifle is a Model 677, lacking sight cuts on barrel or iron sights; built for telescopic sight attachment. *Next*, the Model 68, a companion to the Model 67, is distinguished mainly by the special sights. Rifle at *extreme right*, a Model 47, was a new model appearing in the factory's first price list of 1949, and is the only one of the group without a manually operated cocking knob at the end of the bolt.

195

Variations of the Model 52 repeating rifle. *From the top*, serial number 17. Number 3885 is a slow-lock with its knurled cocking knob visible at end of bolt. Model 52B serial 66477B is a sporter, and was the last one made. With elaborate rear peep sights. Model 52C, a target rifle, bears number 96171C.

Particularly advanced Model 52 target rifles. The International Match at *top* has laminated stock of walnut and maple, special trigger, and Redfield sights, adjustable buttplate, and palm rest. The Model 52E has even more exotic sights and a variant palm rest. The Model 52 International Prone Target Rifle has Redfield International sights and adjustable cheekpiece.

Eric Carmichel, with woodchuck taken with his Model 43 rifle, in .218 Bee caliber.

The Model 54, built c. 1925–36, was the evolutionary predecessor to the celebrated Model 70, and was the first Winchester with a bolt action for centerfire high-velocity, heavy-caliber cartridges. *Top*, a rifle chambered for .220 Swift. At *center*, and showing the bolt open, .30-06 in carbine configuration. *Bottom*, a target version, with Unertl scope and peep sights and chambered for .22 Hornet. The catalogue dates from 1933.

Heralded as a junior variant of the Model 70, the Model 43 bolt-action was chambered for .218 Bee, .22 Hornet, .25-20, and .32-20, and was made only from 1949 to 1957. *From the top*, rifle in .25-20 caliber. A Model 43 in .22 Hornet, with deluxe stock and checkering. Models 75A and 75 were medium-priced to be accompanying models to the Model 52; chambered for .22 Long Rifle, with box magazines. In the line 1938–58.

The Model 70—"The Rifleman's Rifle"

Known as "the Rifleman's Rifle," the Model 70 boasts a production run unmatched by any other Winchester bolt-action: its fiftieth anniversary was celebrated in 1986. When it was initially announced in the January 1937 price list, the new features listed—all improvements over the Model 54—included horizontally pivoting safety, hinged floorplate, adjustable speed lock with a short pull, manually releasable bolt stop, straighter stock with a more robust forearm and superior checkering, triggerguard made from a steel forging, an adjustable sling swivel base for match rifles, and an overall more impressive styling and quality.

Among the myriad variations of the 70 are the Standard, Super Grade, Target, National Match Rifle, and Bull Gun, all announced before World War II, and the Featherweight, Varmint, African, Westerner, Alaskan, Mannlicher, and International Army match (all introduced between the years 1952 and 1970). Calibers range from as small as the .22 Hornet to the .458 Winchester Magnum, and include such classics as the .220 Swift, .243 Winchester, .25-06 Remington, .257 Roberts, .270 Winchester, 7mm, .30-06, .300 Holland & Holland Magnum, .300 Winchester Magnum, .308 Winchester, .338 Winchester Magnum, and .375 Holland & Holland Magnum.

So much variation exists in styling, barrel and sight types, stocks, chambering, weights, and so on that the Model 70 is one of the few Winchesters to have been the subject of its own book: Roger Rule's *The Rifleman's Rifle*. Rule divides the Model 70, 1936–63, into three groupings, Type I (1936–47, serial numbered through approximately 60500), Type II (transition, 1947–48, numbers approximately 60500–87700, standard actions, and numbers approximately 63200–121700, H & H Magnum actions), Type III (1948–63, numbers approximately 87700–581471, standard actions, and numbers approximately 121700–581471, H & H

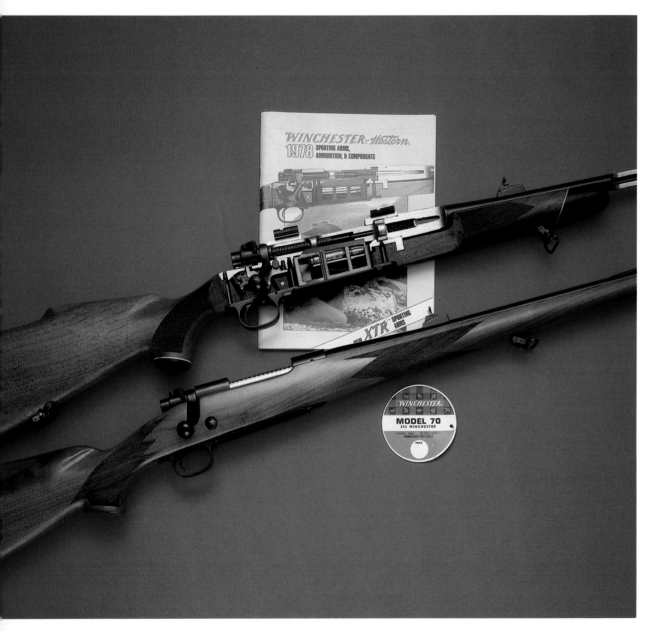

Rare cutaway Model 70, atop the catalogue cover on which it was featured, and accompanied by the Mannlicher variation, offered c. 1969–72.

Unraveling the celebrated pre–1964, 1964, and post–1964 classifications of the Model 70; At *top*, a pre–1964 carbine, serial number 41508, in .30-06 caliber (made in 1941). At *center*, from the first group of the 1964 variation, number 881117 is a .270 and exhibits differences in the stocks (especially checkering), metal finish, rear sight, and safety. *Bottom*, serial number G998832, a .458 Magnum Super Grade, shows a return to quality, with handsome checkering and finish and overall richness.

Magnum actions). Variants differ by such features as markings, tang and other frame details, bolt handles, triggerguards, magazines, finishes, and so forth. Clearly, mastering the evolution of the Model 70 calls for careful observation and an appreciation of mechanical and cosmetic details. Since the 70 was introduced during the Olin period, more information is presented in Chapter IX, and the most recent Model 70s are covered in Chapter XI.

The American Marksman and Sportsman

Marksmanship and a dedication to firearms have been characteristically American for centuries. The sport of target shooting is as old as the beginnings of colonization of the North American continent; some of the first shooting events were intended to impress the Indians. At turkey shoots and other competitions, riflemen demonstrated not only their own skill, but the capabilities of their firearms. Winchesters have excelled not only for the dedicated hunter and professional guide, but in marksmanship competitions and in shooting galleries at state fairs and amusement parks. Still another competition, which had its heyday from the mid-nineteenth century through World War I and—thanks largely to Coors, the Colorado-based brewer—is undergoing a spirited revival, is the *Schuetzenfest*. A most unusual target-shooting event, the concept was brought to America by German and Swiss immigrants, and formal matches were held for many years in a highly social and gregarious festival environment. Standard range was 200 yards, offhand (without aid of slings or benchrests), and the guns had elaborately evolved stocks, butt-

Target Model 70s; *from the top*, a .243 single-shot experimental, with scope bases mounted on barrel and breech. A .300 Holland & Holland with bull (heavyweight) barrel and Redfield Olympic sights. Another .300 H&H, with peep sight and marksman's glove. Note flared stock forends and lack of checkering. Latter two rifles are pre–1964s.

plates, triggerguards, and, often, palm rests. Some of the finest Scheutzen-style rifles were built on such Winchester arms as the single-shot and—in some rare instances—lever actions like the Model 1892 and 1894.

Largely because the national media today pay little attention to the shooting sports, the status of marksmanship and competitive target shooting is hardly known to much of the public. The estimated number of firearms in the United States (1990) is in excess of 225 million, owned by an estimated 60 million citizens. Approximately 13 percent of these own firearms for target shooting. So nearly 8 million—some, of course, more dedicated and involved than others—shoot at targets for recreation. The types of targets include paper bull's-eyes, clay pigeons, tin cans and other objects, silhouettes (metal targets which tip over when hit), and even fruits, vegetables, and packets of exploding gunpowder by exhibition-shooting professionals who carry on the traditions of Annie Oakley and the Topperweins.

Target shooting in America today ranges from the informal get-together to such highly regulated competitions as the National Matches at Camp Perry, Ohio, the Grand American Trap Shoot in Vandalia, Ohio, and the Olympics.

Researchers have also determined that approximately 51 percent of American gunowners are hunters, for a whopping total in excess of 30 million! Also generally unknown except by those who participate is the fact that hunting licenses, excise taxes, and duck stamps raise in excess of $500 million each year in support of wildlife and habitat conservation, educational programs, and the funding of state agencies for fish and wildlife. By 1990, American hunters had contributed over $7.5 billion to wildlife conservation since the Pittman-Robertson Act was passed in 1937 (earmarking a 10 percent excise tax on firearms and ammunition to fund wildlife projects on state and federal levels).

Additionally, an approximate 4 million acres of wildlife habitat have been purchased from these funds.

Clearly hunters and target shooters have played pivotal roles in the remarkable record of wildlife conservation in America. The original conservationists were primarily sportsmen-hunters, such as Theodore Roosevelt. The originators of the modern conservation movement, and its emphasis on the environment, were in such hunting- and conservation-oriented organizations as the Boone and Crockett Club (founded 1887) and the Camp Fire Club of America (founded 1897). It was the patron saint of American conservationists and sportsmen, Theodore Roosevelt, who conceived the former, and he was also a member and driving force of the latter. The founders of the American conservation movement were hunters and fishermen who pursued these sports largely for relaxation and pleasure. As early as the 1870s periodicals like *Forest & Stream*, *Field & Stream* (still published today), and *The American Sportsman* kept hunters and fishermen across the nation informed of current events. These publications, in which W.R.A. Co. often advertised and was otherwise involved, acted to coordinate the interests of readers. The growing identity of sportsmen gave rise to the forming of a number of regional clubs and organizations and to formalized codes of ethics. The first two tenets of the Camp Fire Club's code were (and still are):

> The wild life of today is not ours to do with as we please. The original stock was given us in trust for the benefit of the present and the future. We must render an accounting of this trust to those who come after us.
>
> It is the duty of every person who finds pleasure in the wilderness or in the pursuit of game to support actively the protection of forests and wild life.

The Boone and Crockett Club was the first private group or association which, on a national front, made positive and important achievements

in wildlife and habitat conservation. The club both influenced and initiated enlightened policies on hunting, wildlife, and forest preservations. The New York Zoological Society, Glacier National Park, and scores of federal game preserves were but a few of the Boone and Crockett's innumerable achievements. The pivotal and pioneering role of sportsmen in the conservation of American wildlife and habitat is thoroughly documented in John F. Reiger's *American Sportsmen and the Origins of Conservation*.

Among the members of one of the earliest such clubs, the Hammonassett Fishing Association (Madison, Connecticut), was T. G. Bennett, who joined in 1891, three years after the club was founded. Still other members were his son Winchester Bennett, as well as W.R.A. Co. executive J. E. Otterson. A founding member was Eli Whitney, Jr., whose firm was bought out by Winchester in 1888. And a present member is a great-grandson of Theodore Roosevelt. All have shared the environmental conscience of the dedicated hunter and sportsman.

A Model 70 match rifle in competition, being fired by well-known gun writer the late Pete Kuhlhoff, who was for many years the outdoors editor of *Argosy* magazine. A gentle 6-foot-5 giant, Kuhlhoff had an audience of millions, through his regular writing post and a variety of freelance articles.

Four models of Winchester target rifles. The earliest is at *bottom*, the Model 52, an International Army Match made for a Winchester executive; .22 Long Rifle caliber. At *top*, a Model 75, also in .22 Long Rifle, with military styling; this model was made as a less expensive alternative to the Model 52. *Center* rifles are a Model 70A Police in .308 Winchester caliber and a Model 70 International Army Match in .300 Winchester Magnum, its bolt partially pulled back. Exotic sights are the Redfield Palma Match peep.

Chapter VIII
A Myriad of Shotguns

Winchester's debut in shotguns was not as a maker but as a marketer of a quality double gun made in Birmingham, England. Known as the Model 1879, it was ordered by Winchester agent P. G. Sanford on authority of the main office in New Haven. The New York area had a shortage of shotguns at the time, and Winchester saw an opportunity to fill that void.

Several grades of guns were built, all standard with WINCHESTER REPEATING ARMS CO. and the New Haven address engraved on the barrel rib. The known makers include W. C. Scott & Sons (many years later acquired by Holland & Holland, Lon-

don), C. G. Bonehill, W. C. McEntree & Company, and Richard Rodman. New York being a major firearms market, the guns sold rapidly, and Winchester followed with more orders. At that time the New York store also sold Colt, Remington, and other makes of firearms, including European handguns. Sales of the popular Winchester shotguns prompted the firm to investigate making its own gun, but a *lever-action* repeater.

Approximately 10,000 of these English-made Winchester Model 1879s were sold before the model was discontinued (c. 1884). The first Winchester-made repeating shotgun would appear three years later, a John Browning design known as the Model 1887.

The Lever-Action Repeaters

Two years before the Model 1887 appeared, Winchester bought the design rights and a hand-built model of John Browning's lever-action repeating shotgun. T. G. Bennett had asked Browning to create such a gun when Winchester purchased the model and design rights for the Model 1886 rifle. The astute inventor was in favor of a pump shotgun

rather than a lever, and had been working on such a system. But the tradition-bound Bennett thought of the lever action as so closely identified with Winchester that its first shotgun should be lever-operated. Within half a year's time Browning had the model for his enthusiastic patrons in New Haven.

The 1888 catalogue proudly proclaimed some of the salient features:

> Sportsmen will find this a strong, serviceable arm. The system contains but sixteen parts in all, and can be readily understood from sectional cuts. The breech block and finger lever form one piece, and move together in opening and closing. The hammer, placed in the breech block, is automatically cocked during the closing motion; but can also be cocked or set at half-cock by hand.
>
> The trigger and finger lever are so adjusted that the trigger cannot be pulled prematurely, and the gun cannot be discharged until closed. The barrel can be examined and cleaned from the breech. The magazine and carrier hold five cartridges, which with one in the chamber, make six at the command of the shooter. Anyone accustomed to shooting can readily shoot double birds with this gun.

Four key steps in the evolution of Winchester shotguns. *From the top*, Model 1887, Winchester's first repeater, a lever-action design by John Browning. Slide-action Model 1897, the second and most successful of the factory's repeating shotguns brought out in the nineteenth century; also a John Browning creation. Semiautomatic Model 1911, designed by T. C. Johnson, after efforts to negotiate for the John Browning semiauto had proved fruitless. And the most successful shotgun of all Winchester pumps, the Model 12, hundreds of thousands of which are still in use by shooters worldwide.

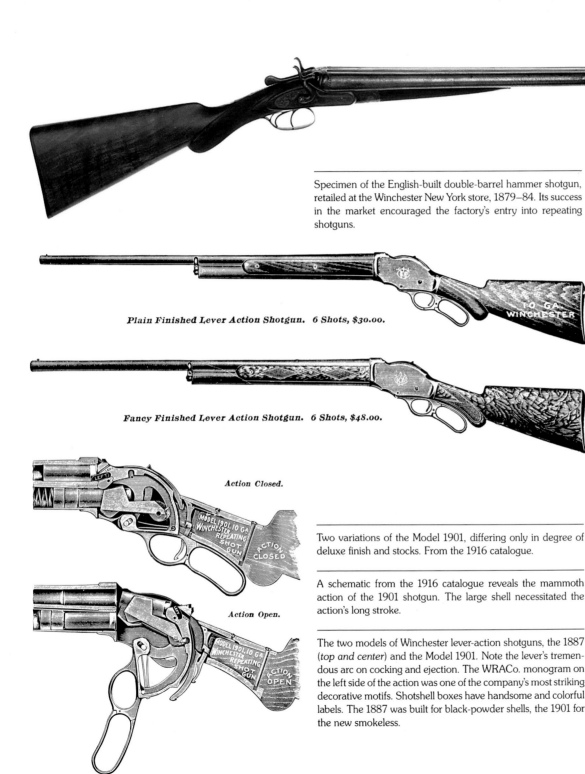

Specimen of the English-built double-barrel hammer shotgun, retailed at the Winchester New York store, 1879–84. Its success in the market encouraged the factory's entry into repeating shotguns.

Plain Finished Lever Action Shotgun. 6 Shots, $30.00.

Fancy Finished Lever Action Shotgun. 6 Shots, $48.00.

Action Closed.

Action Open.

Two variations of the Model 1901, differing only in degree of deluxe finish and stocks. From the 1916 catalogue.

A schematic from the 1916 catalogue reveals the mammoth action of the 1901 shotgun. The large shell necessitated the action's long stroke.

The two models of Winchester lever-action shotguns, the 1887 (*top and center*) and the Model 1901. Note the lever's tremendous arc on cocking and ejection. The WRACo. monogram on the left side of the action was one of the company's most striking decorative motifs. Shotshell boxes have handsome and colorful labels. The 1887 was built for black-powder shells, the 1901 for the new smokeless.

This gun has as yet been very little used in public. On the occasion of its first appearance, the gun divided with one other gun the first prize for fifty birds, February 22nd, 1887, at Plainfield, N.J.

Although the Model 1887 was the first successful lever-action repeating shotgun, it was not the first successful repeating shotgun of any kind—that honor belongs to Christopher Spencer's 1884 pump, made by Bannerman's of New York. Production was limited to 10- and 12-gauges, with black-powder shells only.

While John Browning was on his two-year service as a Mormon missionary, he and a companion went into a sporting goods store in Georgia, and the inventor asked to see a Model 1887 shotgun displayed in the window. His obvious facility at handling the gun aroused the curiosity of the shopkeeper, and even more so as the two missionaries were rather disheveled and rustic. When Browning's companion remarked, "He ought [to know how to handle it], he invented it," the disbelieving and suspicious shopkeeper took the gun from Browning and put it back in the window.

With the transition to smokeless powder, the Model 1887 was phased out, and the Model 1901 lever-action shotgun replaced it. The new design was strengthened to handle smokeless-powder loads, and had other design modifications and improvements as well. One important change was the chambering of the 1901 in 10 gauge only. As Browning had predicted many years earlier to Bennett, the slide or pump action would be preferred over the lever action. And another Browning design, the Model 1897—a pump gun—was proving quite popular.

Posed in a studio, this fur-garbed sportsman, with Labrador and lever-action Winchester, is ready for waterfowl shooting. His rubber boots appear to be waders.

The 158th Model 1887 lever-action shotgun made. Factory records note the barrel as "Good Damascus," with Fancy checkered stock and rubber buttplate; shipped in June of 1887. The new smokeless shells caused functioning problems for the 1887, it having been built for black-powder loads.

This simulated holdup features several Winchesters of Model 1887–1901 type, and several Wells Fargo & Company expressmen. The company was a large buyer of firearms and ammunition.

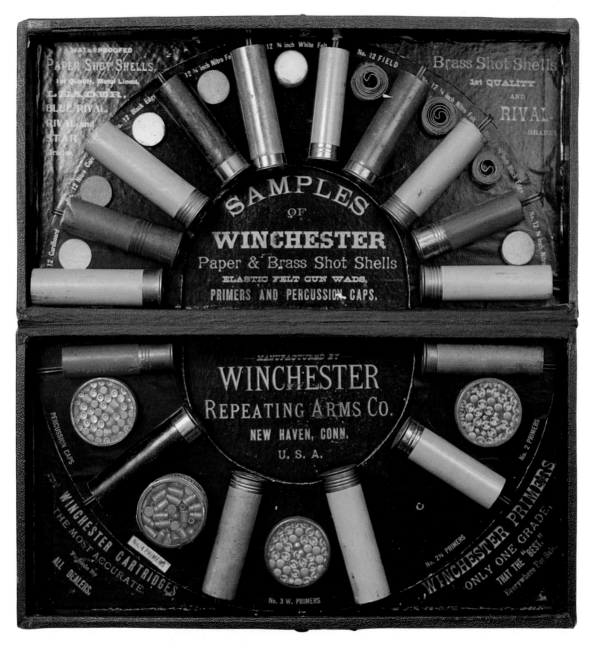

The Model 1893 Slide-Action

Responding in 1890 to competition from the slide-action Spencer and the Burgess shotguns, Winchester bought the John Browning design, an outside-hammer gun with ejection to the side. After improvements to the original concept, the Model 1893, the first Winchester slide-action shotgun, was announced in the June 1893 catalogue:

> This gun is operated by a sliding forearm below the barrel. It is locked by the closing motion and can be unlocked only by pushing forward the firing pin, which may be done by the hammer or by the finger. When the hammer is down, the backward and forward motion of the sliding forearm unlocks and opens the breech block, ejects the cartridge or fired shell and replaces it with a fresh cartridge.
>
> The construction of the arm is such that the hammer cannot fall or the firing pin strike the cartridge until the breech block is in place and locked fast. . . . the hammer cannot be let down except when the gun is locked. Having closed the gun and set the hammer at half-cock, it is locked both against opening and pulling the trigger. While the hammer stands at the full-cock notch, the gun is locked against opening.

Safety was always a hallmark of John Browning designs.

The Model 1893, although well received by the shooting public, had certain failings because of the increasing use of smokeless-powder ammunition.

Salesman's sample kits, often termed "briefcase" samples by collectors, were made from as early as the 1890s (shown here) into the 1930s, as cartridge boards were discontinued, except for occasional special-purpose use. Rifle and handgun cartridges were also used in the briefcase displays.

At *top and center* are the first of Winchester's pump shotguns, the Model 1893, built for black-powder shells. *Top* gun with Damascus barrel and Fancy Grade stock, and accompanied by colorful Winchester promotional envelopes. *Center* gun with standard barrel, but of long length for duck shooting. Model 1897 (*bottom*) has improvements to accommodate the new smokeless shotshells.

WINCHESTER
RIFLES AND SHOTGUNS
ARE MADE FOR ALL KINDS
OF SHOOTING
BY MEN WHO
KNOW HOW

TRY   THE
Red
Gun Oil   W   Rust Remover
Gun Grease   Crystal Cleaner
CLEANING PREPARATIONS
The Kind Used At The Winchester Works

WINCHESTER
REPEATING SHOTGUNS
ENDORSED BY THE U.S. ORDNANCE BOARD
AS SAFE, SURE, STRONG & SIMPLE

FOR SALE BY
W. R. PURNELL CO.,
BERLIN, MD.

25 WINCHESTER 12 ga.

NEW RIVAL
WITH WINCHESTER PATENT CORRUGATED HEAD
LOADED BLACK POWDER SHELLS.
MANUFACTURED AND LOADED BY THE
WINCHESTER REPEATING ARMS CO. NEW HAVEN CONN. U.S.A.

Xpert
Western
Shotgun Shells
BLACK POWDER
MADE IN U.S.A.

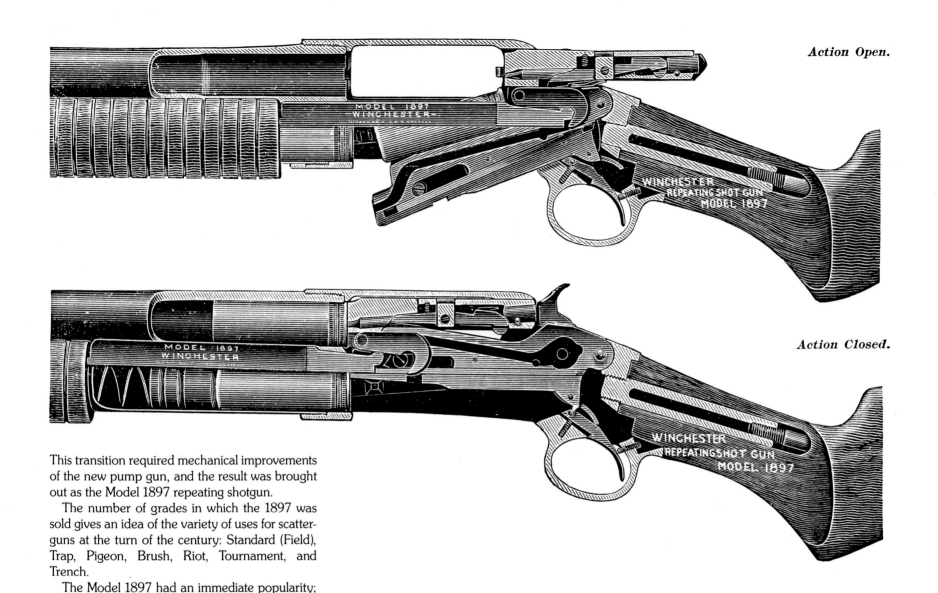

MODEL 1897
WINCHESTER

WINCHESTER
REPEATING SHOT GUN
MODEL 1897

MODEL 1897
WINCHESTER

WINCHESTER
REPEATINGSHOT GUN
MODEL 1897

This transition required mechanical improvements of the new pump gun, and the result was brought out as the Model 1897 repeating shotgun.

The number of grades in which the 1897 was sold gives an idea of the variety of uses for scatterguns at the turn of the century: Standard (Field), Trap, Pigeon, Brush, Riot, Tournament, and Trench.

The Model 1897 had an immediate popularity; the rival Burgess and Spencer guns could not keep up with the Winchester pump, and the 1897 became the best-known and most widely used outside-hammer, slide-action gun in history. Some models of the 1897 were still manufactured as late as 1939, and the trench gun takedown was not discontinued until 1945.

This schematic from the 1916 catalogue shows the mechanical features of the Model 1897 pump. Solid action and exposed hammer have given the 97 one of the longest lives of any of the world's repeating shotguns.

214

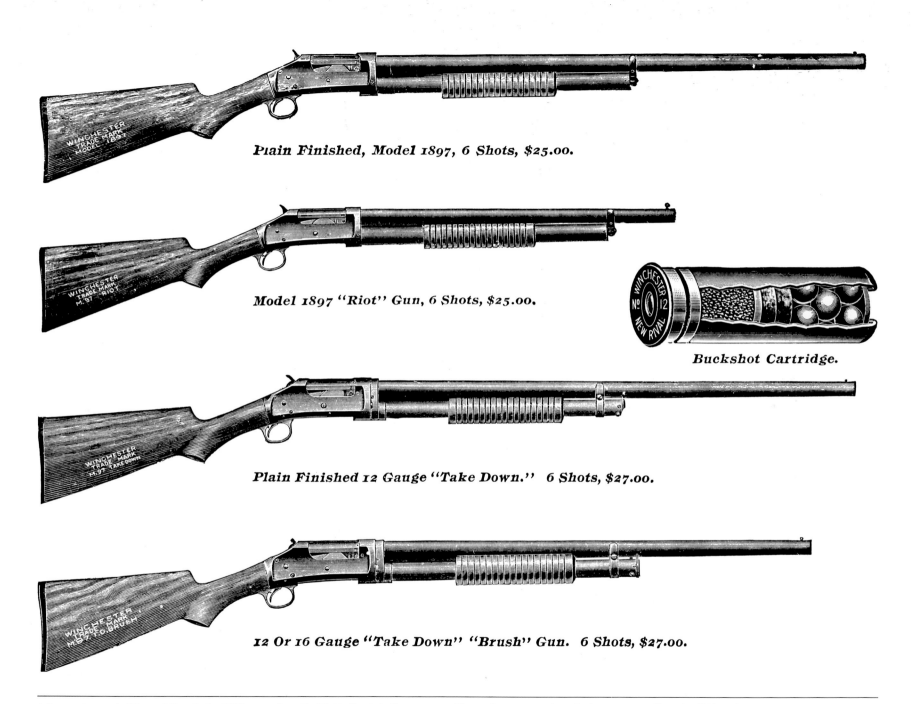

Plain Finished, Model 1897, 6 Shots, $25.00.

Model 1897 "Riot" Gun, 6 Shots, $25.00.

Buckshot Cartridge.

Plain Finished 12 Gauge "Take Down." 6 Shots, $27.00.

12 Or 16 Gauge "Take Down" "Brush" Gun. 6 Shots, $27.00.

A lineup of several of the variations in the 1897 pump, from the Riot to Brush to Tournament to Trap to Pigeon, several in takedown versions. From the 1916 catalogue.

"Tournament" Gun, 12 Gauge, "Take-Down" 6 Shots, $42.00.

12 Or 16 Gauge "Take Down" "Trap" Gun, 6 Shots, $52.00.

12 Or 16 Gauge "Take Down" "Pigeon" Gun, 6 Shots, $100.00.

Continuing the array of several of the Model 1897 variations, from overleaf.

Champions at both trap and live-bird shooting, this team of (*left to right*) G. L. Becker, John Browning, A. P. Bigelow, and Matt Browning was known as the "Four B's." They hold Browning inventions of the 1887 lever-action and 1897 pump shotguns (and an unidentified side-by-side double), and were active shooters in the 1890s.

Exquisite matched pair of Model 1897s, serial numbers 1 and 2, signed by John Ulrich. Dogs and game birds within scrollwork, instead of set in panels, present an unusual treatment.

From the top, Model 1897 in 12-gauge, with Fancy stock, early production, serial number C170510. A 16-gauge with high number 961600. A riot gun, in 12-gauge, takedown, number E931662. Rare factory brochure for guard and riot gun, and colorful box of Speed Loads shells.

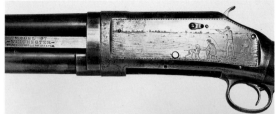

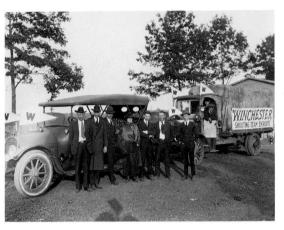

Early live-pigeon-shooting scene engraved on frame of Model 97. Trap lines run to operator, while dog handler awaits to retrieve the pigeon.

Winchester's Shooting Team, c. 1920. At left center, Ad and Plinky Topperwein.

Progression of Model 12s. *From the top*, 16-gauge with solid rib, serial number 849248. A 12-gauge riot gun, number 1251516. Number 1414858 is a 12-gauge with Poly Choke attachment. *Bottom*, 28-gauge skeet gun with ventilated rib, number 1520886.

Further progression of Model 12s. *From the top*, number 1833935F, a 12-gauge Featherweight. A 12-gauge 3″ Magnum duck gun, serial number 1872788. Note the extra riot-gun barrel and the factory-supplied plug to limit cartridge capacity in magazine. Number Y2069835, a 12-gauge skeet gun, with ventilated rib. *Bottom*, serial number Y2010373, 12-gauge, with ventilated rib and rubber buttpad.

12, 16 Or 20 Gauge "Trap" Gun, Model 1912, 6 Shots, $55.00.

12, 16 Or 20 Gauge "Pigeon" Gun, Model 1912, 6 Shots, $105.00.

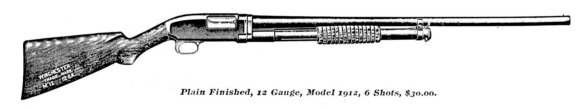

Plain Finished, 12 Gauge, Model 1912, 6 Shots, $30.00.

"Tournament" Gun, 12 Gauge, Model 1912, 6 Shots, $45.00.

The Model 12 and Other Slide-Actions

Continuing the evolution of the Winchester slide-action, the T. C. Johnson–designed Model 12 was the first concealed-hammer repeating shotgun by the company. It is rivaled only by the Model 1894 rifle in renown and production totals; over 2 million Model 12s were made from 1912 through 1980. The 20-gauge gun was touted in company advertising as "The Lightest, Strongest, and Handsomest Repeating Shotgun Made."

So many variations were made and the total production was so substantial that the 12, like the Model 70, is one of the few specific models of American firearms that has been the subject of its own book, *The Winchester Model Twelve*, by George Madis. Though still very much in use in the field, not a few Model 12s have been stocked and/or engraved either by the factory or by renowned independent craftsmen—A. A. White, John E. Warren, and Joseph Fugger among them. The large frame of high-quality steel presented an inviting canvas which challenged the creativity of these master artisans.

A modification standard for all repeating shotguns resulted from a Presidential Proclamation (signed on February 2, 1935) which limited the magazine capacity to two cartridges—a third shell being in the barrel breech—for migratory bird hunting. Since the magazine on the Model 12 held five shells, a wooden plug was devised, thereafter a standard Model 12 feature. Sportsmen were responsible for acquiring plugs for existing guns. Plugs require the shooter to concentrate on marksmanship, reducing the tendency of the uninitiated toward "skybusting."

Joining the ranks of those models of Winchesters which have reached milestone serial numbers, the number 1000000 Model 12 was custom-made in

From the 1916 catalogue, Plain, Tournament, Trap, and Pigeon Grade Model 12s.

Action Open.

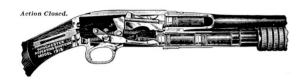

Action Closed.

1943 as a presentation piece to Lieutenant General Henry H. "Hap" Arnold, chief of the Army Air Forces. Number 2000000 was given by the factory to John B. Connally, former secretary of the treasury and Texas governor, in 1973.

A special-variation Model 12 was built in 1975, the Ducks Unlimited Commemorative, serialized 12 DU 001 through 00800. The gun was used by the conservation organization as a fund-raiser for wetlands conservation.

Three distinct models of slide-action shotguns followed the Model 12: the Model 42 (appeared 1933), the 25 (appeared 1949), and the 1200 (1964). The 42 was Winchester's first slide-action made especially for the tiny .410 cartridge. Although it would appear to be a scaled-down Model 12, the 42 was innovatively designed to accommodate the smaller cartridge. In recognition of its distinctive nature, serial numbering was in an individual range, beginning with 1. Nearly 160,000 were built through the year 1963.

Although the Model 25 had a short history—it

The functioning of the Model 1912, as pictured in the 1916 catalogue. The improvements over the 1897 pump are evident in the economy of action and the compactness of parts.

For duck, pheasant, and quail, the Model 12 at *right* in 20-gauge, with stainless barrel, number 480314. At *left*, 12-gauge 3″ Magnum duck gun, serial number 1633054.

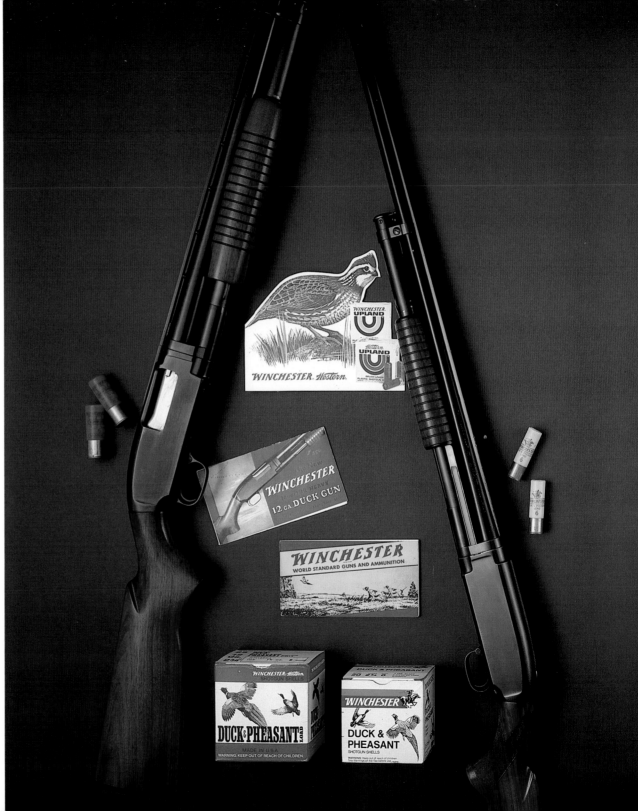

was first shipped in 1949 and was discontinued in 1954—nearly 88,000 were made. It was manufactured in 12 gauge only, with less costly features which were meant to allow it to compete with Remington and others. Thus, the 25 was an economy version of the Model 12.

The Model 1200 featured a rotating bolt with four locking lugs which secured within the barrel extension (the idea was to neutralize any stress on the gun's frame at the time of firing). Another feature of a more revolutionary nature was the Winchoke (1969), a quick-change tube which could be screwed into the muzzle and interchanged in various chokes. Transition from the Model 1200s into the successor Model 1300s took place between 1981 and 1983.

A 1944 advertisement promoting wartime marksmanship training with Winchester shotguns. *Top*, a Model 12, in 12-gauge, with Ordnance bomb and U.S. markings, serial number 990266. With Model 25 serial number 4135, an economy version of the Model 12, made during the Korean War era.

Among the most elegant of Winchesters, the Model 42 pump-action, made c. 1933–63. All three in .410. *From the top*, gun with solid rib and of pre–World War II manufacture. A skeet gun with three shells; late production, as is the *bottom* gun, with engraving by Nick Kusmit of the Winchester Custom Shop and deluxe flame-grain stocks.

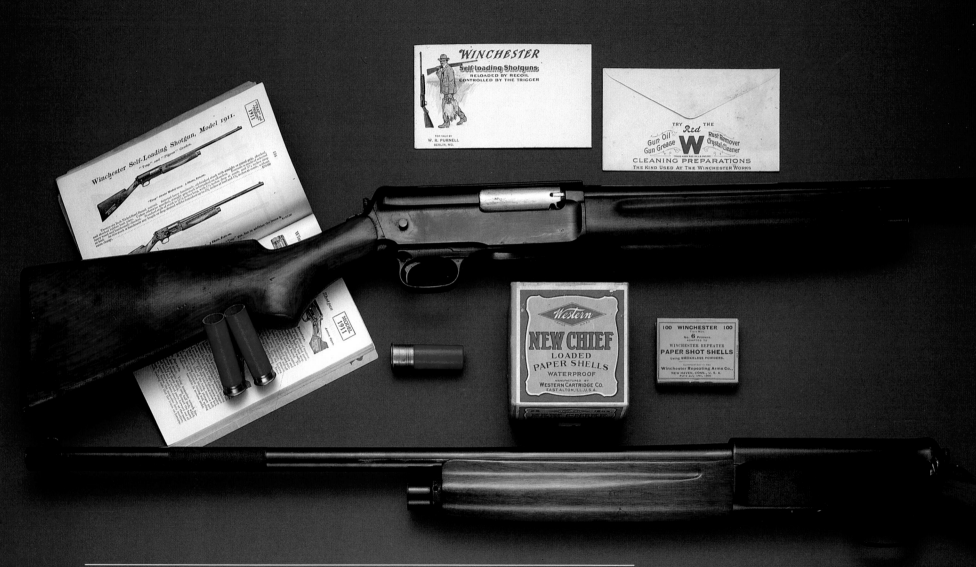

Model 1911s, both from 1912 production, accompanied by the 1916 catalogue, with low- and high-brass paper shells and shell casings, and other related memorabilia. Advertising *envelope* at *left* refers specifically to the Model 1911. The knurled section of barrel is for gripping while cocking the gun for firing. Some clumsy or reckless shooters would put their palm over the barrel to cock, leading to some frightful accidents, and a reengineering of the design.

The Model 1911 and Other Semiautomatics

In the fall of 1889 the Browning brothers were at the Ogden Rifle Club's weekly shoot. John noticed that when a rifle was fired, weeds located a few yards distant swayed with each muzzle blast. He recognized in those blasts a source of energy—energy which could be channeled into operating the mechanism of a repeating firearm.

John gathered brothers Matt and Ed together, and the three Brownings headed back to the shop. On the way John explained his inspiration for what would create a whole new species of guns of his design: automatics. Within a couple of days he had modified a Model 1873 Winchester by attaching to the muzzle a device he termed a "flapper," which automatically operated the modified cocking lever as the gun was fired.* This new concept led to automatic rifles, pistols, machine guns, cannon, and shotguns, with John Browning designs predominant—just as they were in pump- and lever-action sporting arms.

But the long-standing relationship between John Browning and Winchester would come to an end during negotiations for the rights to a semiautomatic shotgun. After years of research and testing, Browning had developed two models of semiautomatic shotguns. In March 1899, brother Matt wrote to T. G. Bennett at Winchester to advise him that the brothers were ready to visit New Haven and show off these new and revolutionary inventions. Bennett was impressed, but months went by as Winchester's patent attorneys investigated the claims and testing and other matters were dealt with.

John Browning was getting increasingly impatient with delays, and a letter of August 1, 1899, to

*"Automatic" and "semiautomatic" are generally used interchangeably, although technically the former refers to continuous fire as long as the trigger is held back, the latter to repeat fire for each time the trigger is repulled after firing an individual shot.

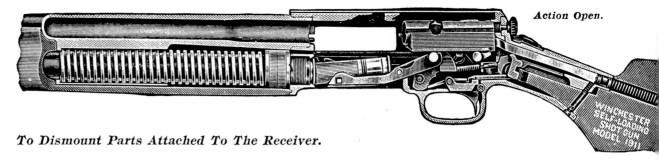

Action Open.

To Dismount Parts Attached To The Receiver.

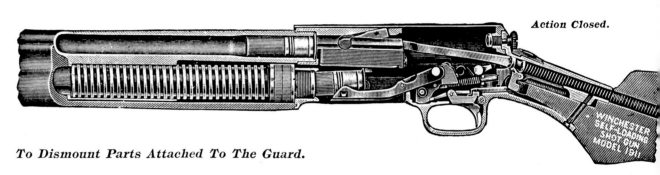

Action Closed.

To Dismount Parts Attached To The Guard.

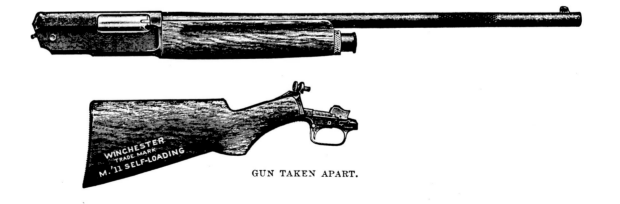

GUN TAKEN APART.

Schematic of the Model 1911 self-loading shotgun, from the 1916 catalogue. The takedown screw is visible at the top rear of breech. Cutaway shows gun taken in half for storage or transport.

Plain Finished, Model 1911. 5 Shots, $38.00.

Fancy Finished, Model 1911. 5 Shots, $56.00.

"Trap" Grade Model 1911. 5 Shots, $70.00.

"Pigeon" Grade Model 1911. 5 Shots, $150.00.

The Model 1911 in Plain and Fancy grades, and in Trap and Pigeon; from the 1916 catalogue.

the Winchester factory included such comments as:

> I see the gun has been worked with considerably by parties who did not understand the system. . . . We have had no mis-fires and think this fault is with the cartridges. By the way, this is a fault that bobs up with the Winchester cartridge more frequent than with any other cartridge we have had any experience with. . . . Our experience has been that a gun gets worse treatment in a draughtsman's office than in a duck hunter's camp.

After nearly two years of delay, Browning decided in 1902 that Bennett and Winchester were stalling on the semiautomatic shotgun, and so he made the long trip to New Haven. The stumbling block was that—for the first time—Browning had asked that the payment be an advance against royalties. Since dealings he had with other arms makers (by then he was doing business with Colt and Fabrique Nationale) were on a royalty basis, he felt justified in requesting royalties from Winchester.

According to Edwin Pugsley, "The word *royalty* was to T. G. Bennett what a red flag is to a bull." Bennett was determined not to enter into an agreement which could have costly repercussions with other inventors and with future agreements. John Browning characterized Bennett's reaction to the royalty proposal as "certainly not diplomatic." Browning did not give in, asked for his models, and left the factory.

Ultimately, Bennett's refusal to pay Browning royalties for the revolutionary concept of the automatic shotgun proved to thwart Winchester from ever dominating that market (at least to date). Browning went to Remington Arms, in January 1902, for a meeting with the firm's president, Marcellus Hartley; on the morning of the 8th, Hartley told Browning he would be pleased to see him that afternoon. On arriving for his appointment, Browning was told by Hartley's secretary that the president would soon be available. Browning waited for about an hour—and in that time Marcellus Hartley had a heart attack, and died. It was a shock to Browning and a blow to Remington.

John Browning then took his extraordinary invention to Belgium and made the deal he wanted with Fabrique Nationale, for world manufacturing rights. U.S. trade restrictions on foreign products (c. 1905) then led to Browning's obtaining a release to permit the Remington Arms Company to manufacture the gun as well. This gun would become the Model 11, the most successful semiautomatic shotgun ever built in the United States—and one to which Winchester and all other manufacturers have yet to catch up. Today the Model 11 continues in production as the Model 1100, and milestone shotgun number 5000000 is due to be made in the early 1990s.

Winchester's auto shotgun, the Model 1911, took years to develop. So comprehensive were John Browning's patented designs that T. C. Johnson was faced with the almost impossible task of circumventing his former colleague's ingenious creation. Johnson finally worked out a manufacturable product, which became Winchester's first semiautomatic shotgun and also the firm's initial shotgun of the hammerless configuration. There were problems which needed correcting during production, and the Model 1911 remained in the line only through 1925; the total produced reached just under 83,000.

There was no automatic shotgun in Winchester's line from 1925 through 1940, when the new Model 40 was announced and shipped. Made only as a 12-gauge, the gun proved to be unreliable. Its lock timing was poor, the magazine tube would mal-

The Model 40, Winchester's bad-luck gun, was made only during 1940–41, and was subject to substantial recalls. Serial number 8381, at *top*, a 12-gauge skeet gun, with a very rare brochure showing the Plain Grade model. *Bottom* gun shows Cutts compensator, and is also a 12-gauge skeet gun, but Fancy Grade; serial number 886.

Made from 1954 to 1961, the Model 50 reached an impressive production total of over 196,000. *From the top*, a 20-gauge, with its original factory tag, and a 12-gauge. *Next*, a 12-gauge skeet gun, with vent-rib barrel. The milestone gun, serial number 16000000, was presented to General Curtis LeMay as Outdoorsman of the Year, 1957, by his friend John Olin. Engraved by John Kusmit in factory pattern 12-5.

The Model 59, Winchester's next semiautomatic shotgun, reached a total run of over 82,000, from 1959 to 1965. At *top*, the rare experimental 14-gauge, with aluminum shells and a box of cartridges. Only about twenty-eight were made. *Next*, a gift to General LeMay from John Olin, at Nilo Farms, Georgia, while on a shoot; 12-gauge. *Bottom*, a gun accompanied by the various steps in producing the unusual fiberglass barrel, from bottom up.

function, and much of the production was subject to factory recall. Perhaps as many as 40,000 were made, but most were scrapped or never completed, and the gun has been termed the most unsuccessful of all Winchester shotguns. Guns returned to the factory were replaced with the tried-and-true Model 12.

The successor to the Model 40 was the Model 51, in the line from 1954 through 1961. Just under 200,000 were made. Serial number 1,000 began the series, and John M. Olin himself was the recipient of that first gun.

Fourth in the sequence of semiautomatic Winchester shotguns was the Model 59, serialized in its own sequence and made from 1959 through 1965. Just over 82,000 were made, and among that number was a novel 14-gauge experimental group. These were tested at Nilo (Olin spelled backward) Farms, the factory's exclusive field-test facility, and although they performed admirably, the concept was dropped. Winchester officials thought that educating the public for the new cartridge would prove an insurmountable task. The cartridge had an aluminum case and was of a special short length.

Winchester's next semiautomatic shotgun was the Model 1400, new to the line in 1964 and serialized from 100000 on up. The total production through 1980 was 750,000; as of 1991 the numbers exceed 1,100,000.

For the years 1974 through 1981, Winchester carried the Super-X semiautomatic shotgun, which was the result of five years of design and special testing. The gas-operated system reduced recoil and eliminated any need for adjusting for low-base or high-base cartridges.

Winchester continued the tradition of special guns honoring key recipients by presenting Super-X serial number 1942 to General Jimmy Doolittle, a keen sportsman and conservationist and a highly decorated aviator. The number honored the year in which Doolittle's Raiders made their daring bombing attack on Tokyo.

William E. Talley, director of sales, introducing the Model 59 to outdoor writers at the 1960 Writers Seminar in Alton, Illinois. Talley went on to become executive vice president and virtually ran Winchester's firearms operations for nearly twenty years. He was also instrumental in the transfer of the Winchester Gun Museum from New Haven to Cody, Wyoming, and was appointed a trustee of the Buffalo Bill Historical Center late in the 1970s.

Promotion of the Super-X, introduced in 1974, was multifaceted. Note specially designed tie, shield-motif display panel, Avon cologne, and etched frame scroll devices. At *top*, special low serial number M23. *Center* gun rests on display panel brackets, made for gun dealer use. At *bottom*, special-order fancy wood, with extra-rich grain. Gun made in 12-gauge only.

Single-Shot Shotguns

The first Winchester single-shot shotgun was an adaptation of the Model 1885 single-shot rifle. The factory chambered the rifle for 20-gauge, with smoothbore barrels, and began the production in 1914. Only about 700 guns were built, serialized in the single-shot range, and they remained in the line only through approximately 1918.

In 1920 a top-break, thumb-lever-released single-shot was announced, the Model 20. It was the firm's first shotgun chambered for .410 gauge as well as its first top-break shotgun. Company literature praised the Model 20 as "an ideal gun for women and the younger members of the family to shoot because of its virtual absence of recoil and its light weight."

The Model 36 also joined the line in 1920, a single-shot, bolt-action smoothbore chambered for 9mm shot cartridges. These guns bore no serial numbers, and the estimated total production (through 1927) was just over 20,300. The 36 is the only U.S.-made shotgun built for the 9mm cartridges. Cocking of the action was not by the bolt, but by pulling back on the cocking head.

Still another new product in 1920 was the Model 41 shotgun, also built without serial numbers. It remained in the line through 1934, with just over

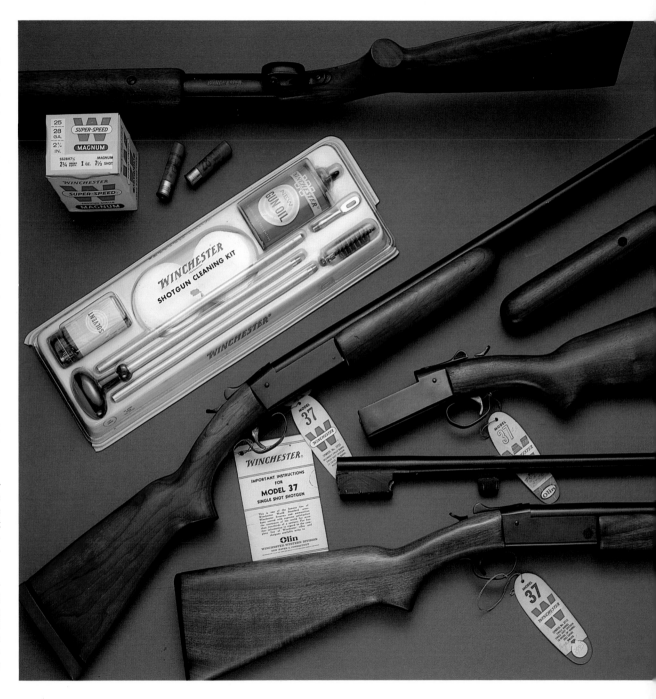

Top-break, single-shot shotgun, at *top*, Model 20, .410; made 1919–24, in a total of about 23,600. *Center and bottom*, the bolt-action Model 41, in the line c. 1920–34, with total of about 22,000, also .410. Accompanied by miscellaneous memorabilia, dating from the same era, which represent the Winchester diversification at the time.

With a twenty seven-year production run beginning in 1936 and totaling over 1,015,000 guns, the Model 37 was the best-selling single-shot Winchester shotgun of all time. Chambered for all gauges between .410 and 12, the Model 37 was all-steel, a simple top-break, with manually cocked outside hammer. Ironically, none bore serial number markings. Note the Winchester logo in red on the bottom of the gun at *top*, a rare feature.

23,000 reported to have been made, all in .410 gauge.

The last Winchester single-shot shotgun was the Model 37, by far the most numerous of any of the series: between 1936 and 1963, over 1,015,000 were made, in 12, 16, 20, 28, and .410 gauges, again without serial numbers. The rarest of all variations is a special snake gun, made on order of John Olin, for use at Nilo Farms, Georgia. These .410 gauge pistols had barrels of about 18 inches and were about 26 inches long overall. Not more than about thirty were constructed.

Double-Barrel Shotguns: The Model 21 and Others

In contrast to such moderately priced shotguns as the 1920s single-shots, Winchester brought out what would become the Cadillac of American side-by-side doubles: the Model 21. Announced some forty-seven years after the English-made hammer doubles (the Model 1879) were discontinued, the Model 21 is the safest, simplest, best-designed, best built, and most reliable side-by-side shotgun ever made in the United States and is still proudly car-

In the line from 1930, the Model 21 has long been the finest side-by-side shotgun of American manufacture. Machined-steel frame at *center* is one reason for its longevity and popularity. At *top*, number 22699, a type supplied to English shooting clubs by Winchester; note precisely milled barrel rib. The double-trigger gun, serial number 4878, is a 12-gauge. *Bottom*, a unique experimental single-barrel trap gun, without a serial number, 12-gauge, built in the early 1930s at the Winchester Model Shop.

Recognizing his contributions to wildlife preservation, Dr. Logan J. Bennett (*left*), executive director of the Pennsylvania State Game Commission, is presented a gold-inlaid and inscribed Model 21 by John M. Olin. In a national balloting of sportswriters, Dr. Bennett, winning out over the likes of Ted Williams and Ernest Hemingway, was elected Winchester's Outdoorsman of the Year, 1956.

ried in the line today. Some of its strongest features were described in the 1933 factory catalogue:

BARRELS—The barrel design of this new Winchester is one of its distinctive features and one that has much to do with the perfection of the barrels themselves. The barrels are dove-tailed together in a mechanical interlock which is far superior to brazing or any other union for there is no distortion or destruction of the temper and strength of the barrel by the terrific heat of brazing. . . . Each barrel with its half lug is a single integral mass forged from Winchester-Proof steel, treated to have a tensile strength of 115,000 pounds per square inch. . . .

THE FRAME of this Winchester Double Gun is made, not of the usual case-hardened material, but of the Winchester PROOF STEEL treated to have a tensile strength of over ninety tons per square inch. We are confident that it will show no evidence of yielding at the breech after a lifetime of shooting with the heaviest modern loads. . . .

At first the Model 21 was priced at $59.50. As of 1991 the least expensive grade, the Custom with matted rib, is $8,100, and all 21s are built to special order.

Among the prime reasons the Model 21 has remained in the Winchester product line for over sixty years are its inherent quality and toughness and the special affection that John Olin had for this model. From the beginning, when the Olins acquired Winchester late in 1931, the Model 21 was a favorite of John Olin's. His own collection included a superb example, beautifully engraved and inlaid by the master R. J. Kornbrath. And when in the late 1970s

---

Rare cutaway Model 21 has 12-inch barrels and bears serial number marking W21X. The complete gun is a Field Grade, number 11168, in 16-gauge.

An economy version of the Model 21, the Model 24 dates c. 1939–57 and totaled over 116,000. Gauges were 12, 16, and 20, with double triggers only. The barrel top rib shown is much plainer than the elegant Model 21's.

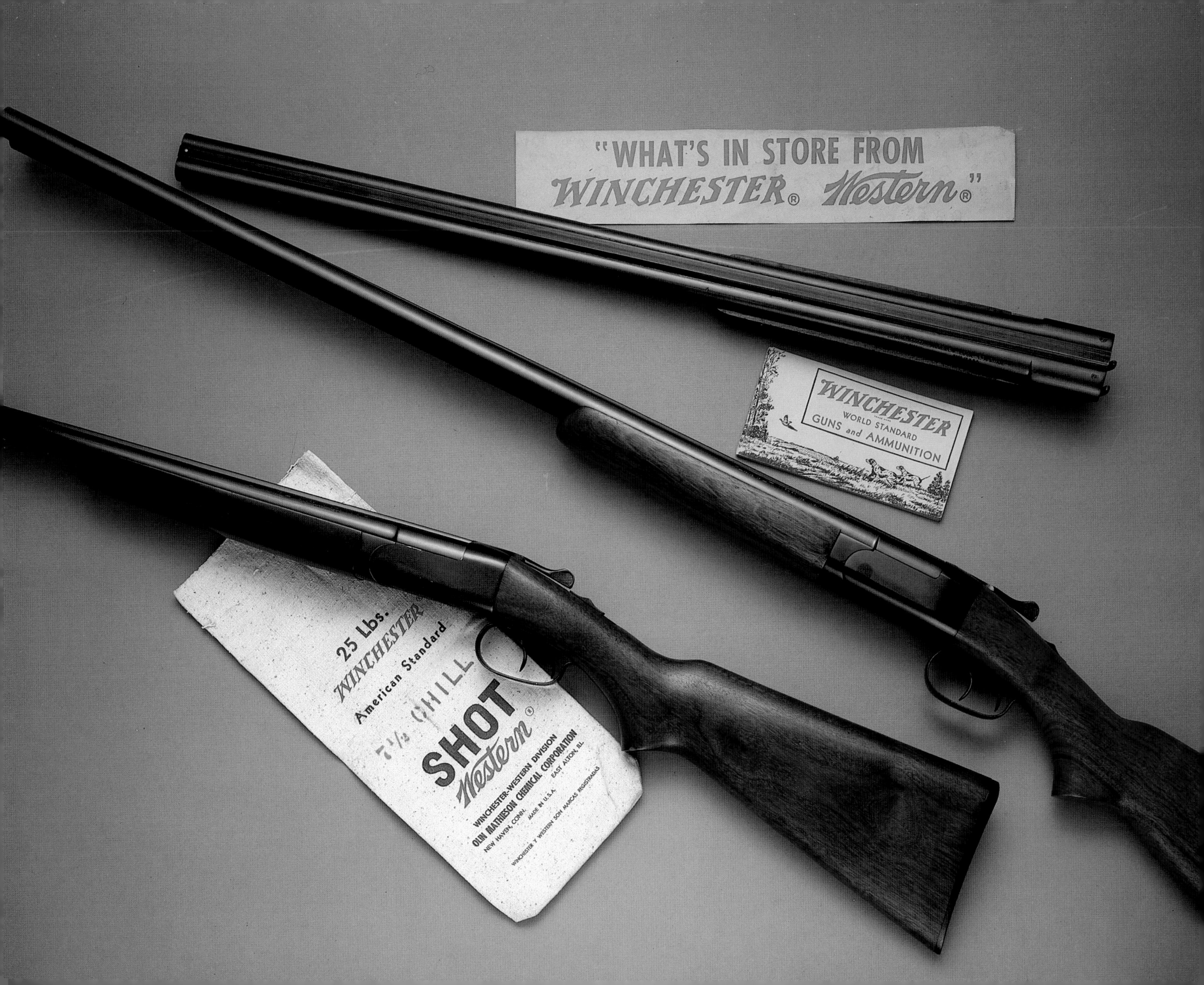
"WHAT'S IN STORE FROM
WINCHESTER® Western®"
WINCHESTER
WORLD STANDARD
GUNS and AMMUNITION
25 Lbs.
WINCHESTER®
American Standard
7 1/2 CHILL
SHOT®
Western
WINCHESTER-WESTERN DIVISION
OLIN MATHIESON CHEMICAL CORPORATION
NEW HAVEN, CONN.
EAST ALTON, ILL.
MADE IN U.S.A.
WINCHESTER Y WESTERN SON MARCAS REGISTRADAS

the board voted to discontinue the Custom Shop, the decision was later reversed in respect for Mr. Olin. The gun remains in the line to this day, and, if anything, the modern-built 21s rival and often surpass those from the 1930s.

Among the grades in which the gun has been built: Standard (Field), Tournament, Trap, Custom Built, Skeet, Duck, Deluxe, Magnum, Custom, Pigeon, Grand American, and, the most exclusive of all, Grand Royal. The first Grand Royal was intended for presentation to John Olin. However, it was not complete at the time of his death and is presently in a private collection in Texas. Of the five Grand Royals ever built, others were for an anonymous enthusiast with the world's leading Model 21 collection, for former Secretary of the Treasury William E. Simon, and for the author. Standard to each gun is a portrait of John Olin, his signature (both in gold), and some of the most exquisite gold inlaying and engraving (both flush and relief) ever applied to an American shotgun.

Sturdy, handsome, reliable, and as well made today as it ever was, the Model 21 is America's answer to the best-quality guns of the London makers, such as Holland & Holland and Purdey. The Custom Shop in New Haven is made up of conscientious and talented craftsmen who make every effort to maintain the standards of quality which were the pride of John Olin himself.

As a middle-class side-by side double shotgun, the Model 24 was a cheaper version of the Model 21 and was made to compete with other manufacturers' economy models. The gun was made from 1939 through 1957, with its own serial range, and had a total production in excess of 116,000.

One of the most complex series of all Winchesters is that built on the Model 101 over-and-under style. The first guns appeared in 1963 and were made in Japan by Olin Kodensha Company, Ltd., a firm set up to build quality guns at a price. Despite the severe restrictions placed on gun ownership in Japan, Japanese mechanics rank among the best gunmakers in the world for factory mass production.

Listed styles include Field, Magnum Field, Skeet, Trap Gun (with Monte Carlo or regular stocks), Trap Gun with single barrel, and Trap Gun with single- and double-barrel combinations. Gauges were 12, 20, 28, and .410. The serial numbering was a bit odd, with the 12-gauge beginning at 50000 and going to 199999; then numbering began anew at 300000. The 101s in 20, 28, and .410 gauge were numbered from 200000.

As in the automobile business after World War II, annual new models seemed to be *de rigueur*. The result is mass confusion for the collector, unless he has been lucky enough to collect catalogues yearly.

Of all the shotguns the author has owned over the years, his 20-gauge 101 Field Grade, a Christmas present in 1969, remains his best-shooting and most reliable American-brand smoothbore. His only improvements were to have custom stockmaker Dennis Martin streak the walnut with india ink (a quick artificial French walnut), recut the factory checkering, and slightly shorten the forend. On the bottom of the buttstock is a gold-inlaid oval, engraved with a duck in flight, by the master K. C. Hunt, of England. On the triggerguard Belgian René Delcour inlaid an RLW monogram. The result: a tribute not only to the Japanese gunmakers, but to American, English, and European craftsmanship.

Gunsmoke's Jim Arness enjoying a day in the field with Winchester's Lloyd Pierce and Tom Henshaw, c. 1960. "Matt Dillon" holds a Pigeon Grade Model 21.

The Models 101 and 1400 successfully used by writer Jim Carmichel on a South American dove shoot. Such hunts help farmers to rid their crops of pests and bring badly needed currency to often deprived countries. Frozen doves are brought back home for gourmet feasts.

From 1963 until c. 1987, the 101 was a steady-selling and highly popular part of the Winchester line. *From the top*, cutaway reveals the basics of the mechanism, solidly built at Olin's Japanese facility, Olin-Kodensha, Ltd. *Next* gun shows hand engraving standard on first years of production. XTR Model has roll-engraved frame embellishments, with detail improved over its hand-engraved predecessor. *Bottom* gun shows etched decoration and continued handsome quality. Mechanical features of the 101 included automatic ejectors and single selective triggers (a switch allows choosing which barrel to fire). Toward the end of the 101's reign, a sporter model was introduced, balanced for sporting clay shooting, a new clay pigeon competition which rapidly gained popularity in England in the 1970s and is becoming increasingly popular in the United States. The sport already has two sanctioning organizations, the National Sporting Clays Association and the U.S. Sporting Clays Association, the latter of which publishes its own monthly magazine (*Sporting Clays*). To shoot 100-straight in sporting clays is so difficult as to be almost impossible.

Chapter IX
Winchester-Western and the Olin Corporation

As of 1931 the role of the Olin family is of equal significance to the Winchester legend as that of Oliver F. Winchester in the firm's formative years, and of T. G. Bennett in its middle years. And the Olin Corporation is bigger now than it ever was—$2.5 billion in sales in 1989—of which the Defense and Ammunition segment (including the largest unit thereof, the Winchester Division) accounted for $665 million, easily the largest net sales year in the entire history of Winchester, with or without the gun-making facility.

When Winchester was purchased by the Olins, it

Representative rifles and shotguns from Olin's post–World War II production. *From the top*, the Model 71 .22 Long Rifle semi-automatic, featuring nylon triggerguard and a cocking lever on left side of action. The Model 88, for centerfire medium-game cartridges, introduced at the same time (1955). Model 70 bolt-action in post–1964 configuration. The Super-X Model 1 semi-automatic, designed to complement the legendary Model 12 pump and brought out in 1974. The 101 over-and-under, made from 1963 by the talented gunsmiths of Olin-Kodensha, Ltd., Japan, primarily for the American market. The *bottom* two guns exhibit custom engraving and gold inlaying.

became a division of their core operation, the Western Cartridge Company, and the transition from the Winchester Repeating Arms Company to Winchester-Western (1931) saw a stumbling giant transformed into what would become a thriving international conglomerate. John Olin's dedication to the firearms field was instrumental in several developments of models and their manufacture, in improvements in the burning qualities of smokeless powder, and in improving the range of shotshells. Advances in primers, powders, and shot would lead to the sensational new Super-X ammunition. And John and Spencer Olin were the impetus behind the new Silvertip rifle ammunition. John Olin himself held patents on some of these cartridge advancements, and he attributed the new Super-X to an altercation he had with a duck hunter in need of an education in sportsmanship. In Olin's own words:

> During that time [c. 1930] I had an experience with a duck shooter, up on the glades club, who shot his ducks on the water, and that disgusted me and I had a hell of a fight with him that time. I told him, you want to get meat, why don't you take one shot . . . and go out

and kill . . . [a] cow. You'll get a thousand pounds of meat from one shell. Anyhow, we had a fight, and during that night I made up my mind I wanted to get something to really teach that man conservation the next season, which I did.

> That was the beginning of SUPER X. We had no idea it would be—I had no idea it would be—a commercial thing, an important ammunition; I wanted to lick this guy, and I did. When I came back the next season, I got on . . . the pattern of ducks coming in. And when they would get fifty yards in the air over me, I'd bang [them]. He didn't get a duck that morning.

Super-X was an immediate success story.

Shortsightedness by the federal government resulted in the next major product coup by Winchester-Western. Dr. Fred Olsen brought to Olin his idea of making smokeless powder in small spheres, underwater, after the government had rejected the concept. Bringing this innovation to Western Cartridge Company, Dr. Olsen was appointed vice president of research and development. His 1936 patent for what was termed ball powder led to a solid competitive advantage, an instrumental step in expanding Western's ammunition operations.

The Winchester-Olin complex in 1949, already for over half a century the most substantial industrial site in New Haven. Its far bigger neighbor, in terms of real estate, is the nontaxable campus of Yale University.

The Model 71 continued the lineage of the Model 1886 in a mechanically strengthened rifle chambered for the powerful .348 Winchester. Over 47,000 were built, 1935–57. *From the top*, the standard sporting rifle, a version lacking checkering. Two checkered-stock variants, the *bottom* in carbine style. Note optional peep sights.

The Model 1892 and its offspring. *From the top*, a 92 saddle-ring carbine, with rifle-style front barrel/magazine tube band and carbine-style rear. The Model 53, initial successor to the 92, made 1924–32, in a total of nearly 25,000 (carbine versions of the 92 continued, however, through 1941). *Bottom* two rifles are the Model 65, which succeeded the 53 and was in the line 1933–47; only about 5,700 were produced. Serial numbering for the 53 and 65 continued along in the 1892 range, and the button magazines (tips visible from forend) were standard. Illustrated calibers are, *from top*, .32-20, .44-40, .32-20, and .281 Bee.

The Model 94 and two of its offspring. *From the top*, a 94 rifle in standard configuration. The Model 55 (1924–32), a button-magazine rifle with shotgun buttplate, of which about 20,500 were made. *Next*, two examples of the Model 64 (1933–57, 1972–73), successor to the Model 55, with pistol-grip stock, longer magazine tube, and changes in sights and trigger pull; total made nearly 67,000. The Model 94 continued throughout, in carbine form, and remains in the U.S. Repeating Arms Company line. Colorful ashtrays are from Olin's European firearms and ammunition sales operation, capitalizing on the popularity of the Old West.

WANTED!

REPORT OF WHEREABOUTS OF THE 123 RARE, HISTORIC GUNS OF THE "ONE OF ONE THOUSAND" WINCHESTER 73 RIFLES

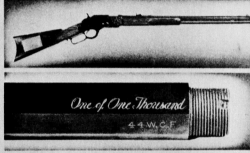

HOW TO IDENTIFY A "ONE OF ONE THOUSAND"
It must be a Winchester lever action repeating rifle Model 73, and MUST have the words "One of One Thousand" engraved on the top of the barrel.

The revolutionary Model 73 developed for Indian fighting and hunting has long been famous in history as "The Gun That Won the West." Of 720,610 of these lever action repeating rifles which were made, only 124 were of the super-accurate variety known as the "One of One Thousand." These were the most sought after guns of their time.

One gun of this variety appears as the "hero" with James Stewart and Shelley Winters in the new Universal-International motion picture "Winchester 73" which glorifies this famous rifle. This prized gun was borrowed for use in the picture from the Museum of the Winchester Repeating Arms Company of New Haven.

Because of their historic interest Universal is now conducting a nationwide search for the whereabouts of the other 123 "One of One Thousand" rifles manufactured from 1875 to 1881.

REWARD! . . . The first 20 persons reporting their ownership of an authentic "One of One Thousand" Model 73 will receive as a gift from Universal a brand new Winchester Model 94 deer rifle which is the modern version of the 73 if they supply the following notarized information: the serial number of the rifle, facts about its previous ownership or history if known, a photograph of the words "One of One Thousand" on the top of the barrel.

If you own one of these guns write to:
Winchester 73 Dept., Universal Pictures Co., Inc.
445 Park Avenue, New York, N.Y.

The postmark will indicate your priority. After the serial number has been authenticated, a new Model 94 will be awarded to you.

This nationwide search began in May with an article in The American Rifleman and will close on Sept. 30, 1950. Remember, we don't want your "One of One Thousand" Model 73. We are only trying to find out how many of them are still in existence.

The proliferation of Western films, starring figures such as Gary Cooper and Burt Lancaster, helped boost Winchester sales and contributed to the marque's historic and colorful image. TV and Hollywood films gave the public an overdose of the Western, but the genre will not die, and a revival was generated beginning in the late 1980s. Cooper and Lancaster are armed with the Model 92 carbine in this still from *Vera Cruz*, a 1954 film which also featured Charles Bronson and Denise Darcel. The Hollywood touch has long added color to Winchester promotions.

One of the 150,000 posters printed in the search by Winchester and Universal Pictures for One of One Thousand rifles in connection with release of the 1950 James Stewart film *Winchester '73*. The pictured rifle was one of three made for film use and does not depict the authentic barrel inscription. These handbills helped uncover twenty-three One of One Thousand 1873s and six One of One Thousand 1876s.

The powder was cheaper to make and has superior burning characteristics.

The federal government, drawn to Western Cartridge by such developments as the new ball powder, contracted to have the firm build and run the St. Louis Ordnance facility. On December 8, 1941 (the day after the attack on Pearl Harbor), finished cartridges came off the new assembly line. To be assured of cartridge metal for the St. Louis Ordnance plant, Western's Brass Mill was expanded, and a new casting shop, tandem mill, hot mill, two annealing furnaces, and two additional finishing mills were added. Further, a new powder plant was constructed, and ammunition facilities were expanded.

With 61,000 employees and over 15 billion rounds produced, Western Cartridge Company was a strong factor in the Allied victory in World War II, and the Army/Navy E Award for excellence in war production was presented to Western Cartridge on June 21, 1945, at a ceremony at which over 6,500 Olin employees were present.

In late 1944 the various other Olin companies were merged with their flagship Western Cartridge Company, and the name was then changed to Olin Industries, Inc., of which John M. Olin was president and Spencer was first vice president. The Olin operations experienced dramatic business growth and expansion, acquiring several firms, including Ecusta Paper Corporation, Frost Lumber Industries, and Ramset Fasteners.

In its December 1953 issue, *Fortune* magazine ran a lengthy article entitled "The Rise of the House of Olin." A trailer for the story noted: "Here, never before told, is the story of a great, family-owned corporation. Olin Industries, Inc., beat off the gunpowder trust at the turn of the century, survived its own internal conflicts, and now, with $250 million in sales, is striding boldly into new technological fields." The article ended by quoting John Olin:

Poster promoting *Winchester '73*. Model 94 carbine in foreground was one of the offered prizes for owners of One of One Thousand rifles who responded to the Universal-Winchester promotion. The first twenty were given Model 94 carbines, compliments of Winchester-Olin.

The whole purpose of our [business] plan is that we can never be attacked, I hope, on all fronts. Our base is broad enough so that we can move in almost any direction.

The Olin-Mathieson Merger
In 1954, Olin Industries took another giant step, by merging with the Mathieson Chemical Corporation to form Olin-Mathieson Chemical Corporation.

The resulting firm had approximately 35,000 employees, in forty-six domestic and seventeen foreign plants, with production and sales in drugs and pharmaceuticals, paper, cosmetics, fertilizer, a wide variety of chemicals, ammonia, hydrazine, pesticides, antifreeze and other automotive specialities, rocket engines, and arms and ammunition. The merger joined technical strengths in metallurgy and chemistry, a combination which has

Landmark 94, serial number 3500000, gold-inlaid and engraved by A. A. White for Winchester, 1978; balance of embellishment by Winchester's Custom Shop. Widespread publicity accompanied this piece, later auctioned at the factory's behest at the Las Vegas Antique Arms Show. One of the best-known of twentieth-century historic Winchesters, and a classic contemporary rifle.

THE MODEL 70 SPORTING RIFLE

The genesis of the Model 70 was covered in Chapter VII. A more comprehensive look at this Winchester classic is presented in this chapter, since most of its history to date has been under the auspices of Olin. The collector and aficionado divide the Model 70 into two periods: before and after 1964, the serial number demarcation coming at the first new model serial number, 700000 (actually, October 1, 1963). The final pre-1964 serial rifle bore number 581471. There thus exist a total of 118,528 serial numbers unassigned.

The purpose of the changeover was to reduce production costs. Changes included some twenty-one components, ranging from the barrel, breech bolt, and bolt sleeve all the way down the list (alphabetically) to the triggerguard bow. The shooting public looked at what the factory considered "improvements" with disdain, and one hears to this day collectors deriding the post-1964 Model 70. Part of this attitude was an objection to the use of precision castings rather than machined parts. Actually, many of the changes are not readily observable. For instance, the frame was machined not from a solid forging of chrome-molybdenum steel, but rather from a billet, which was also of chrome-molybdenum. However, complaints primarily came from a misconception that the frame was a precision casting. And the main objections were based on visual differences: finishes to the metal and wood and especially the checkering (which was akin to a waffle-iron, pressed look).

The criticism of the post-1964 rifles caused values of the earlier rifles to soar. To a certain extent this was due to a lot of tongue-wagging in the firearms field. However, there certainly was room for improvement, and the public outcry inspired a gradual return of quality. A

Cartridge board by Western Cartridge Company, c. 1970, with a wide variety of ammunition, cutaways, and step-by-step component manufacture for shotshell casing, centerfire soft-nosed rifle bullet, and .22 Long Rifle casing and bullet.

listing of technical changes and improvements in quality can be tabulated almost yearly since 1964. A noncosmetic change of interest to collectors is the addition of the prefix G to the serial marking, beginning with number 1028977, in compliance with the marking directed by new federal regulations governing firearms manufacture, sales, and transfers. By 1972 the Model 70 had largely been returned to a competitive status, and in that year a new Super Grade was added, as well as the Ultra Match.

Most noticeable of the stock changes were the addition of a contoured, full-bodied cheekpiece, the addition of a pistol grip (marked with a winged red W), and a new angle applied to the Monte Carlo comb.

In 1978, XTR was introduced almost across the board for all Winchester arms (denoting extra attention paid to quality), and the Model 70 received a richer stock (darker, with a satiny sheen) and a deeper luster to the bluing, which was more black. Both these improvements were attained by new techniques in polishing.

Under the Olin production of the Model 70 during 1964–81, a total of eleven basic styles of complete rifles were presented (not including Models 660, 670, and 70A, and barreled actions). These eleven styles, in chronological order of introduction, are the Standard, Magnum, African, Varmint, Target, Deluxe, Mannlicher, International Army Match, New Super Grade, Ultra Match, and New Featherweight.

A look at Olin's production figures (through 1981) for the post-1964 Model 70 shows a range of sales with a high of about 82,000 rifles (1977) and a low of just under 18,000 (1967). Despite the comments about post–1964 quality, 1964 and 1965 sales were approximately 57,000 and 61,000 respectively.

Interestingly, although serial number 1500000 deluxe rifle was sold at auction in 1979, the actual 1500000 mark wasn't reached until 1981.

By any measure, the Model 70 ranks among the most popular of twentieth-century firearms, proving itself worldwide on a daily basis. It is likely that more professional hunters and guides around the world rely on a Model 70 as their own rifle than any other.

become the corporation's foundation. Headquarters were at 460 Park Avenue, New York, and John Olin was chairman of the board, with Spencer T. Olin a member of the board of directors.

Among important advancements in ammunition in the 1960s were plastic shotshells (1963) and soon thereafter (1967) the beginning of construction of the most modern shotshell facility in the world. And in 1969, the corporate headquarters moved from New York to Stamford, Connecticut.

Over the course of the next decade a new rimfire manufacturing facility was built, then a new warehouse and distribution center and a new ball-powder-manufacturing facility, at St. Marks, Florida. From the Florida site, commencing in 1968, Winchester-Western manufactured gunpowder for military and civilian clients. Still another addition was the extensive modernization of machine shop operations, improved research and development facilities, and completion of a new loading and packing facility for centerfire cartridges.

An aside which is indicative of Olin's versatility: when the federal government decided to eliminate silver from U.S. coinage, the Olin Brass Group developed Posit-Bond clad metal, with a core of copper sandwiched between layers of cupronickel. Olin Brass remains the U.S. Mint's foremost supplier of this material.

Divestiture of Firearms Production
Early in the 1980s the headquarters for Winchester were moved from New Haven to East Alton, Illinois. At the same time Olin began to divest itself of its firearms-manufacturing operations in New Ha-

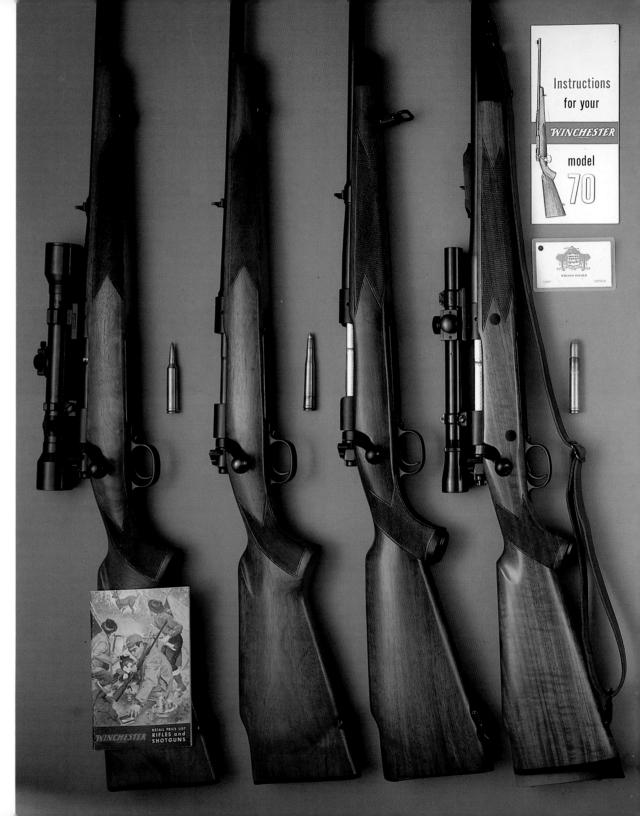

Lineup of pre–1964 Model 70s, beginning with the presentation to General Curtis LeMay at *left*, in .264 Magnum caliber. *Next*, a .308 Featherweight. *Third*, a .300 H&H Magnum rifle (with silver-tipped cartridge above breech), a Super Grade. *Far right*, William Holden's .458 Winchester Magnum, a 1956-era rifle, serial number 391484, in African pattern, accompanied by card with his Mount Kenya Safari Club address, Nairobi.

Top to bottom, the Models 670, 670A, and 770—all derivatives of the Model 70—in economy versions. The 670 (1966–79) had a production total in excess of 287,000 rifles and was made as a sporting rifle, carbine, and Magnum sporting rifle, with seven cartridge chamberings, from .225 to .300 Winchester Magnum. Note the two-position tang safety. The 670A at *center* was an improved version, brought out in 1972; note three-position safety and new checkering pattern. At *right*, Model 770 (1969–72; nearly 21,000 made) offered nine calibers, and medium grade between the Models 670 and 70. The scope is not standard factory fare. Illustrated calibers are (*left to right*) .243, .270, and .30-06.

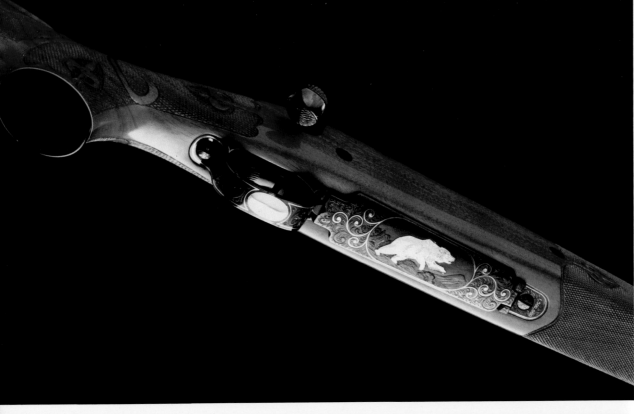

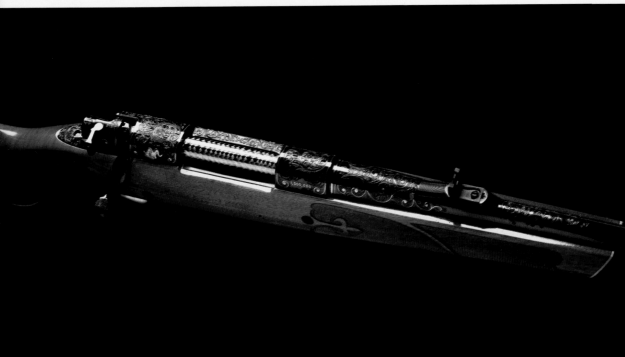

ven (with a satellite factory in Hingham, Massachusetts) and in Japan. Both operations were sold to company employees, the former facility becoming U.S. Repeating Arms Company (1981) and the latter becoming Classic Japan, Ltd. (1987). A separate U.S. sales operation for the Japanese-made guns (including the 101 shotgun) was known as Classic Doubles, headquartered in St. Louis, Missouri.

In 1985 a major achievement was Winchester's winning of the contract to operate the federal government's Lake City Arsenal, in Independence, Missouri. Since the facility's construction in 1941, operation had been by Remington Arms Company, Winchester's chief competitor. Winchester won out in competitive bidding, and in the process took on 3,000 new employees.

The Annual Report of the Olin Corporation for 1990 showed the stockholders a healthy corporation, with solid growth despite changes in the commercial and government markets. With its $2.5 billion in total sales and $124 million in profits, 1989 was a banner year for Olin. In the 1990 report, Chairman, President, and Chief Executive Officer John W. Johnstone, Jr., commented on profitability and on the future:

> I am very pleased to report that in 1989 Olin achieved
> an 18 percent return on equity, and earnings per share

Landmark rifle serial number 1500000 Model 70, gold-inlaid and engraved by A. A. White, with stockwork and finishing by the factory Custom Shop. It was sold at the same auction, the Las Vegas Antique Arms Show, as Model 94 serial number 3500000.

Mechanically and stylistically identifiable as of the same era, these .22-rimfire rifles are all of Olin manufacture. The *top three*, Models 121, 131, and 141 respectively (1967–72, collectively over 104,000 made), differ mainly in being single-shot, clip-loading, or tubular (through butt) magazine. *Bottom two* rifles are Models 310 and 320 (1971–74, totaling approximately 25,000), the former a single-shot, the latter a clip-fed repeater; checkering by pressure equipment.

IMPORTANT
The Winchester Model 74 can be cocked Only when "Safety" is in FIRE position. Do not attempt to cock rifle when "Safety" is ON. Forcing may jam the action. With action cocked, bolt can be retracted easily with "Safety" in either position.

Instructions for your **WINCHESTER** model **77** automatic TUBULAR Self-loading Rifle

Instructions for your NEW **WINCHESTER** model **55** TOP-LOADING, SINGLE-SHOT AUTOMATIC .22 RIFLE PLEASE READ CAREFULLY BEFORE FIRING

Semiautomatic .22s originated by Winchester-Olin. *From the top*, the Model 74 (1939–55, over 406,000 made); *next two*, its successor, the variations of the Model 77 (1955–62, over 217,000 made), differing in having clip or tubular magazines. *Bottom*, the Model 55 rifle, an unusual top-loading, single-shot automatic (1957–61, over 45,000 made), in which the spent cartridge casing was ejected immediately after firing.

The 200 series, in the Winchester-Olin line from 1963 to 1977, with a total production of approximately 2,171,000; all chambered for .22 Short, Long, and Long Rifle. *From the top,* the Model 270 pump; the scope added by buyer. The Model 290 automatic, with Fancy Grade stocks. The Model 190 carbine (economy model of the 290), has its magazine tube cap opened for loading. *Bottom* rifle, the 250 lever-action. Over 80 percent of production was in the automatic.

The Model 100 semiautomatic rifle, in the line from 1960 to 1973. *From the top*, the pre–1964 version. The carbine variant, brought out in 1967 with a 19-inch barrel. The post–1964 Model 100, with characteristic impressed checkering on stock; Aim Point sight attachment (added by buyer) puts red dot on target, showing where bullet should hit. Total production of Model 100s reached nearly 263,000, in calibers .243, .284, and .308.

Lever-action companion to the Model 100, the Model 88 dates from 1955 to 1973 and had a somewhat greater total manufacturing run of nearly 284,000. *From the top*, chambering .243, .308, .284, and .358 cartridges. Pre– and post–1964 stock styles are evident in *top* and *bottom* rifles respectively. Box magazines of the Models 88 and 100 are shown in side and top views.

rose to $6.02. These were record levels for the company and exceeded the prior year's performance by 27 percent and 30 percent, respectively. It also marks the second straight year we exceeded the goals I shared with you in the prior year's annual report. . . . Entering the 1990s is of no small significance to Olin. In 1992 we will celebrate our company's centennial. At that time we want to celebrate an Olin that is much more than a company with a colorful history, rather a company of dedicated people whose best days lie ahead. We have only two more years of performance before we kick off that centennial celebration in April, 1992. I can tell you that I intend to preside over that shareholder's meeting with my head held high. And every Olin employee and shareholder will feel that same pride, because we will have made great strides to improve the company and set it on a clear course to that bright future. We respect Olin's colorful past; we're confident because of our achievements in recent years and we're excited about our prospects for the future. We look forward to that celebration just 26 months from now.

In 1989 the Defense and Ammunition Division had a profit of $31 million (24 percent over its 1988 profit of $25 million). The $665 million in 1989 sales was a 42 percent increase over 1988's $469

Chairman of the Board John Olin (*left*), with board member John W. Hanes (*center*), being shown a new Model 88 rifle by Winchester's Tom Henshaw. Taken at the 1957 Olin stockholders' meeting, East Alton, Illinois.

From 1969 through 1975, Winchester carried a line of "Precision Air Rifles and Pistols," made in West Germany to Winchester's own specifications. Calibers were .177 and .22, and the various models were for every grade and sophistication of shooter. *From the top*, models are the 416, barrels at *left* from the 422 and 423, pistol at *right* the 363, rifle *below* it the 182c, then the Models 427 and 435 with red-finished hardwood stocks, and, at *bottom*, the top-of-the-line 333, with barrel and forend of the 450. Disks at *bottom center* are inserts for front sights of more sophisticated models. Standard features included rifled steel barrels and other advanced details not normally found on air guns. A total of over 19,000 were made.

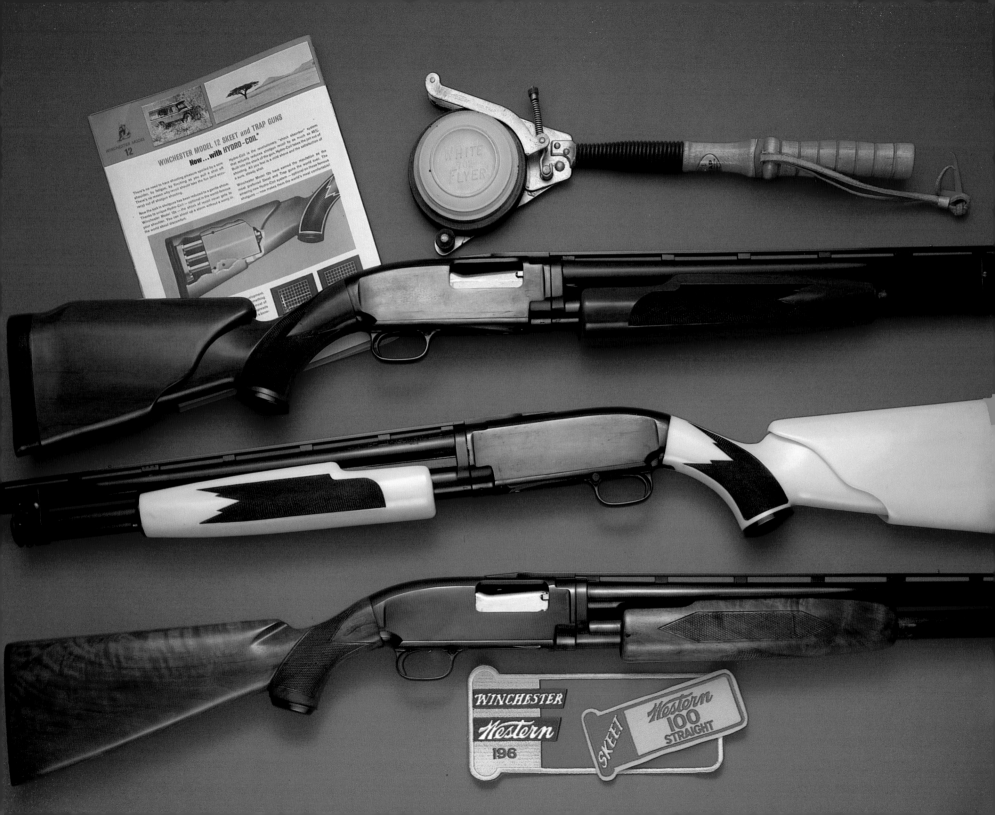

WINCHESTER MODEL 12 SKEET and TRAP GUNS

Now ... with HYDRO-COIL™

WHITE FLYER

WINCHESTER Western 196

SKEET Western 100 STRAIGHT

million total. Donald W. Griffin, executive vice president in charge of the Defense and Ammunition segment, stated (1990 Annual Report):

As a result of the recent changes in Eastern Europe and a new view of the military threat, reductions in U.S. defense spending will occur. We believe each of our businesses, however, has the flexibility and strategies in place to adapt to these changes. . . . Our strategy for *Winchester* sporting ammunition has not changed, and the outlook is favorable. Through prudent investment in cost reduction programs at all levels, we believe we remain the low cost producer. At the retail level, we have seen our strategy to educate our dealers on *Winchester* products result in increased sales.

The report showed that Winchester had achieved its fifth year in a row of record domestic sales of commercial cartridges. There was a particular strength in the target-shooting market.

Winchester Division President Gerald W. Bersett made the following statement for *Winchester: An American Legend*:

John and Franklin Olin would be proud of the strength and vitality of Winchester today, and it is through their foresight and business wisdom back in 1931 that Winchester has survived. The history of Winchester both

---

Model 12s were carried in the Winchester-Olin line through 1963, and thereafter were available by special order, 1963–72 and 1976–79. The high serial number reached in 1980 was 2026721, making it the all-time best-selling pump shotgun in Winchester history, with a production total not equaled by any other manufacturer. *Top and center* 12s were factory-fitted with the Hydro-Coil recoil-reducing device. Plastic stocks were an optional feature. Hydro-Coil was brought out in 1964, and was intended for trap and skeet guns. *Bottom* gun has a walnut stock, which was also available as a Hydro-Coil accessory.

Exhibition shooter Herb Parsons with his array of Winchester longarms. Following in the tradition of Annie Oakley and the Topperweins, showmen like Herb Parsons add spice to the ancient art of shooting. Note vegetables, golf balls, and other targets.

Deluxe Super-X Model 1 auto shotguns, the *top* serial number SXP0017, in Pigeon Grade, and one of only a hundred which were engraved and inlaid. *Lower* gun, serial number SXSP0017, gold-inlaid and engraved with equally elegant select walnut stocks. Shoulder patch part of Winchester-Olin's comprehensive promotion of the Super-X series.

Model 1200 and derivatives, a series brought out in 1964. *From the top*, rare trench gun, in 12-gauge, accompanied by bayonet. Skeet gun, in 20 gauge, with fancy wood and factory brochure. The 12-gauge Model 2200, a Canadian-made variation, was considered an economy model. The Ranger in 20 gauge, introduced for the youth market by U.S. Repeating Arms Co., successors to Winchester-Olin as firearms makers. As the youngster grows up, the adult-size stock can be purchased and fitted in place of the youth-size. At *bottom*, the Winchoke with wrench and carrying capsule, an accessory introduced in 1969.

WINCHESTER
SUPER-X MODEL 1
SHOTGUN

Instructions for your model

1200

WINCHESTER
YOUNG RANGER CLUB
WINCHESTER
LICENSEE

L1441699

Instructions
WINCHO

in time of peace and in time of armed conflict is in a very real sense the history of America, and Olin has played a major role in keeping the legend alive. Today Winchester is indeed "More Than a Gun, an American Legend." Olin is proud that Winchester is the world's largest private ammunition company producing over a billion rounds of ammunition each year and that Winchester operates the U.S. government's small-caliber ammunition plant. Our licensee, U.S. Repeating Arms Company, continues the Winchester firearm legend by making some of the finest sporting rifles available anywhere. Our ammunition plants in Anagni, Italy, and Geelong, Australia, continue to lead their respective markets with high-quality product which consistently wins in international and national competitions. Winchester continues to be one of the world's best-known trademarks, and it is Olin's commitment to meet its customers' expectations all the time that keeps Winchester number one.

The Claybird Tournament Model 1200 (*right*) and 1400 presentation guns, made by Winchester-Olin to encourage competitive skeet and trap shooting, were presented to clubs as awards for top shooters, as part of the 1968 promotional program. Note the shoulder patch indicating international tournaments held in Europe, and Winchester shotshells at bottom made in Italy for the European market.

A selection of models made at Winchester-Olin's Cooey factory, at Cobourg, Ontario. Ted Hazelwood, manager of the works for many years, is pictured at *right* with his trademark cigar. *From the top,* the Model 64 .22 semiautomatic, as a cutaway demonstrator. Model 39, bolt-action, with cutaway breech. Stamp above barrel marked with a variety of trade names used on Cooey-built firearms. The Model 37A single-shot shotgun has its frame roll-engraved. Semiautomatic with nickel-plated frame and trigger is the Model 490 and has special-ordered finish and deluxe walnut stock. At *bottom,* Model 710 bolt-action, an economy version of the Model 70. The factory built both guns and ammunition and even had its own catalogue issues.

Representatives of Winchester-Olin's active European marketing. *From the top*, Super Grade Model 101, made for Continental sale, with straight-stock styling and double trigger. A 101 with pistol-grip stock, built for the European market, also Super Grade. Gold-inlaid deluxe gun at *bottom* is a 101 of presentation quality, also made for the Continent but purchased by an admiring Winchester executive. Horse-and-rider shoulder patch for foreign market, as evidenced by globe motif. Note French-language edition of 1976 catalogue.

Spanish-made Winchesters, built for the international and domestic markets, were introduced in the mid-1970s. *From the top*, a side-by-side 12-gauge, the Model 22. The over-and-under Model 91 was based on the Japanese-made 101. The Model 96 over-and-under and, at *bottom*, the Model 99 (with double trigger) were also 101 derivatives.

New to the line in 1978, the Model 23 Pigeon Grade XTR (*top* and *center*) was the first gun of its type to be marketed in the United States, following classification of the Model 21 as strictly as a custom-order. An eye-catching feature was the gray finish to the frame, triggerguard, and top lever. Sold in 12 and 20 gauge and made by Olin-Kodensha. Each gun was fitted in a carrying case. Contributing to the 23's appeal were its auto ejectors, single selective trigger, automatic safety, and reasonable price. *Bottom*, the new Parker Reproduction by Winchester, made on contract for the Skeuse family of New Jersey (Reagent Chemical Company) and rivaling in quality the original Parker boxlock shotguns. Introduced in 1984.

Among the last firearms brought out by Winchester-Olin were these two over-and-unders. At *top*, a combination rifle and shotgun, c. 1985, chambered for 12 gauge and .30-06. *Bottom*, the Grand Europe, a double rifle in .30-06, made at the Olin-Kodensha works in limited quantities only.

SPORTING ARMS & AMMUNITION
WINCHESTER
CANADA

WINCHESTER
CANADA

WINCHESTER
W
CANADA

WINCHESTER
MODEL 1400 MK II
LEFT-HAND FIELD GUN WITH VENTILATED RIB
AND WINCHOKE
SYMBOL: 140006   12 GAUGE
28 INCH BARREL   MODIFIED WINCHOKE
PRICE

WINCHESTER

HIGH VELOCITY
RABBIT LOAD

25 SHOTGUN SHELLS

WARNING: KEEP OUT OF REACH OF CHILDREN

25 | 12 GA. | 2¾"
W12171 | 70mm - 2 ¾"
3½ DR. EQ. - 30 gram - 1⅛ oz

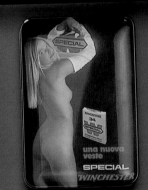

SPECIAL

WINCHESTER
34

una nuova
veste

SPECIAL
WINCHESTER

model 1500 XTR
Semi-Automatic Shotgun
12 Gauge, 28" V.R. barrel
WINCHOKE- (Mod., Full &
Imp. Cyl.)

WINCHESTER

Symbol No. 15085 XTR

European 1500 XTR •
NE004142

WINCHESTER

40 NL

W
SUPER-SPEED
EXTRA

CARTOUCHES DE CHASSE PLASTIQUE
A mettre hors de portée des enfants

modèle 1500 XTR field/chasse
Semi-Automatic Shotgun
Fusil Semi-Automatique
12 Gauge, 28" V.R. barrel
WINCHOKE (Mod., Full & Imp. Cyl.)
12 Calibre, 71 cm B.V. canon

WINCHESTER

G15185 XTRE

CANADA

In 1961 the Olin Corporation purchased the H. W. Cooey Machine and Arms Company, of Cobourg, Ontario, Canada. Cooey had been founded in 1903, in Toronto, and became a leading maker of small arms and machinery. Olin placed the firm under its Winchester-Western Division and launched an expansion program to increase production, including developing a comprehensive ammunition facility and manufacturing the Model 94 rifle. As of 1970 the works was Canada's first and only company manufacturing a complete line of ammunition and firearms. By 1974 the plant had nearly 450 employees. Its operating name was Winchester-Western Canada Limited. Works manager from 1970 to 1980 was Ted Hazelwood, former assistant football coach at the University of North Carolina and a colorful figure in the modern history of Winchester firearms. The plant was closed down in 1980, with the selling of the Winchester firearms models and production to U.S. Repeating Arms Co.

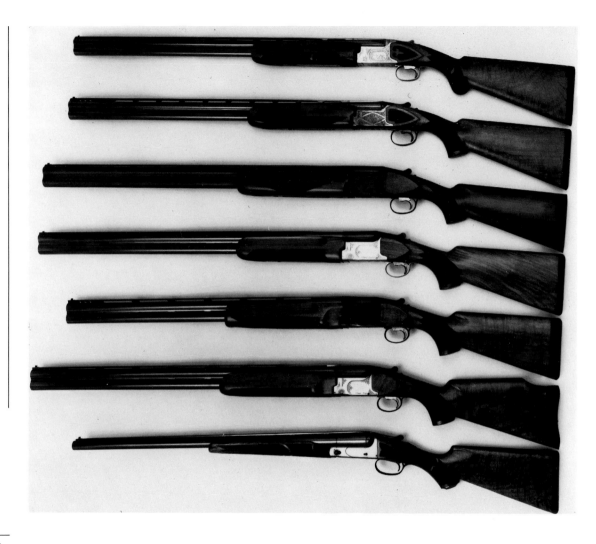

Late models of Winchester-Olin shotguns. *From the top*, the Model 1400, available for both right-handed and (as shown here) left-handed shooters. The cutaway Model 2400, made at the Cooey factory, Canada, was used as a demonstrator. *Bottom two* semiautomatics are the Model 1500 XTR (indicating extra quality, a designation introduced in 1978) and the XTRE (E for European, its intended market). Among the latter's distinguishing features: aluminum frame color on sides, roll-engraved horse-and-rider logo, and sling swivels. The ashtray was one of several racy promotional creations of Winchester-Olin's European operations.

Last of the line for Classic Doubles. *From the top*, Model 101s in Field Grades I and II and Waterfowler, Sporter, Skeet, and Trap variations; at *bottom*, the Model 201 side-by-side. The new firm had hoped to be able to carry on under the new marque, but found the sledding difficult without the strength of the Winchester name. Within two years, Classic Doubles was no more. A somewhat different fate took Parker Reproductions by Winchester: the property on which the factory was located, in Japan, attained such a high real estate value that it was sold, the factory demolished, and the land turned into a golf course. Parker Reproductions, though still in business, has yet to find a factory which could carry on production at a comparable quality and price.

"It's one-of-a-kind . . . and it can be yours" was the headline on the promotional flier widely distributed by the National Shooting Sports Foundation as a fund-raising auction item for the 1984 SHOT (Shooting and Hunting Outdoor Trade) Show. The brochure went on to note: "Measuring nearly three feet by four feet and weighing some 35 pounds, the board not only features nearly every rifle, handgun and shotgun load made by Winchester but also illustrates the various steps in the ammunition manufacturing process. The board features samples of 120 types of ammunition in addition to illustrating more than 50 steps in the ammunition manufacturing process. . . ." It was sold for $3,750, and the funds were applied toward promoting the shooting sports in America.

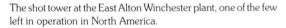

The shot tower at the East Alton Winchester plant, one of the few left in operation in North America.

Winchester knives, made under license from Winchester-Olin, are recreations of the originals made and sold in the 1920s and are marketed under the name Winchester Trademark Knives. Manufacture and sales are by Blue Grass Cutlery Corp., Manchester, Ohio. Approximately twenty-two patterns have been or are being made, the markings including a pattern number and the year of manufacture, to avoid confusion with the originals. Other licensing arrangements include the Italian-made line of leather clothing, shoes, handbags, briefcases, wristwatches, glasses, and stationery goods, each by different specialist manufacturers (c. 1989).

This aerial view shows only part of the Winchester complex of Olin's East Alton facilities, which looks every bit as expansive as the celebrated factory site in New Haven. Shot tower is in foreground and general offices at *left*.

The first factory cartridge board built in the shape of the Winchester W, 3′ × 4′, 30 pounds in weight. Auctioned by sealed bid at the 1985 SHOT Show, it realized $6,000 for the programs of the National Shooting Sports Foundation. It displays 114 different sporting ammunition cartridges (eighty-two rimfire and centerfire cartridges and thirty-two shotshells). Approximately fifteen shotshells are shown in cross-sectional views. Each item is identified by its own nameplate. Only three boards of this pattern were made. Both the 1984 and the 1985 SHOT Show boards were donated by the Winchester Division of Olin.

Chapter X
Commemoratives:
A New Collecting Universe

An innovation of the modern era, the commemorative age in firearms began with Colt's in 1960 (the Geneseo, Illinois, 125th-anniversary derringer). Winchester quickly followed with the 1964 Wyoming Diamond Jubilee Model 94 carbine. The two historic firms have dominated the commemorative field ever since. The total number of Winchester commemorative issues through 1991 has been over fifty, with more than one million guns made—most on the Model 94 action. Two issues, the Centennial 66 and the Buffalo Bill, even capped totals of over 100,000 each; considering volume alone, Winchester became the world's largest manufacturer of commemorative firearms. The popularity of commemoratives meant a whole new market category of arms collectors—a market which was actively promoted by Winchester and Colt by aggressive advertising campaigns, with displays at collectors' shows, sporting goods shows, and the like, and the general proliferation of dealers, all creating new interest in the collecting field. An opinion poll conducted in 1978 determined that 2,400,000 American gun owners considered themselves to be primarily collectors (there were then 50 to 60 million gun owners, and 180 million guns).

This trend of collecting was also spurred on by makers of both shooting and nonshooting firearms. One maker, the Antique Armory, manufactured nonfiring zinc-and-plastic (but authentic-looking) replicas of Winchesters and hundreds of other guns, and the Franklin Mint would eventually bring out a Winchester Buffalo Bill rifle, based on a Model 1873 with plated finishes and elaborate engraving. The active promotion of these issues rapidly elevated the numbers of arms collectors and accelerated the public's interest in firearms for their history and craftsmanship. The investment aspect of collecting was also increasingly emphasized. The buyer of commemoratives preferred his (or her) guns in unused condition, as "new in the box." The new issues often featured beautifully designed slipcovers for the shipping boxes, and Winchester generally commissioned original art for the advertising and promotion of these colorful arms.

The number of categories of commemoratives broadened their appeal, and some buyers bought their first pieces because they wished to be involved in celebrating a particular anniversary honoring a particular person or organization, or even recognizing a special business. The basic categories in commemorative Winchesters are statehood, territory, or country anniversaries; historic events, people, organizations, businesses, or law enforcement groups; American Indians; and Winchester factory anniversaries. All the issues produced to date are published in the Appendix, complete with year of introduction, totals made, and the highest serial number.

The photographs in this chapter were selected to

A collector's print of Norman Rockwell's stagecoach painting, commissioned by U.S. Repeating Arms Company, serves as a backdrop for these four popular Winchester commemoratives. *From the top*, the Centennial 66, second issue made; over 102,000 sold. The Cowboy Model 94; over 27,000 total. The John Wayne, with its rakish giant cocking lever; issue totaling 51,300 in four variations. The Annie Oakley, a 9422 of which 6,000 were made. First two by the Winchester Division of Olin, latter two by U.S. Repeating Arms Company. The Rockwell print was a Winchester promotion at the time of the remake of *Stagecoach*.

show the variety of commemorative issues, the inspired artwork of their packaging, and the innovation of Winchester to create for the collector an entirely fresh field of arms collecting.

In some respects Winchester had made commemorative-type firearms from the early days of production: special presentation or show guns had been built for President Abraham Lincoln, Secretary of the Navy Gideon Welles, and Secretary of War Edwin Stanton. Further, there is the tradition of custom arms made for such signal events as Philadelphia's Centennial Exhibition of 1876, and various world's fairs in Europe and the United States. The custom and deluxe firearms have been celebrated in the author's texts on Winchester engraving, which evidence the factory's emphasis on richly appointed, high-quality deluxe arms.

That tradition continues today not only in the special commemorative issues but in the creations of the Custom Shop. As mass-market and mass-production requirements tended to move handwork more into the background, management and manufacturing relied on the Custom Shop for speciality guns demanding hand engraving, metalwork, and special stocks. In the nineteenth and early twentieth centuries the custom area of the factory was an active entity, staffed with some of the finest talent in the firearms industry. Exquisite examples of this artistry are a featured part of *Winchester: An American Legend.*

But following World Wars I and II, mass production became increasingly predominant. The Custom Shop was a less-active domain where the traditions of Winchester handwork were making something of a last stand.

However, with a burgeoning interest among the shooting and collecting public in richly engraved and stocked firearms—inspired largely by books and magazines featuring deluxe gunmaking, and by collectors' shows, auctions, and gunmakers' promotions—the Custom Shop has made a dra-

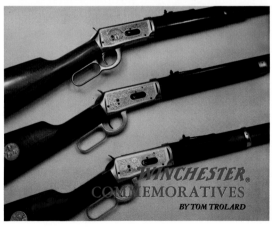

Winchester's Arms Products Committee, c. 1968, Ted Hazelwood standing at left center, with Tom Henshaw holding rifle bolt. A commemorative Model 94 rifle rests on the conference table at right. The committee drew up design concepts for several of the commemorative issues.

Front dust jacket of the standard reference work on Winchester commemoratives, by collector and dealer Tom Trolard.

Earlier issues with slipcase covers standard for several. *From the top,* the Wyoming (1964), Nebraska (1966), Illinois (1968), and Alaska Purchase (1967). Of these only the Illinois was issued in large quantities. Earlier guns had relatively simple cosmetic details, sometimes including medallion stock inlays.

matic and welcome comeback. It is no exaggeration to state that the superb guns emerging from Winchester's Custom Shop since the mid-1970s rival the finest creations of Winchester at any time in its past. Selected examples of these modern gun masterpieces are featured here, a tribute to the high standards of excellence which are hallmarks of the best of contemporary gunmaking. It is the author's firm opinion that the finest artistry and craftsmanship in the history of gunmaking is being done today—and this in an age characterized by such buzzwords as "junk food," "junk bonds," and "planned obsolescence."

The Centennial 66 and Buffalo Bill carbines were accompanied by rifles having 26-inch barrels. These were the two best-selling issues of any commemorative by any gunmaker—each in excess of 100,000. The Centennial 66 began the use of colorful slipcase covers and relied on historic art of the American West, by the likes of Frederic Remington, for the vignettes. Some of the paintings had originally been commissioned by Winchester. Authorized by the Buffalo Bill Memorial Association, the Buffalo Bill issue raised over $500,000 for the Buffalo Bill Historical Center, Cody, Wyoming, through a royalty paid by Winchester.

Winchesters had no little presence in events associated with the Golden Spike (Centennial of the East–West rail connection, Promontory Point, Utah, 1869), the life of sportsman-conservationist Theodore Roosevelt, and the great state of Texas. The last issue celebrated the 125th anniversary of Texas statehood.

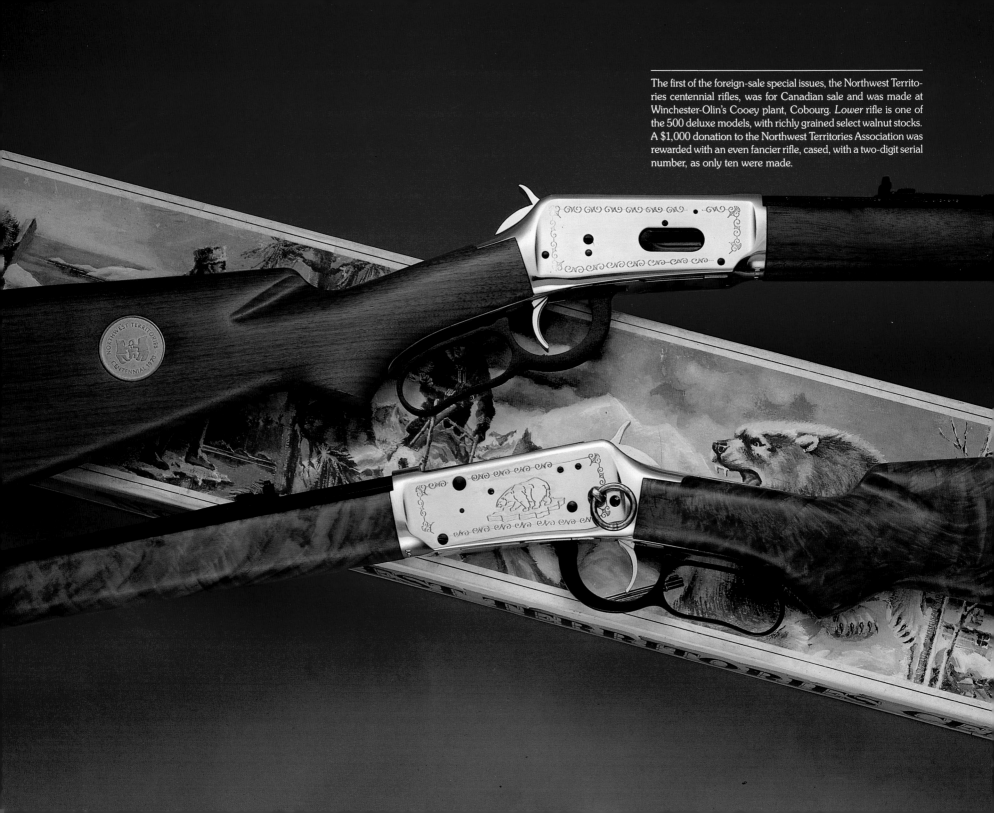

The first of the foreign-sale special issues, the Northwest Territories centennial rifles, was for Canadian sale and was made at Winchester-Olin's Cooey plant, Cobourg. *Lower* rifle is one of the 500 deluxe models, with richly grained select walnut stocks. A $1,000 donation to the Northwest Territories Association was rewarded with an even fancier rifle, cased, with a two-digit serial number, as only ten were made.

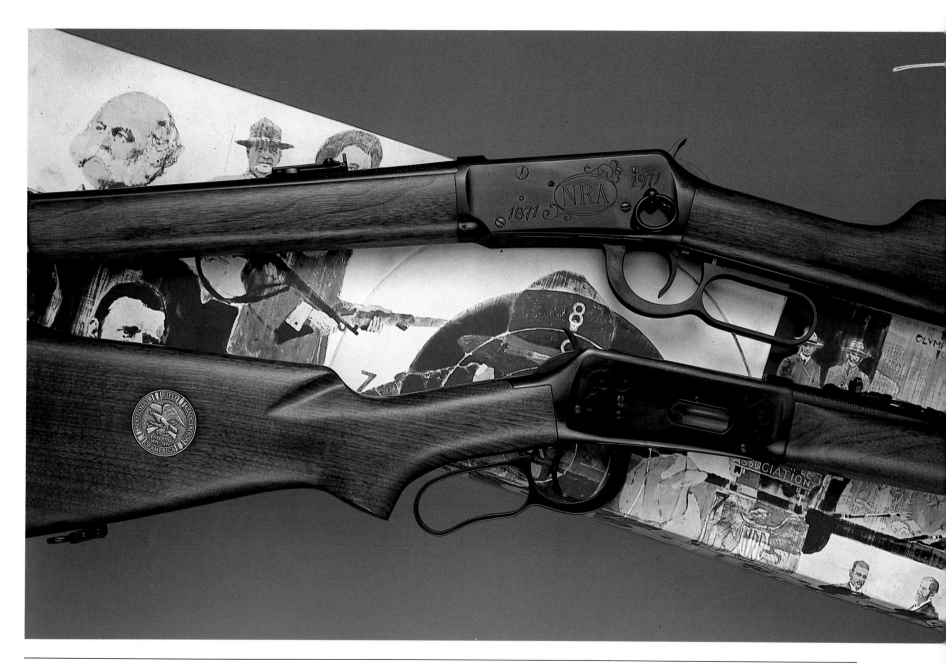

Centennial of the National Rifle Association was celebrated by Colt and Winchester issues, among others. The musket and rifle stylings made for two of the most attractive—and popular—of the commemoratives. The slipcase recognized the contributions of the association to marksmanship, safety, and general firearms education.

Fine Wolf holds a sparkling-new case-hardened Model 1886 rifle, wears a cartridge belt, into which a Colt Single Action revolver is tucked, and—just in case—brandishes a peace pipe. Some of the commemoratives honoring Indians had case-hardened frames.

The Yellow Boy and Royal Canadian Mounted Police were both issues for foreign sale, the former the first commemorative made exclusively for the European market, the latter made specifically for Canada at the Cooey Winchester factory, in four variations. The Texas Rangers carbine honored the Rangers' sesquicentennial and was an exclusive model for Texas sale, issued under authority of the Texas Ranger Commemorative Commission.

From top down, the Apache, Comanche, Sioux, and Little Big Horn were all foreign-sale issues, for the European and Canadian collector market, with manufacture at the Cobourg factory. A few have trickled into the United States. The Little Big Horn was the first of the Winchester commemoratives to be chambered for .44-40 cartridges.

The Klondike Gold Rush carbine was authorized by the Dawson City Historical Society, with a percentage from the sales being assigned to the Dawson City Museum's building fund. Sales were in Canada, production at Cobourg. The U.S. Bicentennial issue was Winchester's salute to 200 years of American independence. Both 94 carbines sported their own ammunition, among the earliest of commemoratives to do so.

The second Trapper's Model commemorative (first was the Texas Ranger Presentation), the Legendary Lawman sported a 16-inch barrel and was accompanied by, as an option, nickel-plated .30-30 cartridges (in the customary twenty to a box). The Wells Fargo issue was in conjunction with the Wells Fargo Bank and honored its 125th anniversary. Bank employees were among the buyers of this issue of approximately 20,000 guns.

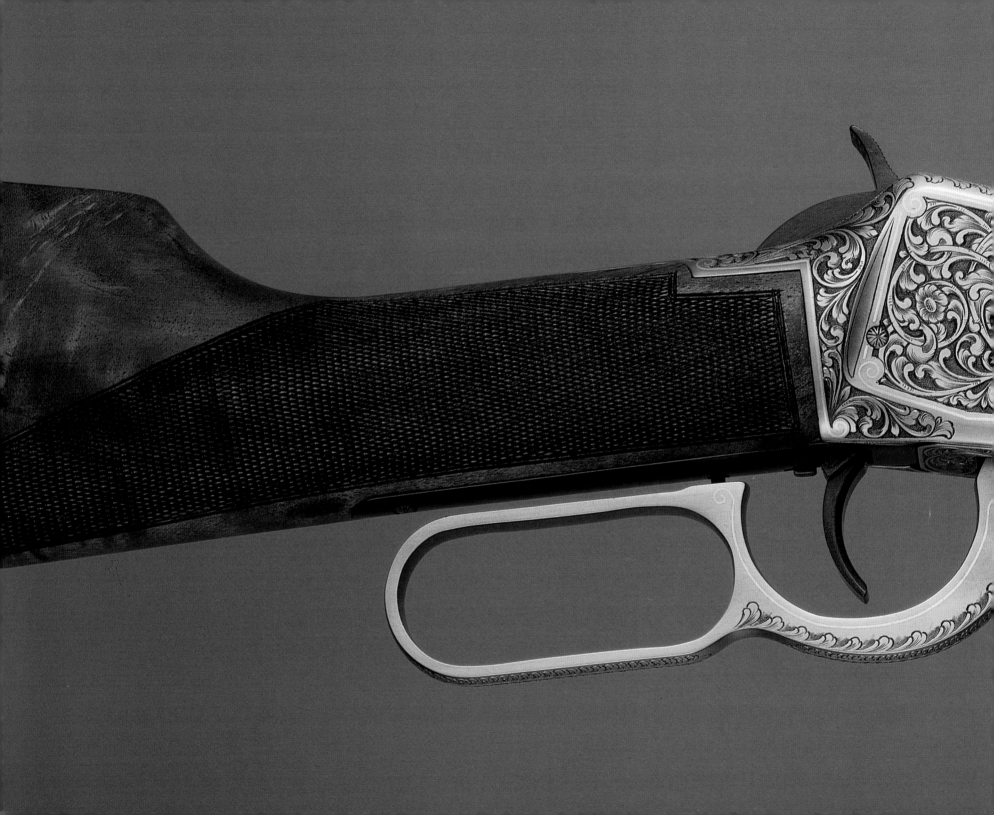

One of the most striking of all issues, the One of One Thousand was a foreign project, each 94 having a serial number ending in 000. Each barrel was gold-inlaid with the prestigious "One of One Thousand" inscription, as was the buttplate, and engraved coverage included the frame, barrel bands, lever, and receiver bottom plate. The left side of the frame was engraved with the Winchester horse-and-rider logo, and "Model 1894 Winchester" was gold-inlaid on the upper tang. Frames are marked from 1 to 250, and each bears the signature of the engraver, Bottega C. Giovanelli. Serial numbers are gold-inlaid on the front bottom of the frame. Deluxe oil-finished walnut stocks; the set in a velvet-lined leather case.

Presentation of a Centennial '66 rifle to H.R.H. Prince Philip, the Duke of Edinburgh, on the set of a western village at 20th Century Fox Studios, Los Angeles. The rifle now in the Royal Collection at Sandringham. Actor Van Heflin made the presentation, on behalf of Winchester.

Known as Canadian Provincial Commemoratives, the Alberta and Saskatchewan Diamond Jubilee 94 carbines were New Haven–made, but for Canadian sale. Likewise for the Canadian market, the Calgary Stampede and Canadian Pacific Centennial were also of New Haven manufacture; both guns were chambered for the .32 Special Winchester cartridge, not previously used with Winchester commemoratives.

Winchester-Olin's Tom Henshaw (*center*), with Michael (*left*) and Patrick Wayne, on launching the John Wayne model. Royalties from the more than 51,000 guns sold provided expanded services for the John Wayne Cancer Clinic at UCLA. Mrs. Ronald Reagan was presented serial number 1 of the John Wayne Standard Model 94.

Resting on its Bianchi saddle scabbard, a John Wayne Standard Model 94. This was Winchester's most popular commemorative in over ten years. It was also the first issue in .32-40 Winchester caliber. A Canadian issue, differentiated by the C prefix accompanying the JW serial number, was made in a limited edition of 1000. With sponsorship of the Fraternal Order of Retired Border Patrol Officers, Winchester brought out the U.S. Border Patrol Trapper's Model, for both civilian purchasers and members. A BP serial prefix identifies the former, and USBP the latter.

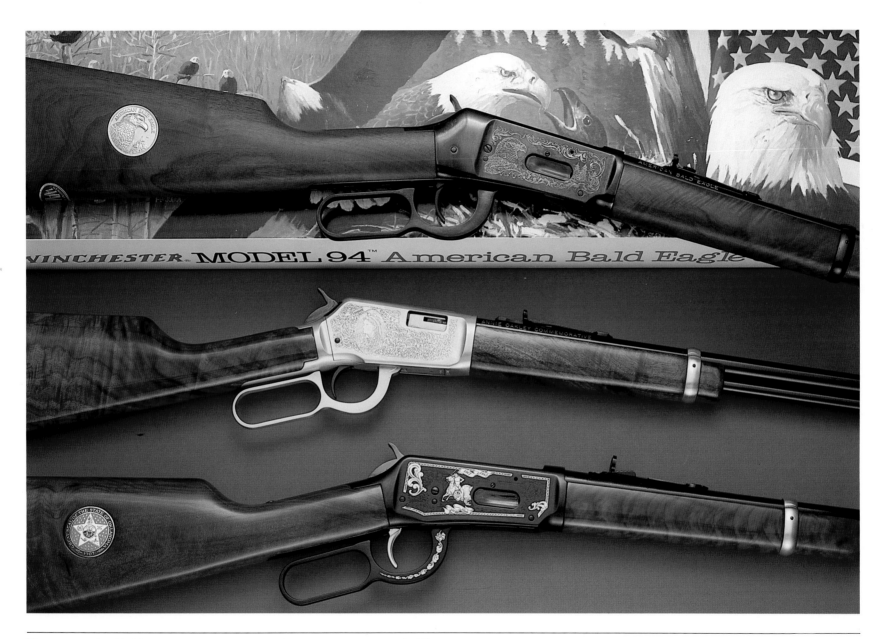

Three variants of the Model 94 were 1982 Winchester issues. *From the top,* the American Bald Eagle (the silver is pictured; a gold was also issued) was built on the new .375 Big Bore and celebrated the 200th anniversary of the bald eagle as the national symbol. *Center,* the Annie Oakley was built on the 9422, and one of the rifles was sold at a Christie's auction, New York, to benefit the U.S. Women's Biathlon Team. The Oklahoma Diamond Jubilee 94 half-magazine rifle included a diamond inlaid on the front sight and a handsome enameled stock plaque. One other issue, the Great Western Artist I, was manufactured in 1982.

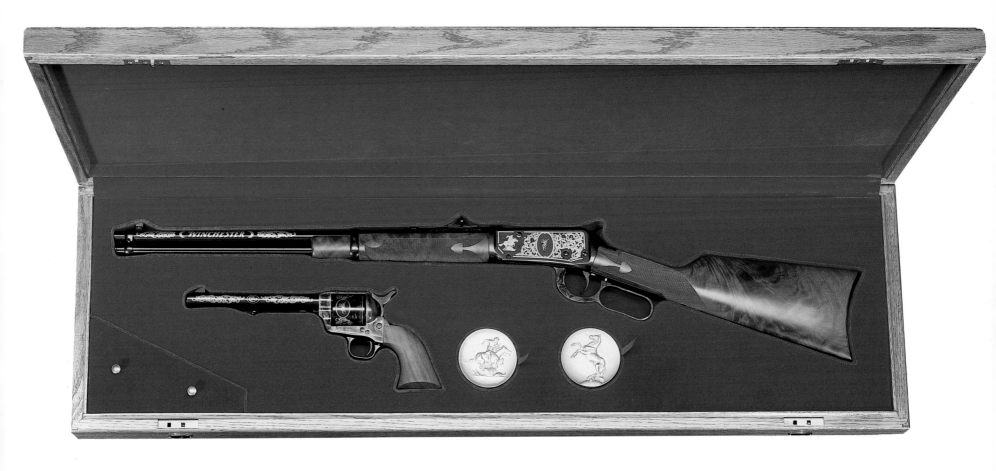

The Colt-Winchester set of matching .44-40 Model 94 and single-action Army revolver was the most ambitious and expensive of all domestic commemoratives, and also the only official joint issue of these two classic objects of Americana. The guns bear identical serial numbers in each set and are elaborately gold-plated and etched; the stocks are of richly grained American walnut.

The art of Frederic Remington was honored in the Great Western Artist II Model 94 (shown) as C. M. Russell's had been honored with series I. The Chief Crazy Horse at *bottom* benefited the Sioux Indians and was authorized by the United Sioux Tribes of South Dakota. Replicas of Sioux artifacts were also available for optional purchase, as accessories to the Crazy Horse rifle.

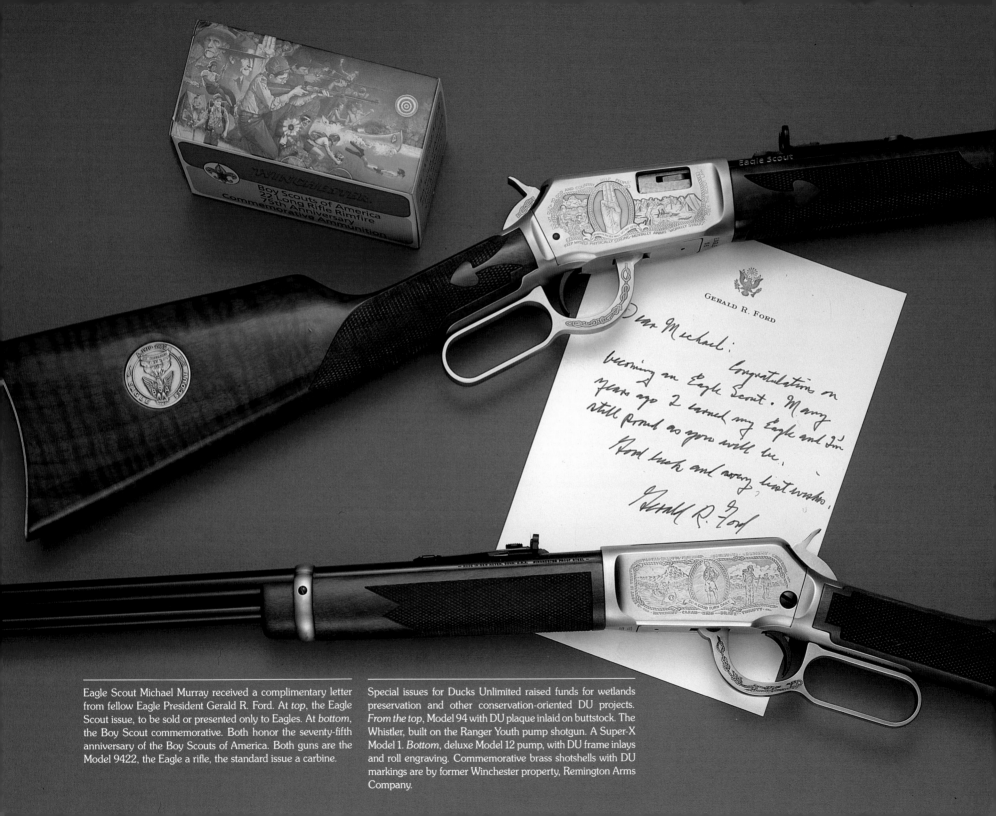

GERALD R. FORD

Dear Michael:

Congratulations on becoming an Eagle Scout. Many years ago I earned my Eagle and I'm still proud as you will be.

Good luck and every best wishes,

Gerald R. Ford

Eagle Scout Michael Murray received a complimentary letter from fellow Eagle President Gerald R. Ford. At *top*, the Eagle Scout issue, to be sold or presented only to Eagles. At *bottom*, the Boy Scout commemorative. Both honor the seventy-fifth anniversary of the Boy Scouts of America. Both guns are the Model 9422, the Eagle a rifle, the standard issue a carbine.

Special issues for Ducks Unlimited raised funds for wetlands preservation and other conservation-oriented DU projects. *From the top*, Model 94 with DU plaque inlaid on buttstock. The Whistler, built on the Ranger Youth pump shotgun. A Super-X Model 1. *Bottom*, deluxe Model 12 pump, with DU frame inlays and roll engraving. Commemorative brass shotshells with DU markings are by former Winchester property, Remington Arms Company.

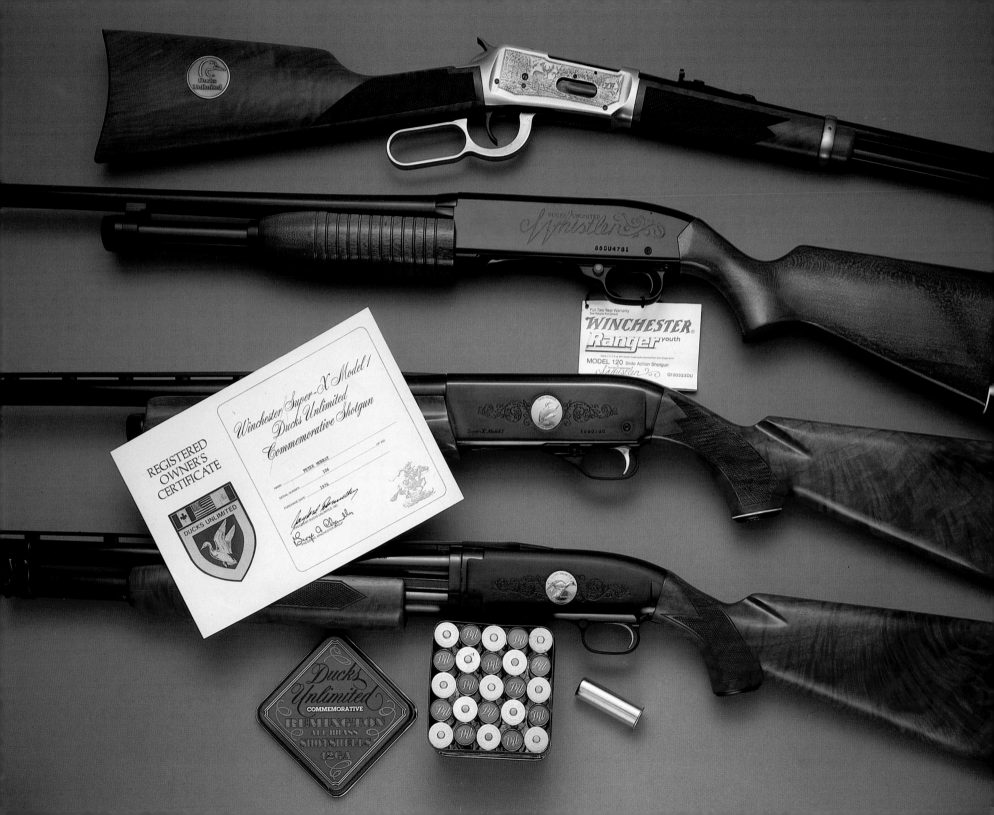

The U.S. Constitution 200th Anniversary Model 94, built exclusively for Cherry's of Greensboro, North Carolina, the world's leading commemorative dealer. Only eight were built, at $12,000 each. Engraving by Bottega C. Giovanelli, with elegant select walnut stocks and blue and gray finishes.

Elegantly engraved and/or inlaid rifles from Winchester's Custom Shop, used on cover of promotional U.S. Repeating Arms Company brochure, 1990. At *top*, Model 70 by Bryson Gwinnell, also pictured full-length on following page. *Center*, Model 94 by Bob Kain, with overall gray finish. Model 70 at *bottom* by Howard Dove.

Model 70 with Bryson Gwinnell gold inlaying and engraving issued in Collector Grade, specifications and price available on request from the Custom Shop. Among the options listed in the 1990 brochure: rust blue, skeleton buttplate, skeleton pistol-grip cap, stock carving, oil finishing, oval initial plate of 14-karat gold, leather-covered recoil pad, and French gray finish.

By the Custom Shop, 1988, this set of 9422s features stocks of bird's-eye maple at *top* and select American walnut at *bottom*; both with pistol grips, classic checkering, and custom oak and leather casing. Latter rifle is the only one made in .22 W.R.F. caliber.

Grand American Grade Model 21, in oak-and-leather casing by Marvin Huey, built on order for collector-shooter Gary Hansen. Serial number W32158, completed early in 1990. On barrel rib: CUSTOM BUILT BY WINCHESTER.

Chapter XI
U.S. Repeating Arms Company:
A New Winchester

The combination of astute business minds and arms and ammunition expertise had thrust Winchester out of bankruptcy and the Great Depression of the thirties, into the high-production demands of World War II, into the two postwar markets of the Cold War and the growing shooting public. The firearms business enjoyed the prosperous years of the 1950s and 1960s, although the years were not without annoying interruptions. Chief among them were severe strikes (c. 1969 and 1979–80) and the city of New Haven's increase of the taxes of Winchester's operations there in the

early 1950s. The Olins' reaction to the increase was immediate: over the weekend following the dark deed of city officials, John and Spencer Olin resolved to move as much of their production and management as possible out of New Haven. Many factory buildings were demolished, thus eliminating much of the real estate tax base. (Only one line of ammunition production was left, and that was a federal government order, and operated on a cost-plus basis.) So the result for New Haven was, ironically, exactly the opposite of what city officials had expected, with the reduced tax base only adding to the decaying city's woes.

In the tradition of Winchester and the Bennetts, the Olins had little to no regard for unions. The strikes were met with steely resolve by Winchester and likely influenced the decision of the Olin Corporation to sell off its domestic firearms manufacturing facility, as announced in December 1980.

The New York Times, on December 13, 1980, noted:

The board of directors of the Olin Corporation de-

cided yesterday to sell the company's Winchester Sporting Arms division, one of the nation's oldest makers of rifles and shotguns.

The move made uncertain the future of Winchester's aged plant in New Haven, which, with more than 1,300 workers, is one of the largest employers there.

John M. Henske, the president and chief executive of Olin, said in an interview yesterday that the company did not have a buyer at this time, although there had been inquiries. . . . He said that . . . if the company could not find a buyer Olin would be prepared to liquidate the business "if we have to do it." But he said, "I don't anticipate that." . . . Mr. Henske . . . conceded that top management shared in the responsibility of the troubles of the division by not modernizing manufacturing techniques sufficiently and in not having kept up in technology and marketing with its competitors, such as the Remington Arms Company. . . .

Sales of the Winchester Group for the first nine months of this year were $218 million, and operating profit before taxes was $20.4 million. Mr. Henske estimated that the arms business was considerably less than half of the total sales of the group.

The board said that the decision to sell the arms

Samplings from the current line of U.S.R.A. Co. *From the top*, the new Super Grade Model 70, serial number G15, with claw controlled-round feeding; .338 Magnum. Model 94 with angle ejection and cocking assist on hammer; standard walnut stocks. The colorful Model 1300 Stainless Marine pump shotgun, corrosion-resistant and with synthetic stocks. The Model 1300 Wild Turkey shotgun, in the Ladies/Youth variation, the stocks of WinCam, specially contoured, and of abbreviated length. The Model 1400 Slug Hunter semiautomatic, with rifled Sabot choke insertable tube.

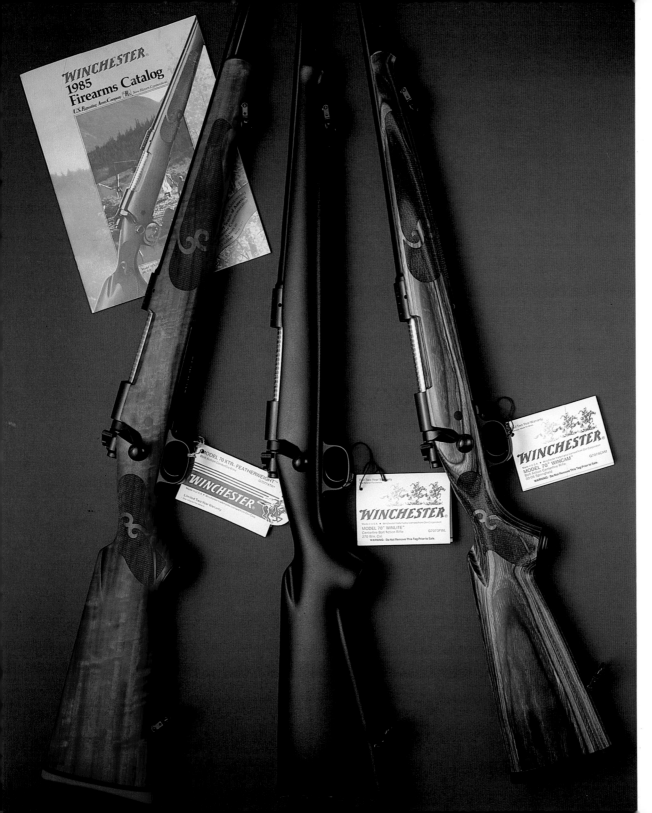

business would enable the Winchester group to focus resources on the remaining lines, made up of such products as ammunition and scopes for rifles.

Six months later a deal had been struck between Olin and a consortium made up of Winchester management which was backed by a $30 million line of credit from the Manufacturers Hanover Bank of New York. The new firm was licensed to use the Winchester name and trademark for rifle and shotgun manufacture and selected the business name of U.S. Repeating Arms Company. A telegram sent to dealers, jobbers, suppliers, and others read:

> OLIN CORPORATION HAS ANNOUNCED THE SALE OF ITS U.S. SPORTING ARMS OPERATIONS TO U.S. REPEATING ARMS COMPANY, NEW HAVEN, CONN.
>
> THE SALE COVERS OLIN'S MANUFACTURING ASSETS IN NEW HAVEN AND HINGHAM, MASS., AND INCLUDES A LICENSE FROM OLIN FOR U.S. REPEATING TO USE THE WINCHESTER TRADEMARK ON RIFLES AND SHOTGUNS PRODUCED BY THE NEW COMPANY.
>
> U.S. REPEATING HAS ASSUMED FULL RESPONSIBILITY FOR SALES, SERVICE, DISTRIBUTION AND WARRANTY REPAIRS FOR ALL U.S. MANUFACTURED FIREARMS. U.S. REPEATING'S RESPONSIBILITY INCLUDES ALL FIREARMS MANUFACTURED PRIOR TO THE DATE OF SALE AS WELL AS ALL FUTURE PRODUCTION. MODELS 101 AND 23, PRODUCED IN JAPAN, ARE EXCLUDED.
>
> OLIN'S RESTRUCTURED WINCHESTER GROUP WILL CON-

Three popular stock selections for the current Model 70. *From the left*, Super Grade with hand checkering as presented on cover of 1985 catalogue. The Winlite stock of fiberglass is virtually indestructible and is a favorite of Alaskan hunters. The WinCam stock is of laminated wood; the "Cam" is a reference to camouflage. The laminated style is also available in WinTuff, with brown coloration.

Target Model 70s, made up in the late 1980s from parts left at factory. *Top* in .30-06 caliber, *bottom* in .300 H&H. Variations are no longer listed in Winchester-U.S.R.A. catalogues.

TINUE TO MANUFACTURE SPORTING AND DEFENSE AMMU-
NITION AND TO MARKET FIREARMS PRODUCED IN JAPAN BY
OLIN-KODENSHA. THE WINCHESTER GROUP ALSO WILL BE
THE EXCLUSIVE MARKETER OF WINCHESTER FIREARMS
MANUFACTURED BY U.S. REPEATING AND SOLD OUTSIDE
THE USA AND CANADA.

CONSISTENT WITH OLIN'S COMMITMENT TO CONCEN-
TRATE ITS RESOURCES ON BUSINESSES IN WHICH IT EN-
JOYS A LEADERSHIP ROLE, OUR NEW WINCHESTER GROUP
IS WELL POSITIONED AS A STRONG AND SUCCESSFUL
COMPETITOR IN THE AMMUNITION BUSINESS. . . .

THROUGHOUT THE NEGOTIATIONS FOR THE SALE OF ITS
U.S. REPEATING ARMS OPERATIONS IT HAS BEEN OLIN'S
OBJECTIVE TO SELL THEM AS AN ONGOING BUSINESS ON A
BASIS WHICH PRESERVES AND MAINTAINS WINCHESTER'S
TRADITIONAL QUALITY AND SERVICE STANDARDS.

WE BELIEVE THAT OBJECTIVE HAS BEEN ACHIEVED, AND
WE WISH U.S. REPEATING ARMS COMPANY THE VERY BEST
OF LUCK IN THE FUTURE.

The two key executives of U.S. Repeating Arms
were C. Hugh Fletcher, president, and Richard M.
Pelton, executive vice president; both had been at
Winchester under Olin and were instrumental in
putting together the purchase package.

The new firm got off to a running start with the
John Wayne Commemorative Model 94 carbine.
Over 51,000 guns were made, and a tremendous
amount of positive publicity was garnered, as well
as handsome profits. The sale of the Winchester
gun-making facility in New Haven was a particularly disappointing event to John M. Olin, who
was then eighty-nine years old. He had been an
owner of Winchester for over fifty years, the gun

Two matched pairs of exceptional Model 70s. *From the left*,
serial numbers G11 and G10 of the new Custom Classic, with
claw controlled-round feeding; .338 Magnum caliber. The pair
at *right* was made to celebrate the Model 70's fiftieth anniversary
in 1986. Serial numbers 50ANV056 and 50ANV057, engraved
actions, floorplates, triggerguards, and barrels, with select walnut Fancy Grade stocks.

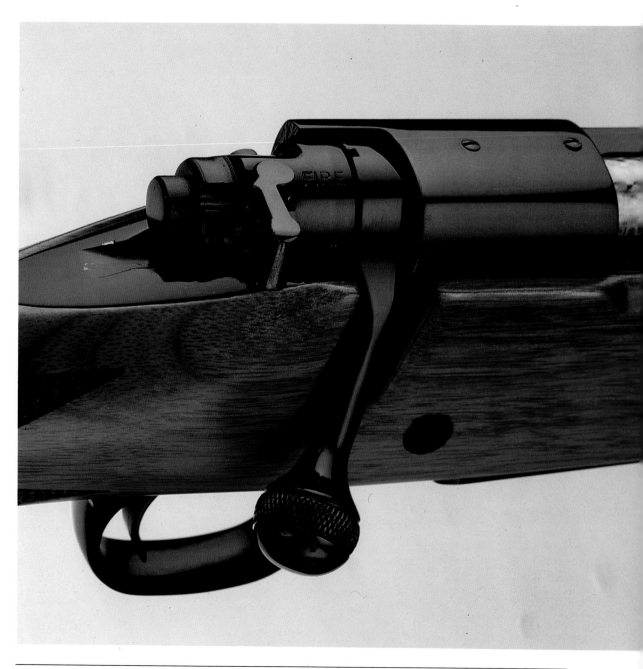

The Model 70's three-position safety, at center position, allowing for locking of trigger but working of bolt.

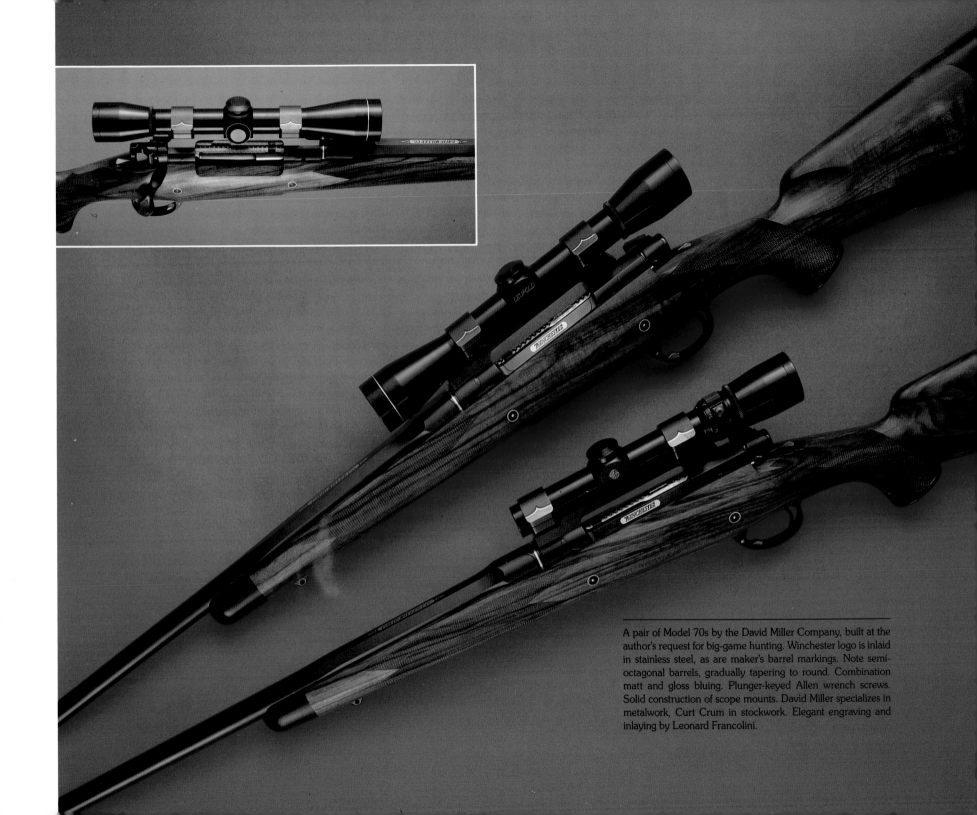

A pair of Model 70s by the David Miller Company, built at the author's request for big-game hunting. Winchester logo is inlaid in stainless steel, as are maker's barrel markings. Note semi-octagonal barrels, gradually tapering to round. Combination matt and gloss bluing. Plunger-keyed Allen wrench screws. Solid construction of scope mounts. David Miller specializes in metalwork, Curt Crum in stockwork. Elegant engraving and inlaying by Leonard Francolini.

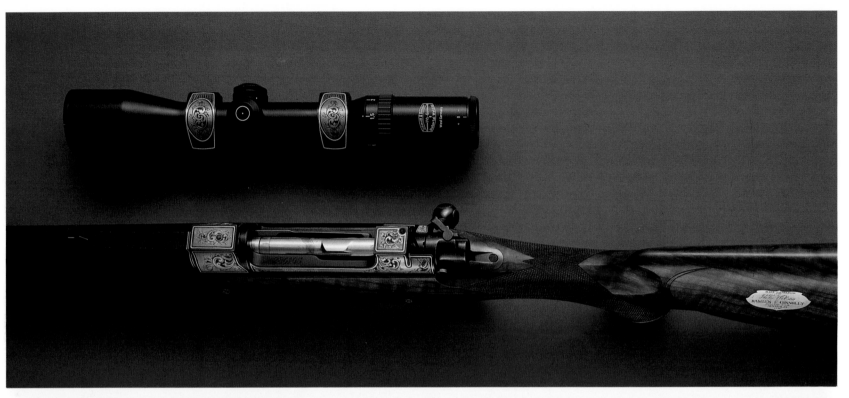

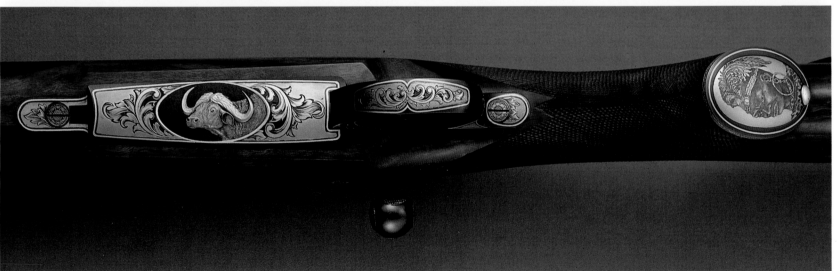

Built for the author by Australian gunmaker-engraver Damien Connolly, Model 70 serial 286105 boasts a number of unusual details. When the quick-detachable scope is removed, engraved and inlaid plates cover the mount apertures; tiny cross-hatched points, when pressed with pointed instrument (or .375 H&H cartridge tip), allow plates to be removed and scope reattached. A hidden hinged pistol-grip cap (engraved with Masai warrior portrait) pivots forward and out, revealing a cavity which is slotted to hold the engraved scope-mount plates. Engraved and sculpted Cape buffalo has striking three-dimensional quality. Proof of the artistry of top contemporary gunmakers.

business being to him and his brother Spencer as much an avocation as it was a vocation. The Winchester business cycle which John Olin oversaw had its glowing achievements, just as the previous seventy-plus years had under O. F. Winchester and the Bennetts. Former Winchester public relations director Jim Rikhoff summed up John Olin's influence on the company in a tribute written in 1982.

> If there hadn't been a John Olin, there wouldn't have been Super-X ammunition, there probably wouldn't have been the Model 21 shotgun, and almost assuredly Winchester wouldn't have been saved in 1931 or have been sustained to survive—we fervently hope—in its latest incarnation as the U.S. Repeating Arms Company.

John Olin was also a firearms collector, and some of his pieces were sold c. 1989–90 to raise funds for the Winchester Museum complex in Cody, Wyoming. Among these were a Henry and Model 1873 rifle, deluxe lever-actions of various models, a Model 21 with JMO gold-inlaid initials, and a custom Springfield sporter with Mannlicher-style stock (which was acquired by the author for his own collection). One of John Olin's finest guns, a deluxe Model 21 engraved by R. J. Kornbrath, was passed down in the family to his great-grandson, himself a dedicated shooter and another generation of Olin "gun men."

Big Bore .375 Winchester carbine, early styling with Monte Carlo stock and sling swivels, c. 1983.

Variants of the Model 94. *From the top*, the Big Bore .375 Winchester, with angle eject, hammer extension, and Monte Carlo stock profile. *Next*, .45 Long Colt Trapper's Model, with case-hardened frame and saddle ring. Another Trapper's Model specially made for the Winchester Arms Collectors Association, with select walnut stocks, long forend, and spade-style checkering. Wrangler, in .38-55 caliber, with large cocking lever inspired by the John Wayne commemorative. *Bottom*, the WinTuff laminated stock, with brown finish; also introduced in WinCam, both c. 1987–88.

WINCHESTER
Made in U.S.A. • Winchester trademarks licensed from Olin Corporation.
Model 94™ XTR® Angle Eject™
Lever Action Centerfire Carbine
G9475AE

FORGED
STEEL
RECEIVER

WINCHESTER
Made in U.S.A. • Winchester trademarks licensed from Olin Corporation.
MODEL 94™ Wrangler II
Lever Action Centerfire Carbine
G9438WRE
WARNING: Do Not Remove This Tag Prior to Sale.

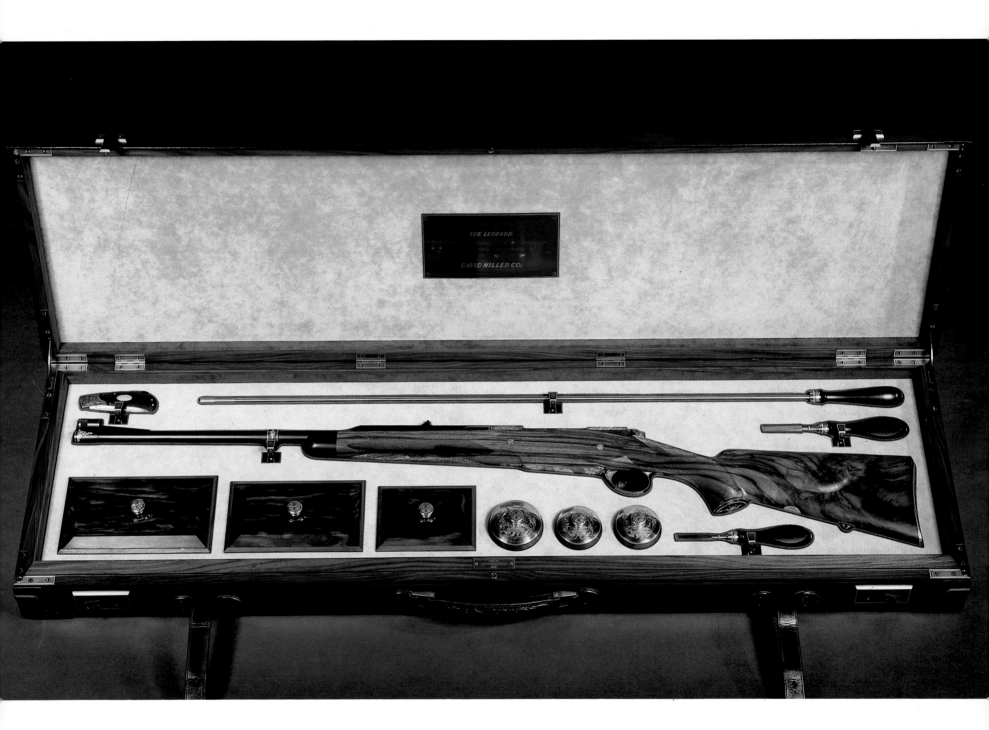

THE LEOPARD

DAVID MILLER CO.

316

Holder of the record auction price for a modern rifle ($201,000, 1986), "The Leopard" by David Miller Company was one of a series made to celebrate Africa's "big five," the rhinoceros, elephant, Cape buffalo, leopard, and lion. Each rifle was sold at auction by Safari Club International at its annual convention. Last of the series, "The Leopard," .338 Magnum caliber, serial number G1, has set the standard of modern gunmaking for any craftsman. Action was supplied by the U.S. Repeating Arms Company and was the first with the new claw controlled-round feeding.

Cased Model 70 Custom Classic rifle, .458 Winchester Magnum caliber, serial number SCI 1990, donated by U.S.R.A. Co. for the Safari Club International annual auction, which raises funds for wildlife conservation. Built by the Custom Shop.

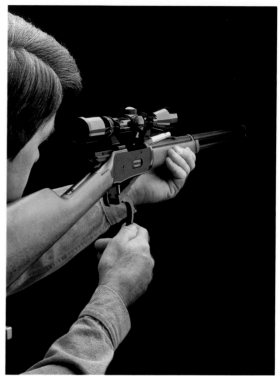

The Angle Eject feature was introduced with the Big Bore 94 in 1983, and on other 94s in 1984. It allows for scope mounting and for firing without empties obscuring the line of sight.

The 9422 was introduced in 1972, and over 600,000 were made by 1991. *From the top*, custom rifle bears gold inlays by factory engraver Nick Kusmit. Classic variation, in .22 Long Rifle, features pistol-grip stock and long barrel; discontinued c. 1988. The WinCam, new in 1987; specimen of lamination beneath butt. At *bottom*, serial number 1, a presentation to Bill Kelly on his retirement in 1971.

Show gun from the Custom Shop, engraved by Robert Burt and featured in the 1990 Custom Shop catalogue.

318

MODEL 9422 XTR CLASSIC
Lever Action Rimfire Rifle
G9422CKTR
WARNING: Do Not Remove This Tag Prior to Sale.
WINCHESTER
Made in U.S.A. • Winchester trademarks licensed from Olin Corporation

MODEL 9422 WINCAM
Lever Action Rimfire Rifle
G9422MCAM
WINCHESTER
Made in U.S.A. • Winchester trademarks licensed from Olin Corp.
Limited Two Year Warranty
SEE RETAILER FOR DETAILS

WINCHESTER.
22 LONG RIFLE CARTRIDGES
HIGH VELOCITY

WINCHESTER GROUP, OLIN CORPORATION
East Alton, Illinois

Like O. F. Winchester's death in 1880 and T. G. Bennett's in 1930, John Olin's passing in 1982 truly marked the end of an era. Although the political atmosphere for firearms has undergone considerable change, the enthusiasm for Winchesters has not faded. The brand has retained its magic, and although the U.S. Repeating Arms Company has had some rough periods—including a change of ownership in 1987, in which a group headed by Peter Alcock assumed control—the marque retains its unique status as an American legend.*

Because of the preponderance of nonprofit, nontaxable organizations in New Haven, the city's tax base is relatively thin. As one of New Haven's largest employers, Winchester–U.S. Repeating Arms has now commanded the interest of politicians for a healthy future. The city is also supportive because of the heavy minority-employment base at the factory.

The modern gun market is marked by heavy competition (both domestic and foreign), the complexities of product liability suits, and increasing insurance and manufacturing costs. However, certain companies are thriving in this atmosphere, among them Sturm, Ruger, and Marlin. Peter Alcock's plans** for the future of U.S. Repeating Arms were stated in his answer to the question "What do you foresee in the next several years?"

> Although no longer called by its original name, the U.S. Repeating Arms Company is the only successor to Oliver Winchester's original company. In fact, most business activities are located on the exact same premises as the original company. U.S. Repeating Arms Company (or USRAC as it is sometimes known) is the only company in the world that manufactures Winchester firearms, which are now made only in the United States.
>
> U.S. Repeating Arms Company as a corporate en-

tity was begun in 1981 when several employees of Olin's Winchester Corporation purchased the Winchester gun-making division. After some tumultuous times in the 1980s, it was purchased by me and other investors in late 1987. We have completed the first phase of a product upgrade program and a manufacturing turnaround.

> As we enter the 1990s, the company is well positioned to expand its market share of sporting rifles and shotguns. Since the turn of the century, no other gun maker has been so innovative in producing guns for hunters and sportsmen. We intend to continue this tradition and expand or change it as the needs of the market change. Our future is tied directly to the future of hunting in America. We believe with the abundant game and increased interest and support of wildlife management, we have a very bright future indeed.

On November 21, 1990, Fabrique Nationale, owners of Browning, and for the previous three years owners of 44 percent of U.S.R.A., made agreements to purchase the shares of Peter Alcock and the other investors. FN thereby became sole owner of U.S.R.A.

Jack Mattan, the new CEO and president, issued a statement on December 10:

> Under FN's auspices we have resumed production of our entire 1991 line of Winchester Shotguns and Rifles [there had been a hiatus while negotiations took place for the takeover by FN]. The "Gun that Won the West" and the "Rifleman's Rifle" are once again rolling off our production lines. In fact, worldwide distribution of our 1991 line has already begun.
>
> At the NASGW (National Association of Sporting Goods Wholesalers) Show this past November, U.S.R.A. received one of eight awards given for total overall performance by a manufacturer during the 1990 sales year. Out of the eight winners we were the only gun company to get one of these awards. It is a testimony of U.S.R.A.'s continuous effort of improving service and quality. In fact, continuing the program of improvements in customer service and product quality are our primary objectives. Our long-term goal is to return Winchester guns to their rightful place of prominence in the worldwide marketplace.

Carl Hummel of Winchester-U.S.R.A. fitting writer Jim Carmichel for a Model 21. Note special "try gun," with adjustable stock, allowing for taking precise measurements to fit individual shooters. Try guns have shooting capability, allowing for field testing and further adjustment prior to doing stockwork.

From the top, an early production model of the 1300 pump, introduced by Winchester-Olin in 1978 and continued by U.S.R.A. The 1300 XTR deer gun, a pump in 12-gauge; two slug shells near forend. The Model 1300 National Wild Turkey Federation gun with WinTuff stocks, and Winchokes (early-style wrench at *right*, with wooden handle and exchange choke). *Bottom* gun, for wild turkey hunting, is fitted with WinCam stocks. All guns in 12-gauge.

---

*At the same time the Winchester Division of Olin continues to record banner years (see Chapter IX).

**August 1990

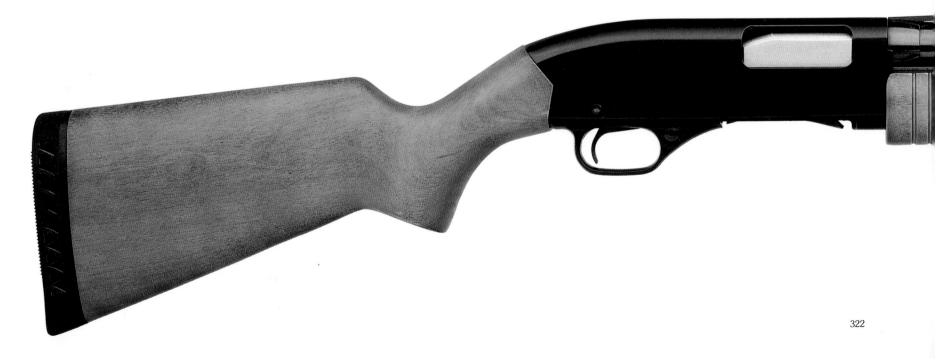

Model 1300 Featherweight, with beavertail-style forend and 20-gauge chambering. Also available in 12-gauge, this styling dates from 1988.

Winchester Ranger Youth slide-action shotgun, first introduced in the 1983 catalogue. Buttstock is replaceable as child grows. A plug is available for training purposes, restricting firing at first to one round; it is segmented to allow increasing tubular magazine capacity. Ladies/Youth buttstocks are not only shorter, but are contoured to accommodate smaller hands. The forend is also farther rearward, reducing the required reach for operating the action.

For wild turkey shooting, Ladies/Youth variation of the Model 1300 with colorful stocks of WinCam, in 20-gauge, 3" Magnum. Floating ventilated rib allows maintaining proper point of impact no matter how hot the barrels become.

The rifled-barrel Model 1300 WinTuff Slug Hunter, new for 1990, in 12-gauge with 22-inch barrel and rifle sights. Matte-finish receiver is drilled and tapped for scope mounting.

Also new for 1990, the Model 1400 Slug Hunter automatic, smoothbore, with rifled Sabot and improved cylinder choke tubes. Sold with scope rings, but scope not included.

Set of Model 21s of mid-1980s manufacture, all three of Custom Grade. *From bottom up*, 12-gauge serial number W32851. Note Monte Carlo stock and cheekpiece. Number W24150, a 16-gauge, shows rich stock grain, especially on cheekpiece. Number W33123, a 20-gauge, has customary inscription for client engraved on rib.

One of the earliest Model 21s (serial number 9, at *bottom*), with one of the most recent made (serial W32532), the latter a Grand American made for the president of U.S.R.A. Co., Peter Alcock. Mechanical differences are noticeable in triggers and frame configurations. Quality has been in evidence with the Model 21s throughout production.

Following a Sporting Clays competition at Migdale Estate, Millbrook, New York, owners Gary and Denise Herman (*center and left*) discuss future competitions with U.S. Sporting Clays Association Chairman and President Robert Davis, of Houston, Texas. Sporting Clays is the fastest-growing shooting sport in America today. Competitors often use expensive guns (like the Model 21s shown here), and the shoots are as classy as driven-bird shooting in England and Scotland.

The Grand Royal, the most deluxe grade of Model 21 and one of the rarest of all Winchesters. Serial number W9190, shown here, was made for presentation to John M. Olin and has his portrait and signature on the left side of frame. A total of four additional Grand Royals were made later (serial numbers W33103, W33104, W33105, and W33121). The concept dates back to c. 1979–80. The John Olin gun is by master engraver-inlayer A. A. White, who also designed the embellishments, based on suggestions of patron Kevin Kurtz and Kurtz Hardware Company, Des Moines. Casing by Marvin Huey.

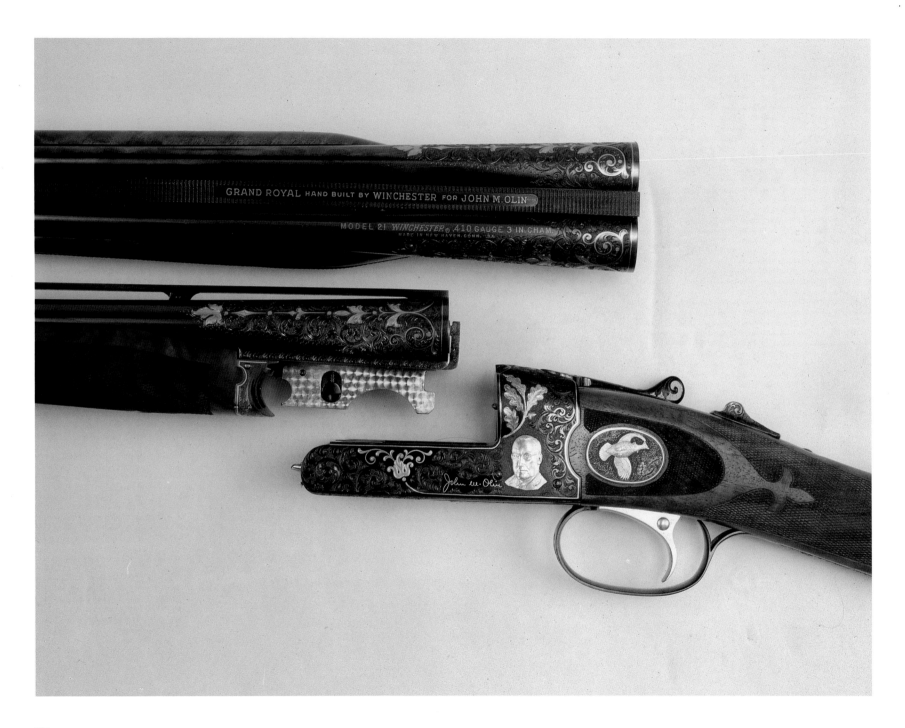

GRAND ROYAL HAND BUILT BY WINCHESTER FOR JOHN M.OLIN

MODEL 21 WINCHESTER® 410 GAUGE 3 IN.CHAM.
MADE IN NEW HAVEN,CONN.U.S.A.

John M. Olin

331

ROLLER SKATES

Chapter XII
Collecting
the Winchester Heritage

The collector of firearms relishes artistry, crafts-manship, history, mechanics, and also romance. Winchesters are awash in such qualities, and are rivaled only by Colts as having the most distin-guished marque in American arms collecting. To-gether they are the "blue chips," and it is not unusual for a collector to be in active and simul-taneous pursuit of guns by both makers.

Winchester collecting is by no means restricted to the United States. Enthusiasts can be found all

over the globe, and not only have Winchesters been sold and shipped worldwide since the first models, but the trade in collectors' guns continues to be international in scope. One of the finest Win-chester collections ever seen by the author was in Australia. Even modern-made arms have an inter-national appeal, as some of the commemorative issues were made for sale in Europe and Canada and were not even advertised in the United States.

Even most collectors of American arms are un-aware that the first Winchester collector was Oliver Winchester himself. In a fascinating letter of Feb-ruary 10, 1871, he wrote to B. S. Lawrence of Hartford, "The 'Jennings' gun came to hand this morning and it is a connecting link in the history of our gun. I should like to keep it in my collection." Typical of collectors, Winchester acquired the piece by trading, in this case, "one of our best sporting guns for it," which was undoubtedly a Model 1866 rifle. He even added that "if you have a few of the balls used in that gun I should be pleased to have them." The lineal descendant of Winchester's col-lection is now displayed at the Cody Firearms Mu-

seum, Cody, Wyoming, much expanded from the modest collection begun by the firm's chief stock-holder and president.

A number of celebrities are Winchester collec-tors, among them Michael and Patrick Wayne (their father, "the Duke," was also a devotée); members of the du Pont, Ford, Olin, and Donnelley families; entertainers Buddy Hackett, Johnny Cash, and Hank Williams, Jr.; publisher Robert E. Petersen; and Bob Lee, founder and president of Hunting World, Inc.

It is impossible to estimate accurately the num-ber of collectors concentrating on Winchesters, but, for commemoratives alone, over 103,000 Model 66 Centennials were sold, and over 112,000 Buf-falo Bills. Based on the estimate of over 2,400,000 collectors in the United States alone, there is plenty of competition for guns. With Winchester and Colt as the top two makes, the numbers are substantial. Some collectors, of course, are more casual about their hobby than others. The number of quite se-rious Winchester devotees—those who are likely to spend at least $10,000 in a single year—is prob-

The Winchester collecting spectrum, from predecessor arms to the contemporary. *Upper left*, the Volcanic, an iron-framed Smith & Wesson, with Jennings self-contained cartridge. The roller skates are a carryover from post–World War I production expansion, which was continued into midcentury by Olin and then Olin-Mathieson. Calendar, with A. B. Frost game scene, promoted W.R.A. Co. arms and ammunition. The Model 1873 musket, with bayonet, represents one of the all-time-great lever-action Winchesters and is in the crisp condition sought by many collectors. The Model 42 is one of the most attractive of twen-tieth-century shotguns. The Oliver F. Winchester rifle is just one of a series of commemorative salutes to events, places, people, and other worthy themes.

Office of the Winchester Repeating Arms Company
New Haven, Conn. February 10th 1871

B. L. Lawrence, Esq
Hartford, Conn.

Dear Sir

The "Jennings' gun came to hand this morning and it is a connecting link in the history of our gun. I should like to keep it in my collection and for this reason will accept your proposition, and give you one of our best sporting guns for it. Will leave the selection with you when you are here again or I will send it to you. If you have a few of the balls used in that gun I should be pleased to have them

Yours truly
O. F. Winchester
President Winchester Rep. Arms Co.

Arms collecting is often a father-son adventure, instilling an appreciation of history, mechanics, art, craftsmanship, and adventure. Author and son Peter with a One of One Thousand and the Henry Brown presentation Model 1873 which was used by the Kansas marshal in a bank holdup.

This letter evidences Oliver F. Winchester's pursuit of a Jennings rifle for his burgeoning arms collection, which was the nucleus of the Winchester Arms Museum. In the mid-1970s, the museum's collection was transferred by the Olin Corporation to the Buffalo Bill Historical Center in Cody, Wyoming, to which it was formally presented in 1989.

Highlights from the John B. Solley III collection, photographed accompanying his widow, Fern. Mr. Solley, an heir to the Lilly pharmaceutical fortune, specialized in the finest nineteenth-century American firearms. Note the fabled "ivory-stocked Winchester" Model 1866, of Mexican President Porfirio Díaz, in *foreground*. The Solley Winchesters were a special favorite, and one of the strong suits in his extraordinary collection.

ably somewhere between 15,000 and 20,000. There is an extraordinary amount of collecting activity, with hundreds of gun shows held annually in the United States, several catalogues by various dealers, advertisements in such journals as *Shotgun News*, *Gun List*, *Man at Arms*, and *The American Rifleman*, and active organizations like the Winchester Club of America and the Winchester Collectors Association, in addition to private contracts among friends and acquaintances.

Sales figures certainly reach—in antique and modern Winchesters—more than $250 million annually, and the current record auction price for a modern American firearm is held by a Winchester Model 70—the superb "The Leopard," pictured on page 316. It was custom-built by the David Miller Company and was sold in 1986 for $201,000.

By any measure the Winchester field is big. Total production of collectible firearms (excluding machine guns, which are federally restricted and were often scrapped) is upward of 20 million, with the number of models in excess of 250. The range is so vast that only a few collectors can try to be complete. A couple from California are among such enthusiasts—their collection has over 5,000 objects, including firearms and memorabilia, in a grouping which rivals the Winchester Arms Museum!

Because of the high value of many examples and the sheer numbers of arms involved, most collectors specialize in specific types, models, and variations. Their choices are based on a combination of particular likes and available funds. Thus, a sportsman is more likely to pursue bird or other game guns, while the more academically oriented collector may concentrate on variations of the lever-actions, single-shot rifles, or even memorabilia. Cartridge boards, for example, have attracted a devoted following.

Often the well-heeled collector will seek embel-

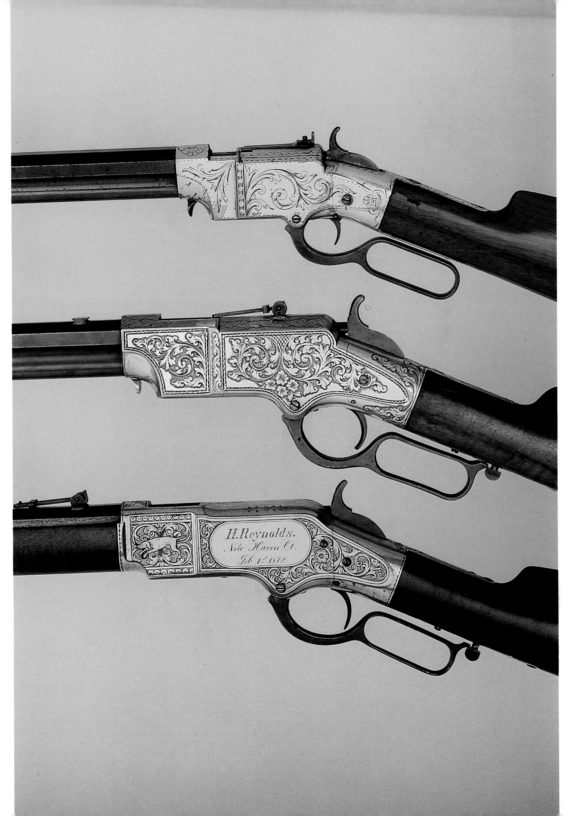

lished, historic, and fine-condition specimens. One on a limited budget may find many of the military arms and most twentieth-century models appealing. Yet many a wealthy collector will include less costly pieces, and the fellow on a budget always has the chance to make that "find" in an attic which he can acquire for far less than true value.

Whatever the quarry, a highly important tool in steeling one for the pursuit is a solid reference library. Later in this chapter the major books will be listed, and a detailed bibliography is at the end of this book. For the money, books are the best investment, and the first investment, any collector should make. These volumes also can be helpful in selecting a speciality in the vast and varied Winchester field.

Categories of Collecting

Because of the wide domain of Winchesters, no absolutes in collecting categories exist. But the major groupings are as follows: pre-Winchesters like the Volcanics and Henrys; major lever-actions of the 1866, 1873, 1876, 1886, 1892, 1894, and 1895; the single-shot rifles; various shotguns (especially Models 12, 42, and 21); militaries such as the Hotchkiss and Lee and U.S. Model 1917; the Model 70 and other bolt-action sporting arms; slide-action rifles like the 1890; the self-loading Models 1903– 1905–1907 et al.; commemoratives and limited editions; cartridges; calendars and other memorabilia; and—generally the *crème de la crème*— engraved firearms and historic firearms. Of course, in most of the above specialities, there is some overlap. This is especially true of engraving, which began in the 1850s and continues through to modern times. That area is especially appealing (and

Three collecting favorites. *From the top,* the Volcanic, the Henry, and the 1866. *Bottom* gun was presented to H. Reynolds, a parts contractor to the Winchester factory. Finishes of the brass frames are in silver and gold plating.

especially expensive), partly because craftsmen today are capable of creating masterpieces which rival or surpass the work of the nineteenth century.

And, of course, a collector can specialize within particular models. Part of the fun of collecting is making choices and, as one's knowledge and experience grows, changing or adapting courses of pursuit. In the author's own experience, even though he has owned One of One Thousands, several historic and engraved pieces, and every model from the Henry through the 1895 (and several beyond), his prized pieces at present are a Grand Royal Model 21 shotgun, two exquisite David Miller Company rifles, and a Damien Connolly rifle, the latter three built on Model 70 actions.

The Pioneer Lever-Actions

The Hunt Volitional Repeater is such a rarity that the only currently known specimen is in the Winchester Arms Museum. Jennings rifles are available, but seldom will they be found in anything better than medium condition. Volcanics are more likely to be found in good condition, but their brass frames, as well as those of the Henry, have tempted certain unscrupulous individuals to "spruce up" examples with engraving. Iron-framed guns are much harder to alter, because of problems of patina and finish.

A major reason why Volcanics in fine condition can be found is that these guns were not particularly practical. There was even remaining stock at Winchester after World War II, and employees are said to have had the opportunity to buy Volcanics

Historic triple presentation from B. Tyler Henry himself (see buttplate inscription). Rifle subsequently presented, with bottom of cartridge carrier block inscribed *Albert M. Root/From/ J. H. Conklin/Christmas 1875*. Finally, the frame was further inscribed, and dated 1877, as illustrated. Deluxe engraved design; gold-plated frame and buttplate; select walnut stock. Made without serial number, sling swivels, or rear sight aperture at barrel breech. Only known Henry presented by the inventor.

Bearing serial number 2681, this elaborate custom Model 1873 rifle was built for General William E. Strong, presentor of the similarly deluxe Model 1876 to General Philip H. Sheridan. Both rifles feature relief-engraved panel scenes, half magazines, and several other details. Both were engraved and signed by John Ulrich.

in their original pasteboard boxes at a price that today would cause a collector terminal apoplexy: some were apparently only 25¢!

Henry rifles—having been manufactured during the Civil War and therefore being in strong demand—are difficult to find in fine condition. Like the Volcanics, only more so, some examples have been engraved in recent years. Fortunately certain researchers, including the author, have extensive serial number listings which date to the 1960s (and some even earlier), recording whether or not an observed Henry was engraved. But caution should always be exercised in the pursuit of brass-framed Henrys purporting to be engraved and/or inscribed.

These early arms, all being made in relatively limited numbers, have survived reasonably well. There have been losses because of wartime scrap drives, fires, and other exigencies, but there is every likelihood that remaining in attics, cellars, and other hideaways are rare and choice examples of pioneer lever-actions.

Do not, however, be fooled by replica firearms, particularly the Henry and the 1866. These guns have been liberally copied since the 1970s, and are of excellent quality. Most have been made by master gunmakers in Gardone, Val Trompia, Italy. But on export they bear proof stampings and other required marks. Some have been altered and otherwise "improved," with the intent to deceive the unwary. A rule of thumb which always works: if in doubt, do without.

The 1866 Through the 1895

By far the area of Winchester collecting which commands the highest average prices and attracts the most high-powered collectors is the Winchester lever-actions, Models 1866, 1873, 1876, 1886, 1892, 1894, and 1895. The Henry can be included in this select category, but exquisite examples are few and far between. The collector has much more opportunity when the total production quantities range from the minimum of 63,871 of the 1876, and over 5 million (and still going strong) in the Model 1894. A basic breakdown for each model has been the carbine, rifle, and musket and the Fancy Grade rifle, plus an engraved example. In filming the *Winchester Firearms Legends* video, the author and director Thomas A. Thornber managed to locate a private collector who had a perfect set of all of the above, which were duly filmed, and selected examples were photographed for color illustration in *Winchester Engraving*. In this instance the collector was keen on condition, so each piece was especially exquisite.

For a price, it is possible to obtain specimens of nearly every variation in excellent condition. However, a mint example of a plain carbine of, say, the Model 1866 might run well into the lower five figures. And a One of One Hundred or One of One Thousand Model 1873 or 1876 in superior condition may go into six figures. Such pieces are of great rarity and are in high demand.

An idea of the high degree of interest in variations for the 1866 through the 1895 is evident in various editions of George Madis's *The Winchester Book*. Some 80 percent of that work, the most recent edition totaling 600-plus pages, concentrates on technical details of these major lever-actions.

The collector who does not demand excellence of condition will be able to assemble his Winchester collection much faster than the mint specialist. However, in all models one should be aware that nonfactory alterations, refinishing, and abused condition generally limits the appeal to most collectors, and therefore the value.

Major reasons for the particular demand for the 1866 through the 1895 are their availability, their popularity in the American West, their aesthetic qualities, and their having often appeared—particularly the 1873, 1892, and 1894—in Western films

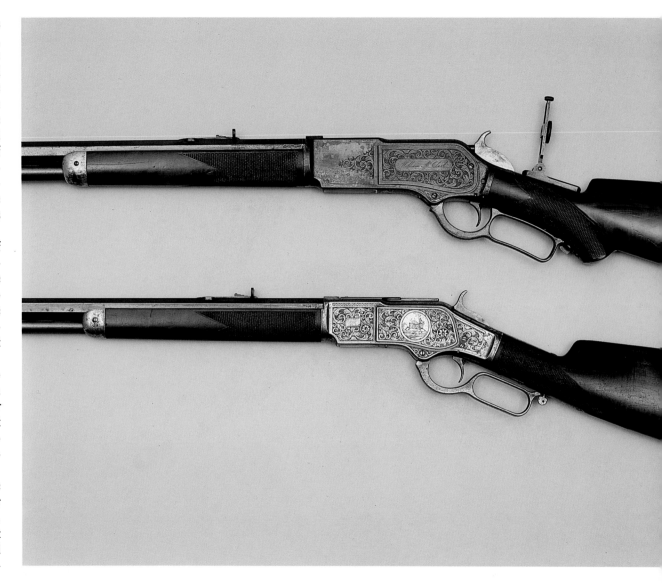

Among the finest One of One Thousand rifles made, the 1873 at *bottom* bears signature stamping J. ULRICH. Model 1876 (*top*) belonged to Senator William A. Clark, of Montana. Both are documented in the factory ledgers, including reference to rare "gold trim" for the Clark rifle. Serial numbers 27727 and 709 respectively. Tang sight on the Senator's rifle needs to be set on absolute vertical prior to shooting.

and on television. John Wayne's use of the large-levered Model 1892 carbine made that style so popular that the U.S. Repeating Arms Company reintroduced the styling for the John Wayne commemorative and for a while made variations of the 94 carbine with the same style of lever.

The Browning Connection

Overlapping with the 1866 through 1895 lever-actions, the "Browning connection" Winchesters are a collecting speciality which pays tribute to the quiet Mormon genius John M. Browning.

An ideal text for the collector to follow in pursuit of these arms is Richard Rattenbury's *The Browning Connection*, published in 1982, which documents an exhibition at the Winchester Museum of the "Models 1885, 1886, 1887, 1890, 1892, 1893, 1894, 1895, 1897 and 1900 . . . all initially conceived and designed by John Moses Browning." The prototype and production guns pictured in the book reveal the extraordinary talent of Browning, and the vision of Winchester in capitalizing on the opportunity to manufacture these mechanical marvels.

The lever-action shotguns, the Models 1887 and 1901, lack the aesthetic appeal of most of the other Browning-designed Winchester production models. However, in craftsmanship they are superb, and are thus quite popular with some collectors. The author remembers serial number 1 of the 1887 Model, which a collector friend was using as part of a lamp stand! But he also had an entire case of mint-condition Model 1895 carbines, and such

Winchester lever-actions from the Henry through the 1895, in one of the most amazing firearms photographs ever. For rarity, quality, embellishment, and condition it would be impossible for a collector or museum to equal this splendid array. Among the historical figures whose guns are represented are Gideon Welles, General Philip Sheridan, the Emperor of Japan and (at *right*) Zane Grey. From the legendary collection of A. I. McCroskie.

exquisite rifles as the Gideon Welles Henry and a complete set of One of One Hundred and One of One Thousand 1873s and 1876s.

With the modern involvement of the Browning Arms Company and U.S. Repeating Arms,* a Browning-connection collection is an ever more appealing category for the collector. On the whole, the cost of such a collection—foregoing patent prototypes, which are supremely rare—does not compare with the cost of a collection of pre-Winchester lever-actions, or the 1866–1895 lever-action group. And one would be less likely to seek engraved specimens, since the mechanical features are primary. The limited editions by Browning of the Models 1895, 1886, 71, 65, and 53 have been handsome tributes to the originals, and are a modern "Browning connection."

Winchester Highly Finished Arms
This particular speciality takes its name from the celebrated Winchester catalogue of 1897, a volume which can serve as the collector's primer for the hunt. Even in worn condition, these guns are not inexpensive, and to acquire a complete set which actually matches the illustrations in the catalogue has—to the author's knowledge—yet to be done.

Since customers used the 1897 publications as a wish book, they often seemed to pick a game scene from one gun, the scroll from another, and the

---

*Browning had a partial investment in the U.S. Repeating Arms Company, and as of December 1990 became sole owner of the firm.

Billed as "Browning commemorates the great levers of yesteryear," these limited editions of (from *left*) the Models 95, 1886, 71, 65, and 53 were issued beginning in 1984 and appeared in the sequence as pictured. Craftsmanship is on a par with that of the Winchester-built originals.

Deluxe 1894s and 1886s, two of several W.R.A. Co. models whose mechanical features came to the firm from the creative genius of John M. Browning.

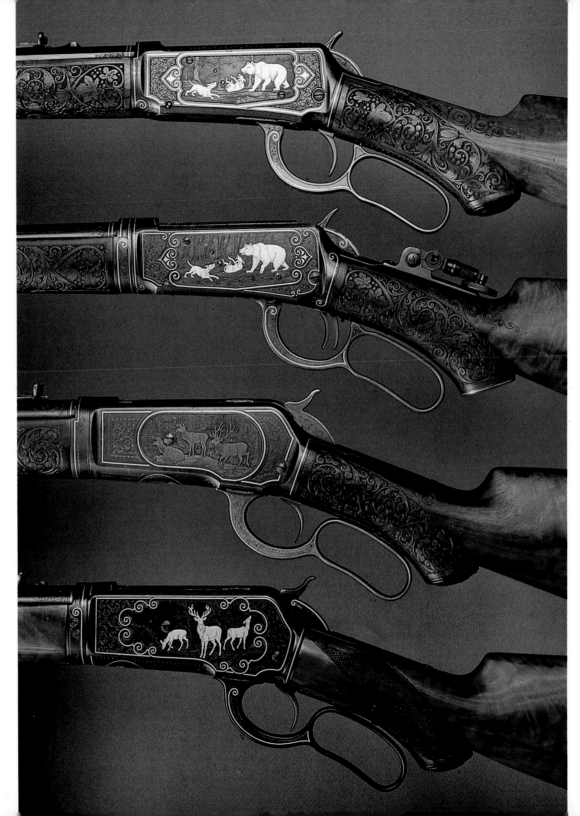

Classics of Winchester engraving. *From the top*, the Gustave Young Model 1866 showpiece. William E. Strong's Model 1876 presentation to his friend General Philip H. Sheridan. A Model 1886 takedown nearly identical to the Style A carving and Style 10 engraving and inlaying shown in "Highly Finished Arms." And the spectacular Model 1892 believed made for the Emperor of Japan. The 1876, 1886, and 1892 are by John Ulrich, and so signed.

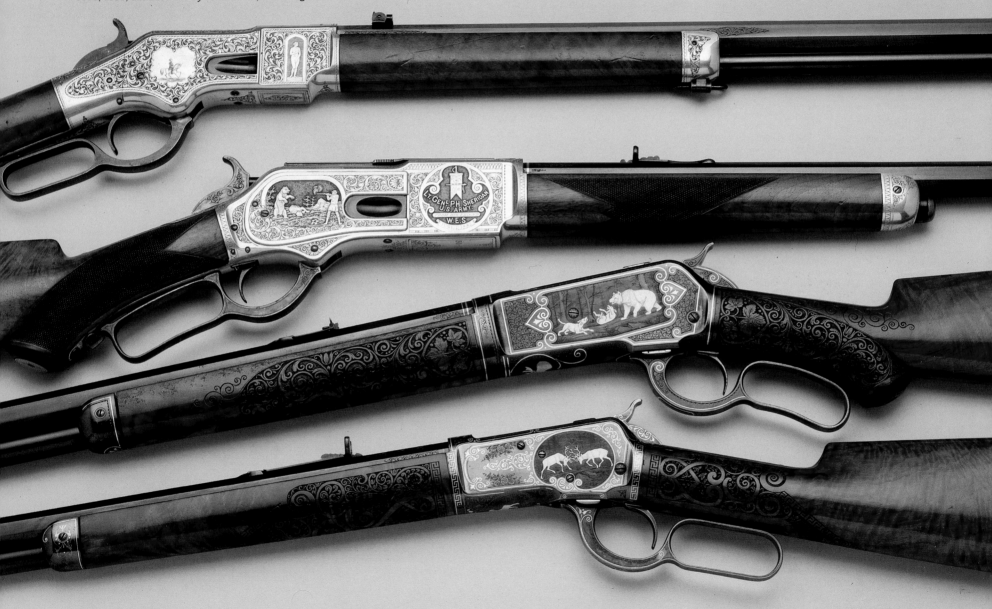

stock pattern from still another. As evidenced in the present volume, and in the author's *Winchester Engraving*, occasionally a gun will precisely match the catalogue illustration of a particular gun. If it predates 1897, that gun was very possibly used by Winchester as the source for that catalogue illustration.

With the high demand—and corresponding prices—for engraved guns, "Highly Finished Arms" presents a challenge to even the wealthiest collectors. They also must exercise caution to be sure the specimens are as authentic as they are claimed to be. It is sometimes difficult to pause for calm and deliberate thought when one discovers, in the midst of the hustle and bustle of a gun show, what appears to be an important gun. The excitement of discovery may color one's judgment. On these superguns, one must be especially sure of not only the gun itself, but its pedigree.

For the author, the most exciting of all Winchesters have been these works of art. A large number of deluxe guns appear in *Winchester: An American Legend* because of their supreme beauty and craftsmanship. They are also featured because the same level of craftsmanship was required to manufacture the standard rifle, carbine, or musket. What made the highly finished arm was the engraving, the select-wood stock, the extra polish for best finish, and any other extras. The basic gun still came off—generally speaking—the same production line.

Single-Shots

Although a Winchester single-shot buff will usually concentrate only on the rifles made by Winchester, he could also be interested in Browning production, and often a general single-shot rifle collector seeks a variety of makers, and Winchester is but one (although an important one) of these. Single-shots are usually moderately priced and offer a wide selection of calibers and technical features.

The spread of calibers, from .22 rimfire to large Express cartridges, was substantial. Further, the selection of options, from elaborate buttplates and stock stylings to a myriad of sights, various finishes, and more, provides an almost endless array of variations.

These arms do not have the glamour of the lever-actions, since they were slow-firing and not preferred as saddle guns or for fighting outlaws and Indians. But their level of craftsmanship, mechanics, aesthetics, accuracy, and impressive target competition history have garnered for them a dedicated following. There is even a national organization of collectors: the American Single Shot Rifle Association.

Rarely will engraved specimens be found, but one is more likely to be able to locate guns in good condition. Owners were more likely to look after their single-shots, using them only in fair weather and not stuffing them into leather scabbards or treating them like a utility, as was all too common with such service-type guns as most lever- and bolt-actions. The single-shots are still quite shootable, and bore condition is therefore of importance to the collector.

A precaution for the collector: target shooters are often inveterate tinkerers. Therefore, care should be taken in ensuring that nonfactory alterations or improvements have not been done on a potential acquisition.

The 22s: Slide, Bolt, and Self-Loading

Since several models of Winchester slide and semiautomatic rifles remain in use to this day, and most were used for plinking and small-game shooting, the majority of surviving specimens are in much-less-than mint condition. The degree of variation is also less than would be found in the more expensive rifles, particularly in comparison with the larger-caliber lever-actions and single-shots.

The author remembers firing, as a boy, a pump

and semiautomatic Winchester, often a popular gallery rifle, at state fairs in Minnesota—before the days of the electronic "rifles" firing light beams that are used at amusement parks today.

A special prize would be a gallery rifle used by the legendary Ad Topperwein, or his wife, Plinky—both deadly accurate with the highly reliable .22 pump or semiautomatic Winchester.

The bolt-action .22 also has a long history, and many remain in use today.

Because of the generally reasonable price, the collector has an edge on trying to put together a group of all the .22s, no matter what the mechanism. And since relatively little has been published on Winchester .22 rifles, the studious collector can enjoy ferreting out information piece by piece.

Self-Loading Rifles

Not in the same league of collector demand as the major lever-actions, the self-loaders, like the Model 1905 and 1907, nevertheless have the appeal as pioneering semiautomatic, high-powered rifles in America. Their use by the Texas Rangers and on the Texas-Mexican border adds a bit of glamour to them. A few were even elegantly engraved, inlaid with gold, and fitted with carved select-walnut stocks. To function properly these rifles required careful machining and fitting, and, from a quality standpoint, they demonstrate Winchester's skills as a precision gunmaker. Incidentally, these rifles are much heavier than they look. These are not models a collector would necessary specialize in, but would fit in with semiautomatics like the Model 1903 and Model 63, in .22 caliber. Of course, they are also for the general collector of Winchesters who pursues a variety of models.

A Note on Post-1898 Firearms

To some collectors, federal, state, and local laws on firearms can be discouraging. However, since arms collectors are as solid a group of citizens as the

Illustration from page 4 of "Highly Finished Arms," matching 1886 number 111070, gold- and platinum-inlaid, and made by Winchester in 1897.

From the "Highly Finished Arms" catalogue of 1897, features of this Model 1886 are nearly identical to engraving Style No. 1 and carving Style A, shown on pages 4 and 5 of that rare and beautiful piece of Winchester literature.

United States can boast, the main concern is simply to avoid inadvertently breaking any laws. A book of federal regulations is published annually by the Bureau of Alcohol, Tobacco and Firearms and is free for the asking. A general guideline is that the Federal Firearms Act of 1968 requires interstate shipments of post-1898 firearms to be between holders of federal firearms licenses. A special license exists for collectors, but most of the estimated 100,000 licenses are held by dealers. Records need to be kept of all relevant shipments, which may be subject to examination by a BATF agent.

Most collectors do not apply for a license, finding it more convenient to have a nearby licensed dealer handle shipments. Forms that may need to be filled out are standard on the federal level, but state and local forms vary considerably. Any local arms dealer can supply details. Whatever may be required, it is the author's opinion that the enjoyment of arms collecting is well worth any amount of paperwork.

Military Winchesters

The amazing production of military arms by Winchester is a theme touched on in various parts of this book. Chapter VI reveals the wide variety, and the often considerable quantity, of these arms. For a patriotic American collector or a foreign enthusiast, these guns, whether the early Hotchkiss and Lee or the later U.S. Model of 1917, or even the Garand and M1 carbine, all pay tribute to both Winchester's extraordinary manufacturing skills and to the soldiers who relied on these arms in warfare. Most of these military rifles, carbines, and rifled muskets will not tax the collector's checkbook. Further, there are so many differing types,

Model 1903 self-loading rifle, the most deluxe factory-embellished example known, the frame inlaid and engraved with a nostalgic outdoor scene, boys with their faithful puppy at a log cabin in the cabin woods.

with so many countries of use and proof or issue stampings, that the research attendant to this speciality can be extensive.

Since government contracts could be highly lucrative and mass production was a key element of success to any gunmaker, the military issues by

Choice Model 1907 self-loading rifle, serial number 16417, its engraver identified by old factory photographs, bearing notations: "Stokes Design F Lab $80.00 Right MO7." Built as a sample piece and retained by the factory, it eventually became part of the museum collection.

Single-shots, a collecting specialty unto themselves. *From the top*, muzzle of a high-wall with No. 3 octagonal barrel, with wind gauge and spirit level front sight. Other barrel of lighter weight and with less complex wind gauge sight. Rifle with Lyman peep tang sight has 36-inch barrel and special-order double-set trigger and spurred triggerguard. *Center* rifle in .22 Long Rifle, with No. 1 half-octagonal barrel and fancy stocks. Different-style set trigger on *center* and *lower* rifles; *bottom*, high-wall with No. 5 barrel (heaviest made), Schuetzen styling including palm rest and midrange vernier peep sight. From the extensive and comprehensive collection of Peter and Patty Murray.

Winchester were extremely important products. In wartime they overshadowed commercial arms, often virtually bringing their production to a standstill.

Collectors of military arms by Winchester are sometimes themselves veterans and may have begun their collecting while still in uniform. The author's service at Fort Dix, New Jersey, begun on enlistment in 1963, was at a time when the Winchester M-14 had not been fully succeeded by the Colt M-16. Most of the members of his unit—city boys from New York—had never fired a rifle, but several of these young men proved to be excellent shots and took to their Winchesters instinctively. The basic training time spent at the rifle range was a subtle introduction to the world of shooting, and—ultimately for some—the appeal of arms as collectors' items.

The Bolt-Action Game Rifle

Although Winchester had been scooped by such pioneer medium- and big-game rifle makers as

Mauser, when the Model 70 appeared the firm was quickly able to make up for its lost market share. Despite its relative youth (born 1936), the Model 70 now has a major percentage of the bolt-action sport/hunting market. By virtue of famous owners, or by embellishment, special serial numbers, or other special features, Model 70s have also come into their own as collectors' items.

A Model 70 reference book with exhaustive information is Roger Rule's *The Rifleman's Rifle*, a tome every Model 70 collector must have.

Having traveled and hunted in several African countries, as well as Alaska, Australia, India, Europe, and the continental United States, the author has seen more Model 70s in use than any other make of sporting rifle. When professional hunters choose a Model 70, generally using the rifle for years and years and depending on its performance for their lives and livelihood, that is not only testimony to a classic rifle, but part of the history of that specific arm.

Author and photographer Peter Beard, whose

book *The End of the Game* is an African classic, has fired thousands of rounds with his trusty .375 H&H Model 70. The author attempted to trade a brand-new, engraved rifle so that Beard's gun could join the RLW arms collection. But Beard was firmly attached to his .375.

The adventures Model 70s like Beard's can tell give these rifles an aura like the prized arms of the great nineteenth- and early-twentieth-century explorers and sportsmen. Most of the author's professional hunters in Africa and Alaska relied on their Model 70s, usually in .458 Winchester Magnum caliber. These were standard with open sights, fitted with simple slings, showing considerable use, but—with luck—seldom fired when on safari with clients. The collector instinct in the author has always led to a try at either buying or trading for the professional hunter's Model 70. But invariably the hunter is too attached to the rifle to sell it.

In such instances, condition is unimportant—except for sharp rifling and deadly accuracy. The more marred and scarred, the more stories the rifle can tell.

Shotguns

With a total of over 7 million shotguns—double- and single-barrel, pump, and semiautomatic—made since the English-built Model 1879, there is much to amuse the Winchester shotgun enthusiast. At the top of the line the aficionado will generally concentrate on the Model 21, the Model 12, and the Model 42. With luck he will have found some of the exquisite pieces made for presentation, perhaps

---

Papoqsi Coyetero, Apache guide and scout for the U.S. Army, photographed by A. F. Randall, in the Arizona Territory. Not being restricted by military dicta for armaments, scouts were often better armed than the troops. Their Indian adversaries also equipped themselves with Winchester repeaters, by any means possible. The rifle is an 1873, which attained substantial export military sales but was never adopted by U.S. Ordnance.

something made for one of the Olin family, or General Omar Bradley, or Gary Cooper, Ernest Hemingway, or Clark Gable. The Model 21 made for aviator Wiley Post and engraved by R. J. Kornbrath was one of the most stunning Winchesters of any model. But the condition of bird-shooting guns—Post's Model 21 among them—often reflect shooting in the marsh, where environmental conditions are unkind to the finish. Post's gun was re-blued many years ago, and, in the process, lost the crispness of the engraving, but it's still a beautiful and quite historic Winchester. The collector wants to be especially careful in his pursuit of such pieces, as shipping and rework records are usually not available. And thus he must depend on a close look at the gun to determine its authenticity. As with all too many sporting arms, private gunsmiths have been tempted to refinish, rebarrel, or otherwise revise or upgrade (sometimes reluctantly, the owner having insisted the gunsmith do the reconditioning). Unless the work was done by a champion engraver the likes of A. A. White, Winston G. Churchill (no relation), or R. J. Kornbrath, the result may be a less valuable gun because of the "improvements." That goes for stockmaking, too, and equally applies to the Model 70 rifle. The great wood craftsmen, such as Al Biesen, Len Brownell, and Monty Kennedy, added value to any rifle or shotgun they stocked. If it's not a factory stock or factory engraving, the added wood or engraving had best be by a top craftsman to give extra value to the gun.

Each year, specific models like the 97 pump shotgun are growing in demand and hence value. The 1988 *Gun Digest* ran a feature article, "Military Shotguns of World War II," which explained the key role of such hard-hitting arms as the Model 97 and the Model 12, as well as the advantage of skeet and trap guns for marksmanship training. All U.S.-military-stamped semiautomatic or pump shotguns made with 18-inch or longer barrels and pre-

dating 1946 are now given "curios and relics" classifications.

And most of the collectible Winchester double- and single-barrel, pump, and semiautomatic shotguns could be taken from their collectors' cabinets and would be perfectly serviceable today. The two reservations to such use would be probable damage to the finish in the field or marsh, and the punishment all-steel shot would give the barrels.

Post–World II Lever-Actions and Commemoratives

For some Winchester collectors the date up to which they collect is determined partly by the perceived quality of the firearms. In gunmaking, speaking in general terms, quality has taken a step downward during wartime. That is to say, the quality of a particular arm made before World War I or II will be better than the same model made after the war. In Winchesters there is a third date which to many spelled misfortune: 1964, when a contingent of former Ford Motor Company executives came into many top management positions, and with them came "improvements," leading to cost-cutting which, to some extent, lowered quality standards. These savings have already been discussed in reviewing the Model 70 (see Chapter VII), but they affected most other products as well. Winchester's advertising and public relations departments have long been rated at the top in the firearms and ammunition business, so not as many gun specialists noticed any decline, or if they did they said nothing about it.

But today's collector is more astute than before. Quality is an increasingly important matter, and lack of quality definitely does not go unnoticed. That is especially so when the superbly machined and finished earlier guns are available for comparison.

Collectors sometimes specialize in commemoratives, but there is often an overlap with the general

Winchester collector, and at times even with the more antiquarian-oriented. One thing all commemorative-seekers share is a liking for mint-condition guns. They also like the idea of being able to own the same numbers in various issues. Further, the issues have, in general, increased in value, a handy point to make to one's wife if she complains about one's spending too much time or money on gun collecting. The list of accepted values is published and updated periodically by Cherry's, giving model name, issue date, quantity, original sale price, and current value. For example, the 1990 issue listed the John Wayne "Duke," of which 1,000 were made, at an issue price of $2,250 and current market value of $2,950.

In recent years, U.S. Repeating Arms Company has made every effort to return quality to its products (as did Winchester-Olin in response to criticism of the post-1964 quality decline). One of the avenues by which U.S.R.A. Co. is proving this resolve is in commemoratives. No further issues will be manufactured unless they are to an overall high standard, and to this end Kevin Cherry, of Cherry's, has been contracted for his firm's involvement in developing future special issues.

The Winchester Custom Shop

The ever-sharper eye of the gun buyers and competition from private custom gunmakers, stockmakers, and engravers have made it clear to gun manufacturers that they must maintain the highest standards or they will not sell product. Nowhere at U.S. Repeating Arms is this dictum more strictly adhered to than in the Custom Shop. Manager Bruno Pardee and his staff make such guns as the Model 21, Deluxe Grade Model 70, and Custom Grade Model 12 with the highest degree of skill the shop has seen since it was formally established in 1960.

And the results are paying off: since before World War II, the shop has never been busier, and had a

greater back order, than now. The timing could not be better as wealthy sportsmen and collectors have recently pushed prices for fine modern guns to new levels. It was U.S. Repeating Arms which supplied the special action for the David Miller Company's "The Leopard" bolt-action Model 70 Safari Club International show gun. Its record price of $201,000 would have been even higher but for an interruption in the rhythm of the auction. The U.S. Repeating Arms displays at various trade shows dazzle both the public and the experts with superb engraving, carving, and metalwork. Today is truly a golden era in American gunmaking, with an emphasis on quality that would warm the heart of O. F. Winchester himself.

An advantage to the collector is that a modern-made piece can be customized by the buyer: he can discuss the details of embellishment, the stock can be made to his measurements (especially important with the custom shotgun), and he can meet the people responsible for handling the order and building the gun. Further, he need have no fear that he will be buying something other than what he ordered, which is a great concern of the collector in virtually any field of antiques (but less so in the firearms field, because most other areas of the dec-

Winchester and the Royal Canadian Mounted Police share over a century of association. The Model 1886 carbine has NWMP marked at center of buttstock in arc; .45-75 caliber, serial number 44172. *Center* carbine is the MPX, one of thirty-two .30-30s made for loan to the RCMP for use in a film documentary on the force for its 1973 centennial; serial number MPX 27. The Model 70, marked RCMP, has special stock and sights; it is a prototype in .308 Winchester. Order followed for service-use rifles, continuing the RCMP-Winchester tradition.

The Winchester-U.S.R.A. Co. Custom Shop produced this matched set of presentation Model 70s, serial numbers G1728300 and G1728301, in .243 (*top*) and .308 calibers. Upper rifle with cheekpiece for left-handed shooter. Presentation walnut casing placed on side for photo.

orative or fine arts are less complex for the accomplished faker).

The author has been a client of the Custom Shop and has enjoyed many an enlightening session with the staff at the New Haven factory complex.

Collecting Cartridges

Unlike most gunmakers, Winchester has had a major involvement in the manufacture of cartridges since the very beginning. Hunt patented his "Rocket-Ball" cartridge even before he had patented the Volitional Repeater gun, and the predecessor Winchester companies did not become successful until the ammunition itself was successful.

B. Tyler Henry developed that first workable cartridge and from then on, ammunition was as important to the firm's progress and profit as were the firearms, and sometimes even more important.

So dominant was Winchester as both a gun and cartridge maker that the firm even marketed cartridges for competitors' guns. Further, it was Winchester's practice to introduce new cartridges for its own newly introduced firearms.

Winchester's history as a cartridge maker is quite impressive. The following list is a summary of cartridges which Winchester introduced to the market, and the models(s) they first appeared with.

.44 Henry (Henry rifle and Model 1866)
.44–40, .38–40, and .32–20 (Model 1873)
.45–75, .45–60, .50–95, and .40–60 (Model 1876)
.22 W.C.F., .38–90 Express, .40–110 Express, .45–110 Express, .45–125 Express, and .50–140 Express (Model 1885 single-shot)
.40–82, .45–90, .50–105, .38–56, .40–65, .40–75 Express, .45–82, .45–85, .50–110, and .33 W.C.F. (Model 1886)
.70–150 (Model 1887 lever-action shotgun)
.22 W.R.F. (1890 pump rifle)
.25–20 W.C.F. (Model 1892)
.25–35 W.C.F., .30 W.C.F., and .32 Winchester Special (Model 1894)

.38–72, .40–72, .35 W.C.F., and .405 W.C.F. (Model 1895)
.22 Win. Auto. (Model 1903 self-loading rifle)
.32 S.L. and .35 S.L. (Model 1905 self-loading rifle)
.351 S.L. (Model 1907 self-loading rifle)
.401 S.L. (Model 1910 self-loading rifle)
.22 R.F. Magnum (Model 61 pump rifle)
.270 Winchester (Model 54 bolt-action)
.308 Winchester, .458 Winchester Magnum, .338 Winchester, .300 Winchester Magnum, .243 Winchester, and .358 Winchester (Model 70 bolt-action)
.357 Magnum (for handgun cartridges, at request of S & W)
.348 Winchester (Model 71 lever-action)
.30 M1 (M1 carbine)
.375 Winchester (Big Bore Model 94)

Memorabilia

The author's book *The Rampant Colt* (1969) is a study of the Colt trademark and also a review of most of the Colt-related memorabilia then known to the collecting world. If anything, an even bigger and more detailed book could be published on "the Winchester Rider," even though the latter trademark has been registered only since 1965.

But Winchester memorabilia, advertising art, and collectibles date back to well before the famous horse-and-rider logo. In the research for this book, the author spent two weeks with the leading private collectors of Winchester products and memorabilia. Their holdings are so overwhelming that their huge gun room is bulging nearly to the point of collapsing the floors.

When a book is published on this subject, the market will expand significantly. The variety of Winchester non-gun products alone is mind-boggling: roller skates, fishing equipment, flashlights, batteries, tools, cutlery, sporting goods (including baseball bats and football gear), paints and brushes, farm and garden tools, auto tool kits, electric irons, lawnmowers, padlocks, and even dishwashers and

refrigerators! To help facilitate the sale of this huge array of merchandise, the company instituted its own stores after World War I. The slogan "As Good as the Gun" was prominent on some of the advertising. At their peak, there were 6,300 Winchester stores nationwide. The author's uncle George Gustafson married the daughter of the owner of one of these, and he ran the store himself for many years: Thielman Hardware, St. Cloud, Minnesota. The author's first modern gun (alas, a Remington Model 511 Scoremaster) was purchased by his parents from Uncle George, as a twelfth-birthday present.

The most expensive category within Winchester memorabilia is that of the cartridge board. A natural outgrowth of cartridge making, the boards are known in six different types and span the years from 1874 through 1897, with later designs (many of them one-offs for special displays or promotions) being produced into modern times. Richard Rattenbury's monograph *Winchester Promotional Arts* (1978) is the best reference on this subject.

The Rattenbury study also deals in some detail with calendar art and posters, a medium begun by Winchester (c. 1887) and employing such prominent artists as Alexander Pope, A. B. Frost, Frederic Remington, Philip R. Goodwin, W. R. Leigh, and N. C. Wyeth. The author remembers going into Winchester's Parts Department office in the late sixties and seeing a fabulous N. C. Wyeth oil, a fixture there for many years, originally painted for the firm's commercial use. In later years, Winchester commissioned works by artists such as John Clymer.

Historical associations lend added appeal to arms and often significantly increase value. Both guns presented to General Curtis LeMay, and so inscribed. At *top*, Model 70 in .375 H&H Magnum, serial number 737056, a Super Grade for big-game hunting. The Model 50 Pigeon Grade, number 182916A, was the sixteen-millionth Winchester made. Presented to the general in a ceremony at which John M. Olin himself was present.

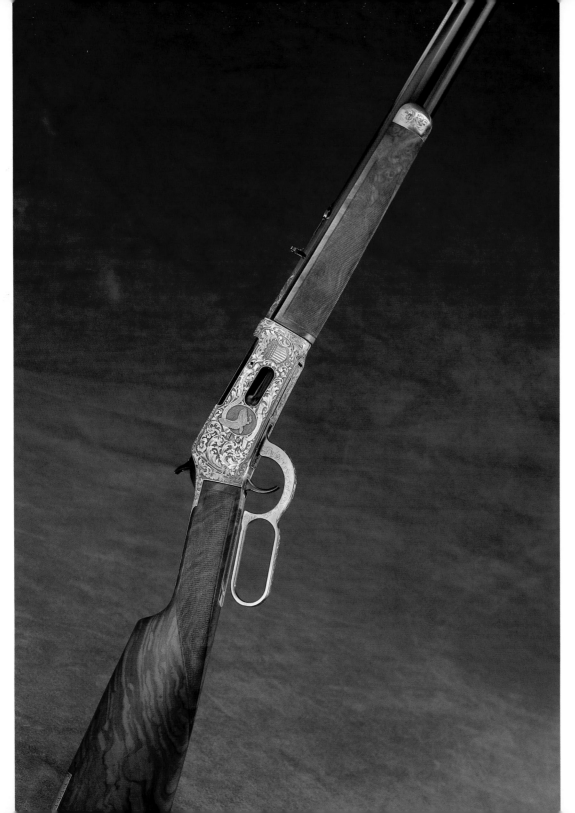

Calendars, cartridge boards, and related illustrations add spice to many collectors' gun rooms and are an aspect of the collecting world which captures the public's general interest. And in calendars and other advertising art, the gun collectors' interests merge with those of connoisseurs of American paintings. It was the firearms industry, beginning with Colonel Samuel Colt's patronage of George Catlin (c. 1851), which first commissioned prominent artists to create paintings for promotional use.

Winchester Arms Museum and Books

The Winchester Arms Museum traces its origin to Oliver Winchester himself, who began collecting firearms at least as early as 1871. Prototypes, experimentals, cutaways, production models, and memorabilia were gathered without a particular plan, until Edwin Pugsley, himself a keen collector, became increasingly influential at the factory. Eventually the bulk of his own collection was sold to Winchester, and the combined holdings of Winchester and Pugsley numbered over 5,000 firearms, plus numerous accessories and other material. As the fortunes of Winchester changed in the 1970s, management sought a new home for the museum. In 1978 the collection, accompanied by many surviving serial number records, was transferred to the Buffalo Bill Historical Center in Cody, Wyoming. It is now a major part of the center's displays and reference holdings. The museum is

U.S. Constitution 200th Anniversary Model 94, the most exclusive commemorative issue in Winchester history (eight guns only), factory-authorized, and made specifically for Cherry's. A superb example of modern gunmaking. Cherry's has a multi-year agreement with U.S. Repeating Arms for joint development of future Model 94 commemoratives.

From the Custom Shop brochure of 1990, two showpiece Model 94s. *Top* rifle engraved and inlaid for the factory by Ben Shostle, stock style classified as A; *lower* by John Vest, with spade-pattern stocks.

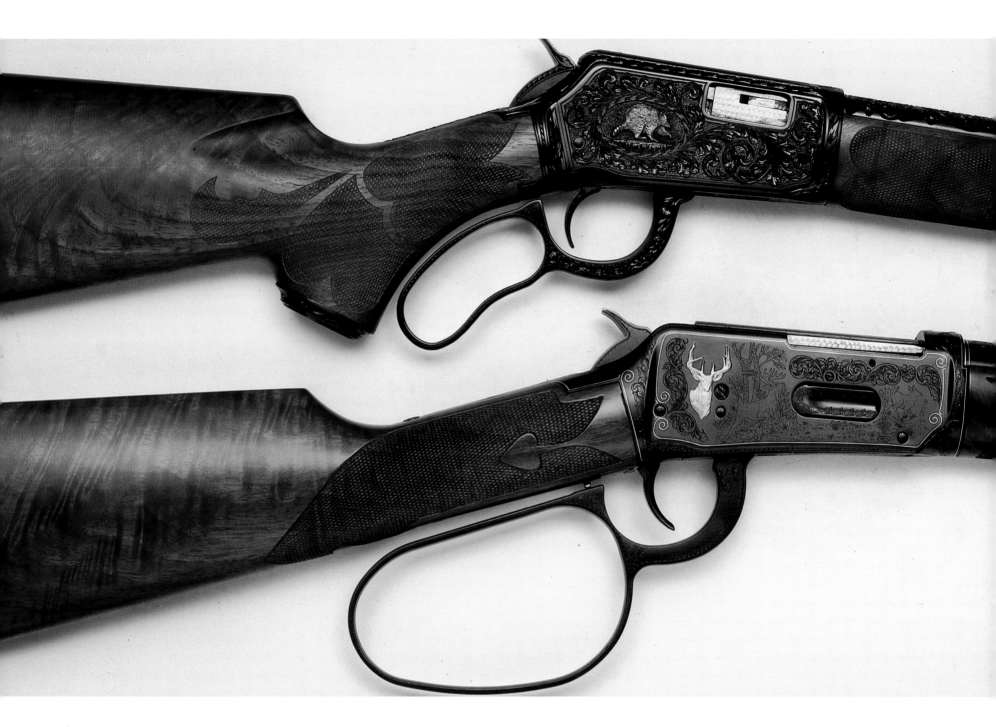

open daily from 8:00 A.M. to 8:00 P.M. in May and September and from 7:00 A.M. to 10:00 P.M. in June, July, and August. Hours during other months should be confirmed with the museum in advance (winters there can be quite miserable). The Winchester Arms Museum is part of a complex known as the Cody Arms Museum, which in turn is a division of the Buffalo Bill Historical Center. For a $35 fee, the museum will research the shipping records of firearms covered by its records. However, the data are restricted to the models listed in the table on page 370.

The standard reference works on Winchester are not yet as numerous as those in the Colt field. But the body of work increases slowly and surely. For general reference, primarily the technical, *The Winchester Book* by George Madis and *The History of Winchester Firearms* by George Watrous, T. E. Hall, Pete Kuhloff, and James Rikhoff are the most widely used; each is periodically updated. For a company business history, the best source, only up through 1952, is Harold F. Williamson's *Winchester: The Gun That Won the West*. For deluxe Winchesters, *Winchester Engraving* and *The Book of Winchester Engraving* are the standard texts. And for the One of One Hundred and One of One Thousand rifles, *Winchester: The Golden Age of American Gunmaking and the Winchester 1 of 1000* is the only source. A variety of other works deal with specifics, such as commemoratives, ballistics, and selected models. An annotated bibliography will be found on page 391.

The dedicated aficionado will find original factory documents, literature, and especially catalogues to be a revealing and fascinating source. These were of prime importance to the author in his research for the Winchester engraving texts, his book on the One of One Hundred and One of One Thousand rifles, and for the present book.

Collecting Winchesters as an Investment

The post–World War II boom in arms collecting has been a continually evolving phenomenon. The two superstars in American arms, throughout the history of arms collecting, have been Winchesters and Colts. Both marques have done famously in return on investments and have given inflation a run for its money. The best Winchester performers have been engraved and historical guns, and fine-condition lever-actions from the Jennings on up through the Model 1895.

The reasons for the collecting boom are many. The appearance of new books and magazine articles has helped the field to grow, and commemoratives help to draw new collectors into the fold. The active participation of Winchester and the U.S. Repeating Arms Company at trade and gun shows, as well as offering support to the Winchester Club of America and the Winchester Collectors Association, has been an instrumental supporting factor. Besides such periodicals as *Man at Arms* and the Winchester club magazines, mainstream gun magazines like *The American Rifleman*, *Guns and Ammo*, *Shooting Times*, and *Guns* carry historical

Custom Super Grade Model 70, from the Custom Shop, in calibers 7mm Remington Magnum, .300 Winchester Magnum, and .338 Winchester Magnum; detailed in factory literature for scope use only, custom-bedded semi-fancy walnut stock (satin-finished and with deep-cut checkering), internal parts hand-honed, barrel hand-lapped with lead for accuracy, bolt and follower engine-turned, flat-sided bolt sleeve, inletted swivel bases, high-luster blue finish, steel triggerguard, floorplate, and pistol-grip cap, and—most important of features—claw controlled feed, extraction, and ejection system.

pieces as well as keep the reader updated on new products.

World travel and the ever-increasing international interest in collector's firearms have also spawned new interest. Gun shows, auctions, videos on Winchester, and the flourishing custom gunmakers and engravers have played a role too.

Considering the estimated 15,000 to 20,000 active collectors and the ever-upward movement in values and prices, a newcomer might think the time to collect was in the distant past. But a great many Winchesters can still be purchased at a reasonable cost (less than $2,000), and there are still discoveries to be made in attics and at flea markets—and even at gun shows.

For value reference the collector should consult Steven Fjestad's *Blue Book of Gun Values* (a comprehensive guide including even modern guns and commemoratives), *Flayderman's Guide to Antique American Firearms*, and C. E. Chapel's *Gun Collector's Handbook of Values*. These works give a general idea of values, are periodically updated,

Writer-photographer Peter Beard, crocodile-cropping for the Kenya Game Department at Lake Rudolf (c. 1967). His studies of crocodiles led to the best-selling *Eyelids of Morning: The Mingled Destinies of Crocodiles and Man*, in which this photograph was published.

Hand and machine work combined in building the Model 21 shotgun. Photographed at the Custom Shop, c. 1983.

The dean of twentieth-century American arms engravers, Alvin White, at his somewhat cluttered bench (à la another firearms genius, John Browning). In a career that began during the Great Depression, White has gold-inlaid and engraved more exquisite Winchester and Colt firearms than any other contemporary engraver, including Model 94 number 3500000, on the dust jacket of this book.

Customized Model 70 by D'Arcy Echols, Providence, Utah, in .338 Winchester Magnum. Note straightened-out bolt knob, English walnut stock, classic styling. Echols is one of the top rifle makers who prove the American mastery of the bolt-action sporting rifle.

Miniature Henry rifle and 1866 carbine, made by Uberti & Co., and illustrated one-half actual size. Scale indicated by .44-40 cartridges.

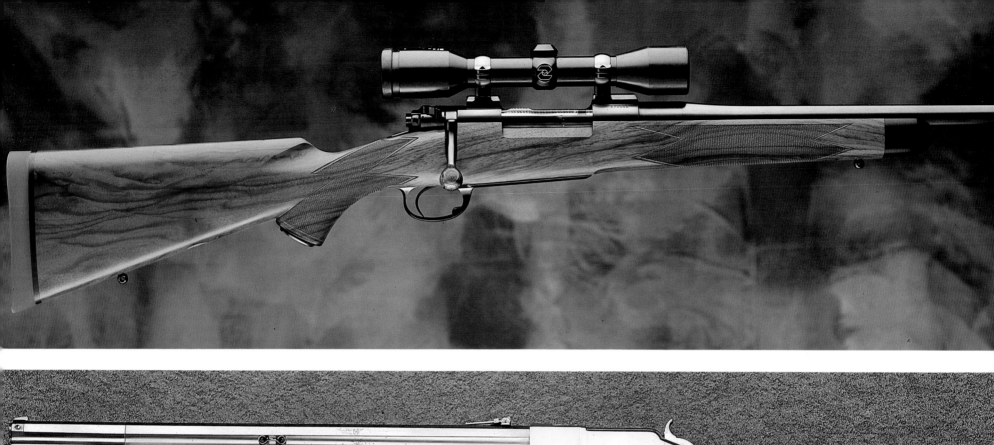

The 1884 cartridge board, 28″ × 38″, held ninety-nine cartridges, in center- and rimfire, the shotshells casings only, since the factory was not yet manufacturing loaded cases. Two primer tins missing at *right* (often the case with nineteenth-century boards, but more often they lack cartridges). This was the third factory board issued, in a total run of six distinctly different patterns.

Miscellany of memorabilia, from Winchester-Olin and U.S. Repeating Arms periods, mainly promotional items rather than factory products. Badges at *right* from the two established Winchester collector groups, each of which issues publications and sponsors guns shows. Winchester Club of America also aided in funding *Winchester Firearms Legends* video, which features several of the guns pictured in this book.

and are available in many bookstores. They also supply basic technical information. However, none presents figures for exotica like presentation or engraved guns, or the ultimate in quality, finish, and other details variant from the norm. Quality and originality, and buying from an impeccable source, will be instrumental in ensuring a fine collection, and one that promises to be a solid return on investment—not only in financial terms, but in sheer enjoyment and pride of ownership.

When researching his *Winchester 1 of 1000*, the author was able to locate only about 25 percent of the total specimens known to have been made. It is unlikely that the balance have been lost over the years; most are still out there. Part of the adventure of collection is the thrill of the chase. Most of these One of One Hundreds and One of One Thousands remain to be discovered, usually in attics of private

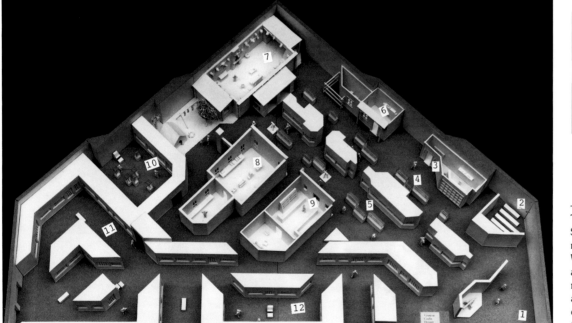

Model of the gallery display area of the new $7 million Cody Firearms Museum complex, which includes the Winchester Arms Museum collections and is part of the Buffalo Bill Historical Center. The Center incorporates three other collections: the Whitney Gallery of Western Art, the Buffalo Bill Museum, and the Plains Indian Museum. Location of Yellowstone Park nearby is an added draw to this uniquely impressive institution, founded in 1917 as a memorial to W. F. "Buffalo Bill" Cody. *1* Entry, *2* Adolph Coors Video Theatre, *3* Colonial Gunsmith Shop, *4* Robert Woodruff Gallery of American Sporting Arms, *5* General James Doolittle Gallery of Military Small Arms, *6* Overland Stage Coach Stop, *7* Boone and Crockett National Collection of Heads and Horns, *8* Nineteenth Century Northern Arms Factory, *9* Old West Gunstore, *10* Woodruff Gallery of Highly Decorated Arms, *11* The Winchester Gallery, *12* Corporate History of American Firearms Manufacturers.

The Winchester Mystery House, a fantasy billed as "The World's Strangest Monument to a Woman's Fears." Designated a California Registered Historical Landmark, the residence was built for William Wirt Winchester's widow, Sarah, who was apparently advised that as long as she never stopped building onto her residence, the spirits of the dead (killed with Winchester firearms) would be appeased. Until her death at age eighty-two, carpenters had been kept hammering for thirty-eight years, twenty-four hours a day! The home has 160 rooms and is on six acres of land (approximately two-thirds of it occupied by the mansion), on Winchester Avenue, San Jose. Some doors and staircases lead nowhere, a window was built into the floor, some columns are upside down, and Mrs. Winchester, obsessed by the number thirteen, signed the thirteen parts to her will thirteen times!

The Supreme line, advertised by Winchester as "The first line of factory-loaded rifle ammunition that can match the performance of cartridges loaded by hand." As of 1990 the Supreme line offered nine centerfire calibers and eleven bullet weights.

homes, but sometimes they are in the hands of individuals who have no idea of the meaning of that magical "One of One Thousand" inscription on the barrel of the rifle standing in a corner or in a closet.

Good advice to make your collecting successful: become an expert, and master your speciality; buy the best-conditioned pieces you can afford; take note of a piece's history, including its pedigree; avoid specimens which have been restored, altered, or (the worst) faked; and keep your reference library up to date. Two further goals: study known genuine specimens, at gun shows, in private collections, and at museums, and, finally, remember the tried-and-true adage "If in doubt, do without."

Were Oliver F. Winchester alive today, one could state with certainty that the canny businessman-entrepreneur would be actively collecting guns and memorabilia bearing his name. He was an admirer of quality, mechanics, and design innovations, and was astute with his investments. And his involvement in collecting would be welcome—albeit strong competition—to the innumerable enthusiasts who actively pursue this blue chip of American longarms:

Top, shelf displays chrome-plated and blackened variants of the Model 1898 breech-loading cannon, firing 10-gauge black-powder blanks. About 18,400 were made through 1958; although they were not serial-numbered, identification numbers do appear on barrels and barrel bands. Rubber tires introduced in 1930. *Lower,* cannon by Bellmore-Johnson Tool Company, licensed by Winchester-Olin from 1976 and still in production. These guns are serial-numbered, as evident on barrel breech. No. P 251 is a Presentation Grade (standard models have S prefix), brass and brass-finished, with stainless-steel fittings and large rubber-tires, in mahogany chest. The standard post–1976 cannon is finished in black and shipped in wood crates emblazoned with red Winchester logo.

Sign at entrance to a main facility at the Winchester Division of Olin complex at East Alton, Illinois. U.S. Repeating Arms Company packaging includes the slogan "More Than a Gun—an American Legend."

Appendix

Winchester Serial Number Research
for Collectors

The Cody Firearms Museum (which houses the Winchester Arms Museum), Buffalo Bill Historical Center, Cody, Wyoming 82414, holds the original factory serial number data. The table which follows shows those models and number ranges which are recorded. Only these models can be researched. The research fee is $35 per letter.

For members of the Center's Patrons Association, research can be done by telephone. When the data are located, the information is supplied to the caller by a collect call; should the party wish a research letter, the $35 fee is required. The Patrons yearly membership fee also provides for free museum admission, a quarterly newsletter, museum store discounts, advance offers on museum publications, and miscellaneous other benefits.

When contacting the museum, include model designation, general information, and, of course, the serial number.

Should the information on a specific gun not be available, the research fee will be refunded.

Winchester Records
Model and Serial Numbers Available

Model 1866   Serial Numbers below 124,995 which are available.

32527	103672	109650	119488	120665	124899
35952	104463	109651	119579	121197	124357
36200	104469	112269	119567	121964	124995
96740	104470	112270	119739	124005	
96743	107208	112274	120072	124876	
96745	107209	119180	120593	124893	

Model Number	Serial Number
1866	124,995 to 170,101
1873	1 to 720,496 (NA 497–610) and (NA 199,551–199,598)
1876	1 to 63,871
Hotchkiss*	1 to 84,555
1885 (S.S.)** (NA 74,459 - 75,556)	1 to 109,999
1886	1 to 156,599 (NA 146,000–150,799)
1887 & 1901 (Shotguns)	1 to 72,999
1890	1 to 329,999 (NA 20,000–29,999) and (NA 126,000–126,699)
1906	1 to 79,999
1892	1 to 379,999
1893 & 1897 (Shotguns)	1 to 34,050 (M/93) to 377,999 (M/97)
1894	1 to 353,999
1895	1 to 59,999
Lee	1 to 19,999
1903	1 to 39,999
1905	1 to 29,078
1906	1 to 79,999
1907	1 to 9,999

*May be referred to in some cases as Model 1879, 1880 or 1883. Most cases Hotchkiss.
**May also be referred to as High Wall or Low Wall.

NA - Not Available.

Serial Numbers and Production Tables

Numerical Listing of Models

Model		Dates of Mfctre.	Approx. No. Made	Serial No. Range
1900	R. F. Rifle	1900–02	105,000	not numbered
Super-X	Model 1 Shotgun	1974–90 (parts cleanup)	87,000	87,700
1901	Shotgun	1901–20	13,500	64,856
1902	R. F. Rifle	1902–31	640,299	not numbered
1903	R. F. Rifle	1903–32	126,000	1–126,000
1904	R. F. Rifle	1904–31	302,859	not numbered
1905	C. F. Rifle	1905–20	29,113	1–29,113
1906	R. F. Rifle	1906–32	727,353	1–727,353
1907	C. F. Rifle	1906–57	58,490	1–58,490
1910	C. F. Rifle	1910–36	20,786	1–20,786
1911	Shotgun	1911–25	82,774	1–82,774
1912	Shotgun	1912–63	1,968,307	1–1,968,307. Custom Shop special order 1963–72, 1976–79; reintro. 1972, dropped 1980; total since 1912: 2,026,721
14	303 British Enfield	1915–17	245,866	1–245,866
M14	U. S. Rifle	1960–63	356,501	NA
1917	U. S. Cal. .30 Rifle	1917–18	545,511	1–545,511
1918	Browning Auto. Rifle	1918	47,123	NA
1920	Shotgun	1919–24	23,616	1–23,616
21	Shotgun	1930–	33,200	1–W33,200
22	Shotgun	1975–NA	NA	NA
23	Shotgun	1978–NA	NA	PWK1–NA
24	Shotgun	1939–57	116,280	1–116,280
25	Shotgun	1949–54	87,937	NA
30	C.F. Rifle	1941 exp	a few only	
31	U.S. 30 M 1	1941–45	818,059	NA
32	U.S. 30 M 2 (Auto)	NA		
33	U.S. Carbine T-3	NA		
36	Shotgun	1920–27	20,506	not numbered
37	Shotgun	1936–63	1,015,554	not numbered
37A	Shotgun	1973–80	395,168	Canadian built
38	Shotgun	c. 1936–38	a few only	NA
39	U.S. 30 Cal. Garand	1940–45	513,582	NA

Model		Dates of Mfctre.	Approx. No. Made	Serial No. Range
40	Shotgun	1940–41	12,000	NA
41	Shotgun	1920–34	22,146	not numbered
42	Shotgun	1933–63	159,353	1–159,353
43	C.F. Rifle	1949–57	62,617	NA
47	R.F. Rifle	1949–54	43,123	not numbered
50	Shotgun	1954–61	196,402	1000–197,402
52	R.F. Rifle	1919–79	125,233	1–125,233
53	C.F. Rifle	1924–32	24,916	with Model 1892
54	C.F. Rifle	1925–36	50,145	1–50,145
55	C.F. Rifle	1924–32	20,580	1–2868, then with Model 1894
55	R.F. Rifle	1957–61	45,060	not numbered
56	R.F. Rifle	1926–29	8,297	NA
57	R.F. Rifle	1926–36	18,600	NA
58	R.F. Rifle	1928–31	38,992	not numbered
59	R.F. Rifle	1930 only	9,293	not numbered
59	Shotgun	1959–65	82,085	1–82,085
60	R.F. Rifle	1930–34	165,754	not numbered
60A	R.F. Rifle	1932–39	6,118	not numbered
61	R.F. Rifle	1932–63	342,001	1–342,001
62	R.F. Rifle	1932–58	409,475	1–99,200. Thereafter Model 62A (1940) to 409,475
63	R.F. Rifle	1933–58	174,692	1–174,692
64	C.F. Rifle	1933–57, 1972–73	66,783 (1933–57)	with Model 1894
65	C.F. Rifle	1933–47	5,704	with Model 1892
1866	R.F. Rifle	1867–98	170,101	prox. 12,000–182,000
66	C.F. Rifle	limited	NA	NA
67	R.F. Rifle	1934–63	383,587	not numbered (except for export)
670	C.F. Rifle	1966–79	287,648	100,000–387,648
677	R.F. Rifle	1937–39	2,239	not numbered
68	R.F. Rifle	1934–46	100,730	not numbered
69	R.F. Rifle	1935–63	355,363	not numbered
697	R.F. Rifle	1937–41	NA	not numbered
70	C.F. Rifle	1935 to date*	1,866,000	1–581,471; 700,000–G1985814
70A	C.F. Rifle	1972–80	NA	with Model 70
71	C.F. Rifle	1935–57	47,254	1–47,254
72	R.F. Rifle	1938–59	161,412	not numbered

*as of 12-90

Model		Dates of Mfctre.	Approx. No. Made	Serial No. Range
1873	C.F. & R.F. Rifle	1873–1919	720,610	1–720,610 (.22 r.f., 1884–1904; 19.552)
74	R.F. Rifle	1939–55	406,574	1–406,574
75	R.F. Rifle	1938–58	88,715	NA
1876	C.F. Rifle	1876–97	63,871	1–63,871
77	Experimental Rifle	1941 Exp.	limited	NA
77	R.F. Rifle	1955–63	217,180	1001–218,181 (stopped numbering, 1959)
770	C.F. Rifle	1969–72	20,938	with Model 70
1883*	C.F. Rifle	1879–99	84,555	1–84,555
1885	Single Shot Rifle	1885–1920	139,725	1–139,725
1886	C.F. Rifle	1886–1935	159,994	1–159,994
1887	Shotgun	1887–1901	64,855	1–64,855
88	C.F. Rifle	1955–73	283,913	1–283,913
1890	R.F. Rifle	1890–1932	849,000	1–849,000
91	Shotgun			Spanish-made
1892	C.F. Rifle	1892–1941	1,004,067	1–1,004,067
1893	Shotgun	1893–97	34,050	1–34,050
1894	C.F. Rifle	1894 to date**	5,616,000	1–5,615,748
9422	R.F. Rifle	1972 to date**	618,000	1–F618,112
1895	C.F. Rifle	1896–1931	425,981	1–425,981
1897	Shotgun	1897–1957	1,024,700	34,151–1,024,700
98†	Cannon	1903–1958	18,400	not numbered
99	R.F. Rifle	1904–1923	75,433	not numbered
100	C.F. Rifle	1960–73	262,838	1–A262838 (A prefix began at 210999)
101	Shotgun	1963–87	NA	‡12ga. from 50,000–199,999 then 300,000–NA
121	R.F. Rifle	1967–72	72,561	not numbered
131	R.F. Rifle	1967–72	16,371	not numbered
141	R.F. Rifle	1967–72	16,592	not numbered
150	R.F. Rifle	1967–73	47,436	not numbered
190	R.F. Rifle	c. 1966–80	2,171,263	numbered together with 200 series below

*Hotchkiss
**as of 12-90

†Reintroduced 1976, built and sold under license from Winchester Division, Olin Corp., by Bellmore-Johnson Tool Co.

‡20,28, .410 from 200,000–NA.

Model		Dates of Mfctre.	Approx. No. Made	Serial No. Range
200** (series)	R.F. Rifles	1963–77		numbered together with 190 series above
310	R.F. Rifle	1971–74	13,544	
320	R.F. Rifle	1971–74	13,544	
333	Air Rifle	1969–74		
353	Air Pistol	1969–74	19,259	
363	Air Pistol	1969–74		
370	Shotgun	1968–72	221,578	Canadian
416	Air Rifle	1969–74		
422	Air Rifle	1969–74		
423	Air Rifle	1969–74		
425	Air Rifle	1969–74	19,259	
427	Air Rifle	1969–74		
435	Air Rifle	1969–74		
450	Air Rifle	1969–74		
490	R.F. Rifle	1975–78	32,893	
1200	Shotgun	1964–	as of 12-90	100,000-L1,340,700
1300	Shotgun	1978–	as of 12-90	LX1,300-LX101,599
1400	Shotgun	1964–	as of 12-90	100,000-N921,547
1500	Shotgun	1978–	as of 12-90	NX1,500-NX49,848

**250	191,264
255	55,310
270	112,716
275	47,657

COMMEMORATIVE MODELS
Listed by Year, Model, Total Produced, and Number
(see Chapters IX, X, XI, and XII)

Collector Code Number		Total Production	High Serial No.
	1964:		
1.	Wyoming Diamond Jubilee	1,500	1,500
	1966:		
2.	Centennial '66 Rifle and Carbine	102,309	102,666
3.	Nebraska Centennial	2,500	2,500
	1967:		
4.	Canadian '67 Centennial Rifle and Carbine	90,301	97,395
5.	Alaska Purchase Centennial	1,500	1,500

Collector Code Number	Total Production	High Serial No.
1968:		
6. Illinois Sesquicentennial	37,648	39,699
7. Buffalo Bill Rifle and Carbine	112,923	112,169
7B. Buffalo Bill Museum Presentation	300	300
1969:		
8. Golden Spike	69,996	73,619
9. Theodore Roosevelt Rifle and Carbine	52,386	56,060
1970:		
10. North West Territories (foreign sale, Canada)	2,500	3,106
10B. North West Territories Deluxe (foreign sale, Canada)	500	500
10C. North West Territories Donation Model (foreign sale, Canada)	10	10
11. Cowboy	27,549	28,904
11B. Cowboy Hall of Fame Presentation	300	300
12. Lone Star Rifle and Carbine	38,385	55,259
1971:		
13. NRA Musket and Rifle	44,400	58,927
1972:		
14. Yellow Boy (foreign sale)	4,903	5,500
1973:		
15. R.C.M.P. (foreign sale, Canada)	9,500	10,442
15B. R.C.M.P. Members Model (foreign sale, Canada)	4,850	5,100
15C. R.C.M.P. Presentation Model (foreign sale, Canada)	10	10
15D. M.P.X. (foreign sale, Canada)	32	32
1974:		
16. Texas Ranger	4,850	4,850
16B. Texas Ranger Presentation	150	150
17. Apache (foreign sale)	8,600	10,200
1975:		
18. Klondike Gold Rush (foreign sale, Canada)	10,500	10,500
18B. Klondike Gold Rush Dawson City Issue (foreign sale, Canada)	25	25
18C. Klondike Gold Rush Presentation (foreign sale, Canada)	15	15
19. Commanche (foreign sale)	11,500	11,511
1976:		
20. U.S. Bicentennial	19,999	19,999
21. Sioux (foreign sale)	10,000	12,000

Collector Code Number	Total Production	High Serial No.
22. Little Big Horn (foreign sale)	11,000	11,350
1977:		
23. Wells Fargo	19,999	19,999
24. Cheyenne .44–40 (foreign sale)	11,225	13,000
24B. Cheyenne 9422 (foreign sale)	5,000	8,221
25. Legendary Lawman	19,999	30,858
26. Limited Edition I	15,000	15,000
1978:		
27. Cherokee .30–30 (foreign sale)	9,000	9,000
27B. Cherokee 9422 (foreign sale)	3,950	3,950
28. Antlered Game	19,999	19,999
29. One of One Thousand (foreign sale)	250	250
1979:		
30. Limited Edition II	1,500	1,500
31. Legendary Frontiersman	19,999	19,999
32. Bat Masterson	8,000	8,000
33. Matched Set of One Thousand	1,000	1,000
1980:		
34. Oliver F. Winchester	19,999	19,999
35. Alberta Diamond Jubilee (foreign sale, Canada)	2,700	2,700
35B. Alberta Diamond Jubilee Deluxe (foreign sale, Canada)	300	300
36. Saskatchewan Diamond Jubilee (foreign sale, Canada)	2,700	2,700
36B. Saskatchewan Diamond Jubilee Deluxe (foreign sale, Canada)	300	300
1981:		
37. Calgary Stampede (foreign sale, Canada)	1,000	1,000
38. Canadian Pacific Centennial (foreign sale, Canada)	2,700	2,700
38B. Canadian Pacific—Employee (foreign sale, Canada)	2,000	2,000
38C. Canadian Pacific Presentation (foreign sale, Canada)	300	300
39. U.S. Border Patrol	1,000	1,000
39B. U.S. Border Patrol, Member Model	800	800
40. John Wayne Standard	49,000	49,000
40B. John Wayne Canadian	1,000	1,000
40C. John Wayne Duke	1,000	1,000
40D. John Wayne Matched Set	300	300

	Collector Code Number	Total Production	High Serial No.
	1982:		
41.	Great Western Artist I	999	999
42.	Oklahoma Diamond Jubilee	1,000	1,000
43.	American Bald Eagle Silver Model	2,800	2,800
43B.	American Bald Eagle Gold Model	200	200
44.	Annie Oakley	6,000	6,000
	1983:		
45.	Great Western Artist II	999	999
46.	Chief Crazy Horse	19,999	19,999
	1984:		
47.	Winchester—Colt Set	3,250	4,440
	1985:		
48.	Boy Scout	15,000	15,000
48B.	Eagle Scout	1,000	1,000
	1986:		
49.	Texas Sesquicentennial Carbine	15,000	15,000
49B.	Texas Sesquicentennial Rifle	1,500	1,500
49C.	Texas Sesquicentennial Set	150	150
	1987:		
50.	U.S. Constitution Bicentennial	50	50
	1990		
51.	Wyoming Centennial Carbine	999	999

Major Ammunition Patents by Olin Corporation

Item	Patent Nos.	Issue Date
General		
1. Ball Powder	2,027,114	01-07-36
2. Lubaloy Plating: Shot Small-Caliber Bullets	1,732,211	10-15-29
Shotshell Ammunition		
1. Battery Cup Foil	1,438,779	12-12-22
2. Super-X	1,757,584	05-06-30
3. Overlay Basewad	1,842,445	01-26-32
4. Cup Over Powder Wad	2,582,124	01-08-52
	2,582,125	01-08-52
5. Mark 5 (Shot Column Liner)	3,055,031	09-25-62
	3,162,124	12-22-64
6. XX Loads (Shot Column Filler)	3,092,026	06-04-63
7. Compression Form Shell	3,171,350	03-02-65
8. Gas Seal Ring (Around Primer-CF)	3,215,077	02-02-65
9. AA Wad (AA Loads)	3,285,174	01-15-66
Centerfire Ammunition		
1. Silvertip Bullets	2,333,091	11-02-43
2. Power Point Bullet	2,838,000	06-10-58
3. Positive Expanding Point Bullet	3,157,137	11-17-64
	3,165,809	01-19-65
	3,311,962	04-04-67
4. Silvertip HP Pistol Bullet	4,193,348	03-18-80
Rimfire Ammunition		
1. Super Match Mark III Bullet (Used in T22)	2,868,136	09-13-59
Priming		

The new lower cost, new chemistry priming mix patent entitled "Method for Making Priming Constituents" is pending. This priming process change represents a significant advance in the state of the art which will improve Olin's primer performance.

Super-X® Centerfire Pistol/Revolver Ammunition

Cartridge	Symbol	Bullet Wt. (grs.)	Type	Velocity (fps) Muzzle	50 Yds.	100 Yds.	Energy (ft-lbs) Muzzle	50 Yds.	100 Yds.	Mid Range Traj. (in.) 50 Yds.	100 Yds.	Barrel Length (in.)
25 Automatic (6.35mm) Expanding Point	X25AXP	45	XP**	815	729	655	66	53	42	1.8	7.7	2
25 Automatic (6.35mm) Full Metal Case	X25AP	50	FMC	760	707	659	64	56	48	2.0	8.7	2
30 Luger (7.65mm) Full Metal Case	X30LP	93	FMC	1220	1110	1040	305	255	225	0.9	3.5	4½
# 30 Carbine Hollow Soft Point	X30M1	110	HSP	1790	1601	1430	783	626	500	0.4	1.7	10
# 30 Carbine Full Metal Case	X30M2	110	FMC	1740	1552	1384	740	588	468	0.4	1.8	10
32 Smith & Wesson Lead Round Nose	X32SWP	85	Lead-RN	680	645	610	90	81	73	2.5	10.5	3
32 Smith & Wesson Long (Colt New Police) Lead Round Nose	X32SWLP	98	Lead-RN	705	670	635	115	98	88	2.3	10.5	4
32 Short Colt Lead Round Nose	X32SCP	80	Lead-RN	745	665	590	100	79	62	2.2	9.9	4
† 32 Long Colt Lead Round Nose	X32LCP	82	Lead-RN	755	715	675	105	93	83	2.0	8.7	4
32 Automatic Silvertip Hollow Point	X32ASHP	60	STHP	970	895	835	125	107	93	1.3	5.4	4
32 Automatic Full Metal Case	X32AP	71	FMC	905	855	810	129	115	97	1.4	5.8	4
38 Smith & Wesson Lead Round Nose	X38SWP	145	Lead-RN	685	650	620	150	135	125	2.4	10.0	4
380 Automatic Silvertip Hollow Point	X380ASHP	85	STHP	1000	921	860	189	160	140	1.2	5.1	3¾
380 Automatic Full Metal Case	X380AP	95	FMC	955	865	785	190	160	130	1.4	5.9	3¾
38 Special Silvertip Hollow Point	X38S9HP	110	STHP	945	894	850	218	195	176	1.3	5.4	4V
38 Special Lead Round Nose	X38S1P	158	Lead-RN	755	723	693	200	183	168	2.0	8.3	4V
38 Special Lead Semi-Wad Cutter	X38WCPSV	158	Lead-SWC	755	721	689	200	182	167	2.0	8.4	4V
† 38 Special Metal Point	X38S2P	158	Met. Pt.	755	723	693	200	183	168	2.0	8.3	4V
38 Special Silvertip Hollow Point + P	X38SSHP	95	STHP	1100	1002	932	255	212	183	1.0	4.3	4V
# 38 Special Jacketed Hollow Point + P	X38S6PH	110	JHP	995	926	871	242	210	185	1.2	5.1	4V
# 38 Special Jacketed Hollow Point + P	X38S7PH	125	JHP	945	898	858	248	224	204	1.3	5.4	4V
# 38 Special Silvertip Hollow Point + P	X38S8HP	125	STHP	945	898	858	248	224	204	1.3	5.4	4V
38 Special Lead Hollow Point + P	X38SPD	158	Lead-HP	890	855	823	278	257	238	1.4	6.0	4V
38 Special Lead Semi-Wad Cutter + P	X38WCP	158	Lead-SWC	890	855	823	278	257	238	1.4	6.0	4V
38 Special Match Lead Mid-Range (Clean Cutting) Match	X38SMRP	148	Lead-WC	710	634	566	166	132	105	2.4	10.8	4V
9mm Luger (Parabellum) Full Metal Case	X9LP	115	FMC	1155	1047	971	341	280	241	0.9	3.9	4
9mm Luger (Parabellum) Silvertip Hollow Point	X9MMSHP	115	STHP	1225	1095	1007	383	306	259	0.8	3.6	4
* 38 Super Automatic Silvertip Hollow Point + P	X38ASHP	125	STHP	1240	1130	1050	427	354	306	0.8	3.4	5
* 38 Super Automatic Full Metal Case + P	X38A1P	130	FMC	1215	1099	1017	426	348	298	0.8	3.6	5
† 38 Automatic (For all 38 Automatic Pistols) Full Metal Case	X38A2P	130	FMC	1040	980	925	310	275	245	1.0	4.7	4½
# 357 Magnum Jacketed Hollow Point	X3573P	110	JHP	1295	1095	975	410	292	232	0.8	3.5	4V
# 357 Magnum Jacketed Hollow Point	X3576P	125	JHP	1450	1240	1090	583	427	330	0.6	2.8	4V
# 357 Magnum Silvertip Hollow Point	X357SHP	145	STHP	1290	1155	1060	535	428	361	0.8	3.5	4V
357 Magnum Lead Semi-Wad Cutter	X3571P	158	Lead-SWC**	1235	1104	1015	535	428	361	0.8	3.5	4V

Note: Tables and data courtesy Winchester Division of the Olin Corporation, © 1989.

Cartridge	Symbol	Bullet Wt. (grs.)	Type	Velocity (fps) Muzzle	50 Yds.	100 Yds.	Energy (ft-lbs) Muzzle	50 Yds.	100 Yds.	Mid Range Traj. (in.) 50 Yds.	100 Yds.	Barrel Length (in.)
# 357 Magnum Jacketed Hollow Point	X3574P	158	JHP	1235	1104	1015	535	428	361	0.8	3.5	4V
# 357 Magnum Jacketed Soft Point	X3575P	158	JSP	1235	1104	1015	535	428	361	0.8	3.5	4V
10mm Automatic Silvertip Hollow Point	X10MMSTHP	175	STHP	1290	1141	1037	649	506	418	0.7	3.3	5½
# 41 Remington Magnum Silvertip Hollow Point	X41MSTHP	175	STHP	1250	1120	1029	607	488	412	0.8	3.4	4V
41 Remington Magnum Lead Semi-Wad Cutter	X41MP	210	Lead-SWC	965	898	842	434	376	331	1.3	5.4	4V
# 41 Remington Magnum Jacketed Soft Point	X41MJSP	210	JSP	1300	1162	1062	788	630	526	0.7	3.2	4V
# 41 Remington Magnum Jacketed Hollow Point	X41MHP2	210	JHP	1300	1162	1062	788	630	526	0.7	3.2	4V
# 44 Smith & Wesson Special Silvertip Hollow Point	X44STHPS2	200	STHP	900	860	822	360	328	300	1.4	5.9	6½
44 Smith & Wesson Special Lead Round Nose	X44SP	246	Lead-RN	755	725	695	310	285	265	2.0	8.3	6½
# 44 Remington Magnum Silvertip Hollow Point	X44MSTHP2	210	STHP	1250	1106	1010	729	570	475	0.8	3.5	4V
# 44 Remington Magnum Hollow Soft Point	X44MHSP2	240	HSP	1180	1081	1010	741	623	543	0.9	3.7	4V
44 Remington Magnum Lead Semi-Wad Cutter (Med. Vel.)	X44MWCP	240	Lead-SWC	1000	937	885	533	468	417	1.2	4.9	6½V
44 Remington Magnum Lead Semi-Wad Cutter (Gas Check)	X44MP	240	Lead-SWC	1350	1186	1069	971	749	608	0.7	3.1	4V
45 Automatic Silvertip Hollow Point	X45ASHP2	185	STHP	1000	938	888	411	362	324	1.2	4.9	5
45 Automatic Full Metal Case	X45A1P2	230	FMC	810	776	745	335	308	284	1.7	7.2	5
45 Automatic Super-Match Full Metal Case Semi-Wad Cutter	X45AWCP	185	FMC-SWC	770	707	650	244	205	174	2.0	8.7	5
# 45 Colt Silvertip Hollow Point	X45CSHP2	225	STHP	920	877	839	423	384	352	1.4	5.6	5½
45 Colt Lead Round Nose	X45CP2	255	Lead-RN	860	820	780	420	380	345	1.5	6.1	5½
# 45 Winchester Magnum Full Metal Case (Not for Arms Chambered for Standard 45 Automatic)	X45WM	230	FMC	1400	1232	1107	1001	775	636	0.6	2.8	5

CENTERFIRE BLANK CARTRIDGES

Cartridge	Symbol		Type									
32 Smith & Wesson Black Powder	32BL2P		Black Powder	—	—	—	—	—	—	—	—	—
† 38 Smith & Wesson Smokeless Powder	38BLP		Smokeless Powder	—	—	—	—	—	—	—	—	—
38 Special Smokeless Powder	38SBLP		Smokeless Powder	—	—	—	—	—	—	—	—	—

FMC–Full Metal Case • JHP–Jacketed Hollow Point • JSP–Jacketed Soft Point • RN–Round Nose
Met. Pt.–Metal Point • XP–Expanding Point • WC–Wad Cutter • SWC–Semi Wad Cutter • HSP–Hollow Soft Point
STHP–Silvertip Hollow Point • HP–Hollow Point
**Lubaloy
*For use only in 38 Super Automatic Pistols.

+ P Ammunition with (+ P) on the case head stamp is loaded to higher pressure. Use only in firearms designated for this cartridge and so recommended by the gun manufacturer.
V-Data is based on velocity obtained from 4" vented test barrels for revolver cartridges (38 Special, 357 Magnum, 41 Rem. Mag. and 44 Rem. Mag.).

Specifications are nominal. Test barrels are used to determine ballistics figures. Individual firearms may differ from test barrel statistics.
Specifications subject to change without notice.
Acceptable for use in rifles also.
† Obsolete in 1989.

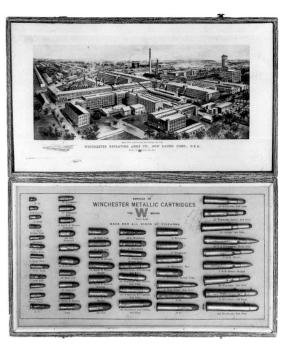

A factory salesman's sample case of c. 1914 (18″ × 10½″).
Winchester Arms Museum Collection.

The 125th Anniversary Tin, Winchester-Olin's salute to "125 years of success." Twenty-five 2¾-inch Super-X #6 shotshells are contained in the six-inch square metal box, embellished with period sporting art and decorative borders. Special tube and head stamps are marked on the limited edition shotshells.

Super-X® Centerfire Rifle Ammunition

Cartridge	Symbol	Game Selector Guide	CXP Guide Number	Bullet Wt. (grs.)	Type	Barrel Length (in.)	Velocity in Feet Per Second (fps)					
							Muzzle	100	200	300	400	500
218 Bee	X218B	V	1	46	HP	24	2760	2102	1550	1155	961	850
22 Hornet	X22H1	V	1	45	SP	24	2690	2042	1502	1128	948	840
22-250 Remington	X222501	V	1	55	PSP	24	3680	3137	2656	2222	1832	1493
222 Remington	X222R	V	1	50	PSP	24	3140	2602	2123	1700	1350	1107
222 Remington	X222R1	V	-	55	FMC	24	3020	2675	2355	2057	1783	1537
223 Remington	X223RH	V	1	53	HP	24	3330	2882	2477	2106	1770	1475
223 Remington	X223R	V	1	55	PSP	24	3240	2747	2304	1905	1554	1270
223 Remington	X223R1	V	-	55	FMC	24	3240	2877	2543	2232	1943	1679
223 Remington	X223R2	D	2	64	PP	24	3020	2621	2256	1920	1619	1362
225 Winchester	X2251	V	1	55	PSP	24	3570	3066	2616 *	2208	1838	1514
243 Winchester	X2431	V	1	80	PSP	24	3350	2955	2593	2259	1951	1670
243 Winchester	X2432	D,O/P	2	100	PP	24	2960	2697	2449	2215	1993	1786
6mm Remington	X6MMR1	V	1	80	PSP	24	3470	3064	2694	2352	2036	1747
6mm Remington	X6MMR2	D,O/P	2	100	PP	24	3100	2829	2573	2332	2104	1889
25-06 Remington	X25061	V	1	90	PEP	24	3440	3043	2680	2344	2034	1749
25-06 Remington	X25062	D,O/P	2	120	PEP	24	2990	2730	2484	2252	2032	1825
# 25-20 Winchester	X25202	V	1	86	SP	24	1460	1194	1030	931	858	798
25-35 Winchester	X2535	D	2	117	SP	24	2230	1866	1545	1282	1097	984
250 Savage	X2503	D,O/P	2	100	ST	24	2820	2467	2140	1839	1569	1339
257 Roberts +P	X257P2	D,O/P	2	100	ST	24	3000	2633	2295	1982	1697	1447
257 Roberts +P	X257P3	D,O/P	2	117	PP	24	2780	2411	2071	1761	1488	1263
264 Winchester Mag.	X2642	D,O/P	2	140	PP	24	3030	2782	2548	2326	2114	1914
270 Winchester	X2701	V	1	100	PSP	24	3430	3021	2649	2305	1988	1699
270 Winchester	X2705	D,O/P	2	130	PP	24	3060	2802	2559	2329	2110	1904
270 Winchester	X2703	D,O/P	2	130	ST	24	3060	2776	2510	2259	2022	1801
270 Winchester	X2704	D,M	3	150	PP	24	2850	2585	2336	2100	1879	1673
284 Winchester	X2842	D,O/P,M	2	150	PP	24	2860	2595	2344	2108	1886	1680
7mm Mauser (7 × 57)	X7MM1	D	2	145	PP	24	2690	2442	2206	1985	1777	1586
† 7mm Mauser (7 × 57)	X7MM	D	2	175	SP	24	2440	2137	1857	1603	1382	1204
7mm Remington Mag.	X7MMR1	D,O/P,M	2	150	PP	24	3110	2830	2568	2320	2085	1866
7mm Remington Mag.	X7MMR2	D,O/P,M	3	175	PP	24	2860	2645	2440	2244	2057	1879
# 30 Carbine	X30M1	V	1	110	HSP	20	1990	1567	1236	1035	923	842
30-30 Winchester	X30301	D		150	HP	24	2390	2018	1684	1398	1177	1036
30-30 Winchester	X30306	D	2	150	PP	24	2390	2018	1684	1398	1177	1036
30-30 Winchester	X30302	D	2	150	ST	24	2390	2018	1684	1398	1177	1036
30-30 Winchester	X30303	D	2	170	PP	24	2200	1895	1619	1381	1191	1061
30-30 Winchester	X30304	D	2	170	ST	24	2200	1895	1619	1381	1191	1061

	Energy In Foot Pounds (ft-lbs)					Trajectory, Short Range/Yards						Trajectory, Long Range/Yards						
Muzzle	100	200	300	400	500	50	⊕100	150	200	250	300	100	150	⊕200	250	300	400	500
778	451	245	136	94	74	0.3	0	-2.3	-7.2	-15.8	-29.4	1.5	0	-4.2	-12.0	-24.8	-71.4	-155.6
723	417	225	127	90	70	0.3	0	-2.4	-7.7	-16.9	-31.3	1.6	0	-4.5	-12.8	-26.4	-75.6	-163.4
1654	1201	861	603	410	272	0.2	0.5	0	-1.6	-4.4	-8.7	2.3	2.6	1.9	0	-3.4	-15.9	-38.9
1094	752	500	321	202	136	0.5	0.9	0	-2.5	-6.9	-13.7	2.2	1.9	0	-3.8	-10.0	-32.3	-73.8
1114	874	677	517	388	288	0.5	0.9	0	-2.2	-6.1	-11.7	2.0	1.7	0	-3.3	-8.3	-24.9	-52.5
1305	978	722	522	369	256	0.3	0.7	0	-1.9	-5.3	-10.3	1.7	1.4	0	-2.9	-7.4	-22.7	-49.1
1282	921	648	443	295	197	0.4	0.8	0	-2.2	-6.0	-11.8	1.9	1.6	0	-3.3	-8.5	-26.7	-59.6
1282	1011	790	608	461	344	0.4	0.7	0	-1.9	-5.1	-9.9	1.7	1.4	0	-2.8	-7.1	-21.2	-44.6
1296	977	723	524	373	264	0.6	0.9	0	-2.4	-6.5	-12.5	2.1	1.8	0	-3.5	-9.0	-27.4	-59.6
1556	1148	836	595	412	280	0.2	0.6	0	-1.7	-4.6	-9.0	2.4	2.8	2.0	0	-13.5	-16.3	-39.5
1993	1551	1194	906	676	495	0.3	0.7	0	-1.8	-4.9	-9.4	2.6	2.9	2.1	0	-3.6	-16.2	-37.9
1945	1615	1332	1089	882	708	0.5	0.9	0	-2.2	-5.8	-11.0	1.9	1.6	0	-3.1	-7.8	-22.6	-46.3
2139	1667	1289	982	736	542	0.3	0.6	0	-1.6	-4.5	-8.7	2.4	2.7	1.9	0	-3.3	-14.9	-35.0
2133	1777	1470	1207	983	792	0.4	0.8	0	-1.9	-5.2	-9.9	1.7	1.5	0	-2.8	-7.0	-20.4	-41.7
2364	1850	1435	1098	827	611	0.3	0.6	0	-1.7	-4.5	-8.8	2.4	2.7	2.0	0	-3.4	-15.0	-35.2
2382	1985	1644	1351	1100	887	0.5	0.8	0	-2.1	-5.6	-10.7	1.9	1.6	0	-3.0	-7.5	-22.0	-44.8
407	272	203	165	141	122	0	-4.1	-14.4	-31.8	-57.3	-92.0	0	-8.2	-23.5	-47.0	-79.6	-175.9	-319.4
1292	904	620	427	313	252	0.6	0	-3.1	-9.2	-19.0	-33.1	2.1	0	-5.1	-13.8	-27.0	-70.1	-142.0
1765	1351	1017	751	547	398	0.2	0	-1.6	-4.9	-10.0	-17.4	2.4	2.0	0	-3.9	-10.1	-30.5	-65.2
1998	1539	1169	872	639	465	0.5	0.9	0	-2.4	-4.9	-12.3	2.9	3.0	1.6	0	-6.4	-23.2	-51.2
2009	1511	1115	806	576	415	0.8	1.1	0	-2.9	-7.8	-15.1	2.6	2.2	0	-4.2	-10.8	-33.0	-70.0
2854	2406	2018	1682	1389	1139	0.5	0.8	0	-2.0	-5.4	-10.2	1.8	1.5	0	-2.9	-7.2	-20.8	-42.2
2612	2027	1557	1179	877	641	0.3	0.6	0	-1.7	-4.6	-9.0	2.5	2.8	2.0	0	-3.4	-15.5	-36.4
2702	2267	1890	1565	1285	1046	0.4	0.8	0	-2.0	-5.3	-10.1	1.8	1.5	0	-2.8	-7.1	-20.6	-42.0
2702	2225	1818	1472	1180	936	0.5	0.8	0	-2.0	-5.5	-10.4	1.8	1.5	0	-2.9	-7.4	-21.6	-44.3
2705	2226	1817	1468	1175	932	0.6	1.0	0	-2.4	-6.4	-12.2	2.2	1.8	0	-3.4	-8.6	-25.0	-51.4
2724	2243	1830	1480	1185	940	0.6	1.0	0	-2.4	-6.3	-12.1	2.1	1.8	0	-3.4	-8.5	-24.8	-51.0
2334	1920	1568	1268	1017	810	0.2	0	-1.7	-4.9	-10.0	-17.1	1.1	0	-2.7	-7.3	-13.8	-33.9	-65.1
2313	1774	1340	998	742	563	0.4	0	-2.3	-6.8	-13.8	-23.7	1.5	0	-3.7	-10.0	-19.1	-48.1	-95.4
3221	2667	2196	1792	1448	1160	0.4	0.8	0	-1.9	-5.2	-9.9	1.7	1.5	0	-2.8	-7.0	-20.5	-42.1
3178	2718	2313	1956	1644	1372	0.6	0.9	0	-2.3	-6.0	-11.3	2.0	1.7	0	-3.2	-7.9	-22.7	-45.8
967	600	373	262	208	173	0.9	0	-4.5	-13.5	-28.3	-49.9	0	-4.5	-13.5	-28.3	-49.9	-118.6	-228.2
1902	1356	944	651	461	357	0.5	0	-2.6	-7.7	-16.0	-27.9	1.7	0	-4.3	-11.6	-22.7	-59.1	-120.5
1902	1356	944	651	461	357	0.5	0	-2.6	-7.7	-16.0	-27.9	1.7	0	-4.3	-11.6	-22.7	-59.1	-120.5
1902	1356	944	651	461	357	0.5	0	-2.6	-7.7	-16.0	-27.9	1.7	0	-4.3	-11.6	-22.7	-59.1	-120.5
1827	1355	989	720	535	425	0.6	0	-3.0	-8.9	-18.0	-31.1	2.0	0	-4.8	-13.0	-25.1	-63.6	-126.7
1827	1355	989	720	535	425	0.6	0	-3.0	-8.9	-18.0	-31.1	2.0	0	-4.8	-13.0	-25.1	-63.6	-126.7

Super X® Centerfire Rifle Ammunition (continued)

Cartridge	Symbol	Game Selector Guide	CXP Guide Number	Bullet Wt. (grs.)	Type	Barrel Length (in.)	Velocity in Feet Per Second (fps)					
							Muzzle	100	200	300	400	500
30-06 Springfield	X30062	V	1	125	PSP	24	3140	2780	2447	2138	1853	1595
30-06 Springfield	X30061	D,O/P	2	150	PP	24	2920	2580	2265	1972	1704	1466
30-06 Springfield	X30063	D,O/P	2	150	ST	24	2910	2617	2342	2083	1843	1622
30-06 Springfield	X30065	D,O/P,M	2	165	SP	24	2800	2573	2357	2151	1956	1772
30-06 Springfield	X30064	D,O/P,M	2	180	PP	24	2700	2348	2023	1727	1466	1251
30-06 Springfield	X30066	D,O/P,M,L	3	180	ST	24	2700	2469	2250	2042	1846	1663
30-06 Springfield	X30069	M,L	3	220	ST	24	2410	2192	1985	1791	1611	1448
30-40 Krag	X30401	D	2	180	PP	24	2430	2099	1795	1525	1298	1128
300 Winchester Mag.	X30WM1	D,O/P	2	150	PP	24	3290	2951	2636	2342	2068	1813
300 Winchester Mag.	X30WM2	O/P,M,L	3	180	PP	24	2960	2745	2540	2344	2157	1979
300 Winchester Mag.	X30WM3	M,L,XL	3D	220	ST	24	2680	2448	2228	2020	1823	1640
300 H. & H. Magnum	X300H2	O/P,M,L	3	180	ST	24	2880	2640	2412	2196	1991	1798
300 Savage	X3001	D,O/P	2	150	PP	24	2630	2311	2015	1743	1500	1295
300 Savage	X3003	D,O/P	2	150	ST	24	2630	2354	2095	1853	1631	1434
300 Savage	X3004	D	2	180	PP	24	2350	2025	1728	1467	1252	1098
303 Savage	X3032	D	2	190	ST	24	1890	1612	1372	1183	1055	970
303 British	X303B1	D	2	180	PP	24	2460	2233	2018	1816	1629	1459
307 Winchester	X3075	D	2	150	PP	24	2760	2321	1924	1575	1289	1091
308 Winchester	X3085	D,O/P	2	150	PP	24	2820	2488	2179	1893	1633	1405
308 Winchester	X3082	D,O/P	2	150	ST	24	2820	2533	2263	2009	1774	1560
308 Winchester	X3086	D,O/P,M	2	180	PP	24	2620	2274	1955	1666	1414	1212
308 Winchester	X3083	M,L	3	180	ST	24	2620	2393	2178	1974	1792	1604
32 Win. Special	X32WS2	D	2	170	PP	24	2250	1870	1537	1267	1082	971
32 Win. Special	X32WS3	D	2	170	ST	24	2250	1870	1537	1267	1082	971
# 32-20 Winchester	X32201	V	1	100	Lead	24	1210	1021	913	834	769	712
8mm Mauser (8×57)	X8MM	D	2	170	PP	24	2360	1969	1622	1333	1123	997
338 Winchester Mag.	X3381	D,O/P,M	3	200	PP	24	2960	2658	2375	2110	1862	1635
338 Winchester Mag.	X3383	M,L,XL	3D	225	SP	24	2780	2572	2374	2184	2003	1832
35 Remington	X35R1	D	2	200	PP	24	2020	1646	1335	1114	985	901
356 Winchester	X3561	D,M	2	200	PP	24	2460	2114	1797	1517	1284	1113
356 Winchester	X3563	M,L	3	250	PP	24	2160	1911	1682	1476	1299	1158
# 357 Magnum	X3575P	V,D	2	158	JSP	20	1830	1427	1138	980	883	809
358 Winchester	X3581	D,M	3	200	ST	24	2490	2171	1876	1610	1379	1194
375 Winchester	X375W	D,M	2	200	PP	24	2200	1841	1526	1268	1089	980
375 Winchester	X375W1	D,M	2	250	PP	24	1900	1647	1424	1239	1103	1011
375 H. & H. Magnum	X375H1	M,L,XL	3D	270	PP	24	2690	2420	2166	1928	1707	1507
375 H. & H. Magnum	X375H2	M,L,XL	3D	300	ST	24	2530	2268	2022	1793	1583	1397

Muzzle	Energy In Foot Pounds (ft-lbs)					Trajectory, Short Range/Yards						Trajectory, Long Range/Yards						
	100	200	300	400	500	50	⊕ 100	150	200	250	300	100	150	⊕ 200	250	300	400	500
2736	2145	1662	1269	953	706	0.4	0.8	0	−2.1	−5.6	−10.7	1.8	1.5	0	−3.0	−7.7	−23.0	−48.5
2839	2217	1708	1295	967	716	0.6	1.0	0	−2.4	−6.6	−12.7	2.2	1.8	0	−3.5	−9.0	−27.0	−57.1
2820	2281	1827	1445	1131	876	0.6	0.9	0	−2.3	−6.3	−12.0	2.1	1.8	0	−3.3	−8.5	−25.0	−51.8
2873	2426	2036	1696	1402	1151	0.7	1.0	0	−2.5	−6.5	−12.2	2.2	1.9	0	−3.6	−8.4	−24.4	−49.6
2913	2203	1635	1192	859	625	0.2	0	−1.8	−5.5	−11.2	−19.5	2.7	2.3	0	−4.4	−11.3	−34.4	−73.7
2913	2436	2023	1666	1362	1105	0.2	0	−1.6	−4.8	−9.7	−16.5	2.4	2.0	0	−3.7	−9.3	−27.0	−54.9
2837	2347	1924	1567	1268	1024	0.4	0	−2.2	−6.4	−12.7	−21.6	1.5	0	−3.5	−9.1	−17.2	−41.8	−79.9
2360	1761	1288	929	673	508	0.4	0	−2.4	−7.1	−14.5	−25.0	1.6	0	−3.9	−10.5	−20.3	−51.7	−103.9
3605	2900	2314	1827	1424	1095	0.3	0.7	0	−1.8	−4.8	−9.3	2.6	2.9	2.1	0	−3.5	−15.4	−35.5
3501	3011	2578	2196	1859	1565	0.5	0.8	0	−2.1	−5.5	−10.4	1.9	1.6	0	−2.9	−7.3	−20.9	−41.9
3508	2927	2424	1993	1623	1314	0.2	0	−1.7	−4.9	−9.9	−16.9	2.5	2.0	0	−3.8	−9.5	−27.5	−56.1
3315	2785	2325	1927	1584	1292	0.6	0.9	0	−2.3	−6.0	−11.5	2.1	1.7	0	−3.2	−8.0	−23.3	−47.4
2303	1779	1352	1012	749	558	0.3	0	−1.9	−5.7	−11.6	−19.9	2.8	2.3	0	−4.5	−11.5	−34.4	−73.0
2303	1845	1462	1143	886	685	0.3	0	−1.8	−5.4	−11.0	−18.8	2.7	2.2	0	−4.2	−10.7	−31.5	−65.5
2207	1639	1193	860	626	482	0.5	0	−2.6	−7.7	−15.6	−27.1	1.7	0	−4.2	−11.3	−21.9	−55.8	−112.0
1507	1096	794	591	469	397	1.0	0	−4.3	−12.6	−25.5	−43.7	2.9	0	−6.8	−18.3	−35.1	−88.2	−172.5
2418	1993	1627	1318	1060	851	0.3	0	−2.1	−6.1	−12.2	−20.8	1.4	0	−3.3	−8.8	−16.6	−40.4	−77.4
2538	1795	1233	826	554	397	0.2	0	−1.9	−5.6	−11.8	−20.8	1.2	0	−3.2	−8.7	−17.1	−44.9	−92.2
2648	2061	1581	1193	888	657	0.2	0	−1.6	−4.8	−9.8	−16.9	2.4	2.0	0	−3.8	−9.8	−29.3	−62.0
2648	2137	1705	1344	1048	810	0.2	0	−1.5	−4.5	−9.3	−15.9	2.3	1.9	0	−3.6	−9.1	−26.9	−55.7
2743	2066	1527	1109	799	587	0.3	0	−2.0	−5.9	−12.1	−20.9	2.9	2.4	0	−4.7	−12.1	−36.9	−79.1
2743	2288	1896	1557	1269	1028	0.2	0	−1.8	−5.2	−10.4	−17.7	2.6	2.1	0	−4.0	−9.9	−28.9	−58.8
1911	1320	892	606	442	356	0.6	0	−3.1	−9.2	−19.0	−33.2	2.0	0	−5.1	−13.8	−27.1	−70.9	−144.3
1911	1320	892	606	442	356	0.6	0	3.1	−9.2	−19.0	−33.2	2.0	0	−5.1	−13.8	−27.1	−70.9	−144.3
325	231	185	154	131	113	0	−6.3	−20.9	−44.9	−79.3	−125.1	0	−11.5	−32.3	−63.6	−106.3	−230.3	−413.3
2102	1463	993	671	476	375	0.5	0	−2.7	−8.2	−17.0	−29.8	1.8	0	−4.5	−12.4	−24.3	−63.8	−130.7
3890	3137	2505	1977	1539	1187	0.5	0.9	0	−2.3	−6.1	−11.6	2.0	1.7	0	−3.2	−8.2	−24.3	−50.4
3862	3306	2816	2384	2005	1677	1.2	1.3	0	−2.7	−7.1	−12.9	2.7	2.1	0	−3.6	−9.4	−25.0	−49.9
1812	1203	791	551	431	360	0.9	0	−4.1	−12.1	−25.1	−43.9	2.7	0	−6.7	−18.3	−35.8	−92.8	−185.5
2688	1985	1434	1022	732	550	0.4	0	−2.3	−7.0	−14.3	−24.7	1.6	0	−3.8	−10.4	−20.1	−51.2	−102.3
2591	2028	1571	1210	937	745	0.6	0	−3.0	−8.7	−17.4	−30.0	2.0	0	−4.7	−12.4	−23.7	−58.4	−112.9
1175	715	454	337	274	229	0	−2.4	−9.1	−21.0	−39.2	−64.3	0	−5.5	−16.2	−33.1	−57.0	−128.3	−235.8
2753	2093	1563	1151	844	633	0.4	0		−6.5	−13.3	−23.0	1.5	0	−3.6	−9.7	−18.6	−47.2	−94.1
2150	1506	1034	714	527	427	0.6	0	−3.2	−9.5	−19.5	−33.8	2.1	0	−5.2	−14.1	−27.4	−70.1	−138.1
2005	1506	1126	852	676	568	0.9	0	−4.1	−12.0	−24.0	−40.9	2.7	0	−6.5	−17.2	−32.7	−80.6	−154.1
4337	3510	2812	2228	1747	1361	0.2	0	−1.7	−5.1	−10.3	−17.6	2.5	2.1	0	−3.9	−10.0	−29.4	−60.7
4263	3426	2723	2141	1669	1300	0.3	0	−2.0	−5.9	−11.9	−20.3	2.9	2.4	0	−4.5	−11.5	−33.8	−70.1

Super X® Centerfire Rifle Ammunition (continued)

Cartridge	Symbol	Game Selector Guide	CXP Guide Number	Bullet Wt. (grs.)	Type	Barrel Length (in.)	Velocity in Feet Per Second (fps)					
							Muzzle	100	200	300	400	500
375 H. & H. Magnum	X375H3	XL	4	300	FMC	24	2530	2171	1843	1551	1307	1126
# 38-40 Winchester	X3840	D	2	180	SP	24	1160	999	901	827	764	710
38-55 Winchester	X3855	D	2	255	SP	24	1320	1190	1091	1018	963	917
# 44 Remington Magnum	X44MHSP2	D	2	240	HSP	20	1760	1362	1094	953	861	789
# 44-40 Winchester	X4440	D	2	200	SP	24	1190	1006	900	822	756	699
45-70 Government	X4570H	D,M	2	300	JHP	24	1880	1650	1425	1235	1105	1010
458 Winchester Mag.	X4580	XL	4	500	FMC	24	2040	1823	1623	1442	1287	1161
458 Winchester Mag.	X4581	L,XL	3D	510	SP	24	2040	1770	1527	1319	1157	1046

† Obsolete in 1989.

	CXP Class	Examples
V–Varmint	1	Prairie dog, coyote, woodchuck
D–Deer	2	Antelope, deer, black bear
O/P–Open or Plains	3	Elk, moose
M–Medium Game	3D	All game in category 3 plus large dangerous game (i.e. Kodiak bear)
L–Large Game	4	Cape Buffalo, elephant
XL–Extra Large Game		

Supreme® Centerfire Rifle Ammunition

Cartridge	Symbol	Game Selector Guide	CXP Guide Number	Bullet Wt. (grs.)	Type	Barrel Length (in.)	Velocity In Feet Per Second (fps)					
							Muzzle	100	200	300	400	500
22-250 Remington	S22250R52	V	1	52	HPBT	24	3750	3268	2835	2442	2082	1755
243 Winchester	S243W100	D, O/P	2	100	SPBT	24	2960	2712	2477	2254	2042	1843
270 Winchester	S270W140	D, O/P	2	140	STBT	24	2960	2753	2554	2365	2183	2009
30-30 Winchester	S3030W150	D	2	150	ST	24	2390	2018	1684	1398	1177	1036
30-06 Springfield	S3006S165	D,O/P,M	2	165	STBT	24	2800	2597	2402	2216	2038	1869
30-06 Springfield	S3006S180	D,O/P,M,L	3	180	STBT	24	2700	2503	2314	2133	1960	1797
308 Winchester	S308W180	D,O/P,M	3	180	STBT	24	2610	2424	2245	2074	1911	1756
300 Winchester Mag.	S300WM190	O/P,M,L	3D	190	STBT	24	2885	2698	2519	2347	2181	2023

	CXP Class	Examples
V–Varmint	1	Prairie dog, coyote, woodchuck
D–Deer	2	Antelope, deer, black bear
O/P–Open or Plains	3	Elk, moose
M–Medium Game	3D	All game in category 3 plus large dangerous game (i.e. Kodiak bear)
L–Large Game	4	Cape buffalo, elephant
XL–Extra Large Game		

Muzzle	Energy In Foot Pounds (ft-lbs)					Trajectory, Short Range/Yards						Trajectory, Long Range/Yards						
	100	200	300	400	500	50	⊕ 100	150	200	250	300	100	150	⊕ 200	250	300	400	500
4263	3139	2262	1602	1138	844	0.3	0	−2.2	−6.5	−13.5	−23.4	1.5	0	−3.6	−9.8	−19.1	−49.1	−99.5
538	399	324	273	233	201	0	−6.7	−22.2	−47.3	−83.2	−130.8	0	−12.1	−33.9	−66.4	−110.6	−238.3	−425.6
987	802	674	587	525	476	0	−4.7	−15.4	−32.7	−57.2	−89.3	0	−8.4	−23.4	−45.6	−75.2	−158.8	−277.4
1650	988	638	484	395	332	0	−2.7	−10.2	−23.6	−44.2	−73.3	0	−6.1	−18.1	−37.4	−65.1	−150.3	−282.5
629	449	360	300	254	217	0	−6.5	−21.6	−46.3	−81.8	−129.1	0	−11.8	−33.3	−65.5	−109.5	−237.4	−426.2
2355	1815	1355	1015	810	680	0	−2.4	−8.2	−17.6	−31.4	−51.5	0	−4.6	−12.8	−25.4	−44.3	−95.5	—
4620	3689	2924	2308	1839	1496	0.7	0	−3.3	−9.6	−19.2	−32.5	2.2	0	−5.2	−13.6	−25.8	−63.2	−121.7
4712	3547	2640	1970	1516	1239	0.8	0	−3.5	−10.3	−20.8	−35.6	2.4	0	−5.6	−14.9	−28.5	−71.5	−140.4

Acceptable for use in pistols and revolvers also.
HSP–Hollow Soft Point • PEP–Positive Expanding Point • PSP–Pointed Soft Point® • FMC–Full Metal Case • SP–Soft Point • HP–Hollow Point • ST–Silvertip® • JHP–Jacket Hollow Point • PP–Power Point

Muzzle	Energy In Foot Pounds (ft-lbs)					Trajectory, Short Range Yards						Trajectory, Long Range Yards						
	100	200	300	400	500	50	⊕ 100	150	200	250	300	100	150	⊕ 200	250	300	400	500
1624	1233	928	689	501	356	−.1	0	−.7	−2.4	−5.1	−9.1	1.2	1.1	0	−2.1	−5.5	−16.9	−36.6
1946	1633	1363	1128	926	754	.1	0	−1.3	−3.8	−7.8	−13.3	1.9	1.6	0	−3.0	−7.6	−22.0	−44.8
2724	2356	2029	1739	1482	1256	.1	0	−1.2	−3.7	−7.5	−12.7	1.8	1.5	0	−2.9	−7.2	−20.6	−41.3
1902	1356	944	651	461	357	.5	0	−2.6	−7.7	−16.0	−27.9	3.9	3.2	0	−6.2	−16.1	−49.4	−105.2
2873	2421	2114	1799	1522	1280	.1	0	−1.4	−4.3	−8.6	−14.6	2.1	1.8	0	−3.3	−8.2	−23.4	−47.0
2914	2504	2140	1819	1536	1290	.2	0	−1.6	−4.7	−9.4	−15.8	2.3	1.9	0	−3.5	−8.8	−25.3	−50.8
2723	2348	2015	1719	1459	1232	.2	0	−1.7	−5.0	−10.1	−17.0	2.5	2.1	0	−3.8	−9.4	−26.9	−54.0
3512	3073	2679	2325	2009	1728	.1	0	−1.3	−3.9	−7.8	−13.2	1.9	1.6	0	−3.0	−7.4	−21.1	−42.2

Rimfire Ammunition

Rimfire Rifle and Pistol					Rifle						Pistol	
Cartridge	Symbol	Bullet Wt. (grs.)	Bullet Type	Game Guide	Velocity (fps) Muzzle	100 yds	Energy (ft-lbs) Muzzle	100 yds.	Nominal Mid-Range Trajectory 100 yds.	Barrel Length (In.)	Muzzle Velocity	Muzzle Energy (ft-lbs)
Super-X High Velocity Cartridges— copperplated bullets												
22 Short	X22S	29	**LRN***	P,S	1095	903	77	52	4.5	6	1010	66
22 Long Rifle	X22LR	40	**LRN***	P,S,V,T,H	1255	1017	140	92	3.6	6	1060	100
22 Long Rifle	X22LR1	40	**LRN***	P,S,V,T,H	1255	1017	140	92	3.6	6	1060	100
22 Long Rifle	X22LRBP	40	**LRN***	P,S,V,T,H	1255	1017	140	92	3.6	6	1060	100
22 Long Rifle Hollow Point	X22LRH	37	**LHP***	P,S,V	1280	1015	135	85	3.5	—	—	—
22 Long Rifle Hollow Point	X22LRH1	37	**LHP***	P,S,V	1280	1015	135	85	3.5	—	—	—
Super-X 22 Winchester Magnum Cartridges— jacketed bullets												
22 Win Mag	X22WMR	40	**JHP**	P,S,V,H	1910	1326	324	156	1.7	6.5	1480	195
22 Win Mag	X22MR1	40	**FMC**	P,S,V,H	1910	1326	324	156	1.7	6.5	1480	195
Winchester Super Silhouette												
22 Long Rifle	XS22LR1	42	**LTC**	P,S,V,T,H	1220	1003	139	94	3.6	6/10	1025/1105	98/114
Winchester T22 Standard Velocity Cartridges												
22 Long Rifle Target	XT22LR	40	**LRN**	P,T	1150	976	117	85	4.0	6	950	80
Other Winchester Rimfire Cartridges												
22 Long Rifle, Wildcat	WW22LR	40	**LRN**	P,S,V,T,H	1255	1017	140	92	3.6	6	1060	100
22 Long Rifle, Shot	X22LRS	37	**#12 Shot**	V	—	—	—	—	—	—	—	—
22 Short Blank	22BL	Black Powder		—	—	—	—	—	—	—	—	—
22 Short C.B.	WW22CBS2	29	**LRN**	P,T	725	—	—	—	—	—	—	—

*Lubaloy coated
Bullet Type: LRN–Lead Round Nose • LHP–Lead Hollow Point • JHP–Jacketed Hollow Point • FMC–Full Metal Case • LTC–Lead Truncated Cone
Game Guide: P–Plinking • S–Squirrel • V–Varmint • T–Target • H–Silhouette

Pattern/Pellet Density and Energy Guide

Look up distance to your game for recommended pellet. Pellets appropriate for longer distance may also be used at shorter range. Use of pellets at distances surpassing their listing is not recommended.

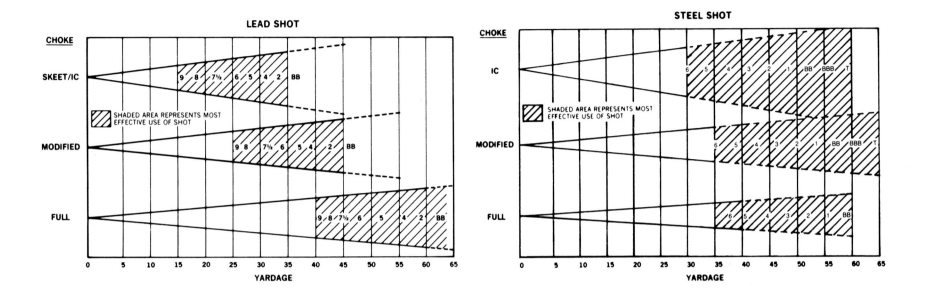

Shotshell Ammunition

Super-X Game Loads

Gauge	Symbol	Length of Shell In.	Powder Dram Equivalent	Velocity Fps @ 3 Ft	Oz Shot	Standard Shot Sizes
12	X12	2¾	3¾	1330	1¼	2, 4, 5, 6, 7½, 9
16	X16H	2¾	3¼	1295	1⅛	4, 6, 7½
20	X20	2¾	2¾	1220	1	4, 5, 6, 7½, 9
New 28	X28H	2¾	MAX	1125	1	6, 7½, 8
28	X28	2¾	2¼	1295	¾	6, 7½
410	X41	2½	MAX	1245	½	4, 6, 7½
410	X413	3	MAX	1135	11⁄16	4, 6, 7½

Super-X Buckshot Loads with Buffered Shot

Gauge	Symbol	Length of Shell In.	Powder Dram Equivalent	Velocity Fps @ 3 Ft	Total Pellets	Standard Shot Sizes
12	X12000B5	2¾	N/A	1325	8	000 Buck
12	X12RB5	2¾	N/A	1325	9	00 Buck
12	X120B5	2¾	N/A	1275	12	0 Buck
12	X121B5	2¾	N/A	1250	16	1 Buck
12	X124B5	2¾	N/A	1325	27	4 Buck
16	X16B5	2¾	N/A	1225	12	1 Buck
20	X20B5	2¾	N/A	1200	20	3 Buck

Winchester Game Loads

Gauge	Symbol	Length of Shell In.	Powder Dram Equivalent	Velocity Fps @ 3 Ft	Oz Shot	Standard Shot Sizes
12	WW12P	2¾	3¾	1330	1¼	4, 6, 7½
12	WW12R	2¾	3¼	1290	1	6
12	WW12D	2¾	3¼	1290	1	7½, 8
16	WW16P	2¾	3¼	1295	1⅛	6
16	WW16R	2¾	2½	1165	1	6
16	WW16D	2¾	2½	1165	1	8
20	WW20P	2¾	2¾	1220	1	6, 7½
20	WW20R	2¾	2½	1210	⅞	6
20	WW20D	2¾	2½	1210	⅞	7½, 8

Field Trial and Blank Loads
Western® Field Trial Popper-Load

12	XP12FBL	2¾	—	—	—	Blank

Blank Loads

10	UW10BL	2⅞	8	Black Powder	—	Blank
12	UW12BL	2¾	6	Black Powder	—	Blank

Super Steel Non toxic Game Loads

Gauge	Symbol	Length of Shell In.	Powder Dram Equivalent	Velocity Fps @ 3 Ft	Oz Shot	Standard Shot Sizes
12	W12SD	2¾	MAX	1375	1	2, 4, 6
12	X12SSL	2¾	MAX	1365	1⅛	1, 2, 3, 4, 5, 6
20	X20SSL	2¾	MAX	1425	¾	4, 6

Super Steel Non toxic Magnum Loads

10	X10SSM	3½	MAX	1260	1¾	BB, 2
12	X12SSM	3	MAX	1265	1⅜	BB, 1, 2, 3, 4
12	X123SSM	3	MAX	1375	1¼	F, BB, 1, 2, 3, 4, 5
12	X12SSF	2¾	MAX	1275	1¼	BB, 1, 2, 3, 4, 5, 6
20	X20SSM	3	MAX	1330	1	2, 3, 4, 5, 6

Super Steel Non toxic Copperplated Magnum Loads

10	XS10C	3½	MAX	1350	1⅝	T, BBB
12	XS123	3	MAX	1375	1¼	F, T, BBB

Winchester AA® Target Loads

Gauge	Symbol	Length of Shell In.	Powder Dram Equivalent	Velocity Fps @ 3 Ft	Oz Shot	Standard Shot Sizes
12	WW12MAAP	2¾	3	1200	1⅛	7½, 8, 9
12	W12SLAA	2¾	2¾	1125	1⅛	7½, 8, 8½, 9
12	WW12AAP	2¾	2¾	1145	1⅛	7½, 8, 9
12	WW12LAAP	2¾	2¾	1180	1	7½, 8, 9
20	WW20AAP	2¾	2½	1200	⅞	8, 9
28	WW28AAP	2¾	2	1200	¾	9
410	WW41AAP	2½	MAX	1200	½	9

Double X Magnum Game Loads—Copperplated, Buffered Shot

Gauge	Symbol	Length of Shell In.	Powder Dram Equivalent	Velocity Fps @ 3 Ft	Oz Shot	Standard Shot Sizes
10	X103XC	3½	4½	1210	2¼	BB, 2, 4
12	X123XC	3	4	1210	1⅞	BB, 2, 4, 6
12	X12MXC	3	4	1280	1⅝	2, 4, 5, 6
12	X123MXCT	3	MAX	1125	2	4, 5, 6
12	X12XC	2¾	MAX	1260	1½	BB, 2, 4, 5, 6
12	X12XCT	2¾	MAX	1260	1½	4, 6
16	X16XC	2¾	3¼	1260	1¼	4, 6
20	X203XC	3	3	1185	1¼	2, 4, 6
20	X20XC	2¾	2¾	1175	1⅛	4, 6, 7½

Double X Magnum Buckshot Loads—Copperplated, Buffered Shot

Gauge	Symbol	Length of Shell In.	Powder Dram Equivalent	Velocity Fps @ 3 Ft	Oz Shot	Standard Shot Sizes
10	X10C4B	3½	N/A	1100	54	4 Buck
12	X123C000B	3	N/A	1225	10	000 Buck
12	X12XC3B5	3	N/A	1210	15	00 Buck
12	X12XC0B5	2¾	N/A	1290	12	00 Buck
12	X12C1B	2¾	N/A	1075	20	1 Buck
• 12	X1231B5	3	N/A	1040	24	1 Buck
12	X12XCMB5	3	N/A	1210	41	4 Buck
12	X12XC4B5	2¾	N/A	1250	34	4 Buck

(• Not Copperplated)

Xpert Field Loads—Improved Upland Game Load

Gauge	Symbol	Length of Shell In.	Powder Dram Equivalent	Velocity Fps @ 3 Ft	Oz Shot	Standard Shot Sizes
12	WW12SP	2¾	3¼	1220	1¼	6, 7½, 8
12	UWH12	2¾	3¼	1255	1⅛	6, 7½, 8, 9
12	UWL12	2¾	3¼	1290	1	6, 7½, 8
16	UWH16	2¾	2¾	1185	1⅛	6, 7½, 8
20	UWH20	2¾	2½	1165	1	6, 7½, 8, 9
20	UWL20	2¾	2½	1210	⅞	6, 7½, 8

Super-X Hollow Point Rifle Slug Loads

Gauge	Symbol	Length of Shell In.	Powder Dram Equivalent	Velocity Fps @ 3 Ft	Oz Shot	Standard Shot Sizes
12	X12RS15	2¾	MAX	1600	1	Rifled Slug
16	X16RS5	2¾	MAX	1570	⅘	Rifled Slug
20	X20RSM5	2¾	MAX	1570	¾	Rifled Slug
410	X41RS5	2½	MAX	1815	⅕	Rifled Slug

Hollow Point Rifle Slug Trajectory

25 yds.	50 yds.	75 yds.	100 yds.
+.2"	0"	−1.8"	−5.5"

Buckshot Specifications

Buckshot Sizes						
Shot Number	#4	#3	#1	0	00	000
Diameter in Inches	.24	.25	.30	.32	.33	.36
Pellets/Lb, Lead	338	299	173	143	130	100

Shot Specifications

Shot Sizes												
Shot Number	9	8	7½	6	5	4	3	2	1	BB	BBB	T	F
Diameter in Inches	.08	.09	.095	.11	.12	.13	.14	.15	.16	.18	.19	.20	.22
Pellets/Oz, Lead	585	410	350	225	170	135	—	87	—	50	—	—	—
Steel	—	—	—	316	243	191	153	125	103	72	61	53	39

Components for Handloading Ammunition

Symbol	Primer	Type
WLR	#8½-120	Large Rifle
WLRM	#8½M-120	Large Rifle Magnum
WSR	#6½-116	Small Rifle
WSP	#1½-108	Small Regular Pistol
WSPM	#1½M-108	Small Magnum Pistol
WLP	#7-111	Large Regular Pistol

Ball Powder® Smokeless Propellants are Available in the Following Sized Containers

Symbol	Type	Unit	Units Per Case	Case Wt. Lbs
231				
2311	Pistol	1 lb	10	14
2313	Pistol	3 lbs	6	24
2318	Pistol	8 lbs	4	38
296				
2961	Mag. Pistol & Shotshell	1 lb	10	14
2963	Mag. Pistol & Shotshell	3 lbs	6	24
2968	Mag. Pistol & Shotshell	8 lbs	4	38
WSL				
WSL1	Shotshell & Pistol	1 lb	10	13
WSL3	Shotshell & Pistol	3 lbs	6	24
WSL8	Shotshell & Pistol	8 lbs	2	19.5
WST				
WST1	Shotshell	1 lb	10	13
WST3	Shotshell	3 lbs	6	24
WST8	Shotshell	8 lbs	2	19.5
452AA				
452AA1	Shotshell & Pistol	1 lb	10	14
452AA3	Shotshell & Pistol	3 lbs	6	24
452AA10	Shotshell & Pistol	10 lbs	1	12

Symbol	Type	Unit	Units Per Case	Case Wt. Lbs
473AA				
473AA1	Shotshell	1 lb	10	14
473AA3	Shotshell	3 lbs	6	24
473AA10	Shotshell	10 lbs	1	12
540				
5401	Shotshell	1 lb	10	14
5403	Shotshell	3 lbs	6	24
5408	Shotshell	8 lbs	4	30
571				
5711	Shotshell	1 lb	10	14
5713	Shotshell	3 lbs	6	24
5718	Shotshell	8 lbs	4	38
680				
6801	Rifle	1 lb	10	14
748				
7481	Rifle	1 lbs	10	14
7488	Rifle	8 lbs	4	38
760				
7601	Rifle	1 lb	10	14
7608	Rifle	8 lbs	4	38

Unprimed Pistol/Revolver	
Symbol	**Caliber**
U357	357 Mag.
U357MAX	357 Rem. Max.
U9MM	9mm Luger (9mm Parabellum)
U9MMWM	9mm Win. Mag.
U38SP	38 Special
U38A	38 Auto. (and 38 Super)
U41	41 Rem. Mag.
U44S	44 S&W Special
U44M	44 Rem. Mag.
U44C	45 Colt
U45A	45 Auto.
U45WM	45 Win. Mag.

Unprimed Rifle	
Symbol	**Caliber**
U218	218 Bee
U22H	22 Hornet
U22250	22-250 Rem.
U220S	220 Swift
U222R	222 Rem.
U223R	223 Rem.
U225	225 Win.
U243	243 Win.
U6MMR	6mm Rem.
U2520	25-20 Win.
U2506	25-06 Rem.
U257P	257 Roberts + P
U264	264 Win. Mag.
U270	270 Win.
U284	284 Win.
U7MM	7mm Mauser
U7MAG	7mm Rem. Mag.
U3006	30-06 Springfield
U3040	30-40 Krag
U300WM	300 Win. Mag.

Unprimed Rifle	
Symbol	**Caliber**
U300H	300 H&H Mag.
U300	300 Savage
U307	307 Win.
U308	308 Win.
U303	303 British
U3220	32-20 Win.
U338	338 Win. Mag.
U348	348 Win.
U356	356 Win.
U358	358 Win.
U375H	375 H&H Mag.
U375W	375 Win.
U4440	44-40 Win.
U44M	44 Rem. Mag.
U4570	45-70 Govt.
U458	458 Win. Mag.
U458	458 Win. Mag.

Shotshell Wads

Symbol	Gauge	Description
WAA12	12	For 1 to 1⅝ ounce loads. White
WAA12R	12	For 1⅛ to 1⅞ ounce loads. Red
WAA12F114	12	For 1¼ to 1⅜ ounce loads. Yellow
WAA12SL (New)	12	For 1⅛ ounce loads but can be used anywhere 1 ounce F1 wad was recommended.
WAA20	20	For ⅞ to 1¼ ounce loads. White
WAA20F1	20	Best in target and field loads with 1 ounce to 1⅛ ounce shot charges. Yellow
WAA28	28	Used in most 28 gauge loads. Pink
WAA41	.410	Used in field and target loads in 2½ or 3 inch cases. White

World War II Production Figures: Olin Industries, Including Winchester and Western Divisions

Item	Quantity
Cartridges	
Rimfire	1,456,217,620
Centerfire Rifle .30-06 Class	8,362,290,537
Centerfire Pistol	1,718,320,461
.50 Caliber	3,052,913,818
20 Millimeter	54,851,309
Shot Shells	346,873,585
Miscellaneous	268,657,924
Total Rounds Ammunition	**15,260,125,254**
Winchester Carbines	818,059
Garand Rifles	513,582
Miscellaneous Rifles & Shotguns	116,587
Total Firearms	**1,448,228**
Other Items Furnished	
Radiator Tubes	1,000,000,000
Radiators	50,000
Batteries	2,212,777
Ignition Cartridges, Primers, Detonators,	
Clips, Traps and Trap Targets	
Targets	162,229,210
Bulk Powder & other Explosives	10,220,667 lbs.
Brass	1,587,254,979 lbs.
Aluminum	105,610,534 lbs.
Alumina	2,711,252 lbs.

Employees

	Peak	Total Hired
New Haven	13,667	45,413
East Alton	12,805	28,283
St. Louis	34,338	86,294
Alumina & Aluminum	600	1,700
Powder & High Explosives	275	750
Total	**61,685**	**162,440**

Data from Harold F. Williamson, *Winchester: The Gun That Won the West*, p. 389.

Bibliography

These titles represent the most useful, reliable, and informative books and monographs published to date on Winchester firearms. Literally thousands of magazine articles, catalogues, field manuals, and other publications could be added. New titles will continue to appear on the species Winchester, not a few of them specific to particular models or types. An up-to-date reference library is a collector's best helpmate.

Browning, John, and Curt Gentry. *John M. Browning American Gunmaker.* Ogden: Browning Arms Co., 1989. Biography of the brilliant inventor and technical commentary on his innumerable firearms inventions.

[No author listed]. *A History of Browning Guns from 1831.* Ogden, Utah: J. M. & M. S. Browning Co., 1942. Sixty-two-page monograph profusely illustrated with Browning inventions, prototypes, and production models and outlining Browning family history and achievements.

Butler, David F. *Winchester '73 and '76.* New York: Winchester Press, 1970. Historical and technical information on the Model 1873 and the Model 1876.

Carmichel, Jim. *Jim Carmichel's Book of the Rifle.* New York: Outdoor Life Books, 1985. Comprehensive volume by one of the world's most experienced and knowledgeable experts on sporting and target rifles.

Fadala, Sam. *Winchester's 30-30 Model 94: The Rifle America Loves.* Harrisburg, Pennsylvania: Stackpole Books, 1986. A sportsman's tribute to the best-selling Winchester of all time.

Garavaglia, Louis A., and Charles G. Worman. *Firearms of the American West 1803–1865.* Albuquerque: University of New Mexico Press, 1984. Historical and technical treatise, profusely illustrated and with prodigious text, with sections on the Jennings, Volcanics, and Henrys.

———— . *Firearms of the American West 1866–1894.* Albuquerque: University of New Mexico Press, 1985. Continuing the detailed and documented presentation of the first volume, with an ever-increasing presence of Winchesters.

Hall, Thomas E. *Sights West.* Cody, Wyoming: Buffalo Bill Historical Center, 1976. Selection of firearms from the Winchester Museum Collection.

McDowell, R. Bruce. *Evolution of the Winchester.* Tacoma: Armory Publications, 1985. Technical and historical review from the Hunt through the Model 1876, and more.

Madis, George. *The Winchester Book.* Brownsboro, Texas: Art and Reference House, various editions since 1961. Profusely illustrated, exhaustively detailed technical history of Winchester firearms and related subjects. Over 600 pages.

———— . *Winchester Dates of Manufacture.* Brownsboro, Texas: Art and Reference House, 1981. More than eighty models listed with serial productions dated by year.

———— . *The Winchester Era.* Brownsboro, Texas: Art and Reference House, 1984. Company history, accompanied by information on models produced.

———— . *The Winchester Handbook.* Brownsboro, Texas: Art and Reference House, 1981. Technical data and illustrations, various models; a handy guide of portable size.

———— . *The Winchester Model Twelve.* Brownsboro, Texas: Art and Reference House, 1982. Detailed work on the most popular Winchester pump shotgun ever made.

Parsons, John E. *The First Winchester.* New York: Winchester Press, 1969 (previous editions 1955, 1960). The Model 1866 Winchester, with background on the Henry and other antecedent arms.

Rattenbury, Richard, and Thomas E. Hall. *Sights West.* Cody, Wyoming: Buffalo Bill Historical Center, 1981. Selections from the Winchester Museum; expanded from the first edition, 1976.

Rattenbury, Richard. *The Browning Connection.* Cody, Wyoming: Buffalo Bill Historical Center, 1982. John Browning's historic connection with Winchester.

———— . *Winchester Promotional Arts.* Cody, Wyoming: Buffalo Bill Historical Center, 1978. Winchester advertising, calendars, cartridge boards, posters, and demonstrator (cutaway) firearms.

Reiger, John F. *American Sportsmen and the Origins of Conservation.* New York: Winchester Press, 1975.

Detailed and documented history of the foundation of the modern environmental movement by U.S. sportsmen-hunters in the nineteenth century.

Rosa, Joseph G. *Guns of the American West*. New York: Crown Publishers, 1985. The subject from the astute point of view of an eminent English historian and arms expert.

Roosevelt, Theodore. *Hunting Trips of a Ranchman*. New York and London: G.P. Putnam's Sons, 1885.

———. *Ranch Life and the Hunting-Trail*. New York: Century, 1888.

———. *The Wilderness Hunter*. New York: G.P. Putnam's Sons, 1893.

———. *Outdoor Pastimes of an American Hunter*. New York: Charles Scribner's Sons, 1905.

———. *African Game Trails*. 2 vols. New York: Charles Scribner's Sons, 1910.

Rule, Roger. *The Rifleman's Rifle: The Model 70*. Northridge, Calif.: Alliance Books, 1982. Comprehensive study of the most renowned of all Winchester bolt-actions, 1936 through 1981.

Schwing, Ned. *The Winchester Model 42*. Lola, Wisconsin: Krause Publications, 1990.

———. *Winchester's Finest, The Model 21*. Lola, Wisconsin: Krause Publications, 1991.

Sharp, Philip B. *The Rifle in America*. New York: Funk & Wagnalls, 1958. Over 800 pages long; history, technical data, and observations from a premier authority. Various editions since 1938.

Stadt, Ronald W. *Winchester Shotguns and Shotshells*. Tacoma, Wash.: Armory Publications, 1984. Detailed reference on the subject, from the double-hammer gun through to the Model 59, with a bibliography of Winchester catalogues and other printed material c. 1867–1981.

Trefethen, James B. *Americans and Their Guns*. Harrisburg, Pa.: Stackpole Books, 1967. History of the National Rifle Association and its role in marksmanship and sportsmanship training and education.

Trolard, Tom. *Winchester Commemoratives*. Plato, Texas: Commemorative Investments Press, 1985. Standard reference book on the subject of commemorative Winchesters.

Watrous, George R., Thomas E. Hall, James C. Rikhoff, Pete Kuhlhoff, and Duncan Barnes. *The History of Winchester Firearms 1866–1980*. Tulsa: Winchester Press, 1980. Model-by-model identification of Winchester firearms production.

Williamson, Clyde. *Winchester Lever Legacy*. Zachary, La.: Buffalo Press, 1988. Practical information and pictures on the shooting of various models and calibers of Winchesters, plus handloading data.

Williamson, Harold F. *Winchester: The Gun That Won the West*. New York: A.S. Barnes; London: Thomas Yoseloff, 1952. A business history of Winchester.

Wilson, R. L. *L.D. Nimschke Firearms Engraver*. Teaneck, N.J.: John J. Malloy, 1965. Facsimile with detailed captions and introductory text on one of America's most prolific and accomplished firearms engravers, active c. 1850–1904.

———. *Theodore Roosevelt Outdoorsman*. New York: Winchester Press, 1971. TR as sportsman, hunter, and arms collector—expert whose special love was for Winchesters.

———. *The Book of Winchester Engraving*. Los Angeles: Beinfeld Publishing, 1975. Detailed review of embellished Winchesters, organized generally by engravers and their specific styles.

———. *Winchester Engraving*. Palm Springs, Calif.: Beinfeld Publishing, 1990. Updated and expanded edition of volume noted above.

———. *Winchester: The Golden Age of American Gunmaking and the Winchester 1 of 1000*. Cody, Wyoming: Buffalo Bill Historical Center, 1983. Detailed study of the One of One Hundred and One of One Thousand rifles, with introductory essay "Deluxe American Firearms and the Winchester 1 of 1000."

Acknowledgments

To Jack Mattan, CEO and President, U.S. Repeating Arms Company, to G.L. Alcock, Jr., formerly President and CEO, U.S. Repeating Arms Company, to George Rockwell, Vice President, Marketing & Sales, to Nicholas G. Maravell, Manager, Advertising & Communications, and to Bruno Pardee, Manager, Custom Shop.

To Gerald W. Bersett, President, Winchester Division, Olin Corporation, and to Bruce E. Burdick, Sr. Counsel, Olin Intellectual Property Law Section.

To Thomas E. Henshaw and Harry H. Sefried, former Winchester employees.

To Peter and Patty Murray, and to their son Michael, Winchester collectors nonpareil.

To Thomas Gillen, for many helpful comments and improvements.

To H.G. Houze, formerly Curator, Cody Firearms Museum, to Dr. Paul Fees, Curator, Buffalo Bill Museum, and to Lawrence C. Means, Buffalo Bill Historical Center.

To Richard Rattenbury, Curator of History, National Cowboy Hall of Fame and Western Heritage Center and formerly Curator, Winchester Arms Museum, who read the manuscript and made several helpful improvements.

To Mrs. Joanne D. Hale, Executive Director, and to James Nottage, Curator, and to Dr. John P. Langellier, Director of Research & Publications, Gene Autry Western Heritage Museum.

To Christopher Brunker, Christopher Austyn, and Elizabeth Haynie, Christie's.

To Frederick S. Calhoun, Historian, U.S. Marshals Service, and Ana-Marie Sullivan.

To Robert J. Chandler, Historical Officer, Wells Fargo Bank.

To Robert T. Delfay, Executive Director, National Shooting Sports Foundation.

To Gaines de Graffenried, Curator, Texas Ranger Museum and Hall of Fame.

To Mrs. Teddy Griffith, Director, Ogden Union Station Museums, and to Linda Balls.

To Wallace Finley Dailey, Curator, Theodore Roosevelt Collection, Harvard College Library.

To Dr. Edward C. Ezell, Curator, Department of Military History, National Museum of American History, Smithsonian Institution.

To Don Snoddy, Director, Union Pacific Railroad Museum.

To Paul Thompson, Browning Arms Company.

To T. G. Bennett, John and Judy Woods, Kevin Cherry, Anstress Farwell, John G. Hamilton, George Jackson, Martin J. Lane, Dr. Edmund Lewis, Greg and Petra Martin, Herb Peck, Jr., Rhonda Redd, Deborah Rindge, Joseph G. Rosa, Peter and Sandra Riva, Paul R. Wells, Arno and Charlotte Werner, and to Heidi, Peter, Christopher, and Stephen Wilson.

And to Robert Loomis and colleagues at Random House, and to Martin Moskof and Associates, designers, who produced a complex volume in record time.

Photographic Note

Allan Brown's studio is in the lower Connecticut River Valley. He has been a photographer in the area for approximately twenty years, specializing in commercial and industrial photography for local and national clients.

His work has appeared in the editorial pages of *Outdoor Life, Audubon, Colonial Homes, Saturday Evening Post, Yankee, The American Rifleman, Man at Arms, Quest, Country Gentleman, Vermont Life, Guns Magazine,* and numerous other periodicals and books. He is a member of the Outdoor Writers Association of America and the Connecticut Art Directors Club. Brown's work has also been shown in a number of one-man shows in New England, and he was named Commercial Photographer of the Year in Connecticut (1984).

For firearms photography, Brown uses a 4×5 combo view camera almost exclusively. He prefers Kodak Ektachrome film (either daylight for outdoors or tungsten for studio work) for consistent quality. Of as much importance as the film is finding a quality lab to process it. Great discrepancies can be found in that area. It takes time, and trial and error, to find a lab that maintains high standards regularly.

For lighting he uses Lowell tungsten lights, 3200° Kelvin, in the studio. The combination of these lights along with various diffusion materials and reflectors produces the lighting he finds complimentary to firearms. Tungsten lights have the added benefit over strobes of allowing one to see the exact lighting that the film will record.

The majority of photographs in *Winchester: An American Legend* were shot by G. Allan Brown. Those that were not were taken by Sid Latham, Sheri Hoem, Richard Rattenbury, S.P. Stevens, Turk Takano, Larry Faeth, Vincent Gengarelly, Jonathan Green, Scott Saunders (Lin Caufield Photographers, Inc.), and Bruce Pendleton.

Owner Credits

Credits not indicated in text or picture captions are as follows: Reproduced through the gracious permission of H.M. Queen Elizabeth II, 43 (*right*); G. L. Alcock, Jr., dust jacket (*back cover*), 329 (Grand American Model 21); Alexander Acevedo, 89 (*bottom right*); Arizona Historical Society, 54 (*center*); author's collection, 21 (*right*), 113, 183, 204, 248 (*left*), 273, 364 (*right*); T. G. Bennett, 7 (*left*), 9, 81 (*right*); Raymond B. Bentley, dust jacket (*bottom*), 36–37, 119, 123; Robert B. Berryman, 57, 337; Joe Bishop, 316; Blue Grass Cutlery Corporation, Winchester Trademark Knives, 275 (*right*); Browning Arms Co., 80 (*left*), 342; Buffalo Bill Museum, Buffalo Bill Historical Center, 48, 90 (*lower left*), 128 (*right*); Jim Carmichel, 198 (*right*), 240 (*bottom*), 321 (*bottom*); Cherry's, Inc., 298; Christie's, 26 (*left*), 56, 89 (*left, top right*), 90 (*right*), 150 (*left*), 338; Chronicle Books, *Eyelids of Morning* by Peter Beard, 361; Cody Firearms Museum, Buffalo Bill Historical Center, 2, 4 (*top*), 5, 10 (*bottom*), 13 (*left*), 15 (*left*), 18 (*left, top right*), 27 (*right*), 38 (*top left*), 42 (*bottom*), 58 (*top*), 64 (*left*), 65 (*left*), 76 (*left and lower right*), 85, 99, 108 (*left*), 131 (*left center*), 134, 159, 164, 189, 208 (*top*), 248 (*right*), 334 (*left*), 347 (*right*), 351, 368 (*left*); Colt Collection of Firearms, Connecticut State Library, 166; David Condon, Inc., 76 (*top right*); Denver Public Library, Western History Department, 75, 102 (*center*), 211; Jim and Theresa Earle, 147 (*top*); D'Arcy Echols, 365 (*top*); Edward C. Ezell, Ph.D., 175, 178, 180 (*left*), 183 (*right, top, bottom*); James S. Fowler, 32, 343; Gene Autry Western Heritage Museum, 65 (*right*), 91, 339; Bottega C. Giovanelli, 290–91; Hagley Museum and Library, 7 (*right*); Gary Hansen, 301; Ivan B. Hart, 11, 131 (*right*); T. E. Henshaw, 162–63, 232, 237, 240 (*top*), 260, 263, 280

(*top*), 293 (*right*); Billy Hodge, Buckhorn Trading Post, 218; Illinois State Library, 19; George Jackson, 71, 352; Kansas State Historical Society, 45, 46 (*right*); Walter Karabian, dust jacket (*top*), 250, 254; Dr. Gerald Klaz, 6 (*right*), 104 (*left center and bottom*); Edward Lewis, 6 (*left*), 47, 61, 63 (*right*), 88 (*left*), 94 (*left*), 103 (*right*), 152 (*left*), 210 (*left*); Lincoln County Heritage Trust, 46 (*left*); John J. Malloy, 101 (*right*); Greg Martin, 34–35; A. I. McCroskie, 15 (*bottom, top rifle*), 24, 29 (*right*), 30, 31, 42 (*center rifle of top illus.*), 49, 59, 66–67, 106 (*left*), 116–17, 119, 141, 310, 311, 340, 341, 344; Montana Historical Society, 17 (*right*); Peter and Patty Murray, endpapers, frontispiece, 26 (*right*), 43 (*left*), 60, 62, 63 (*left*), 78, 82, 84, 92, 93, 96, 97, 98 (*left*), 104 (*top right*), 108 (*right*), 109, 132, 135, 136 (*left*), 137, 139, 140, 142, 143, 145, 146, 148, 149, 150 (*right*), 151, 152 (*right*), 154, 156, 157, 165, 167, 169, 170, 173, 177, 181, 182, 186, 188, 190, 191, 194, 195–97, 198 (*left*), 199–202, 205, 206, 208 (*center and bottom*), 209, 213–16, 219–31, 233–36, 238, 239, 241, 242, 244–47, 252, 253, 255–59, 261, 262, 264–72, 278, 281–85, 286 (*left*), 287–89, 292, 294–97, 300 (*bottom*), 304, 306, 307, 308, 315, 319, 320, 328, 332, 350, 354, 355, 357, 367, 369 (*top right*); Museum of the American Indian, Heye Foundation, 18 (*bottom right*); National Cowboy Hall of Fame, 95, 111; National Museum of American History, Smithsonian Institution, 15 (*top right*); National Shooting Sports Foundation, 274, 276; New Haven Colony Historical Society, 38–39 (*house*); Ogden Union Station Museums, 81 (*left*), 217; Jeff Overington, 114, 115, 118, 120 (*bottom*), 121, 122, 124–27, 129, 130; Herb Peck, Jr., 29 (*left*), 51, 52, 54 (*right*), 58 (*bottom*), 64 (*right*), 73, 88 (*right*), 98 (*right*), 144,

153, 210 (*right*), 286 (*right*); private collections, 8, 15 (*bottom*), 20, 28, 33 (*right*), 40, 42, (*top and bottom rifles, top illus.*), 50 (*left*), 87, 112, 128 (*left*), 131 (*top left*), 249, 346, 347; Gary H. Reynolds, 220 (*top right*), 312–13, 329 (serial no. 9); Theodore Roosevelt Birthplace Collection, 107 (*top*); Theodore Roosevelt Collection, Harvard College Library, 103 (*left*), 107 (*right*), 110; Joseph G. Rosa, 55; Royal Canadian Mounted Police, 27 (*left*), 74; Dr. Lige Rushing, 348–49; Sagamore Hill National Historic Site, 80 (*right*); Charles Scribners Sons, *Ernest Hemingway Rediscovered* by Norberto Fuentes, photograph by Roberto Herrera Sotolongo, 147 (*bottom*); Harry H. Sefried, 23, 336; Robert Shelton, 330 (*left*), 331; Carter N. Short, 94 (*right*); John R. Sweeney, 16 (*top left*); C. W. Slagle, 16, 17 (all but *top left*); John B. Solley III, 10 (*top*), 120 (*top*); State Historical Society of North Dakota, 68 (*left*); Texas Ranger Museum and Hall of Fame, 91 (inset), 100, 101 (*left*), 102 (*right*); Tiffany & Co., 104 (*top left*), 105; Tom Trolard, 280 (*bottom*); Uberti & Co., U.S.A, Maria Uberti, president, 365 (*bottom*); Union Pacific Railroad Museum, 33 (*left*), 106 (*right*); U.S. Repeating Arms Co., 180 (*right*), 184 (*bottom right*), 220 (*bottom right*), 293 (*left*), 299, 300 (*top*), 309, 314, 317, 318, 321 (*top*), 322–27, 358–60, 362, 363, 364 (*left*); University of Oklahoma Library, Western History Department, 72, 86, 136 (*right*); Wells Fargo Bank, 21 (*left*), 53, 102, (*left*); Paul R. Wells, 25, 44, 83, 138, 192, 366; Winchester Division of Olin Corporation, 161, 172, 184 (*left and top right*), 185, 251, 275 (*left*), 277, 368 (*lower right*), 369 (*bottom*); Winchester Mystery House, 368 (*top right*); John R. Woods, 50 (*right*), 69.

Index

References to illustrations are in *italics*